Deviant Maternity

This is the first-ever book to explore illegitimacy in Wales during the eighteenth century. Drawing on previously overlooked archival sources, it examines the scope and context of Welsh illegitimacy, and the link between illegitimacy, courtship and economic precarity. It also goes beyond courtship to consider the different identities and relationships of the mothers and fathers of illegitimate children in Wales, and the lived experience of conception, pregnancy and childbirth for unmarried mothers. This book reframes the study of illegitimacy by combining demographic, social and cultural history approaches to emphasise the diversity of experiences, contexts and consequences.

Angela Joy Muir is a Lecturer in British Social and Cultural History at the University of Leicester.

Routledge Research in Gender and History

The Masculine Modern Woman
Pushing Boundaries in the Swedish Popular Media of the 1920s
Jenny Ingemarsdotter

Gendering Spaces in European Towns, 1500–1914
Edited by Elaine Chalus and Marjo Kaartinen

The Anti-Abortion Campaign in England, 1966–1989
Olivia Dee

British Women Travellers
Empire and Beyond, 1770–1870
Edited by Sutapa Dutta

Married Women in Legal Practice
Agency and Norms in the Swedish Realm, 1350–1450
Charlotte Cederbom

Courtship, Marriage and Marriage Breakdown
Approaches from the History of Emotion
Katie Barclay, Jeffrey Meek and Andrea Thomson

The Impact of World War I on Marriages, Divorces, and Gender Relations in Europe
Edited by Sandra Brée and Saskia Hin

Deviant Maternity
Illegitimacy in Wales, c. 1680–1800
Angela Joy Muir

For more information about this series, please visit: www.routledge.com/Routledge-Research-in-Gender-and-History/book-series/SE0422

Deviant Maternity
Illegitimacy in Wales, c. 1680–1800

Angela Joy Muir

LONDON AND NEW YORK

First published 2020 by Routledge

2 Park Square, Milton Park, Abingdon, Oxon OX14 4RN
605 Third Avenue, New York, NY 10017

Routledge is an imprint of the Taylor & Francis Group, an informa business

First issued in paperback 2021

Copyright © 2020 Taylor & Francis

The right of Angela Joy Muir to be identified as author of this work has been in accordance with sections 77 and 78 of the Copyright, Designs and Patents Act 1988.

All rights reserved. No part of this book may be reprinted or reproduced or utilised in any form or by any electronic, mechanical, or other means, now known or hereafter invented, including photocopying and recording, or in any information storage or retrieval system, without permission in writing from the publishers.

Notice:
Product or corporate names may be trademarks or registered trademarks, and are used only for identification and explanation without intent to infringe.

Publisher's Note

The publisher has gone to great lengths to ensure the quality of this reprint but points out that some imperfections in the original copies may be apparent.

Library of Congress Cataloging-in-Publication Data
Names: Muir, Angela Joy, 1979– author.
Title: Deviant maternity : illegitimacy in Wales, c. 1680—1800 / Angela Joy Muir.
Description: New York, NY : Routledge, 2020. | Series: Routledge research in gender and history ; 41 | Includes bibliographical references and index.
Identifiers: LCCN 2019055339 (print) | LCCN 2019055340 (ebook) | ISBN 9780367896805 (hardback) | ISBN 9781003020516 (ebook) | ISBN 9781000035018 (adobe pdf) | ISBN 9781000035025 (mobi) | ISBN 9781000035032 (epub)
Subjects: LCSH: Illegitimacy—Wales—History—18th century. | Unmarried mothers—Wales—History—18th century. | Wales—Social conditions—18th century.
Classification: LCC HQ999.G7 .M85 2020 (print) | LCC HQ999.G7 (ebook) | DDC 306.87409429—dc23
LC record available at https://lccn.loc.gov/2019055339
LC ebook record available at https://lccn.loc.gov/2019055340

ISBN: 978-0-367-89680-5 (hbk)
ISBN: 978-1-03-217416-7 (pbk)
DOI: 10.4324/9781003020516

Typeset in Sabon
by Apex CoVantage, LLC

For my family.
I fy nheulu, fy hoff bastardiaid bach. Diolch o galon am bopeth. Dwi'n caru chi.

Contents

List of Figures — ix
List of Tables — x
Acknowledgments — xi

Introduction — 1

PART I
Prevalence and Causes — 41

1 Illegitimacy, Paternity, Courtship and Poverty — 43
2 Complicated Relationships and Diverse Identities: Moving Beyond Courtship and Poverty — 73

PART II
The Mortality Penalty — 103

3 Illegitimate Infant and Maternal Mortality — 105
4 Fatal Violence Against Illegitimate Children and Unmarried Pregnant Women — 122

PART III
The Experience of Pregnancy and Childbirth for Unmarried Mothers — 153

5 Reading and Regulating Reproductive Bodies — 155

6	The Provision of Care for Unmarried Mothers	192
	Conclusion	222
	Bibliography	227
	Index	249

Figures

0.1	Comparison of English illegitimacy ratios	9
1.1	Comparison of illegitimacy ratios in Wales and England	45
1.2	Comparison of illegitimacy in mid and northeast Wales with southwest Wales	46
1.3	Comparison of illegitimacy in mid and northeast Wales with west and northwest England	47
1.4	County-level analysis of illegitimacy ratios in Denbighshire, Montgomeryshire and Radnorshire, 1680–1799	48
1.5	Map of illegitimacy ratios by parish, 1790–1799: Denbighshire, Montgomeryshire, Radnorshire and Shropshire	49
1.6	Percentage of baptisms of illegitimate children in which fathers were named, mid/northeast Wales aggregate	51
1.7	Percentage of baptisms of illegitimate children in which fathers were named, Denbighshire, Montgomeryshire and Radnorshire	51
3.1	Percentage of legitimate and illegitimate infants buried within one year of baptism, c. 1759–1799	111
3.2	Percentage of legitimate infants and illegitimate infants (with and without identified fathers) buried within one year of baptism, c. 1759–1799	112
6.1	Sample of payments made by parish poor law officials for pauper births, 1765–1800	201
6.2	Comparison of bastardy bonds drawn up prior to vs after birth in Montgomeryshire and Radnorshire, c. 1700–1799	213

Tables

1.1 Illegitimacy and identified illegitimate paternity in Gresford, Denbighshire, 1750–1799   64
2.1 Occupations of fathers of illegitimate children as listed in baptism registers, bastardy bonds and filiation orders, and quarter sessions records in Denbighshire, Montgomeryshire and Radnorshire   92
3.1 Recorded instances of maternal mortality in Llanrhaeadr ym Mochnant when the cause of death is identified as 'childbed' or 'childbirth', 1759–1799   116

Acknowledgments

This book started as a PhD project in 2014 with funding from the Wellcome Trust and Social Sciences and Humanities Research Council of Canada. With the support from the Institution for Historical Research in the form of an Economic History Society Power Postdoctoral Fellowship, it became a book. The research that went into these pages was carried out at during my time at the University of Exeter, Cardiff University and the University of Leicester, and would not have been possible without these studentships and fellowship.

Research that spans five years and three institutions inevitably leads to a lengthy list of people who are due thanks. First and foremost, I would like to express my sincere gratitude to my doctoral supervisors, Sarah Toulalan and Alun Withey, for their support, guidance and encouragement. A better supervisory team certainly cannot exist. I am also eternally grateful for the comradery of those with whom I had the pleasure of sharing the proverbial PhD trenches, including Emily Bridger, Tom Chadwick, Hannah Charnock, Fred Cooper, Natasha Feiner, Anna Jackman, Simon Mackley, Charmian Mansell, Sharanya Murali, Josh Rhodes, Jon Venn, Michelle Webb and many others. Thank you for the lively, impassioned and thought-provoking debates, as well as the collegiality and friendship that was fostered over many, many hours in the pub.

This book's evolution from a thesis to a monograph began with the support of friends and colleagues in Cardiff. I am indebted to Lloyd Bowen, Emily Cock, David Doddington, Derek Dunn, Rachel Herrmann, Bronach Kane, Jan Machielsen, Gavin Murray-Miller, Kevin Passmore, James Ryan, David Selway, Lara Taffer, Shaun Tougher, Keir Waddington, Garthine Walker, Steph Ward and Mark Williams. An extra special thanks also goes to Mary Heimann for her steadfast confidence and support, and her supply of wine and limoncello. The friendship and support of these colleagues during an otherwise precarious year as an early career researcher has left a deep impression on me.

The finishing touches of this book took place during my first year at the University of Leicester. In addition to being grateful for securing the 'unicorn' that is a permanent job in academic, I am also thankful to Sarah

Goldsmith, Zoë Groves, Zoë Knox, Roey Sweet, Deborah Toner, Richard Butler and Alistair Kefford for their support and collegiality. To the rest of my colleagues in the Centre for English Local History and School of History, Politics and International Relations, I thank you en masse to avoid making these acknowledgements read any more like an Oscar speech than they already do.

My gratitude must also be extended to the staff of the various archives offices I visited over the course of this research, including Flintshire Record Office, Denbighshire Archives Office, Pembrokeshire Record Office, Herefordshire Archive and Records Centre, Shropshire Archives, Greater Manchester County Record Office and The National Archives. Extra thanks go to the staff at Powys County Archives and the National Library of Wales for their expertise and patience in answering my countless queries and fulfilling my endless requests. Special thanks to Anna Brueton for allowing me to incorporate the data she collected and analysed for her study of illegitimacy in Wales, which predates my own.

My thanks also to Rhian Richards, Ian Rees and Rhys Morgan for their assistance with Welsh translations. Thanks also to Siwan Rosser at Cardiff University for reading an early draft of my work and identifying for me the relevant sections of her book and several Welsh ballads. Despite my best efforts, my shortcomings with the Welsh language necessitated their assistance, and I am indebted to them. Diolch yn farw am helpu fi.

On a personal level, I would like to thank my mother, father, brother and late grandmother for their constant support throughout my academic career, and all of my other daft pursuits. Finally, to my partner John, I cannot express my gratitude to you for your patience, encouragement and unwavering confidence in me.

Introduction

Women do not produce illegitimate children, societies do. Women, with the necessary biological contribution of men, produce children and it is the society into which the child is born that determines whether or not that child is 'legitimate'. In European societies a child is traditionally deemed illegitimate based on the acceptability of the relationship between the father and the mother. However, over time and in different communities official and popular opinions about the validity of such relationships vary. Historically, the label of 'illegitimate' carries with it almost universal stigma with potentially negative implications for illegitimate children and their parents.[1] The act of identifying a child as illegitimate is, by its very nature, an act of marking a child, his or her mother, and often father, as a threat to moral and social order. By studying how and why societies construct, problematise and manage illegitimacy we can better understand their broader values, beliefs, tensions and socioeconomic concerns. Illegitimacy is a topic in which social, cultural, religious, legal and economic issues intersect, and it therefore offers a multifaceted approach to the history of British society. This book sheds new light on illegitimacy in eighteenth-century Britain by using previously unstudied sources from Wales, which is a part of the British Isles which has received considerably less attention from historians. The aim is not only to add to our overall understanding of the geographical variations within Britain, but also to look more broadly at the implications of illegitimacy for mothers and their children, and to add to the ongoing discussion about how and why the nature of illegitimacy changed during this period.

This book examines illegitimacy in Wales between approximately 1680 and 1800. It investigates the prevalence and underlying causes of childbirth outside of marriage in the counties of Denbighshire, Montgomeryshire and Radnorshire, and considers the wider context, consequences and experiences of pregnancy and childbirth for unmarried mothers by drawing upon evidence from across Wales. The focus is not only on broad trends revealed in analysis of illegitimacy ratios, but also on the individual identities of those involved in illegitimacy, and the individual experiences of conception, pregnancy and childbirth for unmarried mothers. As one of the first studies to consider evidence from Wales, the aims are twofold: first, to map broader patterns of change in levels of illegitimacy over time, which can be compared to existing data for England; and second, to go beyond quantitative analysis of demographic trends by examining the complex nuances which are often blurred by such approaches. This involves exploring the diverse range of sexual encounters which resulted in childbirth outside of wedlock, the impact illegitimacy had on life expectancy for unmarried mothers and their children, attitudes towards deviant, unregulated reproduction and reproductive bodies and the provision of care and support to unmarried mothers. The central arguments are also twofold: first, in comparison to England, levels of illegitimacy were significantly higher in some, but not all, parts of Wales during the eighteenth century. These overall patterns can be attributed to a combination of courtship-led marriage customs which existed in some parts of Wales, a decline in traditional forms of social control and worsening economic circumstances. The second central argument is that, despite these general trends, there was no singular 'Welsh' experience of illegitimacy, but rather, illegitimacy was a complex phenomenon influenced by a range of individual circumstances, and cultural and socioeconomic factors.

Illegitimacy here refers to any child born outside of lawful wedlock as recognised by the established church.[2] The term 'illegitimacy' will be used throughout this work. Value-laden and outdated synonyms such as 'bastard' or 'bastardy' will only be used in the context of direct quotes, or when referring to documents such as bastardy bonds. The label 'illegitimate' is itself not neutral, as it implicitly demarcates those deemed lawful and valid from those deemed unlawful and invalid based solely on the marital status of their parents. Unfortunately, few suitable alternatives exist in the English language. Whenever possible, terms such as 'non-marital' will be used in its stead; however, use of 'legitimate' and 'illegitimate' are unavoidable.

The study of illegitimacy is not inherently a study of female sexual deviance. If deviance is understood as deliberate behaviours which go against accepted social norms, labelling all forms of illegitimate childbearing as deviant would be an oversimplification, as not all illegitimate childbirths were the result of moral transgression or attempts on the part of mothers to subvert the established social order.[3] If, as many studies of illegitimacy have suggested, the majority of the sexual encounters which led to the birth of an illegitimate child occurred in the context of failed premarital courtships, the births that resulted can hardly be understood as 'deviant'. However, bearing a child outside of formal marriage was, ultimately, interpreted by many as a deviant act. The act of interpreting behaviours as deviant and the consequences of these judgements are in many ways more revealing of social anxieties and the underlying circumstances that inform them than of the behaviours themselves. How illegitimacy was perceived and regulated is of as much interest as the personal relationships and socioeconomic and cultural influences which led to an illegitimate birth. The study of illegitimacy could then, first and foremost, be described as the study of power relationships and of moral, social and economic anxiety and control rather than a study of female deviance.

The birth of a child outside of wedlock was a familiar occurrence in early modern and eighteenth-century Britain, and the demographic studies which have been carried out since the 1970s have been invaluable in revealing just how common these experiences were in some areas.[4] Most studies of illegitimacy in Britain have focused on English parishes, and a smaller, but no less important, body of scholarship investigating illegitimacy in eighteenth-century and nineteenth-century Scotland also exists.[5] Although these analyses have revealed a great deal about patterns of change across many parts of Britain, demographic, social and cultural historians have tended to neglect Welsh material; however Welsh archives are a rich source of evidence, which can be analysed using many of the established frameworks used in the analysis of English data. During this period, England and Wales shared a legal structure and ecclesiastical system, and they became increasingly assimilated in terms of social structure, landholding, education and economy. At the same time, many parts of Wales remained culturally and linguistically unique in ways which directly influenced certain experiences of illegitimacy. Understanding the Welsh context of illegitimacy is therefore not only integral to our understanding of British history, but also demonstrates the extent to which illegitimacy across Britain was a deeply complex phenomenon governed by diverse regionally-specific social and economic influences.

This book combines both quantitative and qualitative approaches to the analysis of Welsh evidence. Quantitative analysis of data taken from parish baptism registers reveals diverse patterns which are central to our understanding of illegitimacy in Wales. Welsh illegitimacy did roughly resemble trends elsewhere in Britain; however, it differed in significant ways, and regional patterns within Wales varied considerably. Although many of these patterns can be attributed to cultural factors such as conjugal courtship customs, and to socioeconomic circumstances, analysis also indicates that there is no single explanation which can account for all instances of illegitimacy in all regions. Analysis of illegitimacy ratios is a necessary starting point as it allows for a quantifiable comparison with demographic studies previously carried out for England, but it has its limitations. The calculation of illegitimacy ratios necessitates an amalgamation of all forms of illegitimate conception into one single category of sexual experience. It seems deeply inappropriate and insensitive to count children born as a result of rape or incest in the same category of sexual experience as consensual premarital sex, or even consensual extramarital sex. Every effort has therefore been made to avoid an over-dependence on quantitative data, in part because of the problems associated with this type of analysis, and in part because of a desire to avoid what Roy Porter described as, 'the risk of creating mists of mythical "averages" which veil the significant contours' of past experience.[6]

The suggestion that illegitimacy in Wales was diverse and complex is by no means an equivocation. As will be demonstrated in the chapters that follow, this argument reflects the diversity of evidence found in Welsh parish registers, poor law accounts and court records. Collecting data used to calculate illegitimacy ratios involves examining thousands of entries in baptism registers. One striking feature of Welsh registers is the frequency with which fathers of illegitimate children are identified in many parishes. This tendency, which will be explored further in Chapter 1, is often not found in English registers, and provides tantalising glimpses of the identities and relationships of those involved in illegitimacy. In the process of counting illegitimate baptisms it became apparent that many of the entries that contribute to the aggregate ratio did not result from the same types of sexual encounter. This multiplicity of sexual encounters is also reflected in poor law accounts, bastardy bonds and court records. To discount these for the sake of an orderly trend that can be explained in terms of a single leading cause requires overlooking the complicated details of lived experiences. Human relationships are often at their most complex when sex is involved, and to study the outcomes of such encounters only in terms of a single motivation seems impractical, if not impossible, and somewhat misguided.[7] The decision was therefore made to give equal voice to these often-marginalised experiences, which may be statistically insignificant, but nevertheless essential to our understanding of the nature of illegitimacy in eighteenth-century Britain.

The diverse circumstances surrounding conception ultimately resulted in divergent experiences of pregnancy and parturition as well. Thus, this work furthers the shift away from considering illegitimacy in terms of prevalence and cause by exploring the experiences of unmarried mothers and their children.[8] However, lived experiences are notoriously difficult to access, particularly when those who lived them left few records of their own. Experiences here are explored through the records of encounters unmarried mothers and their children had with parish and secular authorities. Many of these represent the more extreme consequences of illegitimacy, which is referred to here as the 'mortality penalty'.[9] This penalty is explored both in terms of overall survival chances in the days, weeks and months after birth, and also in terms of how fatal violence against illegitimate children and their mothers was contextualised in court records. Court records are also revealing of the encounters many unmarried women had with neighbours, family and employers when they were suspected of being pregnant or recently delivered. These confrontations reveal the ways in which women's bodies could become the locus of anxieties surrounding deviant reproduction, and thus provide evidence of the broader social and cultural context of illegitimacy in eighteenth-century Wales. The experience of illegitimacy is also explored through an analysis of the range of care provided to unmarried parturient women as revealed in poor law accounts. These experiences could vary considerably depending on a woman's standing within a community, and the circumstances surrounding the conception of the child. Thus, this study also contributes to our understanding of the history of sex, reproductive bodies, and childbirth in eighteenth-century Britain. The skills, reputation and availability of midwifery services in Wales is also explored, as no studies of childbirth of midwifery in Wales during the eighteenth century currently exist. The approaches taken here build upon the work of historians such as Laura Gowing, Adrian Wilson, Tanya Evans, Samantha Williams, Garthine Walker and Emma Griffin, but are novel in that they join together many disparate methodologies and historical fields, including social and cultural history, and the histories of crime, gender and medicine.[10]

The geographic scope of this study covers the historic Welsh counties of Denbighshire, Montgomeryshire and Radnorshire. The choice of these regions is significant for several reasons. This allows for a study which takes into account proximity to, as well as distance from, English communities and other regional variations. The area covered by this study is approximately 1,800 square miles and within this relatively small space there existed a diversity of culture, economy, language and geography. This region therefore lends itself well to an analysis of how the experience of illegitimacy differed in relation to variables such as these. Finally, none of the parishes in these counties have been included in any of the limited studies on illegitimacy in eighteenth-century Wales carried out to date. This study will therefore provide a new perspective on the history of illegitimacy in eighteenth-century Britain by considering evidence from previously unstudied Welsh parishes. Furthermore, and most importantly, by using evidence from a unique region such as this, which contained a distinctive mix of cultural, socioeconomic and geographic influences, this study will demonstrate the heterogeneity of both incidence and experience of illegitimacy in the eighteenth century. This is therefore a study both of Welsh illegitimacy in the eighteenth century and of eighteenth-century illegitimacy more broadly, using examples from specific Welsh parishes.

The years covered by this study are roughly from 1680 to 1800. Few parishes in Wales have records surviving from the late seventeenth century or earlier. The year 1680 represents the earliest date from which half of the parishes studied here have records available, although many are incomplete. A 120-year period was chosen to allow for a mapping of change over several generations. The end point of 1800 was chosen because of the increased momentum in the growth and influence of nonconformity. Although it would have been possible to extend the study past 1800, by that time an increasing number of children were not being baptised in the established Anglican Church, and the majority of nonconformist records from this time have not survived.[11] The timeframe for this study is also important as Wales in the eighteenth century has largely been neglected by historians. Furthermore, this century represents a period of tremendous social, cultural and economic change in Britain brought on by increases in population, industrialisation, religious nonconformity, the growth of empire and the trade and conflicts associated with it and the influence of the scientific revolution and the Enlightenment. The ways in which different regions of Britain experienced these changes varied immensely. Perhaps most relevant to this study is the fact that this is the century in which British society became obsessed with weighing, measuring and quantifying itself, which can provide a tantalising glimpse of demographic trends as well as of contemporary concerns and assumptions.[12]

To date very little research has been carried out on illegitimacy in eighteenth-century Wales, in comparison to a considerable number of works on England and, more recently, Scotland. With the exception of two articles, no Welsh parish data has been considered in any large-scale published quantitative study of illegitimacy in the early modern period, or eighteenth century, nor have any Welsh court records, ballads, diaries or poor law accounts been considered.[13] This omission is surprising given the availability of source material and given that the 1836 *Second Annual Report of the Poor Law Commission* revealed that the former counties of Radnorshire and Montgomeryshire contained the greatest proportion of 'chargeable bastards' per capita in all of Britain, with rates of 1:59 and 1:67 respectively.[14] Denbighshire had the fourth highest proportion of 'chargeable bastards' in Wales at 1:137, tying it with Wiltshire for eleventh overall in England and Wales. In the nearest English counties of Herefordshire and Shropshire the proportion of illegitimate children dependent on poor relief was nearly half of what it was in Radnorshire at 1:108 and 1:109 respectively, but considerably less than Denbighshire. The significance of the ratios in the counties analysed in this study becomes even more apparent when compared to the lowest proportion in all of England and Wales, which was to be found in the county of Hertfordshire with a rate of 1:398.[15]

Moreover, the controversial 1847 *Report of the Commission of Inquiry into the State of Education in Wales*, or 'Blue Books', suggests that some parts of Wales purportedly contained a large number of illegitimate children. The Report also provides insight into the concerns this situation raised for the authors, who were English, as well as local clergymen, officials and other social commentators. Several local individuals of standing are quoted, such as Reverend James Morgan, the Vicar of Talgarth, who stated that,

> the standard of morality is certainly low; illegitimate children are by no means rare, and pregnancy before marriage is of common

occurrence. It scarcely seems to be considered a sin, or even a disgrace, for a woman to be in the family-way by the man to who she is engaged to be married.

Or Reverend Rees Price of St. John's and St. David's Brecknock, who believed that, 'chastity does not appear to be highly valued by the younger portion, as may be learned . . . from the number of illegitimate children presented for baptism.' And finally, Richard Williams, a medical doctor and coroner, who attested that, 'the youth of both sexes are very unchaste, and do not consider promiscuous intercourse any disgrace, which is chiefly owing to the want of proper education.'[16] Concerns about illegitimacy and sexual morality made up a small but significant part of the overall argument for educational reform.[17]

The idea that illegitimacy was prevalent in Wales became part of the cultural stereotype, as can be seen in a satirical article from 1959 which took the form of a guide for foreign students living in Wales. The article cautioned that, 'whereas English villages are inhabited only by pure yokels in smocks, thatching roofs and not hurting a fly, Welsh villages are noisome with revolting hypocrites beetling in and out of slummy houses and burying illegitimate babies under the rhubarb.'[18] This article was a response to a handbook for foreign students arriving in Britain entitled, 'How to Live in Britain: A handbook for students from overseas' published by the British Council, which was challenged for its patronising tone, colonialist assumptions and civilising intention. The fact that comment about illegitimacy was included in this satire which plays on stereotypes of the Welsh is quite telling of popular assumptions, which were in part a legacy of the impact of the 'Blue Books'. This evidence does much to suggest that Welsh sources warrant their own dedicated study, or at least inclusion in the historiography of illegitimacy in Britain.

Historiographical Context

Illegitimacy in Wales

In one of the only studies of historic illegitimacy in Wales published to date, I analysed the baptism registers of the parishes of Hawarden in Flintshire, and St Peters in Carmarthen, and considered the significance of identified paternity in relation to high levels of illegitimacy.[19] In the period 1700 to 1800 fathers of illegitimate children were listed in baptism registers 72 per cent of the time in Hawarden, and 65 per cent of the time in Carmarthen, which is significantly higher than in many parts of England. This study did not chart change over time, but instead attempted to analyse the language used to identify fathers in Carmarthen, which had a more detailed register, as a means of determining the nature of the relationships between mothers and fathers. Where a father's name

8 *Introduction*

was listed alongside the mother's, or where a child was listed as the base, illegitimate or bastard son of a named man, the relationship between mother and father was assumed to be more stable, established or at least known to the community, which may be indicative of more permissible unions, whereas terms such as 'stranger', 'stroller' and 'reputed' were used to indicate less established and therefore less acceptable sexual relationships. This quantitative analysis of illegitimate taxonomy found that 64 per cent of all illegitimate baptisms where fathers were listed possibly resulted from relationships between men and women who were involved in some form of established union, such as a courtship, or a form of marriage or cohabitation which may have been acceptable within the community but did not meet the church's standards for marriage. This was a small study which considered the data from two parishes and tested a hypothesis about the nature of non-marital sexual relationships using the data from one parish, so the results are far from conclusive. This hypothesis does not hold up against the data collected from the 45 parishes considered in this book. The language used by officials in different parishes varies considerably, and probably does not reflect the nature of conjugal relations between men and women who were not married to one another.

Illegitimacy in Britain

The first large-scale studies of illegitimacy in Britain emerged from the work of the Cambridge Group for the History of Population and Social Structure, which was founded in the 1960s. Early studies were concerned primarily with demographic analysis of parish records and attempted to establish aggregate national averages from the beginning of the parish registration period to the present day. Attempts were also made to explain the changes in these rates over time. A team from the Cambridge Group, headed by Peter Laslett, presented some of their earlier findings in shorter works, but their first volume on the subject, *Bastardy and its Comparative History*, reported the results of an analysis of 98 parishes across England. Although it is now clear that some of the data and collection methods used were defective, Laslett and his team were able to establish a trend which has roughly been supported by later demographic research.[20] They found that there had been a steady, cyclical, upwards trend in levels of illegitimacy in England from the late sixteenth to late twentieth centuries.[21] For the years relevant to this study, they found that levels of illegitimacy increased steadily from approximately 1.5 per cent of all baptisms in 1680, having dropped off during the latter half of the seventeenth century, to just over 5 per cent by 1800.[22] This is a pattern which has been generally supported by larger studies by later authors, such as Richard Adair and his study of 250 English parishes.[23] Adair's study ends in 1754, however his findings do corroborate Laslett's earlier work (see Figure 0.1).[24] Leah Leneman and Rosalind Mitchison found

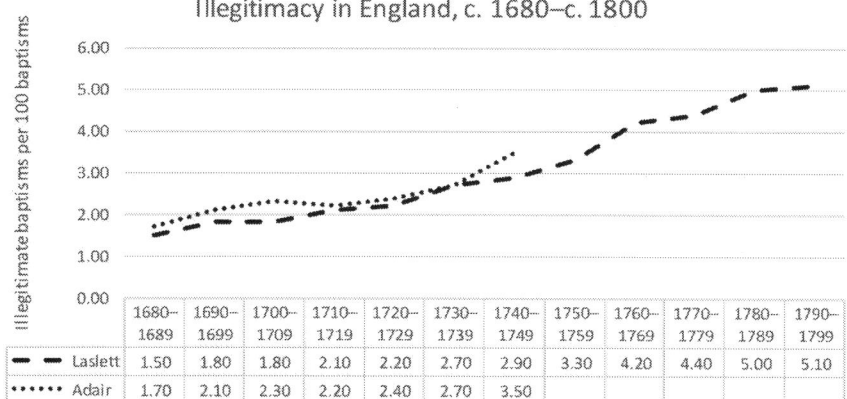

Figure 0.1 Comparison of English illegitimacy ratios taken from Laslett, 'Introduction', p. 14 and Adair, Courtship, p. 50. Laslett's decadal date format is 00–09 and Adair's in 01–10. The data has not been altered.

that a similar pattern was not present in Scotland.[25] Studies of Scotland are more difficult than English studies due to different ecclesiastical administrative systems and the poor survival of records. However, using kirk session records they were able to determine that, during roughly this same period (1660 to 1780), the level of illegitimate births overall in Scotland remained surprisingly consistent throughout most of the eighteenth century. Levels fluctuated between a high of 5 per cent and a low of 3 per cent, which they attributed to stricter forms of ecclesiastical discipline.[26]

A trend which was evident to Laslett, and made even more apparent by Adair, is the distinctive regional nature of illegitimacy. For the later years of his study Laslett identified and ranked the top ten and bottom ten parishes which consistently reported the highest and lowest levels of illegitimacy. In doing so he demonstrated that there was both regional variation and local persistence in patterns of illegitimacy.[27] Parishes in the north and west of the country consistently had higher levels of illegitimacy than areas in the south and east, and parishes which reported high illegitimacy for one period tended to consistently report levels higher than the national average, although with some fluctuations. Leneman and Mitchison also found regional differences in Scotland. The central lowland regions were areas of significant consistency, whereas northeastern regions followed a downward pattern from considerably high levels to much lower instances of illegitimacy, and south-western regions followed a more upward trend which resembled patterns in England.[28] The significance of regional variations are even more apparent in Adair's work, and he has argued that regional variations may have more of an influence on illegitimacy than any other demographic variable.[29] Adair grouped his 250 parishes into six regions, and although the basic national pattern was apparent across all regions, overall higher levels of illegitimacy were found in northwestern regions and lower levels in the southeast.[30] Adair made a further geographic distinction between highland and lowland regions, which are roughly divided by a line running from Exeter to Hull, with the highland regions to the northwest and the lowlands to the south. When looked at this way, overall regional distinctions become even more apparent, with levels of illegitimacy consistently greater in highland regions across the entirety of Adair's study.[31] Laslett and Adair's findings and their resulting hypotheses relating to courtship will be considered against Welsh evidence in Chapter 1.

One hypothesis relating to potential causes of illegitimacy proposed by Laslett is the 'bastardy prone sub-society.'[32] This is a hypothetical group of deviant women, connected through networks of kinship, who bore multiple illegitimate children, and who were likely themselves to have been illegitimate. Laslett's treatment of this subject in his early works is somewhat problematic and chauvinistic, as can be seen in his reference to female members of the Hoare family in Colyton, who appear to have given birth to several illegitimate children over multiple generations. Laslett remarks,

> there could be no more appropriate name for a family selected as an instance of a situation which could be succinctly described as the claim that when illegitimacy increased it was due more to the activities of whores, or to women whose procreating activities look unmistakably like those of whores, than to any other identifiable influence.[33]

Judgemental language such as this does not appear in his later discussions on the subject. Some studies of individual parishes have supported the hypothesis that there may have been some family groupings that had a tendency to produce more illegitimate children, however there is little evidence to suggest they were self-identified as such, and in reality may have been more connected by poverty than by sexual nonconformity.[34] Although records do reveal that some women were 'repeaters', meaning they bore more than one illegitimate child, they did not contribute significantly to overall illegitimacy levels. Moreover, the circumstances which led to women bearing multiple illegitimate children could be quite varied, and there is no evidence linking repeaters with promiscuity. The data available strongly indicates that the majority of illegitimate children born in England and Wales prior to the nineteenth century were 'singletons'.[35] This will be explored further in Chapter 2.

One of the central questions historians of illegitimacy have attempted to answer is why so many children were born outside of wedlock, and why this number increased so dramatically in some regions during the eighteenth century. Historians such as Nicholas Rogers, Thomas Nutt, Adrian Wilson, Emma Griffin, Edward Shorter, Nigel Goose, and Louise Tilley, Joan Scott and Miriam Cohen have all utilised a combination of demographic, social and economic methodologies to account for rising levels of illegitimacy in Britain.[36] Other historians, such as Tim Hitchcock, Thomas Laqueur, Randolph Trumbach and Faramez Dabhoiwala have argued in various ways that the increases in illegitimacy seen in the eighteenth century resulted from the unmarried men and women increasingly engaging in more 'higher risk' sexual activities, such as penetrative sex, which could result in more children born out of wedlock. These hypotheses will be discussed in greater detail in Chapter 1 within the context of Welsh data. What is central to all of these approaches is the presumption that something significant changed during this period which resulted in more illegitimate children being born, as reflected in an increasing illegitimacy ratio. This is typically attributed to a convergence of economic, social and cultural influences. Although this is also the approach taken throughout this book, an alternative hypothesis will be presented for consideration later in the introduction.

Identities and Experiences

In recent years some historians have shifted their focus away from the incidence and causes of illegitimacy towards understanding who the mothers and fathers of illegitimate children were, and their individual experiences of illegitimacy. Illegitimate paternity has gained limited but increasing attention from historians over the past 20 years. Adair suggested that the recording of fathers in baptism registers was indicative of more stable, serious relationships such as established courtships or non-conforming marriages which were not recognised by the church. He used this hypothesis to explain why regions, such as the northwest of England, experienced higher levels of illegitimacy.[37] Some of the most interesting research to date has been by John Black and Thomas Nutt in their respective chapters in *Illegitimacy in Britain, 1700–1920*.[38] Nutt's chapter investigates some of the problems associated with identifying and holding accountable the fathers of illegitimate children under the old poor law.[39] Black's chapter is the first body of research undertaken to try to determine who the fathers of illegitimate children in the eighteenth century actually were. His study focuses on London and uses settlement and examination records from three London parishes. Through his analysis Black was able to determine that the sexual relationships which produced illegitimate children were not only licit, but that the fathers of illegitimate children did not come from an impoverished sub-society. Instead, Black found that the occupational pattern amongst fathers of illegitimate children proportionately represented the occupational makeup of the parishes included in his study, although the proportion of fathers from elite backgrounds declined towards the end of the eighteenth century.[40] A similar methodology will be employed in Chapter 2 for an analysis of occupations and social statuses of fathers in Welsh parishes. More recently, Alexandra Shepard has made a meaningful contribution to the study of illegitimate paternity by considering the social role of fatherhood as it relates to illegitimacy. Shepard argues that historians have been all too quick to assume putative fathers could not, or did not, take up the social role of fathers.[41] Rather, she demonstrates that although the link between biological paternity and the social role of fatherhood could be severed, the nature of care and support arrangements made for illegitimate children demonstrates some of the expectations placed on unmarried fathers.[42] Furthermore, although evidence is limited, some fathers did provide willing support, and felt affection for their illegitimate children.[43]

It is often difficult to determine the socioeconomic background of parents of illegitimate children given the lack of information about fathers found in parish records. However, it is generally accepted by historians that most of those recorded as such in parish registers were primarily from the lowest orders of society.[44] Black found that the socioeconomic profile of fathers of illegitimate children roughly matched that of the population in London at large, which meant that, although they came from all classes, the majority were in lower-paying occupations such as domestic service and manufacture.[45] Leneman and Mitchison found that the majority of mothers of illegitimate children brought before the kirk sessions in Scotland were domestic or farm labourers. In many cases the fathers of their children were also employed as servants.[46] The frequent appearance of mothers of illegitimate children as recipients of payments in poor law accounts does suggest that a significant portion of mothers may have been from poorer economic backgrounds.[47] However, it may not necessarily be the case that poorer people were more prone to bearing illegitimate children, but that illegitimate children born into an already precarious economic situation were of greatest concern to parish officials. The correlation between illegitimacy and poverty will be discussed in Chapter 2.

An increasing amount of excellent scholarship has been produced in recent years that focuses on the lived experience of illegitimacy. This shift is both a trend and an aim noted by the editors of *Illegitimacy in Britain, 1700–1920*, a collection of essays which discuss various aspects of the lived experience of illegitimacy including mortality, paternity and stigmatisation in popular literature.[48] In her work on illegitimacy in London, Tanya Evans highlights the complex nature of illegitimacy, which varied widely and cannot be explained in terms of a simple, single cause, and both experiences and official responses to it were not uniform within communities or throughout regions.[49] Evans effectively demonstrates that there was 'no simple path to unmarried motherhood.'[50] She also argues that single mothers were able to employ a range of survival strategies for them and their children.[51] Laura Gowing and Samantha Williams have both focused on the experience of illegitimacy for unmarried mothers in London.[52] Gowing has explored the treatment of unmarried mothers and their children and argues that the financial threats associated with illegitimacy could negatively affect women's access to support and jeopardise their place within urban parishes.[53] Gowing also explores some of the ways in which single mothers could create their own sense of belonging through hard-fought negotiations which could involve adapting or subverting rituals, such as churching and christening, to suit their individual needs.[54]

Women's experiences of pregnancy and childbirth have also been the subject of historical research. Adrian Wilson and Sharon Howard have both written detailed accounts of women's experiences, their fears and anxieties and the rituals surrounding childbirth.[55] As valuable as these studies are, they have focused on the experience of married women, often from the middling and upper classes. Unmarried women's experiences have received considerably less attention. Gowing was one of the first historians to explore the ways in which single women's experiences of pregnancy and childbirth could vary from those of married women, and found that they were often characterised by fear, conflict and confrontation.[56] Using infanticide trial records, Gowing examined the lengths to which single pregnant women would go in an attempt to conceal their pregnancies and deliveries, and the strategies neighbours, families and employers used to discover them. Gowing argues that these experiences are central to our understanding of broader social and cultural anxieties surrounding the female reproductive body. Samantha Williams has also used infanticide trial records to reconstruct the experiences of the later stages of pregnancy and childbirth for unmarried women in London.[57] Williams analysed the ways in which the birthing bodies of women who had been charged with concealing their pregnancies and deliveries were described in terms of deviance and extrapolated from this what was considered acceptable birthing practice. For example, evidence often focused on how these women had given birth secretly and alone, which demonstrates there was a clear expectation that birth required witnesses.[58] Chapters 4, 5 and 6 are built upon the work of Gowing and Williams.

Mortality Penalty

Historians have also considered the extent to which illegitimacy could have an impact on infant and maternal survival chances in early modern and eighteenth-century Britain. Peter Kitson has demonstrated that, during the parish registration period of the sixteenth through nineteenth centuries, illegitimate infant mortality could be as high as 70 per cent in some market towns.⁵⁹ The concept of the 'mortality penalty' used in Chapters 3 and 4 is borrowed from Alysa Levens's chapter in *Illegitimacy in Britain, 1700–1920*.⁶⁰ Levene analysed data from London during the eighteenth century and determined that children born out of wedlock experienced an increased risk of dying, and suggests this may have been the consequence of maternal poverty and malnutrition, which may have resulted in lower birth weights for some illegitimate children.⁶¹ None of these studies have considered the correlation between infant survival chances and identified illegitimate paternity, which will be explored in Chapter 3. Roger Schofield and Irvine Loudon have explored maternal mortality in early modern and eighteenth-century England.⁶² Loudon has demonstrated that childbirth was one of the leading causes of death for women prior to the advent of sulphonamides and antibiotics in the twentieth century.⁶³ However, Schofield has also demonstrated that, despite this reality, and the widespread belief that childbirth was a precarious time for women, statistically speaking, women were at no greater risk of dying during childbirth than they were of dying from common infectious diseases.⁶⁴ Neither of these studies differentiated between married and unmarried women, and no studies to date have considered the impact of illegitimacy on maternal mortality levels.

The mortality penalty associated with illegitimacy can also be understood in terms of fatal violence. One manifestation of this—the crime of infanticide—has received significant attention from historians.⁶⁵ To a greater or lesser degree, these studies of this period have been framed around the broad changes which occurred between the enacting of the 1624 'Act to prevent the Destroying and Murthering of Bastard Children' and its repeal in 1803, and consist primarily of different readings of the extensive legal records which exist for most high courts across England and Wales.⁶⁶ Broadsides, ballads and newspapers have also provided historians with popular representations of these crimes.⁶⁷ Some studies, such as those carried out by Keith Wrightson and Nick Woodward, have attempted to quantify the phenomenon and identify broad trends and patterns, whereas historians such as Mark Jackson, Laura Gowing and Anne-Marie Kilday have sought to delve into the complex social, medical and legal experiences and understandings of infanticide. Infanticide in Wales is one of the few subjects associated with illegitimacy which has been studied. Nick Woodward analysed records from the Court of Great Sessions between 1730 and 1830, and found that recorded incidences of the crime, patterns of conviction and acquittals closely resembled infanticide in England.⁶⁸ In his conclusion, Woodward noted that the relatively small number of cases, and low conviction rates found in Wales are noteworthy given that Wales is associated with higher levels of illegitimacy, which often results in higher instances of infanticide.⁶⁹ He then postulates that this may be due to illegitimacy carrying less stigma in Wales.⁷⁰ Woodward's study predates any of the work that has now been done on illegitimacy in Wales, so he was not able to explore this hypothesis further.

This book also considers the mortality penalty for mothers of illegitimate children in terms of murder. To date, very little research has been carried out on fatal violence against unmarried women in early modern Britain. Historians such as Garthine Walker, Elizabeth Foyster, and many others have studied gender and homicide, but these studies have typically focused on men who murder other men, husbands who kill their wives, and on women who kill their infants and occasionally other women.[71] The history of intimate partner violence as a distinct, complex social and cultural phenomenon is still very much in its infancy, and has focused almost exclusively on the use of physical force by husbands as a means of disciplining wives.[72] As so little research has been done, this book will incorporate the work of these historians with modern social science research into intimate partner homicide published by bodies such as the World Health Organisation. These will be used in Chapter 4 to examine the ways in which anxieties surrounding deviant, unregulated reproduction could be manifest in fatal violence against unmarried pregnant women in eighteenth-century Wales.

Primary Sources

This book draws upon a range of official documents and popular literature: first, parish registers, which are one of the chief sources for the study of illegitimacy in Britain prior to the nineteenth century. From the 1530s onwards, England and Wales shared similar secular and ecclesiastical legal systems, which aids in a comparative study as like can be measured against like. In 1538 Thomas Cromwell issued a mandate requiring each parish in England and Wales to record every baptism, marriage and burial which took place within their boundaries.[73] Where these records survive they serve as a rich but limited source of information about the lives of ordinary people in centuries past. The format for recording baptisms in parish records was similar across England and Wales. Registers were kept in Latin until the early eighteenth century and were then replaced with English in both England and Wales in accordance with the language clause in the 1536 Act of Union.[74] For the study of illegitimacy ratios, registers of baptisms are the most relevant, although marriage and burial registers, overseers of the poor records and churchwarden accounts can also provide important details. Parishes were required regularly to submit copies of registers to their bishop, and these Bishops' transcripts can serve to fill in the blanks where surviving parish registers have gaps. The details recorded in baptism registers typically include the given name of the child, the name of one or both parents and the date of baptism. Additional information may include the sex of the child, the date of birth, the status or occupation of the parents and their village or parish of residence.

Baptism was an ecclesiastical rite which marked the social birth of a child.[75] Parish officials were never required to record whether a child was legitimate, however in the vast majority of registers in England and Wales such a distinction was made.[76] That parish officials saw fit to include information on the legitimacy of children brought forward for baptism indicates the significance of illegitimacy. It was through baptism that the label of 'illegitimate' was applied which for many either represented or created an increased level of disadvantage and stigma which potentially carried long-term consequences for children and parents. The fact that so many illegitimate children were brought forward for baptism—a ritual act which conformed to social norms and expectations—further demonstrates that illegitimate childbirth was not inherently a deviant act. Baptism was the act of welcoming a child into the community of the parish, and was therefore an act of acceptance on the part of the church and community, and an act of social conformity on the part of the parent or parents.[77] Until well into the nineteenth century local poor relief was the responsibility of individual parishes, and relief was mainly provided in one's parish of legal settlement.[78] For illegitimate children, this was the parish of birth until the 1740s, and the mother's parish of settlement thereafter.[79] Children born to unwed mothers were at particular risk of poverty, and therefore parish officials were keen to establish which parish was responsible for their maintenance.[80] The recording of illegitimacy therefore may have had as much, if not more, to do with economic concerns than moral control.

Prior to 1812 when standardised forms for recording baptisms were introduced the information recorded in baptismal registers varied widely. Even within a single parish the amount and quality of data could vary over time due in part to the idiosyncratic priorities of individual record keepers. Details recorded may reflect individual biases or may be reflective of broader attitudes in the community, and such differences must be interpreted with caution. We cannot know for certain if higher rates of recorded illegitimacy were due to the actual occurrence of more illegitimate births or to an increased bias or meticulousness on the part of the recorder; this is a point to which I will return at the end of the introduction.[81] However, some means of mitigating these challenges are available. One means of diminishing the risk of rogue variations and individual bias is creating an aggregate using a broad sample of consistent records from parishes in close geographic proximity, thus relying less on individual records and more on trends over time. However, as discussed earlier, aggregated data can blur the unique realities of individual circumstances.

Richard Adair has set out several ways of identifying illegitimate children in parish baptism registers in England, and these have been adapted to suit Welsh registers.[82] The most obvious indicators are when terms such as 'illegitimate', 'base', 'supposed', 'natural', 'reputed', 'putative' and 'spurious' are recorded in baptism entries.[83] However not all use any distinguishing label, but rather list the child's given name with the surname of one parent followed by a second surname, sometimes listed as 'alias' or sometimes in parentheses.[84] The use of the term 'alias' was a common convention in early modern records and was used to denote the name of a father not married to the mother of a child, thus identifying a child as illegitimate. In Wales, however, the use of 'alias' could frequently indicate a nickname, and often refers to a personal characteristic of a parent rather than a non-marital union. The registers for the parish of Carno, Montgomeryshire contain entries for mothers with aliases such as *'Dew'* (fat or thick), *'Drol'* (Cart), *'Fawr'* (great or big), or the alias of 'Bessy Tudor' for a woman named Elizabeth Tudor.[85] The parish of Gladestry, Radnorshire contains similar records, such as 'Mary Thomas (Otherwise Molly ye Maid)' and 'Elizabeth Evans (alias Betsy come last)'.[86] These women were all mothers of identified illegitimate children, but their nickname alone would not have been enough to determine this. An additional complicating factor for the use of alias in Wales is the traditional use of patronymics, or 'ap' for son of and *'ferch'* for daughter of.[87] Patronymics were clearly on the decline in the eighteenth century, but they do still appear in some registers, and it is possible that parish officials substituted *'ferch'* or with 'alias' when listing mothers in baptism registers, even if the parents were married. 'Alias' entries have therefore only been counted as illegitimate when additional supporting evidence is available.[88]

For an illegitimate child to be recorded in parish registers a series of events must have occurred.[89] A man and a woman who were not formally married had to engage in sexual intercourse, resulting in the conception of a child; the monthly probability of conception occurring for women engaging in regular sexual intercourse has been estimated at between 15 and 50 per cent.[90] Prior to birth the mother must not have married any man, as that would have legitimised the child. The pregnancy would have to go as near to full term as necessary for a viable live birth without having been terminated by a natural miscarriage or an induced abortion. The probability of a fertilised ovum naturally surviving to nine months was roughly 50 per cent.[91] The infant would then have to survive the precarious first few hours and days of life when it was most at risk of succumbing to death by natural causes, which typically claimed between 110 and 170 newborn lives per 1,000 births.[92] This does not take into account the small fraction of children who were victims of abandonment or infanticide. A parent or guardian, such as a grandparent, would then have to bring the child to his or her parish church for baptism. Finally, parish officials must have had enough information about the parent or parents to be able to identify the child as illegitimate and feel compelled to record the child as such. For these reasons, it is highly likely that there were countless other occurrences of illegitimate conception and birth that do not appear in any available source.

If only the mother's name is given in a register it is presumed the child is illegitimate because in most registers across England and Wales the standard convention was to list paternal affiliation, with mothers being of secondary importance. For example, in Carno in 1702 Joyce Evans, a pauper, had her illegitimate twin daughters baptised, and they were identified as such in the register. In 1704 her son was baptised and although he was not identified as illegitimate no father was listed, and there was no record of her marrying between 1702 and 1704.[93] If the parents were married but the father was absent at the time of birth the reason for his absence was frequently noted. Therefore, if only a mother is listed it is assumed the father was not known.[94] Similarly, if a mother is listed as a widow and a burial record for the father cannot be found within the previous ten months the child is considered illegitimate. Finally, if a mother is listed as a 'concubine', 'whore' or as the 'reputed wife' of the father, then the child is counted as illegitimate. Each parish appears to have its own ways of recording details of illegitimate births, which may have reflected anxieties about individual parents. Illegitimate children born into more impoverished circumstances may have been branded as such more frequently because of its potential future dependence on poor law support. Single mothers in more stable financial positions may not have elicited as much concern, which might explain variations in records.

During the parish registration era, illegitimacy is measured by calculating the proportion of illegitimate baptisms to legitimate baptisms over five or ten year periods.[95] This number can be expressed per 1,000 baptisms, but is often expressed per 100, and thus as a percentage. For clarity, the illegitimacy ratio will be discussed in the text throughout this book in terms of percentage. This is not to be confused with an illegitimacy rate, which refers to the number per 1,000 unmarried women of childbearing age. This type of analysis is not possible prior to the official census, so illegitimacy rates will not be considered here. When twins or triplets are identified they are counted as one entry as they represent one conception. It is also possible to express the illegitimacy ratio. Older children and adults, whether legitimate or illegitimate, are not counted. Only data collected from baptism registers has been included in the ratios. Unbaptised illegitimate children can often appear in other records such as poor law accounts and burial registers; however, these children have not been counted.[96] The reasons for this are twofold: first, the ages of children are frequently not given in burial registers, so it is not always possible to know in which birth year to include an illegitimate burial. Second, and most importantly, including illegitimate infants found in burial registers risks inflating the illegitimacy ratio because it is not always possible to identify and include unbaptised legitimate burials. Since no adjustment can be made to include both legitimate and illegitimate burials, no burials have been included in the ratios. It should be noted that many of the family reconstitution techniques used by historical demographers for the study of illegitimacy and family structure, such as calculating prenuptial pregnancy, and identifying 'repeaters', or women who bore more than one illegitimate child, cannot be applied to Welsh sources.[97] This is due to the limited pool of Welsh surnames which makes it difficult or impossible to differentiate between different individuals who carry the same names.[98]

Few of the parishes studied have a consistent, uninterrupted run of records available for the entire period under consideration. Many registers have intermittent gaps of one or more years, either due to under-recording or to damage to the original documents. Data was calculated per decade, and, if any register had a gap of more than three years in one decade, the data from that decade was excluded from the aggregate figures. The data represents approximately 130,000 baptisms over the entire period increasing from just below 7,500 in the first decade of the study to nearly 14,000 in the last, which provides evidence of the growth in population in this region over the eighteenth century. For comparison, data was also collected from 11 additional parishes in the neighbouring county of Shropshire.

The interval between birth and baptism is not always knowable, however when date of birth is also provided it appears that most baptisms occur within a few days of birth, and typically not more than two weeks.[99] This raises one important problem when dealing with parish registers. The only source of quantitative data on illegitimate births available rarely records actual births and using records of an ecclesiastical event to map sexual encounters seems deeply problematic. Parish registers are not detailed records of vital events but are an ecclesiastical administrative record of baptisms which historians can only use as a proxy for births.[100] From these records we must cautiously glean the information relevant to our study while remaining vigilant and cognisant of the fact that the records we are using were not kept for our purposes and do not tell the whole story. We cannot know how many individuals went unbaptised, or were baptised outside the established church, nor can we know how many church officials kept meticulous records, or how many recorded selectively or haphazardly. The patterns discovered may in fact reveal more about compilers' biases and assumptions than actual demographic trends.[101] This is not to say that quantitative analysis of proxy sources is futile, but they should not be used exclusively and should not be assumed to be infallible.

Parish records are also used here to analyse illegitimate paternity. Fathers of illegitimate children can be identified in records in two primary ways. The first is when their names are given in parish baptism registers, either alone or alongside the mother's names. Frequently only a name is given, but in many entries an occupation is also listed. The second way in which fathers are identified is in parish churchwarden and overseers of the poor records, primarily in bastardy bonds and filiation orders. Details given in these documents frequently include occupation, and when appropriate, title. These records will be analysed in two ways. In Chapter 1, the frequency of named fathers in baptism registers will be used for a quantitative analysis and geographic mapping using a similar method employed to establish illegitimacy ratios. These findings will be compared to regional patterns of illegitimacy. In Chapter 2, details about the occupations and social status of fathers found in 212 bastardy bonds and filiation orders from 11 parishes in Montgomeryshire and Radnorshire are used to explore the broad and diverse range of occupations and ranks of fathers of illegitimate children.

This book also uses evidence from parish burial registers to calculate levels of illegitimate infant and maternal mortality. These records carry many of the same problems as baptism registers, such as under-registration. Many infants who perished soon after birth may have died unbaptised or without having been formally baptised in the church, and therefore would be almost completely absent from the historical record.[102] Infants may still be recorded in burial registers, but details of such burials are frequently vague, and simply list 'child of' without providing the given name. It is therefore apparent that many stillborn infants, or newborns who died shortly after birth cannot be accounted for statistically. However, parish registers are the only sources of information available relating to mortality prior to the nineteenth century. As with baptisms, any challenges relating to these records must be mitigated through the use of large samples of the high-quality data and, more importantly, must be balanced out and contextualised through the thorough use of qualitative analysis of available records. Maternal mortality is more difficult to calculate. Without evidence of an infant, it is impossible to differentiate in most burial registers between the deaths of women of childbearing age who died as the result of complications during childbirth and those who died from any other cause. For this reason, analysis of maternal mortality will only use the exceptionally detailed burial records of one parish, Llanrhaeadr ym Mochnant, which recorded a cause of death for every burial from 1759 onwards.[103] This will be used as a case study to compare the mortality levels of married and unmarried parturient women.

Bastardy bonds and filiation orders are also a rich source of evidence. These documents were drawn up shortly before or after the birth of an illegitimate child that was perceived by officials to pose a financial risk to the parish, and therefore served a specific purpose in the management of illegitimacy. Thus, they must be used with caution. Samantha Williams has argued that such documents were only produced when an unmarried mother was either impoverished or at risk of becoming so.[104] Thus, the motive for producing such a document was financial. Parish officials frequently went out of their way to ensure reputed fathers were bound for the maintenance of their children. Countless entries in account books list expenses for warrants and journeys to pursue fathers who either lived in other parishes or had fled.[105] Once a man was named in a bond as a father, the onus was on him to prove that he was not, should he choose to do so.[106] It is therefore possible that some of the men named in bonds were not the biological father, but were implicated because their financial circumstances would have enabled them to provide support. Officials were apparently aware of this risk but appear to have been more concerned with financial indemnity than accuracy.[107] However, it cannot be assumed that the identification of fathers in all cases were fabricated. The evidence for these documents was taken under oath, and therefore most information contained in them should be considered credible.[108]

Bastardy bonds and filiation orders also provide a means of accessing details about the relationships between the mothers and fathers of illegitimate children. It is rarely possible to interrogate baptism registers for additional information about the circumstances surrounding conception, but through analysis of these documents, evidence about the experience of conception for some women can be uncovered. Although not explicit in descriptions of sexual violence, or accusations of rape and exploitation, bastardy papers can provide strong indications of sexual encounters resulting from male abuses of power.[109] As will be discussed in Chapter 2, this is evident in bonds which hold men higher up the social order accountable for fathering children with female servants in their household, or when multiple men in the same family are all bound as fathers of illegitimate children born to different pauper women in their community. In each of these instances it is impossible to determine the precise nature of the relationships between these men and the women they fathered children with, but in all cases, relationships of courtship seem highly implausible.

Also revealing of complex and diverse relationships and circumstances surrounding illegitimacy are court records. Although this book draws upon both quarter sessions and Court of Great Sessions records, the latter are used to a much greater degree due to the detailed nature of depositions which have survived. The Court of Great Sessions was the highest criminal court in Wales and was similar to the English Assizes.[110] Witness depositions from cases relating to murder and infanticide provide a detailed glimpse of some of the fraught circumstances in which illegitimate children were conceived. The records of the Court of Great Sessions not only reveal the general circumstances surrounding these crimes, but through closer analysis can also reveal more about the experience of being single, pregnant and lacking in tangible support from family and the community. Depositions are invaluable resources for accessing popular involvement in legal processes, and they give voice to those who may otherwise have remained silent. However, these records are not without their problems.[111] Depositions and confessions were recorded as part of the pre-trial process by local justices of the peace or coroners, who committed to paper, sometimes post hoc, the statements of those who were predominantly non-literate, and cannot be read as verbatim accounts of what witnesses or suspects actually said.[112] Furthermore, in Wales the official language of the courts, which was Latin until the 1730s and English thereafter, was likely not to have been the language of the majority of those involved as suspects or witnesses in cases.[113] Testimony given verbally to local magistrates or coroners in Welsh would have been translated into English during the recording process and then forwarded to courts. Welsh translations of words or phrases were only retained if the meaning was seen to be significant, and beyond these instances it is impossible to determine what language a deponent spoke.[114] However, it is unlikely that even in translation officials would have intentionally distorted many details in depositions, as they were only one part of the legal process leading up to a potential trial where evidence would be given by witnesses in person.[115]

What seems more likely to have occurred is that accounts of events would have been reshaped along more formulaic legal or fictional lines which conformed to eighteenth-century understandings of crime. This process, which both witnesses and recorders may have engaged in, should not be read as deceitful, nor as acts of falsification, but rather as a process of conforming to familiar narrative formats which assigned meaning, and thus can provide insight into mentalities.[116] One example of this is the use of supernatural idioms of providence in witness statements which functioned to confirm community convictions about the details of certain crimes, and also to conform to broader cultural conventions about how stories of fatal violence should be understood and recounted.[117] Examples of this can be found in the records of Welsh murder trials. Several witnesses in the murder trial of Mary Brown of Flintshire, who in 1731 was accused of poisoning her brother, Thomas, over a disagreement between them about who she should marry, told of how Thomas's two dogs died shortly after consuming his vomit.[118] Examples of animal providence such as this were a common device used in popular accounts of murder throughout the early modern period.[119] Similar tropes can also be found in infant murder trials. In 1763 servant named Thomas Jones testified on two occasions that he had led his master's horse to a water-filled gravel pit so the horse could drink. However, the horse refused to drink, having been frightened, according to Thomas, by something in the water. Thomas then searched for what this might be and discovered what initially looked like a partially submerged dog carcass but turned out to be the body of an infant. Devices which use providence such as these help to reveal violent crimes which otherwise may have remained undiscovered: had Thomas Brown's dogs not died, his death could have been ruled natural, and had Thomas Jones's master's horse not been frightened, the body of the infant may not have been discovered. The relevance here is not in the veracity of accounts about dead dogs or frightened horses, but rather in the fact that these details were deemed important enough to the narrative of these crimes to be recorded. Thus, the specific details recorded in depositions relating to infanticide can be understood to carry particular meanings.

The importance of these meanings is not that they always conform to literary formats, as they often do not, but that they are the details which those who recounted events, and those who recorded them, believed were essential to understanding the circumstances surrounding these acts of violence against newborn infants, and are therefore central to our understanding of how these events were experienced. Chapter 4 analyses some of the key narrative details revealed in witness depositions and confessions of several cases of infanticide in eighteenth-century Wales which have received less attention from historians, but are significant nonetheless. The significance of these narratives lies in the ways in which specific details about these women and their dead infants were conveyed and recorded. Moreover, as discussed in Chapter 5, infanticide trial records from the Court of Great Sessions also demonstrate the extent to which women's bodies served as a locus of broader social anxieties about deviant reproduction in the eighteenth century. By their very nature, legal documents represent acts of regulation, intervention and surveillance, and thus they offer vital clues to the social and cultural priorities and perceptions that inform them.[120] Witness depositions, confessions and inquests all reveal diverse interpretations, negotiations and confrontations between uncertainty, secrecy, and authority that are all directly related to early modern understandings of the reproductive body.

This book also draws upon evidence found in account books kept by overseers of the poor and churchwardens. Accounts do not survive for each of the 50 parishes considered here; however, records do exist for several other parishes not included in the illegitimacy ratio. Evidence has therefore been collected from every parish across these counties which have surviving records from the eighteenth century. In eighteenth-century Britain, the responsibility of care for the poor fell on parishes. Based on legislation from 1662 individuals were eligible for support from their parish of legal settlement, which was obtained through birth or marriage, residence and employment for a set period of time, or holding of property over a certain value.[121] Parish officials collected poor rates from better-off residents, and distributed support to their poor either in the form of cash, tangible goods such as clothing, shoes or basic food stuffs, or by paying other parishioners to house and nurse the sick and poor during their time of need. Poor law accounts were the records kept by the overseers of the poor in each parish of this expenditure. These records are thus a valuable source of evidence about the everyday lives of the lower orders of British society. These documents are used here to further explore the identities and socioeconomic circumstances of the mothers and fathers of illegitimate children, and the support provided to impoverished illegitimate children and their parents. One key problem with these documents is that they only reflect the support provided to paupers, or those experiencing temporary instances of extreme need. Thus, they are not necessarily representative of the experiences of all unmarried mothers and their children. Although, as will be demonstrated in Chapters 1 and 2, there is a strong correlation between poverty and illegitimacy, the experience of bearing, begetting, or being an illegitimate child was not limited to the poorest stratum of society. The abundance of evidence found in poor law records should not be taken as evidence that the poor were the only ones involved in illegitimacy.

Poor law accounts also provide evidence of the nature of care provided to unmarried parturient women in the period of time immediately before, during, and after childbirth. This evidence will be used in Chapter 6 to explore the experience of giving birth outside of wedlock in eighteenth-century Wales. Evidence about the lived experience of childbirth for most early modern women, both married and unmarried, is scarce However, these documents do provide enough evidence to reveal the nature of care available to the poorest women in eighteenth-century Welsh society. Details found in poor law accounts include payments made to midwives and other birth attendants, to families, and to unmarried mothers for support during lying-in. Accounts also contain details of payments made to remove pregnant paupers from one parish to another in an attempt to prevent the woman and her child from becoming a burden on the parish. This evidence can then be compared with parish expenditure on married pauper mothers, and allows for the reconstruction of the 'ceremony of childbirth'. Parish resources were limited, and the support provided under the poor law often covered only what was considered absolutely necessary. Analysis of what overseers of the poor deemed essential for the safe delivery of illegitimate infants found in account books is yet another means of exploring the diversity of experiences of childbirth outside of marriage.

Payments made by poor law officials to midwives, birth attendants and male medical practitioners also allows for an examination of the nature of midwifery and obstetric care available in eighteeth-century Wales. Childbirth in early modern England has received considerable attention from historians, but no similar studies of childbirth or midwifery in early modern Wales exist. Poor law documents have therefore been used to construct an overview of midwifery in Wales within the context of eighteenth-century British childbirth practice. Evidence for this analysis will also be drawn from limited number of surviving applications for licences to practise midwifery. As Chapter 6 demonstrates, these sources provide ample evidence to suggest that the services of at least one woman experienced in delivering babies were readily available to most women across Wales, and that every parish appears to have had at least one woman on hand to deliver those in need.

Finally, this book also examines popular literature such as travel writing and ballads. During the eighteenth century, several English travellers published accounts of their journeys across Britain. Many of these included descriptions of the customs and habits of the people who inhabited various parts of Britain, including Wales. Some of these accounts include descriptions of unique courtship rituals, such as bundling, as discussed in Chapter 1. Although often tantalisingly detailed, these accounts were recorded by English visitors travelling through Wales who were seeking to tell their readers about the antiquities and novelties of 'Welshness'. The 'authenticity' of writers' accounts of customs which they may not have understood fully, or even personally witnessed, is difficult to ascertain. However, when considered alongside evidence from court records and official reports, such as the 1834 *Poor Law Report*'s *Rural and Town Queries*, they do provide compelling perspectives on Welsh culture and society in the eighteenth century.[122] Popular attitudes towards illegitimacy and crimes such as infanticide can also be gleaned from ballads. Hundreds of Welsh-language ballads survive from the eighteenth century, and they are some of the few documents available in Welsh which address many of the themes covered in this book.[123] Many ballads do not discuss specific cases, nor report on crimes committed in England or further afield, but at least six surviving Welsh ballads appear to respond to real cases of infanticide in Wales during the eighteenth century.[124] As with English ballads, Welsh ballads that address topics such as illegitimacy and infanticide are often cautionary and highly judgemental of deviant female sexuality, and thus serve as a fascinating contrast to some of the narratives found in court records relating to similar crimes.

Structure

This book is divided into three parts, each of which contains two chapters. The first section explores the prevalence and underlying causes of illegitimacy. Chapter 1 analyses levels of illegitimacy and identified illegitimate paternity using data collected from the baptism registers of 50 parishes, as well as 11 additional parishes in Shropshire. This data is analysed in relation to explanatory frameworks used in the analysis of illegitimacy in England, which account for illegitimacy in terms of courtship practices and economic hardship. Chapter 2 moves beyond courtship to explore the diversity of identities and sexual encounters which resulted in the birth of a child outside of wedlock and reassesses the correlation between illegitimacy and poverty.

The second section focuses on different manifestations of the mortality penalty of illegitimacy for children and mothers. Chapter 3 utilises quantitative methods to compare illegitimate and legitimate infant mortality in several of the study parishes, and also considers the influence of identified paternity on infant survival chances. Illegitimate maternal mortality is also examined using the detailed burial register from one Welsh parish. Chapter 4 focuses on fatal violence against illegitimate infants and unmarried pregnant women by examining narratives found in witness depositions from the Court of Great Sessions. These records reveal the complex processes of stigmatisation and social control which operated against unmarried women, and reflect broader anxieties about the deviant female reproductive body.

Section 3 explores the experience of pregnancy and childbirth for unmarried mothers. Chapter 5 examines narratives of pregnant, parturient and infant bodies found in infanticide trial records revealing the ways in which women, their families, communities and authorities attempted to regulate reproduction outside of wedlock. Although these cases are rare and extreme, many of the negotiations and confrontations would have been experienced in very similar ways by unmarried women whose pregnancies and deliveries were not concealed, and therefore they are central to understanding experiences of bearing a child outside of wedlock. Chapter 6 focuses on the provision of care to unmarried parturient pauper women. As no major studies of childbirth customs and practice in Wales have been carried out previously, this study will also take into account evidence of the birth of legitimate children.

Illegitimacy: A Social Problem

Until very recently the study of illegitimacy in Britain has been the study of demographic data: it has been a study of numbers conducted in an attempt to better understand family formation amongst the lower orders of society for whom we have few other details. The earliest works such as those published by Laslett in the 1970s are the product of social history's mandate to democratise history.[125] Although these analyses have revealed a great deal about patterns of change across Britain, Europe and many other countries, they are also problematic. The model for studies of illegitimacy established by Laslett and utilised by later historians such as Adair set out to calculate levels of illegitimacy and to attempt to explain the changes observed in their data sets. Few of the major works on illegitimacy in Britain have considered illegitimacy as a social construction which carried consequences for parents and children.[126] Before analysing evidence found in Welsh records, it is worth challenging some of the assumptions which underpin the traditional quantitative approach to illegitimacy.

Historians who use parish data are careful to acknowledge that their sources are inherently flawed due to any number of issues, such as clerical laziness, damage to records or the use of proxies where the desired information is gleaned from the nearest approximation, such as using baptisms as a proxy for births. From these sources, demographic historians construct compelling and convincing statistical averages and graphs, which ultimately lend an enhanced air of authority to their arguments. When enough of these averages corroborate, they are taken to represent a demographic reality. It is assumed that the results of analysis provide answers to the specific questions asked of the data. In the case of illegitimacy, more illegitimate baptisms must mean more illegitimate births. However, this information can also be indicative of other forces at play. Perhaps the evidence of illegitimate baptisms in the eighteenth century can serve as more than just proxies for illegitimate births and can be read as a symptom of increasing anxiety about the potential socioeconomic consequences of illegitimacy. The rise in recorded illegitimacy can therefore be understood not solely in terms of a demographic reality but rather as the invention of a social problem.

Britain was not the only European country to experience increases in reported rates of illegitimacy in the eighteenth century, but no single explanation can account for this.[127] Most theories either attribute this rise to changes in sexual behaviour, which meant more young people were engaging in penetrative sex during courtship, or to changes in the size of the population which were most likely to engage in premarital sex.[128] Few have considered the possibility that the increase in recorded illegitimacy may be reflective of a broader paradigm shift brought on by social, economic and political change and unrest. Patricia Crawford has suggested that an increase in reported illegitimacy in England in the early 1600s may represent anxieties about the growing number of poor, rather than an actual increase in children born out of wedlock.[129] The rapid change seen over the eighteenth century produced anxieties about the stability of society, which in turn increased concern for social control and moral regulation. It could be argued that these axieties were then reflected in changing administrative priorities which put more emphasis on keeping greater track of moral and sexual transgressions. The fact that illegitimacy levels were seen to increase in both Catholic and Protestant countries which had varying levels of industrialisation and urbanisation suggests that its root cause was a broad trend rather than a single economic or demographic factor, such as change in age of first marriage or lower mortality rates. Different countries may not have shared religion or economics, but they may have shared similar anxieties which ultimately led to illegitimacy being perceived as a social problem. Changes in levels of reported illegitimacy may not necessarily reflect changes in sexual activity, but instead may reflect changes in concerns about sexual behaviour which were seen to undermine the stability of society.

The evolution of illegitimacy as a social problem is a concept which can be traced back to Michel Foucault, and has since been developed more fully by historians such as Gail Reekie.[130] Before the eighteenth century, illegitimacy was seen first and foremost as a personal and moral problem, the impact of which was primarily economic and extended no further than the boundaries of parishes and immediate networks of kin.[131] There is much to suggest that illegitimacy did not register as a significant category of concern to those who were surveying British society in the late seventeenth and early eighteenth centuries. Early statisticians such as Gregory King and John Graunt took no account of illegitimacy in their measures, and, unlike later versions, the first edition of *Encyclopaedia Britannica*, published between 1768 and 1771, carried no reference to illegitimacy or bastardy.[132] This is not to suggest that illegitimacy was of no concern to people who considered themselves respectable, but rather that it was not considered by the educated upper and middling sorts to be a problem which required measuring and solving. Throughout the early modern period sexuality had been regulated by the church, which oversaw marriage and birth, and sexual transgressions were dealt with in church courts.[133] However, from the late seventeenth century onwards the authority of church courts began to wane, and subsequently levels of reported illegitimacy in some areas began to rise.[134] It is, of course, very easy to draw a connection between the decline in church authority and the rise in illegitimacy, as will be discussed in Chapter 1. However, it may not be as straightforward as this, especially when other developments of the eighteenth century are taken into account.

A thorough analysis of illegitimacy requires more than a basic definition of the term: it also requires an examination of the institutions which generate the idea of illegitimacy and give rise to the legitimate/illegitimate dichotomy.[135] It is not coincidental that illegitimacy came to be seen as a social problem during the eighteenth century. Increased emphasis on scientific methods and rational thinking combined with efforts to mitigate the risk of social, economic and political unrest, and conflicts such as the Seven Years' War, the American War of Independence and the French Revolution meant that this was a century which became increasingly obsessed with counting and measuring itself.[136] For Foucault, this was manifested in a growing need to 'take sex into account,' which produced new discourses on sex derived not just from morality, but rationality. Sex became something which needed to be policed and consolidated for the benefit of the state.[137] Foucault attributed this to the emergence of 'population' as an economic and political problem. It became more and more essential to keep tally of the workforce which supplied growing nation states, which meant governments became increasingly obsessed with measuring birth rates, marriages, and legitimate and illegitimate births. This was done to 'ensure population, to reproduce labour capacity, to perpetuate the form of social relations: in short, to constitute a sexuality that is economically useful and politically conservative.'[138] Births which occurred outside the acceptable confines of family structures, and which resulted from unsanctioned sexual relationships were not in the best interest of the state. Foucault was, of course, referring to Revolutionary France, but similar ideas can be seen in Britain. As Lisa Forman Cody has argued, concerns about plebeian sexual behaviour in Britain, which had previously been regulated by ecclesiastical authorities, by the mid-eighteenth century had become the concern of political economists, and through this, illegitimacy came to be seen as a drain on the nation.[139]

The long eighteenth century saw the birth of a number of charitable societies and reform movements which were concerned with improving the morality and welfare of Britain through the improvement of the morals and welfare of individuals. These ranged from the Society for the Reformation of Manners, which was founded in London in the 1690s, and Society Promoting Christian Knowledge, which was active in Wales through Griffith Jones's circulating schools, to the movement for the abolition of slavery led by William Wilberforce, whose other legacies include the 1787 Royal Proclamation *For the Encouragement of Piety and Virtue and for Preventing and Punishing of Vice, Profaneness and Immorality*.[140] These were projects of moral regulation led by the middling and upper classes who sought to maintain social control by regulating the morality of the people. They were motivated by anxieties generated by events such as the Industrial and French Revolutions which led to greater gulfs between the propertied classes and growing industrial elite, and the labouring classes who were increasingly worse off economically and socially.[141] From a sociological perspective, such projects can be seen as a process of governance which occurred within a political context with the purpose of controlling other social entities. They were undertaken by 'agents' such as parish officials acting against 'targets' such as unmarried mothers who deployed 'tactics' or 'techniques' of control such as registering and recording illegitimate children.[142] For Peter Burke, projects such as this occur when one social stratum seeks to assert dominance over another by first moralising some part of the culture of the lower social strata, then by acting upon it as something which can be reformed.[143] Thus, the increased registration of illegitimate baptisms could be understood in terms of a project of moral regulation in the sociological sense rather than as an actual demographic phenomenon.

Further evidence of the development of illegitimacy as a social problem in the eighteenth century can be seen in the establishment of institutions such as the Foundling Hospital. Thomas Coram's motivation for establishing the Hospital in London the 1740s was to preserve the lives of vulnerable infants who he believed were being abandoned in large numbers by their unmarried mothers. This was not simply a humanitarian effort, but rather a desire to preserve the economic prospects of a growing empire which was dependent upon a growing population to serve it at home and abroad. Through his charitable institution, illegitimate children could be salvaged and trained to work in respectable occupations which served Britain's broader economic interests.[144] Forty years later, Joseph Townsend also voiced concerns about the economic problems associated with illegitimacy. He believed that poor law support of illegitimate children incentivised sex outside of marriage, which led to the birth of more illegitimate children, which added pressure to an already strained poor relief system.

Perhaps most importantly, in his 1798 *An Essay on the Principle of Population* Thomas Malthus argued that because the population of Britain was growing beyond its ability to support itself the state could no longer afford to support illegitimate children, and therefore illegitimacy was detrimental to the wellbeing of Britain.[145] This was the first treatise in English to present illegitimacy as a social problem, and, significantly, it did so using statistics. Malthus's work must be understood as part of the 'discourse of statistics', which emerged in the eighteenth century and was arguably the most crucial catalyst in the transformation of illegitimacy into a social problem.[146] The systematic collection of statistical data on births provided a means for early social scientists to think about illegitimacy on a national scale, thus turning it into a national problem. For Foucault, mathematics provide the simplest means of conveying knowledge about individuals and societies with scientific form and justification.[147] As a result, it is accepted as fact that illegitimate births and unmarried mothers exist as naturally occurring, measurable phenomena rather than as cultural artefacts created for a particular political purpose.[148]

A connection can be made between these increasing anxieties and the Welsh context of illegitimacy. In 1788 Lloyd Kenyon was appointed Lord Chief Justice of England and Wales.[149] Kenyon was notoriously puritanical in his views towards sexual transgressions, which historians have attributed to growing anxieties about social order inspired by conflicts such as the French Revolution, and general political and economic instability.[150] Following his appointment, the number of cases of criminal conversation (female adultery) brought to trial increased dramatically.[151] Although these cases were restricted to the upper orders of society, they do reflect a broader 'sex panic' of the late eighteenth century which viewed female sexual transgressions as a threat to the stability of society.[152] These anxieties are also reflected in the growing number of pamphlets and tracts which addressed the perceived increase in problems such as divorce and adultery.[153] Lloyd Kenyon was born in Flintshire, and educated in Hanmer and Ruthin before pursuing a legal career. Prior to his appointment to Lord Chief Justice, he presided over the North Wales Circuit of the Court of Great Sessions.[154] His son, George Kenyon, inherited his father's title as well as his harsh stance on what he viewed on sexual immorality. The younger Lord Kenyon appears in the churchwarden accounts from the parish of Hanmer in 1809. The account book contains a record of a meeting called by Lord Kenyon on 11 January of that year to consider his proposed plan 'for the virtue and the prevention of all dissolute habits, fornication in particular.'[155] One of the motions recorded by the vicar of Hanmer, who chaired the meeting, noted:

> That it is the opinion of this meeting that as the plan proposed may not be wholly adequate to the total prevention of the evil; as it would leave the most crying side of the question open to those deaf

to shame and decency, unless the vice is severely punished, as well as virtue rewarded, it is therefore the earnest desire of the meeting that the Magistrates would exercise their utmost power in punishing those persons who are brought before them in cases of Bastardy.[156]

The details of what this plan involved were not recorded. Although ecclesiastical authorities were involved, the initatitive to reform plebeian sexual behaviour was implemented by a secular authority. This demonstrates that broader anxieties about the risks of sexual transgression amongst the ruling elite, which have been observed at a national level, had spread to more remote parts of Britain, such as Flintshire. Thus, vitriolic opinions about illegitimacy and fornication could have been one of the influences behind the increased numbers of illegitimate children recorded in baptism registers in Wales, and elsewhere.

Historians of gender have gone so far as to argue that statistical discourses can be deeply and problematically political in that they provide authoritative support to particular constructions of male and female identities which reinforce inequalities.[157] This is not to say that illegitimacy is not a worthy or suitable subject for study, but rather that caution should be taken when using statistics because they imply empirical certainty but depend on data which was recorded with a specific moral agenda. Unlike the study of demographic patterns such as fecundity or mortality the study of illegitimacy is not neutral, although it has been treated as such by many demographic historians.[158] Parish records can exhibit prejudices, as can be seen in the condemnatory language used by officials. In February 1751 in the parish of Marchwiel, Denbighshire Denbighshire an infant named Mary was baptised, and her mother was identified as the father's whore. This couple married two months later.[159] In New Radnor, Radnorshire, in 1730 the daughter of Judith Hoddall was baptised. Parish officials chose to label Judith as 'the infamous whore', and she continued to be listed as such in subsequent illegitimate baptism records.[160] When fathers are identified they rarely, if ever, have any moralising labels applied to them, which is due, in large part, to the paucity in the English language of condemnatory labels for a man who is perceived to act with sexual impropriety. The label 'illegitimate' was applied to children born in circumstances which did not conform to accepted ideals of proper sexual behaviour, and ultimately it was female sexuality which was seen to be the problem. To construct a model of analysis which depends largely on prejudices such as these could arguably be seen as complicit acceptance of these discriminations. Historians have since recognised that many of the earlier studies of illegitimacy, such as the work carried out by Laslett, were heavily value-laden, and added modern prejudices to historic ones, thus perpetuating the perception that unregulated female sexuality is inherently deviant.[161]

Introduction

However, despite the inherent flaws in the statistical analysis of illegitimacy, this data can still prove useful, but different questions must be asked of it. A social science approach to the statistical analysis of a historical social problem can still prove immensely useful, but only if the purpose is to better understand the effect rather than the cause.[162] Thus, this book will use the illegitimacy ratio only as a starting point for a more in-depth analysis of the broader context and experience of illegitimacy. It is clear from the evidence presented in Chapter 1 that the levels of reported illegitimacy in some regions of Wales did increase significantly over the course of the eighteenth century, but in other regions levels remained consistently low. By shifting the focus away from the qualification of causes to the quantification of effects such as infant mortality, and the qualitative experiences of illegitimacy for unmarried mothers, the remaining chapters will seek to better understand what these patterns of change can tell us about illegitimacy in eighteenth-century Britain.

Notes

1. Richard Adair, *Courtship, Illegitimacy and Marriage in Early Modern England* (Manchester: Manchester University Press, 1996), p. 90.
2. Adair, *Courtship*, p. 8.
3. Alysa Levene, Thomas Nutt and Samantha William, eds, *Illegitimacy in Britain: 1700–1920* (Basingstoke: Palgrave Macmillan, 2005), p. 11.
4. Peter Laslett, *Family Life and Illicit, Love in Earlier Generations: Essays in Historical Sociology* (Cambridge: Cambridge University Press, 1977); Peter Laslett, Karla Oosterveen and Richard M. Smith, eds, *Bastardy and Its Comparative History* (London: Arnold, 1980); Adair, *Courtship*.
5. For example, see: Andrew Blaikie, *Illegitimacy, Sex and Society in Northeast Scotland, 1750–1900* (Oxford: Clarendon Press, 1993); Rosalind Mitchison and Leah Leneman, *Girls in Trouble: Sexuality and Social Control: Scotland 1660–1780* (Edinburgh: Scottish Cultural Press, 1998).
6. Roy Porter, *English Society in the Eighteenth Century*, revised edn (Basingstoke: Palgrave Macmillan, 1990), p. 5.
7. Barry Reay, *Microhistories: Demography, Society and Culture in Rural England, 1800–1930* (Cambridge: Cambridge University Press, 1996), p. 212.
8. Several historians have already begun to consider illegitimacy as more than merely a demographic phenomenon, most notably Tanya Evans, *'Unfortunate Objects': Lone Mothers in Eighteenth-Century London* (Basingstoke: Palgrave Macmillan, 2005); Samantha Williams, *Unmarried Motherhood in the Metropolis, 1700–1850: Pregnancy, the Poor Law and Provision* (Basingstoke: Palgrave Macmillan, 2018); and the authors who contributed to the edited collection, Levene, et al, *Illegitimacy*.
9. The phrase, 'mortality penalty' is borrowed from Alysa Levene, 'The Mortality Penalty of Illegitimate Children: Foundlings and Poor Children in Eighteenth-Century England', in *Illegitimacy*, ed. by Levene, et al, pp. 34–49.
10. Evans, *Unfortunate Objects*; Laura Gowing, 'Secret Births and Infanticide in Seventeenth-Century England', *Past & Present*, 156 (1997), 87–115; Emma Griffin, 'Sex, Illegitimacy and Social Change in Industrializing Britain', *Social History*, 38 (2013), 139–161; Garthine Walker, 'Rape, Acquittal

and Culpability in Popular Crime Reports in England, c. 1670–c. 1750', *Past and Present*, 222 (2013), 115–142; Samantha Williams, 'The Experience of Pregnancy and Childbirth for Unmarried Mothers in London, 1760–1866', *Women's History Review*, 20 (2011), 67–86; Adrian Wilson, 'The Ceremony of Childbirth and Its Interpretation', in *Women as Mothers in Pre-Industrial Britain*, ed. by Valerie Fildes (Abingdon: Routledge, 2013), pp. 68–107; Adrian Wilson, *Ritual and Conflict: The Social Relations of Childbirth in Early Modern England* (Farnham: Ashgate, 2013).
11. David Howell, *The Rural Poor in Eighteenth-Century Wales* (Cardiff: University of Wales Press, 2000), p. 15; Melvin Humphreys, *The Crisis of Community: Montgomeryshire, 1680–1815* (Cardiff: University of Wales Press, 1996), p. 70 citing EA Wrigley and RS Schofield, *The Population History of England, 1541–1871: A Reconstruction* (London: Arnold, 1981), table 7.8.
12. Porter, *English Society*, p. 4.
13. Angela Muir, 'Illegitimacy in Eighteenth-Century Wales', *Welsh History Review*, 26 (2013), 351–388.
14. House of Commons, *Second Annual Report of the Poor Law Commissioners for England and Wales, Appendices A, B, C, D and E* (19th Century House of Commons Sessional Papers, 1836), Appendix D, pp. 507–508.
15. House of Commons, *Second Annual Report of the Poor Law Commissioners*, Appendix D, pp. 507–508.
16. House of Commons, *Reports of the Commissioners of Inquiry into the State of Education in Wales* (19th Century House of Commons Sessional Papers, 1847), pp. 57–61.
17. Gwyneth Tyson Roberts, *The Language of the Blue Books: The Perfect Instrument of Empire* (Cardiff: University of Wales Press, 1998), p. 22.
18. Jean Ware, 'How to Live in Wales: A Guide to Foreign Students, Including the English and Scots', *Wales*, 38 (1959), 57–61.
19. Muir, 'Illegitimate in Eighteenth-Century Wales'.
20. Adair, *Courtship*, pp. 48–49.
21. Laslett, *Family Life*, p. 113; Peter Laslett, 'Introduction', in *Bastardy*, ed. by Laslett, et al, pp. 14–16.
22. Laslett, 'Introduction', p. 18.
23. Adair, *Courtship*.
24. Figure 1: Comparison of English illegitimacy ratios taken from Laslett, 'Introduction', p. 14 and Adair, *Courtship*, p. 50. Laslett's decadal date format is 00–09 and Adair's in 01–10. The data has not been altered.
25. Rosalind Mitchison and Leah Leneman, 'Girls in Trouble: The Social and Geographical Setting of Illegitimacy in Early Modern Scotland', *Journal of Social History*, 21 (1988), 483–497 (p. 484); Rosalind Mitchison and Leah Leneman, 'Scottish Illegitimacy Ratios in the Early Modern Period', *Economic History Review*, 2nd ser., 1 (1987), 41–63 (p. 53).
26. Mitchison and Leneman, 'Girls in Trouble', p. 484; Mitchison and Leneman, 'Scottish Illegitimacy', p. 53.
27. Laslett, 'Introduction', p. 30.
28. Mitchison and Leneman, *Girls in Trouble*, p. 76; Mitchison and Leneman, 'Scottish Illegitimacy Ratios', pp. 51–53.
29. Adair, *Courtship*, p. 52.
30. Adair, *Courtship*, pp. 52–64.
31. Adair, *Courtship*, p. 63.
32. Peter Laslett, 'The Bastardy Prone Sub-Society', in *Bastardy*, ed. by Laslett, et al, pp. 217–240; Laslett, *Family Life*, p. 149.
33. Laslett, *Family Life*, p. 149.

Introduction

34. Steven King, 'The Bastardy Prone Sub-Society Again: Bastards and Their Fathers and Mothers in Lancashire, Wiltshire, and Somerset, 1800–1840', in *Illegitimacy*, ed. by Levene, et al, pp. 66–85 (p. 85).
35. Adair, *Courtship*, pp. 7, 68–76.
36. Nigel Goose, 'How Saucy Did It Make the Poor? The Straw Plait and Hat Trades, Illegitimate Fertility and the Family in Nineteenth-Century Hertfordshire', *History*, 91 (2006), 530–556; Griffin, 'Sex, Illegitimacy and Social Change'; Thomas Nutt, 'Illegitimacy, Paternal Financial Responsibility, and the 1834 Poor Law Commission Report: The Myth of the Old Poor Law and the Making of the New', *Economic History Review*, 63 (2010), 335–361; Nicholas Rogers, 'Carnal Knowledge: Illegitimacy in Eighteenth-Century Westminster', *Journal of Social History*, 63 (1989), 355–375; Edward Shorter, 'Illegitimacy, Sexual Revolution, and Social Change in Modern Europe', *The Journal of Interdisciplinary History*, 2 (1971), 237–272; Louise A Tilley, Joah W Scott and Miriam Cohen, 'Women's Work and European Fertility Patterns', *Journal of Interdisciplinary History*, 6 (1976), 447–476; Adrian Wilson, 'Illegitimacy and Its Implications in Mid-18th Century London: The Evidence of the Foundling Hospital', *Continuity and Change*, 4 (1989), 103–164.
37. Adair, *Courtship*, p. 79.
38. John Black, 'Who Were the Putative Fathers of Illegitimate Children in London?' in *Illegitimacy*, ed. by Levene, et al, pp. 50–65; Thomas Nutt, 'The Paradox and Problems of Illegitimate Paternity in Old Poor Law Essex', in *Illegitimacy*, ed. by Levene, et al, pp. 102–121.
39. Nutt, 'Paradox and Problems', pp. 104–106.
40. Black, 'Putative Fathers', pp. 54–58.
41. Alexandra Shepard, 'Brokering Fatherhood: Illegitimacy and Paternal Rights and Responsibilities in Early Modern England', in *Remaking English Society: Social Relations and Social Change in Early Modern England*, ed. by in Steve Hindle, Alexandra Shepard and John Walter (Woodbridge: Boydell Press, 2013), pp. 41–63.
42. Shepard, 'Brokering Fatherhood', p. 63.
43. Shepard, 'Brokering Fatherhood', p. 58.
44. Alan Macfarlane, 'Illegitimacy and Illegitimates in English History', in *Bastardy*, ed. by Laslett, et al, pp. 71–85 (p. 81).
45. Black, 'Putative Fathers', p. 54.
46. Mitchison and Leneman, 'Girls in Trouble', p. 486.
47. King, 'Bastardy Prone Sub-Society Again', p. 66.
48. Levene, et al, *Illegitimacy*.
49. Evans, *Unfortunate Objects*, p. 4.
50. Evans, *Unfortunate Objects*, p. 203.
51. Evans, *Unfortunate Objects*, pp. 173–202.
52. Laura Gowing, 'Giving Birth at the Magistrate's Gate: Single Mothers in the Early Modern City', in *Women, Identities and Communities in Early Modern Europe*, ed. by Stephanie Tarbin and Susan Broomhall (Aldershot: Ashgate, 2008), pp. 137–150; Williams, 'Experience of Pregnancy'; Williams, *Unmarried Motherhood*.
53. Gowing, 'Giving Birth', pp. 137–150.
54. Gowing, 'Giving Birth', pp. 148–150.
55. Sharon Howard, 'Imagining the Pain and Peril of Seventeenth-Century Childbirth: Travail and Deliverance in the Making of an Early Modern World', *Social History of Medicine*, 16 (2003), 367–382; Wilson, 'Ceremony of Childbirth'; Wilson, *Ritual and Conflict*.

Introduction 35

56. Gowing, 'Secret Births', p. 90.
57. Williams, 'Experience of Pregnancy'.
58. Williams, 'Experience of Pregnancy', pp. 74–76.
59. Peter Kitson, 'Differentials in Infant Survivorship Between Illegitimate and Legitimate Children: Case Studies of Two English Market Towns, ca. 1670–1830' (unpublished doctoral thesis, Cambridge, 2003) cited in Levene, 'Mortality Penalty'.
60. Levene, 'Mortality Penalty'.
61. Levene, 'Mortality Penalty', p. 44.
62. Roger Schofield, 'Did the Mothers Really Die? Three Centuries of Maternal Mortality in "The World We Have Lost"', in *The World We Have Gained: Histories of Population and Social Structure*, ed. by Lloyd Bonfield, Richard M Smith and Keith Wrightson (Oxford: Blackwell, 1986), pp. 231–260 (p. 260); Irvine Loudon, 'Deaths in Childbed from the Eighteenth Century to 1935', *Medical History*, 30 (1986), 1–41 (p. 6).
63. Loudon, 'Deaths in Childbed', p. 6.
64. Schofield, 'Did the Mothers Really Die?' p. 260.
65. See: Peter C Hoffer and NEH Hull, *Murdering Mothers: Infanticide in England and New England 1558–1803* (New York: New York University Press, 1981); Gowing, 'Secret Births'; Russell Grigg, 'Getting Away with Murder? Infanticide in Wales, 1730–1908', *Local Historian*, 44 (2014), 115–133; Mark Jackson, *New-Born Child Murder: Women, Illegitimacy and the Courts in Eighteenth-Century England* (Manchester: Manchester University Press, 1996); Mark Jackson, ed., *Infanticide: Historical Perspectives on Child Murder and Concealment, 1550–2000* (Aldershot: Ashgate, 2002); Anne-Marie Kilday, *A History of Infanticide in Britain, c. 1600 to the Present* (Basingstoke: Palgrave Macmillan, 2013); Garthine Walker, *Crime, Gender and Social Order in Early Modern England* (Cambridge: Cambridge University Press, 2003); RW Malcolmson, 'Infanticide in the Eighteenth Century', in *Crime in England 1550–1800*, ed. by JS Cockburn (Princeton: Princeton University Press, 1977), pp. 187–209; Nick Woodward, 'Infanticide in Wales, 1730–1830', *Welsh History Review*, 23 (2007), 94–125; Keith Wrightson, 'Infanticide in Earlier Seventeenth-Century England', *Local Population Studies*, 15 (1975), 10–22.
66. 21 James I c. 27, *An Act to Prevent the Destroying and Murthering of Bastard Children* (1623/4); 43 George III c. 58, *An Act for the Further Prevention of Malicious Shooting, and Attempting to Discharge Loaded Fire-Arms, Stabbing, Cutting, Wounding, Poisoning, and the Malicious Using of Means to Procure the Miscarriage of Women; and also the Malicious Setting Fire to Buildings; and also for Repealing a Certain Act, Made in England in the Twenty-First Year of the Late King James the First, Intituled, an Act to Prevent the Destroying and Murthering of Bastard Children; and also an Act Made in Ireland in the Sixth Year of the Reign of the Late Queen Anne, also Intituled, an Act to Prevent the Destroying and Murthering of Bastard Children; and for Making Other Provisions in Lieu Thereof*.
67. Jennifer Thorn, ed., *Writing British Infanticide: Child-Murder, Gender and Print, 1722–1859* (Newark: University of Delaware Press, 2003), p. 112.
68. Woodward, 'Infanticide in Wales', p. 124.
69. Woodward, 'Infanticide in Wales', p. 124.
70. Woodward, 'Infanticide in Wales', p. 124.
71. See: JM Beattie, *Crime and the Courts in England: 1660–1800* (Oxford: Oxford University Press, 1986); Annie Cossins, *Female Criminality: Infanticide, Moral Panic and the Female Body* (Basingstoke: Palgrave Macmillan,

2015); Elizabeth A Foyster, *Manhood in Early Modern England: Honour, Sex and Marriage* (London: Longman, 1999); Elizabeth A Foyster, *Marital Violence: An English Family History, 1660–1857* (Cambridge: Cambridge University Press, 2005); Anne-Marie Kilday and David S Nash, eds, *Histories of Crime: Britain 1600–2000* (Basingstoke: Palgrave Macmillan, 2010); James A Sharpe, *Crime in Seventeenth-Century England: A County Study* (Cambridge: Cambridge University Press, 1983); Walker, *Crime, Gender and Social Order*; KJ Kesselring, 'Bodies of Evidence: Sex and Murder (or Gender and Homicide) in Early Modern England, c. 1500–1680', *Gender and History*, 27 (2015), 245–262.

72. See: Randolph Roth, 'Gender, Sex, and Intimate-Partner Violence in Historical Perspective', in *The Oxford Handbook of Gender, Sex, and Crime*, ed. by Rosemary Gartner and Bill McCarthy (Oxford: Oxford University Press, 2014); Joanne Bailey, ' "I Dye [sic] by Inches": Locating Wife Beating in the Concept of a Privatization of Marriage and Violence in Eighteenth-Century England', *Social History*, 31 (2006), 273–294; Leah Leneman, ' "A Tyrant and Tormentor": Violence Against Wives in Eighteenth- and Early Nineteenth-Century Scotland', *Continuity and Change*, 12 (1997), 31–54; Elizabeth A Foyster, 'Male Honour, Social Control and Wife Beating in Late Stuart England', *Transactions of the Royal Historical Society*, 6 (1996), 215–224; Margaret R Hunt, ' "Great Danger She Had Reason to Believe She Was in": Wife-Beating in the Eighteenth Century', in *Women & History: Voices of Early Modern England*, ed. by Valerie Frith (Toronto: Coach House, 1995), pp. 81–102.
73. Laslett, 'Introduction', p. 48; RW McDonald, 'The Parish Registers of Wales', *National Library of Wales Journal*, 19 (1976), 399–429 (p. 399).
74. Janet Davies, *The Welsh Language* (Cardiff: University of Wales Press, 1993), p. 23.
75. Wilson, 'Ceremony of Childbirth', pp. 79–80.
76. Laslett, 'Introduction', p. 48; Adair, *Courtship*, p. 31.
77. Adair, *Courtship*, p. 42.
78. Richard Connors, 'Poor Women, the Parish and the Politics of Poverty', in *Gender in Eighteenth-Century England: Roles, Representations and Responsibilities*, ed. by Hannah Barker and Elaine Chalus (London and New York: Addison Wesley Longman, 1997), pp. 126–147 (pp. 134–135).
79. 14 Charles II c. 12, *An Act for the Better Relief of the Poor of This Kingdom* (1662); 17 George II c. 5, *An Act to Amend and Make More Effectual the Laws Relating to Rogues, Vagabonds and Other Idle and Disorderly Persons, and to Houses of Correction* (1743).
80. Macfarlane, 'Illegitimacy and Illegitimates', p. 81; Connors, 'Poor Women', p. 131; Adair, *Courtship*, p. 11.
81. Laslett, 'Introduction', p. 50.
82. Adair, *Courtship*, p. 32.
83. Adair, *Courtship*, pp. 32–35.
84. Anthea Newman, 'An Evaluation of Bastardy Recordings in an East Kent Parish', in *Bastardy*, ed. by Laslett, et al, pp. 141–157 (p. 145).
85. MGS (Carno) MGY/MR/PR/115, 1784, 1790, 1792, 1793.
86. PFHS (Gladestry) POW PR/17CD, 1778, 1783.
87. McDonald, 'Parish Registers', p. 411.
88. McDonald, 'Parish Registers', p. 412; Adair, *Courtship*, p. 35.
89. Laslett, *Family Life*, pp. 109–110.
90. Barry Reay, 'Sexuality in Nineteenth-Century England: The Social Context of Illegitimacy in Rural Kent', *Rural History*, 1 (1990), 219–247 (p. 221).

91. Reay, 'Sexuality', p. 221.
92. RE Jones, 'Infant Mortality in Rural North Shropshire, 1561–1810', *Population Studies*, 30 (1976), 305–317 (p. 313).
93. MGS (Carno) MGY/MR/PR/114 1702 and 1704.
94. Newman, 'An Evaluation', p. 142.
95. Laslett, *Family Life*, p. 120.
96. Adair chose to include illegitimate children found in burial registers in his analysis. See Adair, *Courtship*, p. 32.
97. For example, see Karen Oosterveen, Richard M Smith and Susan Stewart, 'Family Reconstitution and the Study of Bastardy', in *Bastardy*, ed. by Laslett, et al, pp. 86–140; Wrigley and Schofield, *Population History of England*.
98. Lawrence Stone, 'Kinship and Forced Marriage in Early Eighteenth-Century Wales', *Welsh History Review*, 17 (1995), 356–364 (p. 356); Michael Anderson, ed., *British Population History: From the Black Death to the Present Day* (Cambridge: Cambridge University Press, 1996), p. 113.
99. Although Wilson suggests that women who participated in extended lying-in periods which ended with churching may have delayed their child's baptism to allow them to be present, which meant public baptisms could occur up to four weeks after birth, however this was probably only true for higher-status women who could afford extended periods of lying-in. See Wilson, 'Ceremony of Childbirth', pp. 79–80.
100. Pat Hudson, *History by Numbers: An Introduction to Quantitative Approaches* (London: Arnold, 2000), p. 15; Humphreys, *Crisis of Community*, p. 70.
101. Porter, *English Society*, pp. 4–5; Adair, *Courtship*, p. 36.
102. Wrigley and Schofield, *Population History of England*, p. 96.
103. CFHS (Llanrhaeadr ym Mochnant) CLD-21809, 1759–1812.
104. Samantha Williams, '"They Lived Together as Man and Wife": Plebeian Cohabitation, Illegitimacy, and Broken Relationships in London, 1700–1840', in *Cohabitation and Non-Marital Births in England and Wales, 1600–2012*, ed. by Rebecca Probert (Basingstoke: Palgrave Macmillan, 2014), pp. 65–79 (p. 72).
105. For example, see Llandrindod Wells, PCA (Aberhafesp) M/EP/2/O/RT/1 (1751). In 1751 officials paid 18s. 6d. for a warrant and two journeys to Llanfyllin to pursue a father. Discussed further in Chapter 2.
106. Nutt, 'Paradox and Problems', p. 109.
107. Laura Gowing, 'Ordering the Body: Illegitimacy and Female Authority in Seventeenth-Century England', in *Negotiating Power in Early Modern Society: Order, Hierarchy and Subordination in Britain and Ireland*, ed. by Michael J Braddick and John Walter (Cambridge: Cambridge University Press, 2001), pp. 43–62 (pp. 56–57); Black, 'Putative Fathers', pp. 102–103.
108. For an excellent discussion about the problems of oath taking and credibility in early modern England, see Barbara J Shapiro, 'Oaths, Credibility and the Legal Process in Early Modern England: Part One', *Law and Humanities*, 6 (2012), 145–178; Barbara J Shapiro, 'Oaths, Credibility and the Legal Process in Early Modern England: Part Two', *Law and Humanities*, 7 (2013), 19–54.
109. Patricia Crawford, *Blood, Bodies and Families in Early Modern England* (Harlow: Pearson Education, 2004), p. 125.
110. Jackson, *Infanticide*, p. 37; Katherine D Watson, 'Women, Violent Crime and Criminal Justice in Georgian Wales', *Continuity and Change*, 28 (2013), 245–272 (p. 249).

38 *Introduction*

111. Malcolm Gaskill, 'Reporting Murder: Fiction in the Archives in Early Modern England', *Social History*, 23 (1998), 1–30 (p. 2).
112. Gaskill, 'Reporting Murder', p. 2.
113. Watson, 'Women, Violent Crime', p. 247.
114. Watson, 'Women, Violent Crime', pp. 247–248.
115. Gaskill, 'Reporting Murder', p. 3.
116. Natalie Zemon Davis, *Fiction in the Archives: Pardon Tales and Their Tellers in Sixteenth-Century France* (Stanford: Stanford University Press, 1987), pp. 3–4 cited in Gaskill, 'Reporting Murder', p. 4.
117. Gaskill, 'Reporting Murder', p. 4.
118. Aberystwyth, NLW 4/1000/8 (Mary Brown, Flintshire, 1731).
119. Gaskill, 'Reporting Murder', p. 6.
120. Sara D Luttfring, *Bodies, Speech, and Reproductive Knowledge in Early Modern England* (Abingdon: Routledge, 2016), p. 5.
121. KDM Snell, *Parish and Belonging: Community, Identity, and Welfare in England and Wales, 1700–1950* (Cambridge: Cambridge University Press, 2006), p. 85; 21 James I c. 27.
122. House of Commons, *Royal Commission of Inquiry into Administration and Practical Operation of Poor Laws* (1834), Appendix B.2, 'Answers to Town Queries', p. 180a.
123. John Humphrey Davies, *A Bibliography of Welsh Ballads Printed in the Eighteenth Century* (London: Honourable Society of Cymmrodorion, 1911).
124. As listed in Davies, *Bibliography of Welsh Ballads*. My thanks to Dr Siwan Rosser for her identifying these cases for me, and to Rhian Richards and Ian Rees for their help in translating these cases. See also, Siwan M Rosser, *Y Ferch ym Myd y Faled: Delweddau o'r Ferch ym Maledi'r Ddeunawfed Ganrif* (Cardiff: University of Wales Press, 2005), p. 90.
125. Laslett, *Family Life*.
126. The introduction to *Illegitimacy*, ed. by Levene, et al does describe illegitimacy as a social construction, p. 5.
127. Laslett, et al, *Bastardy*.
128. Mitchison and Leneman, *Girls in Trouble*, pp. 4–5; Anna Clark, 'Heterosexuality: Europe and North America', in *A Cultural History of Sexuality in the Enlightenment*, ed. by Julie Peakman (London: Bloomsbury, 2015), pp. 33–56 (p. 33).
129. Patricia Crawford, *Parents of Poor Children in England: 1580–1800* (Oxford: Oxford University Press, 2010), pp. 35–36.
130. Michel Foucault, *The History of Sexuality Volume 1: An Introduction*, trans. by Robert Hurley (London: Penguin, 1990), pp. 23–25; Gail Reekie, *Measuring Immorality: Social Inquiry and the Problem of Illegitimacy* (Cambridge: Cambridge University Press, 1998), p. 21.
131. Reekie, *Measuring Immorality*, p. 21.
132. Reekie, *Measuring Immorality*, pp. 23–25.
133. RB Outhwaite, *The Rise and Fall of English Ecclesiastical Courts 1500–1860* (Cambridge: Cambridge University Press, 2007), pp. 78–94.
134. Clark, 'Heterosexuality', p. 43; Anna Brueton, 'Illegitimacy in South Wales, 1660–1870' (unpublished doctoral thesis, Leicester, 2015), p. 28.
135. Jenny Teichman, *Illegitimacy: A Philosophical Examination* (Oxford: Blackwell, 1982), p. 10.
136. Evans, *Unfortunate Objects*, p. 42; Porter, *English Society*, p. 4.
137. Foucault, *History of Sexuality*, pp. 23–25.
138. Foucault, *History of Sexuality*, pp. 36–37.

139. Lisa Forman Cody, *Birthing the Nation: Sex, Science, and the Conception of Eighteenth-Century Britons* (Oxford: Oxford University Press, 2005), p. 284.
140. Reekie, *Measuring Immorality*, p. 66.
141. Alun Hunt, *Governing Morals: A Social History of Moral Regulation* (Cambridge: Cambridge University Press, 1999), pp. 57–60.
142. Hunt, *Governing Morals*, p. 28.
143. Hunt, *Governing Morals*, p. 31; Peter Burke, *Popular Culture in Early Modern Europe* (London: Temple Smith, 1978), pp. 207–243.
144. Reekie, *Measuring Immorality*, p. 52.
145. Reekie, *Measuring Immorality*, p. 49.
146. Reekie, *Measuring Immorality*, p. 27.
147. Michel Foucault, *The Order of Things: An Archaeology of the Human Sciences* (New York: Vintage Books, 1973), p. 351 cited in Reekie, *Measuring Immorality*, p. 48.
148. Reekie, *Measuring Immorality*, pp. 7–17.
149. Katherine Binhammer, 'The Sex Panic of the 1790s', *Journal of the History of Sexuality*, 6 (1996), 409–434 (p. 423).
150. Binhammer, 'Sex Panic', p. 423.
151. Lawrence Stone, *Broken Lives: Separation and Divorce in England, 1660–1857* (Oxford: Oxford University Press, 1993), p. 23 cited in Binhammer, 'Sex Panic', pp. 422–423.
152. Binhammer, 'Sex Panic', p. 423.
153. Binhammer, 'Sex Panic', p. 414.
154. George T Kenyon, *The Life of Lloyd, First Lord Kenyon, Lord Chief Justice of England* (London: Longmans, 1873), p. 109.
155. Hawarden, FRO (Hanmer) P/27/1/27 (1809).
156. FRO (Hanmer) P/27/1/27 (1809).
157. Reekie, *Measuring Immorality*, p. 26.
158. Teichman, *Illegitimacy*, p. 10.
159. CFHS (Marchwiel) CLD-22103 (1751 & 1752).
160. PFHS (New Roadn0r) POW/PR/16CD (1730, 1731).
161. Evans, *Unfortunate Objects*, p. 4.
162. Teichman, *Illegitimacy*, p. 21.

Part I
Prevalence and Causes

1 Illegitimacy, Paternity, Courtship and Poverty[1]

This chapter examines in detail the illegitimacy ratios from the 45 study parishes in mid and northeast Wales.[2] Quantitative analysis of illegitimacy ratios demonstrates that Welsh patterns of illegitimacy did roughly resemble trends elsewhere in Britain, but they differed in significant ways. Two important patterns emerge from this data: levels of illegitimacy were much higher in certain, but not all, parts of Wales in the eighteenth century, and levels of identified illegitimate paternity were consistently high in some regions, and fell considerably in others. As one of the first large-scale studies of Welsh data it is important to consider this evidence in relation to some of the extensive research on illegitimacy in England. For the purposes here, Welsh data is considered against two explanatory frameworks: those which attribute rising levels to cultural changes that influenced premarital sexual behaviour, and those which associate increases in illegitimacy with economic opportunities created by industrialisation.[3] The data presented here were considered in relation to other potential influencing factors, such as parish-level sex ratios, language and geographic features such as elevation; however no meaningful patterns or correlations emerged.[4] The two explanatory frameworks used in the analysis that follows have been chosen because they relate to significant cultural and socioeconomic changes that, in many ways, defined Britain in the eighteenth century.

Welsh evidence appears to challenge these understandings: because Wales was linguistically different and lacked certain cultural markers which some historians have associated with an eighteenth-century 'sexual revolution' And, furthermore, because the highest levels of illegitimacy are found in agricultural regions of Wales which experienced little or no industrial change. What the evidence examined here indicates is that Welsh illegitimacy was influenced by a combination of courtship-led marriage customs, a decline in traditional forms of social control and worsening economic circumstances. Surprisingly, these patterns appear remarkably similar to those found in London during the same period. Central to understanding these patterns are the cultural and economic contexts within which these changes occurred.

One of the biggest questions that historians of illegitimacy have tried to answer is why so many unmarried women bore children outside wedlock, particurarly towards the end of the eighteenth century. Hypotheses have included Laslett's 'bastardy prone sub-society', theories which relate either to non-marital cohabitation and irregular marriage, conjugal courtship customs whereby intended marriages were either delayed or thwarted as a result of changing socioeconomic circumstances and changes in sexual practice resulting from shifting attitudes towards penetrative sex.[5] Theories related to the bastardy prone sub-society, cohabitation and irregular marriage will be explored in Chapter 2. For the purposes of this chapter, Welsh evidence will be considered in relation to changes in sexual practice, and to theories about socioeconomic influences on courtship. Historians such as Tim Hitchcock, Thomas Laqueur, Randolph Trumbach and Faramerz Dabhoiwala have argued that the types of heterosexual sexual activity men and women engaged in changed during the eighteenth century, displacing activities such as mutual masturbation with penetrative sex, which resulted in more children being conceived and born outside of marriage.[6] Other historians, such as Peter Laslett, Richard Adair, Thomas Nutt and Nicholas Rogers have utilised various demographic, social and economic approaches to parish and court records to account for rising levels of illegitimacy.[7] Central to these approaches is the understanding that most illegitimacy resulted from courtships in which couples engaged in penetrative sex with the intention (or at least promise) of marriage, but failed to marry when pregnancy occured.[8] Such failures are often attributed to economic circumstances which prevented couples from marrying, and thus the influence of industrialisation in the eighteenth century is often central to these discussions.[9]

These two broad explanatory frameworks are not entirely at odds with each other, and do help shed light on different aspects of the tremendously complex phenomenon of plebeian sexual culture in the eighteenth century, which is notoriously difficult to access. It is therefore useful to consider these in tandem.[10] The extensive work which has been done within these broad approaches is compelling and convincing, and contributes a great deal to our understanding of illegitimacy in eighteenth-century England. Both Emma Griffin and Adrian Wilson have integrated elements of these two broad approaches to explore the ways in which sexual practice intersected with changing economic circumstances to produce a larger number of illegitimate children in the eighteenth century.[11] These integrated approaches provide a useful starting point for analysis of Welsh illegitiamcy, and also allow for the Welsh context to be drawn into the debates about illegitimacy in Britain more broadly. Levels of illegitimacy will be analysed first, followed by an examination of patterns of identified illegitimate paternity. The significance of these demographic trends will then be considered in relation to sexual culture and courtship in Wales, and an examination of economic circumstances within which these activities took place. What this analysis reveals is the extent to which illegitimacy levels were acutely sensitive to economic hardship, the effects of which were amplified when certain types of courtship practices were present.

Comparative Illegitimacy Ratios

Figure 1.1 compares the aggregate data from the 45 Welsh parishes to Laslett's 98 English parishes.[12] This comparison indicates that levels of reported illegitimacy in Wales during the eighteenth century were consistently, and at times significantly, higher than the overall average for England. The illegitimacy ratio in mid-Wales- rose 2 per cent to 7.5 per cent over the 120-year period, with one early peak of 4 per cent in the decade 1700–1709, dropping back to roughly 2.9 per cent in the 1720s before steadily increasing. This early peak may provide evidence that fluctuations in illegitimacy in Wales are attributable to less than favourable economic circumstances, as these years saw a series of poor harvests due to long winters and cold summers which resulted in famine, particularly in the celtic periphery of Britain.[13] During this decade, Montgomeryshire experienced three years of 'crisis mortality' when the number of burials outnumbered the number of baptisms by at least 10 per cent. In 1709 crisis mortality in the county reached 20 per cent, and in 1700 and 1708 this rose to over 30 per cent.[14] Other than the early peak, the trend in Wales appears to have followed roughly the same pattern as in England, with increasing divergence over the course of the period. In the 1680s the

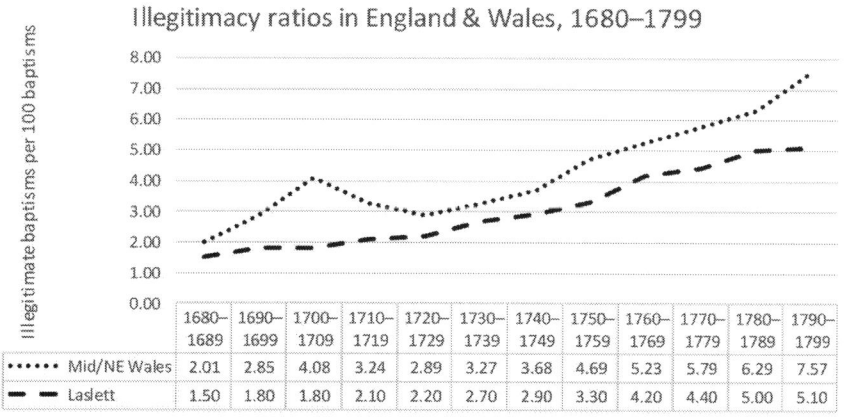

Figure 1.1 Comparison of illegitimacy ratios in Wales and England.

Source: English data taken from Laslett, 'Introduction', Bastardy, p. 14.

46 Prevalence and Causes

difference between Wales and England was approximately 0.5 per cent, whereas by the end of the eighteenth century it had increased to nearly 2.5 per cent.

These findings are consistent with evidence presented by Anna Brueton in her doctoral research on south Wales. She found illegitimacy ratios in the regions she examined fluctuated in an increasing trend from just below 2 per cent in the 1680s to just below 8 per cent in the late 1790s (Figure 1.2).[15] Illegitimacy in south Wales in the 1680s was comparable to the aggregate for England as a whole, however it increased steadily in the 1690s and 1700s and then dropped before reaching an early peak in the 1720s. The ratio then fell more markedly in the 1730s than it did in mid and northeast Wales, dropping slightly below the English average before continuing on a similar upward and increasingly divergent trend over the remaining decades of the century. The continuinity in trend between south, mid and northeast Wales is striking, particularly from the 1740s onwards. Based on Brueton's findings and the data presented here, it is now possible to say with a sufficient degree of certainty that levels of recorded illegitimacy across Wales were noticeably on the increase from the second quarter of the eighteenth century onwards, and gained increased momentum as the century progressed. Although illegitimacy in England was also on the rise during this period, overall levels in Wales were consistently higher, and the marked differences noted by poor law reports in the 1830s were evident in some parts of Wales at least 100 years before this date.

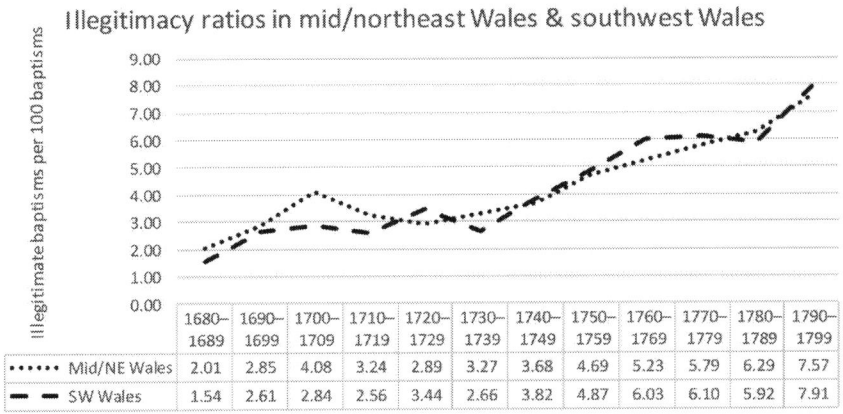

Figure 1.2 Comparison of illegitimacy in mid and northeast Wales with southwest Wales.

Source: Southwest Welsh data taken from Brueton, 'Illegitimacy in South Wales', p. 49.

Regional Trends

In his study of 250 English parishes between the 1530s and 1750s, Adair distinguished between highland regions in the north and west, and lowland regions in the south and east of England, and found that highland regions consistently experienced higher levels of illegitimacy throughout the period covered by his study.[16] All of the Welsh parishes considered here are in Adair's highland zone, so his highland/lowland distinction is not appropriate to this study. However, regional variations which may not be linked to topography are still evident. Comparisons can be made with Adair's regional data for the latter part of the seventeenth and early eighteenth centuries. The most relevant regions for comparison are Adair's west and northwest regions, as the western region includes the county of Shropshire, which borders Denbighsire, Montgomeryshire and Radnorshire, and the northwest region shows a roughly analogous pattern of change over time (see Figure 1.3).[17] Although illegitimacy ratios in mid and northeast Wales were constantly higher than in western England, particurarly between 1690 and 1710, the upward trend across both regions from the 1720s is notably similar in both level and trajectory. All three regions began with a ratio of between 2 and 3 per cent in the 1680s, and ended with between 3 and 4 per cent in the 1740s, which was the last complete decade studied by Adair.

When ratios are disaggregated to the level of the county (Figure 1.4) regional variations become even more apparent, and it is evident that

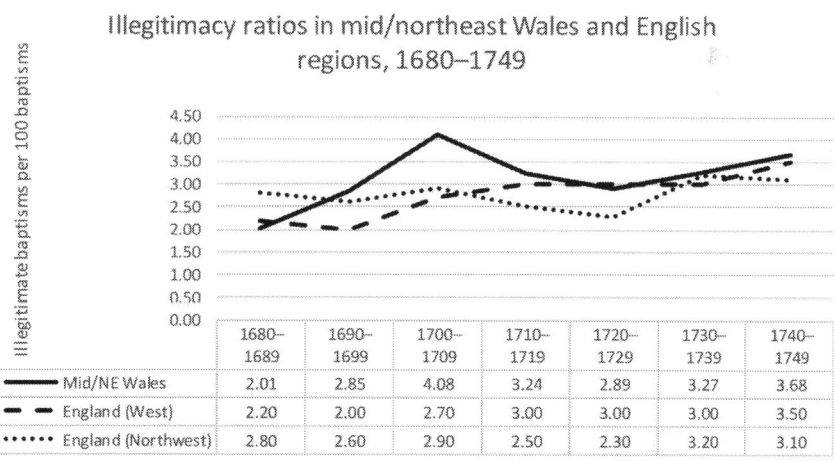

Figure 1.3 Comparison of illegitimacy in mid and northeast Wales with west and northwest England.

Source: English data taken from Adair, *Courtship*, pp. 51–62.

48 *Prevalence and Causes*

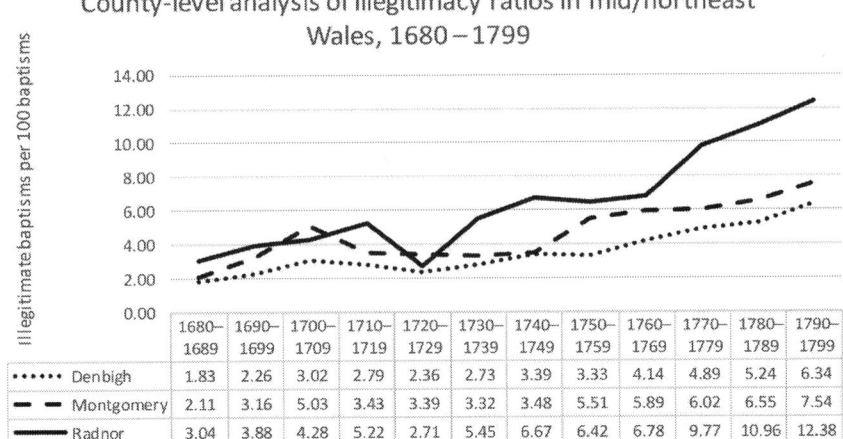

Figure 1.4 County-level analysis of illegitimacy ratios in Denbighshire, Montgomeryshire and Radnorshire, 1680–1799.

reported illegitimacy in Radnorshire was considerably higher than both Denbighshire and Montgomeryshire. This suggests that there was not a singular 'Welsh' experience of bearing a child outside of wedlock. Levels in all three counties were relatively comparable in the last two decades of the seventeenth century, and, with the exception of a drop in the 1720s, the ratio of illegitimate baptisms in Radnorshire increased substantially, especially from the 1730s onwards, with a sharp increase between 1770 and 1799. The early peak in the 1700s is evident in Montgomeryshire, and precedes a similar peak in Radnorshire in the follwing decade. However, levels in Denbighshire remained relatively consistent from the 1690s until the 1750s, afterwhich illegitimacy increased steadily across all three counties. By the end of the century all three counties had higher illegitimacy ratios than than the national average in England, with Denbighshire and Montgomeryshire 1.2 and 2.4 per cent, respectively. The early and sustained increase in illegitimacy in Radnorshire from the 1730s is particurarly striking, and suggests significant continunity with the levels reported in the 1830s. Radnorshire ended the century with levels of reported illegitimacy nearly two and a half times greater than England, which indicates significant regional variations existed within Wales that cannot be explained by a single cultural variable.

Considerable variation is also apparent within each county. As Figure 1.5 demonstrates, the parishes which experienced the highest levels of illegitimacy are in Radnorshire and the southeastern parts of Montgomeryshire, and are closest to the border regions with England.[18] The parishes

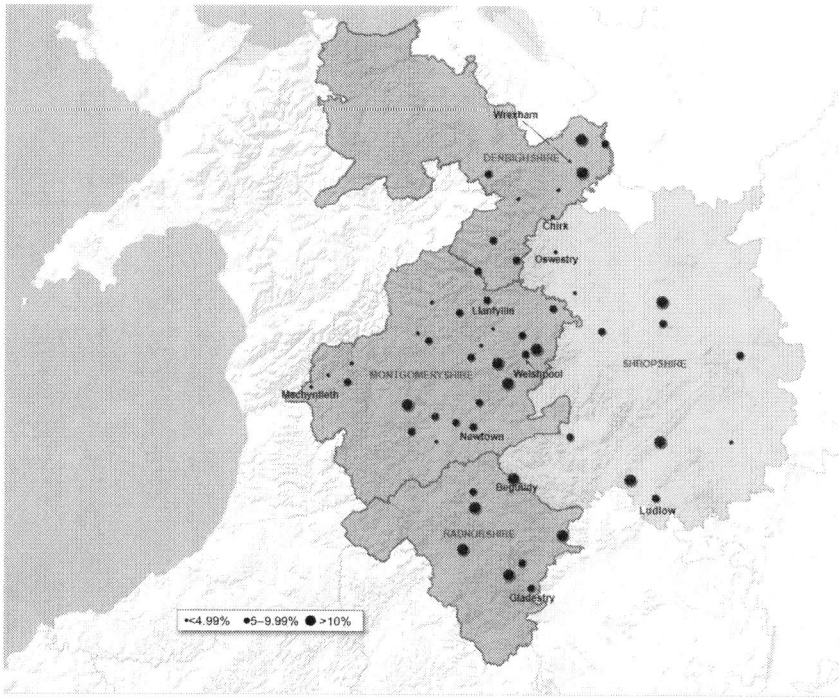

Figure 1.5 Map of illegitimacy ratios by parish, 1790–1799: Denbighshire, Montgomeryshire, Radnorshire and Shropshire.

Source: Map by author.

with the lowest levels of illegitimacy are scattered across Montgomeryshire and Denbighshire. The concentrated areas of lower illegitimacy in western Montgomeryshire roughly correlate with areas involved in the wollen trade.[19] Similarly, the areas of lower illegitimacy in Denbighshire roughly correspond coalmining areas, although higher levels were still to be found in mineral-rich regions along the English border.[20] The limited correlation between these economic factors and illegitimacy levels will be explored further later. Perhaps most notably, in the last decade of the eighteenth century many parishes located within the boundaries of the English county of Shropshire had illegitimacy ratios which exceeded the ratios of some Welsh parishes. This strongly suggests that the factors which contributed to increased levels of illegitimacy in England and Wales were tied to more diverse, regional socioeconomic variables rather than distinctive 'national' characteristics. These local and regional variations, which are frequently masked by broader statistical trends, are significant and warrant further investigation. In understanding the diversity of reproductive experiences in the eighteenth century the outliers are arguably as important as the average.

Taking into account the exceptionally high levels of illegitimacy seen in the later eighteenth century across mid and northeast Wales, and Radnorshire in particular, it is clear that something changed which either enabled or encouraged Welsh men and women to have more procreative sex outside of marriage. Instances of recorded illegitimacy do not represent every instance of sex outside of marriage which took place, and therefore baptism registers under-represent the amount of sex unmarried men and women were having.[21] When this list of requisite circumstances discussed in the introduction is considered alongside an illegitimacy ratio of between 6 and 12 per cent it becomes apparent that a sizeable proportion of unmarried men and women in Wales were engaging in considerably more pre- or extramarital sex by the end of the eighteenth century than their counterparts a century earlier. Such a significant shift was likely not caused by a single phenomenon, but rather by a confluence of influences.

Identified Illegitimate Paternity

Another compelling pattern which is apparent in many Welsh baptism registers is the frequency with which unmarried fathers were identified at the time of baptism. In many parts of England, unmarried fathers were identifiable in fewer than 50 per cent of cases and in some areas in as few as 7 per cent of cases.[22] However, some Welsh parishes identified unmarried fathers in over 80 per cent of cases. This phenomenon is significant for two reasons: first, as will be explored in Chapter 2, it provides clues about the socioeconomic background of fathers, and the relationships between the unmarried men and women who begat and bore children in the eighteenth century. Second, as with patterns of illegitimacy, the evidence of identified illegitimate paternity reveals marked regional variation, and both continuity and change over time. When considered in relation to the cultural and socioeconomic circumstances within each county, these patterns provide vital clues to some of the causes which influenced the dramatic changes in levels of illegitimacy seen in Wales during the eighteenth century.

Analysis of levels of identifiable illegitimate paternity in this study considers data from the years 1700 to 1799. Evidence from the earlier period has not been included here due to inconsistencies in the information recorded in parish baptism registers. The level of identified illegitimate paternity is calculated by decade as a percentage of the total number of illegitimate baptisms in a given parish over the same period. The level of identifiable paternity has been calculated at the level of the county and parish. When taken in aggregate, the level of identified illegitimate paternity across the 45 Welsh parishes fluctuated considerably, and with the exception of the 1760s, consistently remained at or above 60 per cent throughout the century (see Figure 1.6). The aggregate level of identified

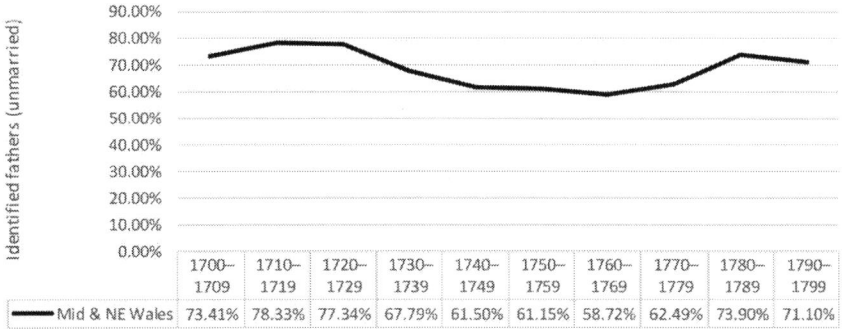

Figure 1.6 Percentage of baptisms of illegitimate children in which fathers were named, mid/northeast Wales aggregate.

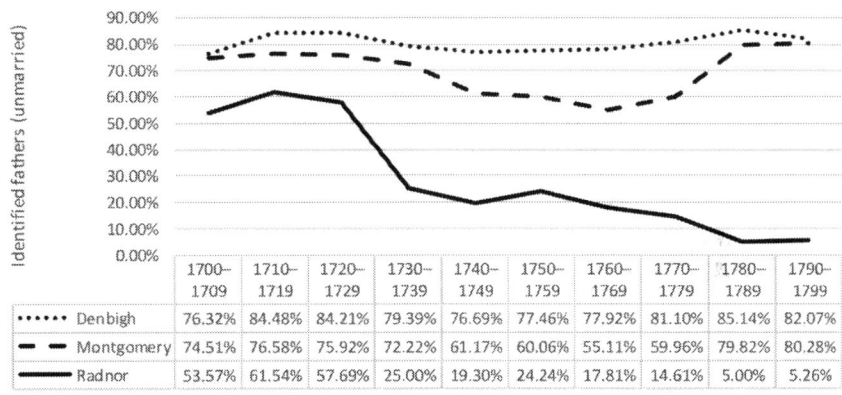

Figure 1.7 Percentage of baptisms of illegitimate children in which fathers were named, Denbighshire, Montgomeryshire and Radnorshire.

paternity peaked at just above 78 per cent in the 1710s then decreased steadily to as low as 58 per cent in the 1760s before recovering to over 70 per cent in the final two decades of the century. However, a disaggregate county-level analysis reveals that this overall trend is somewhat misleading, as levels of identified illegitimate paternity in Radnorshire were markedly lower (see Figure 1.7). As will be seen, disparity between all three counties is considerable, and demonstrates how the amalgamation of data from smaller areas into larger-scale studies can obscure the nuances of regional variation.

Fathers of illegitimate children in Denbighshire were consistently identified in over 75 per cent of illegitimate baptisms across the century. In Montgomeryshire, fathers were identified in between approximately 72 and 77 per cent of baptisms in the first four decades of the century before declining to 55 per cent in the 1760s, and increasing to approximately 80 per cent in the 1780s and 1790s. The situation in Radnorshire was considerably different. Levels of identifiable paternity in the first three decades of the century were markedly lower, ranging between 53 and 62 per cent before falling dramatically to between 19 and 25 per cent between 1730 and 1759, then continuing on a pronounced downward trajectory, reaching a low of approximately 5 per cent in the last two decades of the century. At no point over the 100-year period did overall levels of identifiable paternity in Radnorshire meet or exceed levels in Denbighshire or Montgomeryshire. Although levels of identification in Montgomeryshire and Radnorshire declined between the 1720s and 1760s, when levels began to identification began to increase in Montgomeryshire in the 1760s, the rate of decline in Radnorshire increased. When considered in relation to broader cultural and economic circumstances, this phenomenon may be central to our understanding of the causes and nature of illegitimacy in eighteenth-century Wales.

Courtship in Wales

Many historians maintain that courtship was the leading cause of childbirth outside of marriage in eighteenth-century Britain, and Richard Adair has suggested that high levels of identified illegitimate paternity may be indicative of conjugal courtship customs.[23] Any unmarried woman of reproductive age was at risk of bearing an illegitimate child.[24] That risk increased substantially if she was engaging in regular sexual contact, even if penetrative sex only took place during the latter, most serious stages of courtship, because interruption in the marriage process could have resulted in a child being born outside of wedlock. Unfortunately, the vast majority of men and women involved in illegitimacy in the eighteenth century left no accounts of their own experiences. As discussed in Chapter 2, not all illegitimate children were conceived under similar circumstances, which makes accounting for broad trends and change over time problematic. Ample evidence of exploitative sexual relationships exists, and it seems deeply inappropriate to count children born as a result of rape or incest in the same category of sexual experience as consensual premarital sex.[25] Moreover, many men and women who were not married to each other possibly engaged in consensual sexual activity with no intention of marrying at all, as can be seen in cases of adultery or prostitution. With the exception of only the most detailed entries, parish registers unfortunately provide no way for modern researchers to distinguish between different types of consensual and non-consensual procreative sex. It is therefore important to bear in mind that considering illegitimacy ratios in aggregate obscures the diversity of lived sexual experiences, and that there can be no universal explanation for why children were conceived outside of wedlock. Nevertheless, it is highly probable that many, if not most, illegitimate children born in eighteenth-century Britain were conceived with the intention to marry on the part of one or both parties.

Emma Griffin's analysis of plebeian autobiographies found that unmarried men and women did sometimes engage in sexual activity either on promise of marriage, or in hopes of securing a marriage.[26] Unfortunately, similar first-hand accounts do not exist for Wales. However, certain Court of Great Sessions records do indicate that sex was very much a part of premarital courtship for some couples, at least from 1750 onwards. The most compelling evidence comes, perhaps surprisingly, from murder trials.[27] These cases will be explored in much greater detail in Chapter 4, but certain shared features warrant briefly outlining here. Between 1750 and 1800 five pregnant single women were murdered, and in each of the cases the accused was the supposed father of the child, and the relationship between victim and accused was understood to be one of courtship.[28] In the 1764 murder of Elizabeth Evans by Evan Jenkins, Jenkins's employer deposed that he believed the two were intending to marry as the banns had been published.[29] In the 1788 murder of Margaret Thomas, a witness deposed that she had heard the accused, William Williams, asking Margaret to publish banns so the two could marry.[30] In 1756, Margaret Matthews was murdered, and the lone suspect was Edward Pugh, who witnesses said was courting her. One witnessed deposed that on the night she disappeared, Margaret went searching for Edward, 'to know his answer . . . whether he would have her or take care of her and her child.'[31] Caution should be taken when considering these cases in terms of the broader experience of courtship in Wales as they are in many ways exceptional. These women were all murdered by men who they had hoped to marry, and those sentiments were clearly not reciprocated. For example, Evan Jenkins confessed to his gaoler that he 'would rot in iron before he would marry [Elizabeth].'[32] However, it is entirely plausible that the victims and their communities genuinely believed these relationships would eventually be solemnised, and perhaps these women had hoped that by becoming pregnant their partners would be compelled to marry them.[33] Although both tragic and exceptional, these examples do demonstrate that premarital penetrative sex was taking place in Wales within the context of courtship, and communities were aware of these relationships.

Welsh courtship customs which could have involved sexual contact include practices such as bundling, which are sometimes referred to as *caru ar* [or *yn*] *y gwely*, or 'love on [or in] the bed'.[34] Bundling entailed a young couple spending an evening, and frequently an entire night, together in bed, unsupervised, typically in the home of the young woman.[35] If and when the woman conceived, marriage was the expected outcome. The origins of the custom are not clear, but it has been argued that it was either a form of fertility testing or trial marriage to test a couple's compatibility.[36] Although not unique to Wales, it is the courtship custom most frequently associated with the country.[37] Evidence of the practice and what it involved is scarce. As a popular custom of the rural poor no first-hand written accounts of bundling in the eighteenth century exist, but reference to it can be found in some official nineteenth-century accounts. Evidence from the eighteenth century is scarce, but the accounts that do exist are richer in detail. Intriguingly, some English travel writers who claimed to have witnessed the custom depicted it as a polite one which did not involve any sexual contact at all. An English traveller described the bundling he witnessed while staying as a guest in a Welsh home in Merionethshire in 1772 as completely modest, contrary to accounts of Welsh virtue he had previously heard.[38] An anonymous writer described the ritual as explained to him by locals in Harlech as retiring to bed together and saying 'the same things there as are generally said under less favourable circumstances, but it is to be noticed the friends of both are frequently present and the lady is only half undressed.'[39] Another particularly detailed account described bundling as an innocent ritual, while also providing further insight into the socioeconomic background of those who participated in it:

> The lower order of people do actually carry on their love affairs in bed, and what would extremely astonish more polished lovers, they are carried on honourably, it being, at least, as usual . . . to go from the bed of courtship to the bed of marriage, as unpolluted and maidenly . . . and yet, you are not to conclude that this proceeds from their being less susceptible of the belle passion than their betters.[40]

Other accounts describe the ritual as not entirely innocent, but generally acceptable amongst the labouring classes, as long as the couples marry:

> Much has been said of the innocence with which these meetings are conducted, but it is a very common thing for the consequence of the interview to make its appearance in the world within two or three months after the marriage ceremony has taken place. The subject excites no particular attention among the neighbours, provided the marriage be made good before the living witness is brought to light. Since this custom is entirely confined to the labouring classes of the community, it is not so pregnant with danger as, on a first supposition, it might seem.[41]

These accounts are recorded by English visitors travelling through Wales commenting on the antiquities and novelties of 'Welshness'. It is difficult to know if the accounts of outside observers represent an 'authentic' description of customs which they may not have fully understood, or to which they may not have been completely privy. However, these conflicting descriptions may also be indicative of changes in sexual practice that took place during the century and which may account for increasing levels of illegitimacy.

The authors of the 1834 *Rural and Town Queries*, which heavily influenced subsequent poor law reform, identified bundling as a 'powerful cause' behind the high levels of illegitimacy reported in nineteenth-century Wales.[42] The report described bundling as 'the way in which all courtships amongst the lower class have been carried on from time immemorial', and it was not considered 'either immoral or indecent.'[43] Similarly, nineteenth-century commentators in the Blue Books attributed the substantial number of illegitimate children and pregnant, unmarried mothers they observed in Welsh communities to the relative acceptability of premarital sex between courting couples, which included the practice of staying up all night without supervision. Other than referring to bundling as 'courting in bed', the report offered no description of what courting couples actually did, although we can implicitly assume the authors believed some were engaging in penetrative sex, as the practice often resulted in pregnancy. Fragments of evidence can also be found in court records from the nineteenth century. In Carmarthenshire in 1816 a yeoman and lay preacher named Rees Thomas Rees from Llangadog was convicted of murdering Elizabeth Jones, his 19-year-old lover. Elizabeth's father testified that Rees had been 'in the habit of sitting up with the deceased in [her] house for the purpose of courting her as was customary in the county.'[44] Elizabeth became pregnant, and Rees convinced her to consume a mixture of arsenic and mercury in an attempt to induce an abortion; Elizabeth died as a result. Although not referred to specifically by name as bundling or *caru ar y gwely*, it is probably the same practice mentioned by the authors of *Rural and Town Queries*. Eight years later in Anglesey, a labourer named Griffith Roberts was charged with burglary for unlawfully entering a dwelling.[45] His defence was that he had entered the property with the intention of courting a servant in the household, and he was never indicted. Such a defence would only be possible if it was customary for young men to secretly enter the homes of the women they were courting at night. It is highly plausible, therefore, that bundling was part of plebeian courtship in some parts of Wales, at least in the nineteenth century. In certain circumstances, it clearly did create an opportunity for couples to engage in penetrative sex, but how many actually did so is impossible to ascertain.

A Welsh Sexual Revolution?

Much has been written about heterosexual sex in the seventeenth and eighteenth centuries.[46] Some historians have argued that the type of sex men and women were engaging in changed, and such changes were part of a broader sexual revolution which was brought on by the economic growth and social change resulting from increasing industrialisation, the Enlightenment, and the decline in ecclesiastical regulation of sexual behaviour.[47] As a result, perceptions about male and female sexuality shifted between the late seventeenth and early eighteenth centuries, whereby women went from being understood in cultural, medical and legal terms as sexually aggressive and lustful to being perceived as sexually passive.[48] This was mirrored by a correlative emergence of a new active male sexuality, which emphasised penetrative sex. Tim Hitchcock describes this as a shift away from non-penetrative sexual activity, such as mutual masturbation, towards more 'phallo-centric' sex.[49] Such a shift would have been particularly significant for unmarried couples engaging in sexual activity, as more penetrative sex outside of marriage would have resulted in more childbirths outside of marriage. This change in sexual practices is used to account for, at least in part, the increasing levels of illegitimacy seen in the eighteenth century. Hitchchock maps these changes onto the growing popularity of proscriptive literature which increasingly denounced the sin of Onan, associated particularly, but not only, with male masturbation.[50] The earliest English-language example of this type of literature was *Rebuke of the Sin of Uncleanness* by Josiah Woodward, which was published by the Society for the Promotion of Christian Knowledge (SPCK) in 1704.[51] Later and more popular examples include the anonymous *Onania, or the Henious Sin of Self-Pollution, and all its Frightful Consequences in both Sexes . . .*, which was published in 1708, and Tissot's *Onanism: or a Treatise upon the Dissorders Produced by Masturbation*, which was published in French in 1758 and subsequently translated into English in 1766.[52] Other advice literature, such as *Aristotle's Master-piece: or, the Secrets of Generation Displayed in all the Parts Thereof*, which was first published in 1684, and Nicholas Venette's *Tableau de l'amour conjugal*, first translated into English in 1703, were manuals of reproductive knowledge. These works were not so much anti-masturbatory as they were 'pro-natalist'.[53] *Onanism* and *Aristotle's Masterpiece* remained in publication until the twentieth century.[54] The significance of this type of literature was that it propagated a type of sexual knowledge which emphasised the importance of the penis in reproduction, and resulted in a profound shift in sexual practice.[55] How far these ideas disseminated throughout society is impossible to measure, but the persistent and increasing popularity of the text would indicate a wide reception.

The presence of similar literature in Wales may therefore be an indicator of whether Wales experienced a similar revolution in sexual practice. Rising levels of illegitimacy, and conflicting descriptions of bundling may suggest that sexual culture changed during the eighteenth century, particularly for courting couples. It is possible that descriptions such as Mr Pratt's reflect earlier non-penetrative manifestations of bundling which, by the nineteenth century, had evolved to include penetrative sex. However, the types of evidence Hitchcock uses in his analysis of sexual change in England is conspicuously absent in Wales. Before 1800, Wales remained predominantly monoglot Welsh, although areas such as Pembrokeshire, communities closer to the English border, and industrialising regions of the south, would have had larger English-speaking populations, and many would have been bilingual.[56] The existence of these texts in Welsh would therefore provide persuasive evidence of a similar shift in Wales. An increasing number of printing presses dedicated to the printing of Welsh-language materials were founded from the early 1700s, and by 1800 virtually every Welsh town had at least one press.[57] Despite there being the means to reproduce such texts, the vast majority of works published by these presses were of a religious nature.[58] Crucially, not a single Welsh translation of any of these works were produced during the eighteenth century, and there was no original Welsh-language equivalent.[59] *Aristotle's Masterpiece* was translated into Welsh as *Gwaith Aristotle*, but not until 1826. The SPCK, which was active in Wales in the eighteenth century, did translate some of Josiah Woodward's works into Welsh, however *Rebuke of the Sin of Uncleanness* does not appear to be one of them.[60] There is therefore no clear link between the ideas communicated in these genres of literature and Welsh sexual culture in the eighteenth century. It is possible that ideas about anti-masturbatory, pro-penetrative sex were disseminated throughout Wales via oral culture. Research into medical knowledge in eighteenth-century Wales has provided convincing evidence that information about medicine and remedies found in popular medical texts were translated and passed through oral communication, and then transcribed in personal diaries and household accounts.[61] However, given the complete absence of any proscriptive literature about sexual conduct in the Welsh language in the eighteenth century, its impact on the types of sex unmarried Welsh men and women were having should not be overstated.

Despite the absence of pro-penetrative Welsh literature, it is still possible that sexual culture in Wales changed during the eighteenth century, but for entirely different reasons. Moreover, that illegitimacy levels in Wales increased without a clear correlation with the types of literature examined by Hitchcock, it may be that these texts were not as instrumental as he suggests. It is worth nothing that not all historians are convinced by Hitchcock's hypothesis. In her analysis of seventeenth-century pornography, Sarah Toulalan has demonstrated that phallo-centrism existed much earlier than Hitchcock suggests. Furthermore, Toulalan argues that the popular sex manuals cited by Hitchcock actually arose out of a seventeenth-century culture and society which already favoured penetrative, procreative heterosexual sex.[62] Alternatively, Faramerz Dabhoiwala has identified the decline in legal regulation of sex outside of marriage as one of the central features of what he sees as an eighteenth-century sexual revolution.[63] To suggest that the changes which occurred in Wales amounted to a sexual 'revolution' would be an overstatement, but connection between the decline in ecclesiastical regulation and rising levels of illegitimacy can still be made. Throughout the early modern period, English and Welsh plebeian sexual activity had been regulated by the Church, and sexual transgressions were dealt with by church courts.[64] However, from the late seventeenth century onwards the authority of church courts began to wane, and by the late eighteenth century local ecclesiastical authorities were increasingly reluctant to prosecute for sexual transgressions such as premarital fornication and bastardy.[65] Subsequently, levels of reported illegitimacy in some areas began to rise.[66] Throughout the eighteenth century moral reformers did make repeated attempts to legislate against certain types of illicit sexual activity, but by the middle of the eighteenth century most consensual sex outside of marriage was no longer the concern of the courts.[67] Furthermore, the religious changes associated with the rise of nonconformity in Wales would have had little influence on plebeian sexuality in eighteenth-century mid-Wales. The vacuum created by the decline in the authority of ecclesiastical courts was not immediately filled by the moral strictures of Methodism. Although Wales in the nineteenth century is synonymous with staunch religious nonconformity, it is easy to exaggerate its impact prior to 1780.[68] The rise of Methodism was slow and fitful, and its message appealed more to the middling sort, particularly in towns, than to the poor labourers and paupers who constituted the bulk of the population. The circulating schools of Griffith Jones, which led to substantial increases in literacy and nonconformity, were not overly active in the area covered by this study.[69] Nonconformity did increase in the latter decades of the eighteenth century, and chapels began to be established in Montgomeryshire as early as the 1790s, but their numbers would not have been statistically significant enough to influence plebeian sexual behaviour more widely, especially earlier in the century.[70] In the later decades of the eighteenth century the population in poorer rural areas would have adhered to the established church.[71]

The decline in formal moral regulation of sexual behaviour likely did result in increased sexual freedom for courting couples, and perhaps even accelerated the speed with which some couples progressed to penetrative sex.[72] The existence of customs which already allowed young couples a degree of freedom and privacy during courtship may well have accentuated the impact of this decline. However, the waning of ecclesiastical authority over pre- and extramarital sexual behaviour on its own cannot entirely explain the changes in illegitimacy levels observed in Wales, as a similar decline occurred across England and Wales. Moreover, families and neighbours would still have viewed illicit sexual activity as a cause for concern. Communities would have played an active role in monitoring the behaviour of young, unmarried men and women, as few would have welcomed an increase in illegitimate births.[73] This is evident in an 1842 notice from the Board of Guardians of the Llanfyllin poor law union, who accused local farmers of, 'allowing a free intercourse between the female servants and men, after bed time,' which they attributed to the increasing costs of supporting illegitimate children in their workhouse.[74] The steps taken by poor law officials, such as these, as well as secular courts to regulate and manage illegitimacy demonstrate the extent to which illegitimacy was seen as a significant problem throughout the eighteenth century. However, their concerns were practical rather than moral, as children born outside of wedlock posed a financial risk to communities.[75] Sex within courtship may have been more acceptable to communities than other types of non-marital sexual relationships, but only if it resulted in marriage.[76] However, a significant proportion of children conceived under these circumstances in Wales were not born to married parents, which raises the question of why so many Welsh couples were engaging in courtship practices but never marrying.

The Economics of Marriage and Illegitimacy

The most widely explored explanations for why courting couples failed to marry are related to economic circumstances. Peter Laslett codified one version of this in his 'courtship intensity' hypothesis, which assumes that couples based their courtship decisions on their financial prospects and ability to establish their own home and independence. This hypothesis, which also correlates with changes in the age of first marriage, posits that during periods of perceived economic stability marriage prospects for young people would appear good, therefore the age of marriage would drop, and more couples would engage in intensive courtship which involved penetrative sex. Increased sexual activity resulted in increased prenuptial pregnancy when the courtship was successful, and increased illegitimacy when the courtship failed or was interrupted. A significant proportion of illegitimate births were therefore 'accidents of courtship' which resulted from intensified courtship activity under more prosperous economic circumstances.[77] Conversely, when economic prospects seemed poor, young people refrained from intensive courtship practices. Therefore, higher levels of illegitimacy should correlate with improved economic circumstances. Not all historians are convinced by the courtship intensity hypothesis. David Levine has argued that although economic changes may have delayed the age at which couples married, economic factors may not have influenced sexual behaviour outside of marriage.[78] Emma Griffin has argued that this broad theory cannot account for the diverse variations found in regional studies and, furthermore, it is impossible to know how many couples within a community were actively engaging in courtship at any given time.[79] Adrian Wilson has found more convincing evidence of a correlation between precarious economic circumstances, as evidenced by increasing grain prices resulting from bad harvest, and higher levels of illegitimacy in London manifested in the number of women seeking reprieve from the Foundling Hospital.[80] Wilson argues that these circumstances were compounded by courtship practices which differed to those found in rural England. This model may work in relation to Welsh evidence, and will be explored further later.

Economic explanations for increases in illegitimacy have also considered the influence of industrialisation on courtship and marriage patterns. Edward Shorter was the first to explore this correlation by suggesting that industrialisation resulted in higher illegitimacy by granting women economic independence, and therefore greater sexual freedom.[81] The central assumption of Shorter's argument, the notion that increased illegitimacy resulted from female emancipation, was quickly rejected by historians.[82] In their response to Shorter, Tilly, et al argued that increasing levels of illegitimacy actually resulted from 'structural and compositional changes associated with urbanisation and industrialisation.'[83] According to them, illegitimacy was a by-product of the geographic mobility caused by industrialisation and urbanisation, which led to more women moving away from the support of their families, and more men facing economic instability resulting in more broken marriage promises.[84] Nigel Goose has argued that slightly higher levels of illegitimacy in counties where women were employed in the straw plait trade could plausibly be connected to the effects of the trade on female employment, but also suggested this correlation should not be overstated.[85] Emma Griffin also refutes Shorter's claim of eighteenth-century female sexual liberation; however, her study of plebeian autobiographies does reveal an increase in sexual freedom for young, unmarried men and women. She also found that female employment opportunities created by industrialisation could grant some women greater economic freedom, which enabled some to support children outside of marriage.[86]

These analyses are useful for understanding illegitimacy within the context of urbanisation and industrialisation to some degree, but do little to further our understanding of illegitimacy in rural contexts. Many studies have found that levels of illegitimacy in the nineteenth century were lowest in rural areas where traditional forms of domestic and agrarian employment persisted, and where long-established networks of family and community surveillance existed.[87] However, Radnorshire and Montgomeryshire had some of the highest levels of illegitimacy in the eighteenth and nineteenth centuries, yet remained almost exclusively rural and sparsely populated. Moreover, Denbighshire, which did possess small but expanding ironworks and coalfields in the later eighteenth century, experienced a mix of very high and very low levels of illegitimacy. Clearly, economic circumstances in rural, agrarian areas and in fledgling mining areas were different to those in urban and more expansive industrial areas, but this does not preclude the application of certain parts of these approaches to rural and protoindustrial contexts. As has repeatedly been found, illegitimacy is a compound phenomenon which manifests differently in different regions, and therefore regional responses to changing socioeconomic variables would also differ.[88] Given the nature of the available evidence, the most useful approaches for comparison in this preliminary analysis of Welsh evidence are ones that consider changes in courtship practice within the context of the socioeconomic climate, as both Griffin and Wilson have done for urban and industrial regions.

Industrial developments began to expand in south Wales in areas such as Merthyr in the 1760s, but similar developments did not take place in Montgomeryshire and Radnorshire.[89] Although lead mining was a feature in Montgomeryshire near Llanidloes and Llangynog, mines and smelteries declined in the early eighteenth century and were not an important feature of the economic landscape of the region.[90] Montgomeryshire was predominantly agricultural, but parts of the county were also heavily involved in the woollen trade throughout the eighteenth century. However, the woollen trade in the county remained a scattered, domestic industry dominated by the Shrewsbury Drapers Company, and only gradually became mechanised from the 1780s.[91] Even the poorest cottages in Montgomeryshire could probably afford a spinning wheel, and many would have been involved in carding and weaving, which could have helped to supplement incomes.[92] The economy in Radnorshire was also predominantly agricultural, but unlike Montgomeryshire, was not actively involved in the woollen trade. The bulk of the population would have been poor peasants.[93] Denbighshire was generally much more mineral-rich than parts of Montgomeryshire and all of Radnorshire, but not nearly to the same degree as the south Wales coalfields. Iron mining and smelting in the county had enabled exploitation of a relatively small coalfield in the east around Wrexham, Ruabon and Chirk.[94] However, poor transportation and lack of access to the sea meant that mining in Denbighshire in the late eighteenth century was not of the same commercial importance as south Wales, and instead served more local markets.[95] Despite this, by the end of the eighteenth century employment opportunities around the coalfield did result in higher population density, and economic circumstances for labouring classes in these areas were likely better than in Radnorshire.[96] However, southern and western Denbighshire lacked similar resources, and instead featured an upland, pastoral, woollen-producing rural economy similar to Montgomeryshire.[97]

The key characteristics which have emerged thus far are as follows: the relatively harsh economic circumstances across the region studied (as described in the Introduction), with some pockets of wool production, coalmining and iron smelting which may have improved economic circumstances in those areas; and the presence of established courtship customs which increasingly allowed for, and likely involved, sexual contact.

Given these circumstances, Adrian Wilson's analysis of illegitimacy in eighteenth-century London proves particularly useful. Wilson found that, in general, the number of children admitted to the Foundling Hospital corresponded strongly to changes in grain prices.[98] Wilson argued that most foundlings were illegitimate, and their conceptions resulted from a particular model of courtship which existed in the capital but not in rural areas.[99] In this model, marriages in London were 'courtship-led', meaning courting couples engaged in sex before a promise to marry had been made, and committed to marriage only after conception had occurred.[100] The inverse of this, which Wilson argues prevailed elsewhere in rural areas of pre-industrial England, was courtship that was 'marriage-led', meaning a decision to marry preceded sexual contact.[101] Marriage in both models was still very much contingent on economic circumstances. However, in the marriage-led model, sexual activity did not take place until after the couple was financially able to marry and set up a household. The combination of a courtship-led model of marriage and economic instability meant that many unmarried couples in London ended up conceiving but not marrying because of their financial circumstances, thus resulting in the birth of more illegitimate children.

The evidence from mid and northeast Wales points to a similar courtship-led model of marriage within the context of poor economic circumstances. Evidence from all three counties supports this, as to differing degrees Denbighshire, Montgomeryshire and Radnorshire experienced deteriorating economic conditions which corresponded to differential increases in the illegitimacy ratio. Radnorshire experienced the cumulative effects of harsh weather and crop failure between 1727 and 1730, which saw the poor rate double, and in the following decade death rates increased substantially.[102] The 1760s also saw periods of hardship, reflected in increased demand on relief from poor law officials, and the 1770s experienced further deficient harvests and considerable increases in poor rates.[103] These decades roughly correspond with the more marked increases in the illegitimacy ratio in Radnorshire found in Figure 1.4. The early peak in illegitimacy in Montgomeryshire between 1700 and 1709 corresponds with a series of poor harvests due to long winters and cold summers which resulted in famine, and which probably also affected conditions in neighbouring Radnorshire.[104] This is the decade which also experienced crisis mortality in at least three years, as discussed earlier. The plateau in illegitimacy between 1710 and 1749 roughly corresponds with a similar plateau in the number of poor law claimants throughout the county, which suggests a period of relative economic stability.[105] However, the rise in illegitimacy from 1740 onwards is not matched by a rise in poor law claimants until midway through the 1760s.[106] This correlation suggests that economic circumstances were a significant contributing factor to increases in childbirths outside of wedlock in Wales. Levels of illegitimacy in Denbighshire remained relatively consistent, and increased at a slower rate than Montgomeryshire and Radnorshire, following a pattern similar to England. Economic conditions in Denbighshire were also deteoriating in the late eighteenth century, but the limited economic opportunities provided by mining and smelting likely resulted in the labouring classes being somewhat more resliant to the adverse conditions that affected those in agricultural regions.[107] Thus, courting couples in Denbighshire were likely better placed to marry than couples in Montgomeryshire and Radnorshire if and when pregnancy occurred.

Additional links between economic circumstances, illegitimacy and marriage can be found in the areas of Montgomeryshire where the woollen trade was clearly active. In terms of the woollen trade, women would have been employed at the domestic level in activities such as combing, carding and spinning.[108] In a study of marriage patterns, Bridget Hill examined evidence from the wool-producing parish of Culcheth, Lancashire, where by the 1760s the illegitimacy ratio had reached 8.1 per cent, and it continued to increase, reaching 10 per cent by the early nineteenth century. In some years, illegitimacy could be as high as 30 per cent of all baptisms.[109] The majority of these women were handloom weavers who, Hill argues, made a conscious decision to separate childbearing from marriage by remaining in their parents' home after the birth of their illegitimate children. This decision was beneficial for both the mothers and their families as it was less expensive than establishing a new home within marriage, and it allowed the young woman's parents to retain her labour within the home. Griffin also found evidence to suggest that increased employment opportunities for women could have provided the mothers of illegitimate children with the means to support themselves and their children without having to marry.[110] Although less technologically advanced, the woollen trade in Montgomeryshire could possibly have provided similar opportunities for unmarried mothers. However, this appears to have not been the case. Not only did the wool-producing county have lower levels of illegitimacy than Radnorshire overall, but parishes where the woollen trade was established, such as Meifod and Machynlleth, had some of the lowest levels of illegitimacy.[111] The illegitimacy ratio in both parishes in the 1790s was 4.4 per cent, which was considerably lower than the 7.5 per cent county aggregate, and slightly lower than the national average 5.1 in England.[112] This evidence would suggest that, when economic circumstances allowed, the courtship-led model of marriage in Wales could, and frequently did, lead to marriage rather than illegitimacy.

To a lesser and more complex extent, similar connections between economic circumstances, marriage and illegitimacy can be found in some of the coalmining areas of Denbighshire. Several of the parishes considered here are situated in or near the coalfield in the northeastern part of the county. In the final decade of the century, Gresford and Marchwiel both had high levels of reported illegitimacy, at 11.1 and 11.9 per cent respectively.[113] However, the parishes of Ruabon, Llangollen and Chirk all recorded considerably lower levels of illegitimacy, at 4.7, 4.5 and 3.9 per cent respectively. Unlike in Montgomeryshire, all of these parishes were located relatively close to the boarder with England, again confirming that difinitive Welsh/English distinctions cannot be made. Moreover, this evidence suggsts that improved employment opportunities did not inevitably result in marriage for couples who engaged in conjugal courtship practices.

The link between illegitimacy and marriage can be found in the parish of Gresford, where poor law officials made considerable efforts to ensure that unmarried couples who had conceived actually married. Levels of illegitimacy in Gresford began to increase dramatically from the 1760s, along with the proportion of unmarried fathers named in baptism registers (Table 1.1) The correlative rise in identified illegitimate paternity is particularly interesting when considered alongside evidence from overseers of the poor account books. From the 1760s onwards parishes officials began pursuing and apprenehding fathers through legal chanels, and then paying the costs associated with marriage. For example, in 1763, officials paid 2s. 6d. for 'expenses attending Edward Gabriel who was under confiendment in the house of correction and afterwards married.'[114] In May of 1764 Edward Gabriel's daughter Elizabeth was baptised.[115] Similarly, in 1790 officials paid 9s. 9d. to apprehend Edward Jones, and a furher £2 6s. 3d. for a marriage by licence.[116] In May of that year Edward's son, who bore his name, was baptised.[117] Similar expenses occur in limited numbers across the last four decades of the eighteenth century in Gresford, although not all can be tied to baptism records. Other than preventing illegitimacy there is no reason why parish poor law officials would have concerned themselves with promoting marriage amongst its parishioners. Therefore, this is fascinating evidence of how different parishes chose to manage illegitimacy. Gresford is the one of the only parishes considered here with surviving poor law records that reveal these efforts, but is is possible that similar efforts were made by other parishes. A poor law entry from the parish of Henllan, located in northwestern Denbighshire is one such example, and indicates that relationships between

Table 1.1 Illegitimacy and identified illegitimate paternity in Gresford, Denbighshire, 1750–1799.

Decade	Illegitimacy Ratio (%)	Identified Illegitimate Paternity (%)
1750–1759	4.8	61.5
1760–1769	6.6	77.5
1770–1779	8.1	85.0
1780–1789	8.1	90.2
1790–1799	11.1	87.5

apprehended men and the women they were compelled to marry could be genuine. In 1794 officials paid 6s. to apprehend Thomas Roberts after a servant woman named Dinah swore her child to him, and a further £1 6s. to pursue Dinah so the two could be married, 'according to the desire of her sweetheart who is in gaol.'[118]

Parishes may also have resorted to alternative methods of managing illegitimacy, and the recording of illegitimate partenity may have been one such method. Regional sensitivities to economic circumstances may account for the disparity in the frequency with which fathers in Denbighshire, Montgomeryshire and Radnorshire were identified. In addition to having relatively low levels of illegitimacy, the parishes of Meifod and Machynlleth reported some of the highest levels of identified paternity. Despite significant variation in levels of illegitimacy, most parishes in Denbighshire also reported high levels of identified paternity in the last decade of the century. As previously noted, some historians have suggested that the frequent identification of fathers may indicate community awareness, and even acceptance, of the relationship between courting couples. Caution must be taken with this assumption, though, because these identified fathers included men who had committed rape, incest and adultery, or had exploited their positions of power to take advantage of women subordinate to them.[119] Therefore, not all identified fathers can be interpreted as suitors. An alternative hypothesis may be that the identification of fathers represents a more-established means of formal affiliation, which existed for financial reasons. Poor law legislation had held both parents financially accountable for the support of their children since the sixteenth century, but because mothers were often sole carers, the financial burden most often fell to fathers.[120] An Act of 1733 established the formal legal mechanism that would, in theory, ensure fathers would indemnify the parish against the cost of supporting illegitimate children.[121] The more frequent recording of fathers in Denbighshire and Montgomeryshire could represent one component of the affiliation system as it operated there, which may have been absent in Radnorshire.

A further indication that this may be the case can be found the responses to *Rural and Town Queries*. Parish officials were asked three questions relating to illegitimacy, one of which was this: 'What number of bastards have been chargeable to your parish? And what has been the expense occasioned by them during each of the last five years? And how much of the expense has been recovered from the putative father? And how much from the mothers?'[122] Three Denbighshire parishes, ten Montgomeryshire parishes and two Radnorshire parishes returned responses to these questions.[123] Most reported having spent between £100 and £1,000 on the maintenance of illegitimate children over the preceding five-year period, and most recovered between £50 and £240 from fathers. Only six parishes reported recovering any costs from mothers, which was considerably less than any amounts recovered from fathers. In total, the limited number of responses do not allow for quantitative analysis similar to Thomas Nutt's study of paternal financial responsibility under the old poor law, however some inferences can be made.[124] Most parishes appear to have recouped less than one-third of what they spent on the maintenance of illegitimate children, which is considerably less than the amounts recouped in England.[125] This is likely to be indicative of the persistent poverty experienced to different extents across all three counties. What is perhaps most significant is the scarcity of answers to these questions from Radnorshire. The parish of Clyro was the only one in the county to provide amounts for actual annual expenditure and costs recovered, which were comparable to Denbighshire and Montgomeryshire.[126] However, the response from the parish of Old Radnor may be more telling. Officials there reported paying 2s. per week per chargeable illegitimate child, with fathers contributing an additional 1s. The reason given for the practice was that 'if more were demanded it would force the father on the parish.'[127] This response presents the intriguing possibility that endemic poverty throughout the county may have rendered futile any formal affiliation processes, which is also reflected in patterns of paternal identification at the time of baptism. The high levels of illegitimacy and low levels of identification experienced in Radnorshire therefore demonstrate just how closely illegitimacy and economic circumstances were linked, especially when the marriage process was courtship-led.

A further related factor which warrants consideration is migration, as it could have played a role in the very high levels of illegitimacy found in these regions of Wales, particularly in the last three decades of the eighteenth century. Economic circumstances in poorer agricultural areas, such as Radnorshire, may have meant that a greater number of people lived relatively mobile lives, often travelling considerable distances to find work in new areas as old opportunities dried up.[128] The economy of Wales was dependent on both male and female servants and farm labourers, and the number of day labourers increased throughout the eighteenth century.[129] Age of marriage in these areas was relatively late as it was expected marriage would only take place when a couple was able to establish a degree of economic independence, which was dependent on servants and labourers amassing sufficient savings.[130] Contracts for farm labourers typically only lasted one year, and, as a result, younger agricultural workers were much more likely to move between communities in search of work without settling for longer periods of time. It is likely that young unskilled labourers could travel a fair distance into England to find work, and some even went as far as London to seek employment, and others may have enlisted in the army or navy.[131] It is possible that many couples engaged in courtship which involved penetrative sex, which they may have fully intended would lead to marriage. However, if employment opportunities dried up before a formal marriage took place, one or both partners could have been compelled to move on, perhaps even before a pregnancy was detected. In contrast, in Denbighshire, the nature of the economy may have resulted in different, more predictable patterns of migration which meant that unmarried fathers could be pursued if pregnancy occurred. Mining in northeastern Denbighshire in the late eighteenth century typically drew migrants from within northeast Wales rather than from longer distances, and typically migration took place along established routes.[132] Thus, unmarried fathers who, either knowingly or unknowingly, left a pregnant partner behind to pursue opportunities in the coalfield could likely be tracked once the pregnancy been discovered.

Conclusion

Although manifested in different ways, and in significantly different measures, patterns of illegitimacy across Wales were governed by a combination of cultural and economic factors surprisingly similar to those found in eighteenth-century London. Many different sexual encounters can result in an illegitimate birth, but it is likely that one of the chief causes of illegitimacy in Wales during the eighteenth century were conjugal courtship practices. Courtship-led marriage processes, which included practices such as bundling, were likely a significant contributing factor to the increased levels of illegitimacy seen across mid-Wales during the century. The sexual experiences of Welsh courting couples changed over this period, but not because of a sexual revolution led by profound shifts in sexual knowledge. Rather, the changes can be ascribed to a decline in the traditional modes of regulation enforced by the ecclesiastical courts. Central to our understanding of why these changes in sexual practice had such a considerable impact on levels of illegitimacy are the specific regional economic circumstances in which these courtship practices took place. These couples probably engaged in penetrative sex with the intention of marrying should conception occur, however once faced with that reality, their personal circumstances prevented them from doing so. In Wales, patterns of illegitimacy reveal the realities of life in a predominantly agrarian and protoindustrial economy which existed, to varying degrees, on the edge of subsistence. Patterns of illegitimacy are therefore an important indication of the ways in which the broad changes which occurred during the eighteenth century were experienced at the local level.

However, regional variations in levels of illegitimacy in these Welsh counties, and across Britain, make it abundantly clear that there is no satisfactory explanation which addresses all circumstances in all locations. The experience of illegitimacy in mid and northeast Wales is only one manifestation of the dynamic interplay between sexual practice and socioeconomic reality. Although these are the most apparent, and therefore most useful as a starting point for a preliminary study of Welsh evidence, they are not the only variables which need to be considered. Seeking a leading cause is relevant, particularly in an initial analysis such as this, but the diversity of experiences should also be considered. There are many other types of experiences beyond courtship which resulted in the birth of an illegitimate child, which also warrant further study. In effect, the study of illegitimacy may be better approached as a study of illegitimacies. The following chapters will therefore move beyond broad quantitatitive analysis of ratios, which necessitates aggregating all non-marital sexual encounters into a single category of 'illegitimacy', to consider the diverse identities, sexual relationships and experiences of the men and women involved in illegitimacy.

Notes

1. An earlier version of this chapter was, in part, first published as Angela Joy Muir, 'Courtship, Sex and Poverty: Illegitimacy in Eighteenth-Century Wales', *Social History*, 43 (2018), 56–80. © 2017 The Author(s). Published by Informa UK Limited, trading as Taylor & Francis Group.
2. Denbighshire (parish register transcripts published by the Clwyd Family History Society): Bryneglwys, Chirk, Gresford, Holt, Llanarmon Dyffryn Ceiriog, Llangollen, Llansilin, Marchwiel, Ruabon; Montgomeryshire (parish register transcripts published by the Montgomeryshire Genealogical Society unless otherwise stated): Aberhafesp, Berriew, Bettws Cedewain, Buttington, Carno, Castell Caereinion, Cemmaes, Darowen, Garthbeibio, Guilsfield, Llandinam, Llandrinio, Llanfair Caereinion, Llanfihangel-yng-Ngwynfa, Llanfyllin, Llangadfan, Llangyniew, Llanrhaeadr ym Mochnant (Clwyd Family History Society), Llanwddyn, Llanwnog, Llanwrin, Machynlleth, Meifod, Newtown, Trefeglwys, Welshpool; Radnorshire (transcripts published by the Powys Family History Society): Beguildy, Gladestry, Glascwm, Llanbadarn Fawr, Llanbadarn Fynydd, Llanbister, Llanfihangel Nant Melan, Llansantffraed-in-Elwel, New Radnor, Norton.
3. Other possible correlations were considered, including parish-level comparisons with the sex ratio, and with topographical features such as elevation, however no meaningful patters or emerged.
4. Many thanks to Professor Keith Snell for his assistance in the analysis of sex ratio data.
5. Laslett, *Family Life*, pp. 105–107; Laslett, 'Introduction', p. 3; Adair, *Courtship*, pp. 15–16, 79; John R Gillis, *For Better, for Worse: British Marriages, 1600 to the Present* (Oxford: Oxford University Press, 1985), pp. 128, 219; David Levine and Keith Wrightson, *The Making of an Industrial Society: Whickham, 1560–1765* (Oxford: Clarendon Press, 1991) as cited in Rebecca Probert, 'Introduction', in *Cohabitation*, ed. by Probert, pp. 1–9 (p. 3).
6. Tim Hitchcock, 'Redefining Sex in Eighteenth-Century England', *History Workshop Journal*, 41 (1996), 72–90; Randolph Trumbach, *Sex and the Gender Revolution, Vol 1: Heterosexuality and the Third Gender in Enlightenment London* (Chicago: University of Chicago Press, 1998); Thomas Laqueur, 'Sex and Desire in the Industrial Revolution', in *The Industrial Revolution in British Society*, ed. by P O'Brien and R Quinault (Cambridge: Cambridge University Press, 1993), pp. 100–123; Faramerz Dabhoiwala, *The Origins of Sex: A History of the First Sexual Revolution* (London: Allen Lane, 2012).

7. Laslett, 'Introduction'; Adair, *Courtship*; Nutt, 'Paternal Financial Responsibility'; Rogers, 'Carnal Knowledge'.
8. Wilson, 'Illegitimacy and Its Implications', p. 134; Rogers, 'Carnal Knowledge', p. 369; Laslett, 'Introduction', pp. 53–61.
9. Rogers, 'Carnal Knowledge', p. 39; Laslett, 'Introduction', pp. 53–61.
10. Griffin, 'Sex, Illegitimacy and Social Change', p. 143.
11. Griffin, 'Sex, Illegitimacy and Social Change'; Wilson, 'Illegitimacy and Its Implications'.
12. Laslett, 'Introduction', p. 14.
13. Humphreys, *Crisis of Community*, p. 64.
14. Humphreys, *Crisis of Community*, pp. 72–73.
15. Brueton, 'Illegitimacy in South Wales', p. 49; Laslett, 'Introduction', p. 14. Brueton's decadal date format is 01–10 and Laslett's is 00–09. Many thanks to Anna Brueton for sharing her raw data.
16. Adair, *Courtship*, p. 63.
17. Adair, *Courtship*, pp. 51–62 (Regions are as follows: west includes Derbyshire, Gloucestershire, Herefordshire, Monmouthshire, Shropshire, Staffordshire, Warwickshire, Worcestershire, northwest includes Cheshire, Cumberland, Lancashire, Westmorland).
18. English parishes: Shropshire (transcripts held by Shropshire Archives): Astley, Bishops Castle, Cardeston, Kinnerley, Ludlow, Middleton Scriven, Munslow, Onibury, Oswestry, Stirchley and Uffington.
19. J Geraint Jenkins, 'The Welsh Woollen Industry', in *Wales in the Eighteenth Century*, ed. by Donald Moore (Swansea: C Davies, 1975), pp. 89–108 (p. 95).
20. Samuel Lewis, *A Topographical Dictionary of Wales* (London, 1849), pp. 36–47, 241–248, 356–368; British History Online <www.british-history.ac.uk/topographical-dict/wales> [accessed 22/8/2019].
21. Reay, 'Sexuality', p. 221.
22. Oosterveen, et al, 'Family Reconstitution', p. 104; Adair, *Courtship*, pp. 78–79.
23. Laslett, *Family Life*, pp. 105–107; Laslett, 'Introduction', pp. 3, 20–22; Adair, *Courtship*, pp. 15–16, 64–65, 79.
24. Gowing, 'Ordering the Body', p. 8.
25. Reay, 'Sexuality', p. 237.
26. Griffin, 'Sex, Illegitimacy and Social Change'.
27. See also: Elizabeth Hurren and Steven King, 'Courtship at the Corner's Court', *Social History*, 40 (2015), 185–207.
28. NLW 4/523/4 (Radnorshire, Margaret Matthews, 1756); 4/53/3 (Denbighshire, Mary Jones, 1762); 4/188/1 (Montgomeryshire, Elizabeth Evans, 1764); 4/388/5 (Breconshire, Margaret Thomas, 1788); 4/390/4 (Breconshire, Ann Watkin, 1797).
29. NLW 4/188/1 (Montgomeryshire, Evan Jenkins, 1764).
30. NLW 4/388/5 (Breconshire, William Williams, 1788).
31. NLW 4/523/4 (Radnorshire, Edward Pugh, 1756).
32. NLW 4/188/1 (Montgomeryshire, Evan Jenkins, 1764).
33. Griffin, 'Sex, Illegitimacy and Social Change', p. 149.
34. Catrin Stevens, *Welsh Courting Customs* (Llandysul: Gomer, 1993), p. 104.
35. Stevens, *Welsh Courting Customs*, pp. 83–87.
36. Stevens, *Welsh Courting Customs*, p. 82; Laslett, 'Introduction', p. 8.
37. Muir, 'Illegitimate in Eighteenth-Century Wales', p. 370; Adair, *Courtship*, p. 6.
38. J Jackson, *Letters from and Relating to North Wales, 1742–1792* cited in Stevens, *Welsh Courting Customs*, pp. 86–87.

39. NLW MS 20073A, Anonymous, *Journal of a Tour of Wales and Parts of England* (1793), pp. 31–32.
40. Mr Pratt (Samuel Jackson), *Gleanings Through Wales, Holland and Westphalia* (London, 1797), p. 105.
41. William Bingley, *North Wales: Including Its Scenery, Antiquities, Customs, and Some Sketches of Its Natural History* (London, 1804).
42. 'Town Queries', p. 180a.
43. 'Town Queries', p. 180a.
44. NLW 4/760/4 (Carmarthenshire, Rees Thomas Rees, 1816).
45. NLW 4/259/5 (Anglesey, Griffith Roberts, 1824).
46. Hitchcock, 'Redefining Sex'; Dabhoiwala, *Origins of Sex*; Laqueur, 'Sex and Desire'; Sarah Toulalan, *Imagining Sex, Pornography and Bodies in Seventeenth-Century England* (Oxford: Oxford University Press, 2007).
47. Hitchcock, 'Redefining Sex', p. 76. Not all historians are convinced by Hitchcock's hypothesis. Sarah Toulalan's analysis of seventeenth-century pornographic texts demonstrates that a favouring of penetrative heterosexual sex existed prior to the eighteenth century.
48. Hitchcock, 'Redefining Sex', p. 78; Dabhoiwala, *Origins of Sex*, pp. 141–142.
49. Hitchcock, 'Redefining Sex', pp. 79–80.
50. Hitchcock, 'Redefining Sex', p. 81.
51. Hitchcock, 'Redefining Sex', p. 81.
52. Hitchcock, 'Redefining Sex', pp. 82–84.
53. Hitchcock, 'Redefining Sex', p. 83.
54. Hitchcock, 'Redefining Sex', p. 82.
55. Hitchcock, 'Redefining Sex', p. 83.
56. Geraint H Jenkins, *The Foundations of Modern Wales, 1642–1780* (Oxford: Oxford University Press, 1993), p. 398.
57. Eiluned Rees, 'Developments in the Book Trade in Eighteenth-Century Wales', *Library*, 5th ser., 24 (1969), 33–43 (p. 34).
58. Rees, 'Book Trade', p. 39.
59. Eiluned Rees, *Libri Walliae: A Catalogue of Welsh Books and Books Printed in Wales 1546–1820* (Aberystwyth: National Library of Wales, 1987).
60. Eryn M White, *The Welsh Bible: A History* (Stroud: The History Press, 2007), p. 62. Other works by Woodward which were translated by the SPCK into Welsh include *Cyngor yr eglwyswr: i ŵr ieuangc newydd dderbyn conffirmasiwn gan yr Esgob. Neu'r hyn a elwir yn gyffredinol, Bedydd-Esgob* (*Council of the Churchman: A Young Man Receiving Confirmation from the New Bishop*) (1703) and *Llaw-lyfr y Gwir Gristion* (*Handbook of the True Christian*) (1716).
61. Alun Withey, *Physick and the Family: Health, Medicine and Care in Wales, 1600–1750* (Manchester: Manchester University Press, 2011), pp. 58–63.
62. Toulalan, *Imagining Sex*, pp. 66–67. See also Foyster, *Manhood in Early Modern England*, pp. 72–73.
63. Dabhoiwala, *Origins of Sex*, pp. 71–78.
64. Outhwaite, *The Rise and Fall*, pp. 78–94.
65. Outhwaite, *The Rise and Fall*, p. 83.
66. Clark, 'Heterosexuality', p. 43; Outhwaite, *The Rise and Fall*, p. 84.
67. Dabhoiwala, *Origins of Sex*, pp. 71–77.
68. Jenkins, *Foundations*, pp. 347, 356, 367.
69. Jenkins, *Foundations*, p. 376.
70. Howell, *Rural Poor*, p. 15; Humphreys, *Crisis of Community*, p. 176.
71. Humphreys, *Crisis of Community*, p. 70, citing Wrigley and Schofield, *The Population History of England*, table 7.8.

72. Griffin, 'Sex, Illegitimacy and Social Change', p. 154.
73. Gowing, 'Ordering the Body'; Laura Gowing, 'Knowledge and Experience, c. 1500–1750', in *The Routledge History of Sex and the Body: 1500 to the Present*, ed. by Sarah Toulalan and Kate Fisher (Abingdon: Routledge, 2013), pp. 239–255 (p. 242).
74. London, The National Archives, MH 12/16543/316, Folio 449, Llanfyllin Poor Law Union (1824).
75. Nutt, 'Paternal Financial Responsibility'.
76. Griffin, 'Sex, Illegitimacy and Social Change', p. 146.
77. Laslett, 'Introduction', pp. 54–55.
78. David Levine, *Family Formation in an Age of Nascent Capitalism* (New York: Academic Press, 1977), p. 5.
79. Griffin, 'Sex, Illegitimacy and Social Change', p. 143.
80. Wilson, 'Illegitimacy and Its Implications'.
81. Shorter, 'Illegitimacy, Sexual Revolution'.
82. Tilley, et al, 'Women's Work'.
83. Tilley, et al, 'Women's Work', p. 470.
84. Tilley, et al, 'Women's Work', pp. 472–476.
85. Goose, 'How Saucy Did It Make the Poor?'
86. Griffin, 'Sex, Illegitimacy and Social Change', pp. 156–157.
87. Reay, 'Sexuality'; King, 'Bastardy Prone Sub-Society'; Laslett, 'Introduction'.
88. Reay, 'Sexuality'; Adair, *Courtship*; Levine and Wrightson, *Industrial Society*.
89. RO Roberts, 'Industrial Expansion in South Wales', in *Wales in the Eighteenth Century*, ed. by Donald Moore (Swansea: C Davies, 1975), pp. 109–126.
90. Humphreys, *Crisis of Community*, pp. 23–24.
91. Jenkins, 'Welsh Woollen Industry'.
92. Jenkins, 'Welsh Woollen Industry', p. 97.
93. OS Ashton, 'Eighteenth Century Radnorshire: A Population Survey', *Radnorshire Society Transactions*, 40 (1970), 40–55 (p. 40).
94. Bethan Lloyd Jones, 'Profile of a Welsh County Coalfield: The Denbighshire Coalfield, 1850–1914' (unpublished doctoral thesis, Cardiff, 2008), pp. 27–30; Lewis, *Topographical Dictionary*.
95. Jones, 'Welsh County Coalfield', pp. 28–29.
96. WTR Pryce, 'Industrialism, Urbanization and the Maintenance of Culture Areas: North-East Wales in the Mid-Nineteenth Century', *Welsh History Review*, 7 (1975), 307–340 (p. 331).
97. Gareth Elwyn Jones, *Modern Wales: A Concise History*, 2nd edn (Cambridge: Cambridge University Press, 1994), p. 13.
98. Wilson, 'Illegitimacy and Its Implications', p. 131.
99. Wilson's argument that most foundlings were illegitimate has been challenged. See: Alysa Levene, 'The Origins of the Children of the London Foundling Hospital, 1741–1760: A Reconsideration', *Continuity and Change*, 18 (2003), 201–235.
100. Wilson, 'Illegitimacy and Its Implications', pp. 134–136.
101. Wilson, 'Illegitimacy and Its Implications', p. 136.
102. Ashton, 'Eighteenth Century Radnorshire', p. 51.
103. Ashton, 'Eighteenth Century Radnorshire', p. 52.
104. Humphreys, *Crisis of Community*, p. 64.
105. Humphreys, *Crisis of Community*, p. 89.
106. Humphreys, *Crisis of Community*, p. 89.
107. C Neville Hurdsman, *History of the Parish of Chirk* (Wrexham: Bridge, 1996), p. 111.

108. Jones, *Concise History*, p. 13.
109. Bridget Hill, 'The Marriage Age of Women and the Demographers', *History Workshop Journal*, 28 (1989), 129–147 (p. 143).
110. Griffin, 'Sex, Illegitimacy and Social Change', pp. 157–158.
111. Jenkins, 'Welsh Woollen Industry', p. 99.
112. Source: sample (1790–1799 Meifod: 453 baptisms, 20 of which illegitimate, 16 fathers identified; Machynlleth: 573 baptisms, 25 of which illegitimate, 25 fathers identified); Laslett, 'Introduction', p. 14.
113. Data for Wrexham is not available for the 1790s.
114. Ruthin, DAO (Gresford), PD/34/1/320 (1763).
115. CFHS (Gresford) CLD-20703 (1764).
116. DAO (Gresford), PD/34/1/320 (1790).
117. CFHS (Gresford), CLD-20704 (1790).
118. DAO (Henllan), PD/38/1/68 (1794).
119. Evidence of this is limited, but can be found in baptism registers and other parish documents including bastardy bonds. For example, the 1743 baptism register for Llansilin, Denbighshire, includes an entry for a child named Richard Morris, born to Matthew Morris and his daughter Elizabeth, 'by incest' (CFHS (Llansilin) CLD-21918 (1743).
120. Nutt, 'Paradox and Problems', p. 103.
121. 6 George II c. 31, *An Act for the Relief of Parishes and Other Places from Such Charges as May Arise from Bastard Children Born Within the Same* (1732).
122. 'Town Queries', Appendix B.2, part V, question 59.
123. 'Town Queries', pp. 643e–644e, 650e–656e, 661e–662e.
124. Nutt, 'Paternal Financial Responsibility'.
125. Nutt, 'Paternal Financial Responsibility', p. 346, northern parishes were far more successful than their southern counterparts in recouping bastardy cost from putative fathers (82.6 per cent of bastardy costs vs 41.5).
126. 'Town Queries', p. 661e.
127. 'Town Queries', p. 662e.
128. Humphreys, *Crisis of Community*, pp. 8–29; Clark, 'Heterosexuality', p. 43.
129. Humphreys, *Crisis of Community*, p. 83.
130. Humphreys, *Crisis of Community*, p. 53.
131. Evans, *Unfortunate Objects*, pp. 27, 53.
132. Pryce, 'Industrialism', pp. 334–335.

2 Complicated Relationships and Diverse Identities
Moving Beyond Courtship and Poverty

Quantitative analysis of parish records can only go so far in revealing the level of illegitimacy and identified illegitimate paternity. For a deeper understanding of the complex diversity of illegitimate experiences a much broader range of sources must be considered. The evidence presented in the previous chapter does indicate a strong correlation between courtship, poverty and illegitimacy in Wales, however, not everyone who bore or begat a child outside of wedlock was necessarily an impoverished unmarried man or woman engaging in premarital sex with the intention of marrying. Qualitative analysis reveals that circumstances for many Welsh men and women were much more complicated, their socioeconomic backgounds were more varied, and the relationships which resulted in an illegitimate birth were potentially more fraught. This chapter examines many of these alternative circumstances by analysing a range of parish records which reveal information about the identities and relationships of the parents of illegitimate children, and where possible, the identities of illegitimate children themselves. It is only through examining the diverse spectrum of those who bore and begat children outside of wedlock that a far greater understanding of the social context and consequences of illegitimacy can be gained.

The first part of this chapter will examine details about the mothers and fathers of illegitimate children named in parish registers, bastardy bonds, poor law accounts and courts records, which reveal the diverse range relationships which cannot be attributed to courtship. This evidence will be used to engage with some of the oft-cited hypotheses relating to illegitimacy in early modern Britain not explored in Chapter 1. These include Laslett's 'bastardy prone sub-society', and theories which attribute higher levels of illegitimacy to cohabitation and irregular marriage. Although there is little Welsh evidence to suggest that either contributed significantly to illegitimacy in Wales, they serve as useful starting points for a discussion of the relationships and identities of those involved in illegitimacy. In searching for evidence of these explanatory frameworks, evidence emerges that is indicatitive of sexual encounters often overlooked in historical studies of illegitimatecy, such as rape, incest, adultery, prostitution and casual sexual encounters with no pretense of marriage. These relationships are impossible to quantify as they leave few traces in the historical record. However, the evidence that does exist warrants close examination. The quantification of illegitimacy inevitably results in the aggregation of diverse sexual experiences into one single statistical figure which is typically taken by historians to represent consensual sex as part of a courtship process. Such assumptions are deeply problematic. The aim here is to address this misrepresentation by examining evidence, however limited, which presents alternative narratives. Illicit and non-consensual sex were very much a part of early modern and eighteenth-century British life. The consequences of these encounters could be the birth of a child outside of wedlock. Even if they only account for a small portion of illegitimacy overall, these experiences should nonetheless be included in studies such as this.

The second part of this chapter will analyse the identities and socioeconomic background of parents of illegitimate children in Wales. It has long been argued that illegitimacy was most prevalent amongst the poorer orders of British society, which has been based primarily upon the abundance of evidence pertaining to illegitimacy available in poor law records.[1] However, closer analysis of these records reveals considerable information about the occupations and social status of many of the fathers of illegitimate children. Rather than being drawn exclusively from a single, impoverished sub-society prone to begetting illegitimate children, it appears that fathers, in fact, came from a diverse range of occupational and social origins which reflects the diversity of Welsh society at the time.[2] The mothers of illegitimate children will also be considered as, to a lesser degree, similar evidence is available for them. Although not as revealing in detail, parish and poor law documents do yield some evidence pertaining to the socioeconomic circumstances of women and the potential implications for women's lives of bearing an illegitimate child. Finally, the significance of the label 'illegitimate' and the length of time it was attached to individual parents and children will also be considered.

This chapter has three principle aims: the first is to move away from traditional approaches to the study of illegitimacy which associate it primarily with pauper courtship, and frame it as a broader phenomenon which could result from a range of sexual encounters between individuals across the social spectrum. This requires moving away from the search for a single leading cause of illegitimacy to consider instead the broad range of sexual encounters which could result in the birth of an illegitimate child. The second is to further the shift away from studies which consider illegitimacy in terms of a female-only problem by framing it instead as a community problem through examining the identities and socioeconomic backgrounds of fathers in more detail. Although it has never been stated explicitly, this presupposition is evident in the inclusion of only women (until recently) in the 'bastardy prone sub-society'.[3] This bias appears unreasoned when we consider the basic fact that women cannot create children—illegitimate or otherwise—on their own. The third is to reconsider the relationship between poverty and illegitimacy. It will be demonstrated that, although there is a strong correlation between poverty and illegitimacy overall, the experience of begetting and bearing an illegitimate child was not limited to the poorest social stratum alone. Concerns about poorer people who bore illegitimate children found in the abundant poor law records does not necessarily mean they were the only ones having children out of wedlock, although it will be suggested that bearing an illegitimate child in certain circumstances may have created disadvantage for some women.

Cohabitation, Irregular Marriage and the Bastardy Prone Sub-Society

As the previous chapter explored, there is a clear link between many instances of illegitimacy and courtship. The association between illegitimacy and courtship has been made by many historians based on the observation of additional patterns as well, such as a correlation with increases in bridal pregnancy in some regions, as well as the implicit understanding that young, unmarried men and women have probably always had sex with people they see as potential long-term partners.[4] However, additional hypotheses have also posited a link between illegitimacy and different types of conjugal relationships. Historians, such as John Gillis and Richard Adair, have also suggested that increased levels of illegitimacy and identified illegitimate paternity may be indicative of non-marital cohabitation, or irregular forms of marriage which were stable, but not recognised by church officials.[5] Gillis went so far as to argue that during the eighteenth century as many as one in seven couples were living together without being officially married due to the costs associated with marrying in church, which for the poorest individuals would have been prohibitive.[6] Gillis's view has been criticised by numerous historians, but he has not been the only historian to suggest the connection between irregular marriage and illegitimacy.

Other historians have suggested that marriage was a relatively weak institution in places such as Wales which had higher levels of illegitimacy, but the evidence they provide for this is scarce and unconvincing.[7] Peter Laslett argued that, prior to Lord Hardwicke's Marriage Act of 1753, marriage could be understood as more of a process than a single event delineating a clear distinction between married and unmarried.[8] Various regional customs existed that allowed men and women to enter into espousals. To all intents and purposes, they were a legally binding form of marriage giving licence for conjugal relations to take place, although they were not formally recognised by the established church. These typically preceded a formal church wedding, but the argument is that, for various financial and customary reasons, many people would have felt this level of commitment sufficiently constituted a marriage and not continued to definitively formalise the relationship with a church wedding. Gillis found evidence of these and similar types of informal marriage in the work of early twentieth-century folklorist Gwenith Gwynn, who claimed to have uncovered informal marriages in parish registers in Wales through the administrative practices of listing 'lawful wife' vs simply 'wife', however his methodology has since been discredited.[9] Despite this, numerous historians have relied on Gillis's account of Gwynn's research as evidence of informal marriage.[10]

In the parishes considered in this study, very little direct evidence survives which supports hypotheses that cohabitation caused the high levels of illegitimacy and identified illegitimate paternity in Wales. By their very nature, informal relationships would not be well documented, as marriage registers would only record banns and the final solemnising of vows. Arrangements made outside the church would not be recorded. However, if couples were conceiving children outside of official wedlock this would manifest itself in the registers in one of three ways: they would marry before the child was born, thus bearing a legitimate child; they would marry sometime after the child was born and baptised as illegitimate, and would subsequently be entered in the marriage register at a later date, or they would never marry at all, but might bear multiple illegitimate children. Another alternative would be that they would choose not to formally solemnise their marriage. Couples who either placed little value on, or could not afford the cost of a marriage in church might choose not to officially baptise their children for the same reasons, which would therefore have little effect on illegitimacy ratios found in baptism registers. Many of the individuals listed in bastardy bonds do not then appear in parish baptism registers, which, in the case of bonds drawn up prior to birth, could be because the infant did not survive. Bonds which were drawn up after the birth of an illegitimate child and which do not have a corresponding entry in the baptism registers may represent parents' lack of incentive or financial means to have their child baptised, although parishes did, on occasion, pay the baptism expenses of pauper children. For example, in the parish of Kerry, Montgomeryshire in 1796 officials paid for the baptism of Martha Tuders's child and in the same year in Tregynon, Montgomeryshire officials paid for the baptism of John Richard's legitimate child.[11]

Parish reconstruction techniques which allow for mapping bridal pregnancy are not practical in Wales due to Welsh patronymics, which make it difficult to differentiate between individuals who share common names with much of their community, so it is not possible to estimate how many couples had engaged in prenuptial sex.[12] However, if bridal pregnancy were widespread it would be expected that many couples would find themselves delivered of a baby before they had an opportunity to marry, and therefore illegitimate baptisms would precede a formal marriage. There is some evidence of this, such as in Machynlleth in 1765 where Abraham Pugh and Bridget Jones baptised their illegitimate daughter, Elizabeth, and then married afterwards as the baptism register contains a note stating that Bridget was 'now' Abraham's wife.[13] On 24 September 1768, in the parish of Llangadfan, Thomas Jones married a widow named Margaret Pugh approximately six weeks after the baptism of their illegitimate son Evan.[14] In the same parish in 1774, William Morris and Catherine Harry baptised their illegitimate daughter, Jane, on 8 February.[15] The couple then married on 31 May, nearly four months later.[16] However, when a bride was pregnant at the time of her wedding, the marriage was not necessarily between her and the biological father of her child. For example, in Hawarden in 1748 churchwardens recorded an 'expense in the service of the parish to promote the marriage of one Edward Evans (a stranger) with one Elizabeth Allday, als Williams (a pregnant woman & notoriously wicked and lewd) in order to destroy her legal settlement which here took effect).'[17] Such coercion cannot be seen as a courtship-led marriage custom. It is possible that the promotion of marriage at the expense of the parish of Henllan discussed in the previous chapter are instances of this. Although examples are scarce, they do provide evidence that bridal pregnancy did occur to at least some extent in Wales during the eighteenth century.

Likewise, limited evidence of irregular marriage and cohabitation also exists. In New Radnor, the register for 1698 contains a note stating, 'Hugh Saunders cohabits with a woman with whom he pretends marriage.' The same couple's child is baptised as legitimate in 1699.[18] Another note in the same register in 1701 states, 'Thomas Ranson & Elizabeth Massy are co-habitors since married.'[19] These are the only examples from parish registers which explicitly identify couples as cohabiting. Bastardy bonds sometimes yield similar information, such as in Llandegley, Radnorshire, where in 1761 Ann Miles was said to inhabit with David Povah, the alleged father of her child.[20] Other records list couples as reputedly married, such as in Wrexham in 1682 Anne Bowen was listed as the 'supposed wife' of Roger Jones in the baptism record for their illegitimate son.[21] Similarly, in Buttington where in 1780 and 1782 Mary Evans baptised twins and then a son who were all identified as illegitimate, and whose father was listed as Samuel Evans, her presumed husband.[22] Less explicit examples may be when the same couple bears more than one illegitimate child together over a number of years. For example, in Llanfair Caereinion John Jones and Mary Griffiths baptised illegitimate sons in 1788 and 1790, or in Llangyniew, where Evan Pryce and Catherine Jones baptised illegitimate daughters in 1785 and 1788, and John Lloyd and Elizabeth Rogers baptised illegitimate daughters in 1787, 1789 and 1795.[23] Likewise, in Wrexham Samuel Hughes and Jane Reeves baptised two illegitimate children in 1766 and 1767, and Edward

Edwards and Sarah Samuel baptised two illegitimate children in 1773 and 1782.[24] Margaret Matthews, who died in New Radnorshire in 1756, was noted as having been, 'supposed to be married'.[25] This may have been the same Margaret Matthews who baptised three children between 1688 and 1700, only one of whom was listed as a 'bastard', however no father was named in any of the records. Most extraordinarily, Thomas Parry and his 'concubine' Elizabeth Lloyd baptised seven illegitimate children in the parish of Glascwm between 1699 and 1720.[26] As with bridal pregnancy, these instances are rare. With the exception of the three parishes in Radnorshire discussed later, only a few examples of unmarried couples bearing more than one illegitimate child together exists in each of the parishes studied here.

Bastardy bonds provide evidence to suggest that some poorer couples may have chosen to enter into conjugal relationships without marrying at all. In Holt in 1771 Watkin Maddock was identified in a bond as the father of Deborah Axon's illegitimate daughter.[27] The child was baptised on 11 April of that year, although no name was given for either the child or the father.[28] Another bond was drawn up the following year as Deborah was again pregnant, and Watkin Maddock was identified and bound as the father.[29] No baptisms record for their second child exists, but an entry in the burial register on February 1773 for an unnamed child identified only as the base child of 'Maddocks' suggests the infant was either stillborn or died shortly after birth.[30] In Trefeglwys in 1752 Oliver David was officially named by Jane Owen as the father of her daughter Sarah, who was born the year earlier. Three years later, Oliver David is again named and bound for the maintenance of another illegitimate daughter, Mary, also born to Jane Owen.[31] Oliver is identified in the 1751 baptism record for Sarah, but not the 1755 record for Mary, however given his prior affiliation it seems unlikely parish officials did not know who the father was at the time of baptism. If the bonds are taken at face value then it appears that this couple had a long-standing sexual relationship of some sort, but the nature of their relationship remains unclear. Based on the available evidence it is impossible to determine if such a relationships were the result of stable but irregular marriages, casual, consensual sexual relationships, extended courtships or something more sinister.

Another much-debated explanation for the prevalence of illegitimacy in early modern Britain is Laslett's 'bastardy prone sub-society'. Historians such as Steven King have found evidence of familial networks of individuals who, over several generations, engaged in numerous 'illegitimate events', frequently with different partners, with an apparent disregard for any legal or social consequences.[32] In the two communities King studied he found that 'repeaters' did account for the increased level of illegitimacy. However, patterns such as this appear to be limited elsewhere, as other historians have conducted similar studies for regions such as London and Scotland, and have not found evidence of such a bastardy prone sub-society.³³ The parishes of Llanfihangel Nant Melan, Glascwm and New Radnor in Radnorshire, which are within 11 miles of each other, do appear to have a higher frequency of repeaters at different times throughout the century which can account for some of the instances of reported illegitimacy, and a small portion of identified paternity in this region, but by no means all of it. The nature of Welsh surnames makes it difficult to map family networks, or to know with certainty if repeated names are actually evidence of 'repeaters' or simply the popularity of certain names. For example, it is plausible, yet highly unlikely, that the Mary Foulkes listed as bearing six illegitimate children over a 25-year period from 1757 to 1789 in the parish of Llanfyllin is the same individual.³⁴ Likewise, it is impossible to know if the Anne Swift of the same parish who bore six illegitimate children to at least three different fathers is, in fact, one individual. Both the forenames Mary and Anne and surnames Foulkes and Swift are common in the parish. In Llanfyllin in 1747 and 1751 Mr Evan Rice had illegitimate children baptised.³⁵ The use of 'Mr' in baptism registers is not common, and suggests some level of elevated rank, so the repeated use of this prefix means it is probable that these children were fathered by the same man. The mother of the child born in 1751 was a widow named Margaret Ellis; however, the mother of the child born in 1747 was identified only as 'Mrs RG'. The redaction of the mother's full name was probably done to protect her identity and prevent future shame and scandal, as she was likely to have been a woman of some rank or standing, as indicated by the use of the title 'Mrs'. In the mid-eighteenth century the prefix 'Mrs', which was short for mistress, was used to denote a woman of rank, or who possessed authority over servants, apprentices or employees.³⁶ It was used by both married and unmarried women of status well into the nineteenth century.³⁷ Therefore, it is likely the relationship between Mr Evans and Mrs RG was a sexual liaison between a man of some rank and an unmarried woman whose social standing warranted the use of the title 'mistress'.³⁸ Courtship or cohabitation were unlikely. Mr Rice could be classified as a 'repeater' and although contemporaries may have viewed his sexual behaviour as reprehensible he could hardly be seen to have been part of an illegitimacy-prone under-class.

There is at least one example which may indicate the sort of familial link sought by historians such as Laslett and King. In Glascwm in 1752 and 1753 Elizabeth Parry and John Davies baptised two illegitimate children. The aforementioned Thomas Parry and Elizabeth Lloyd who bore seven illegitimate children baptised a daughter named Elizabeth in 1718, and there is a possibility this may be the same Elizabeth Parry more than 30 years on, but given the commonality of both her first and surname it is difficult to know for certain.³⁹ Although there is no evidence to suggest that they were the greatest contributors to the overall level of illegitimacy in these areas, it is likely that some women bore multiple illegitimate children, possibly with more than one man. For example, in Llanfihangel Nant Melan, women named Phoebe Price and Ann Davies, both of whom were identified as paupers, bore six illegitimate children between them between 1791 and 1810, but the remaining 16 illegitimate baptisms during this time were 'singletons' born to women who only baptised one illegitimate child.[40] However, to assume that all instances of repeaters are evidence of a socially cohesive sub-society is an oversimplification.[41] In some parishes at certain times 'repeaters' can account for a portion of illegitimate baptisms, but there is no evidence that they formed a sub-stratum of society united by 'inherited' behaviours which produced illegitimate children. Similarly, Anna Brueton found that in south Wales repeaters were only responsibly for a small portion of illegitimate children who appeared in baptism records.[42] In the majority of parishes studied here, most couples and individuals listed in baptism registers as the parents of illegitimate children do not appear more than once.

One particular problem is that the language used to denote relationships between couples in parish registers can be misleading. A modern reader may understand terms such as 'cohabit' and 'concubine' to mean very specific things, such as living together as a couple in the same dwelling, or a woman who is kept as a man's sexual partner, however the usage of these terms in the eighteenth century is far more ambiguous.[43] This may create an impression that a large proportion of couples who bore illegitimate children were engaged in stable, conjugal unions. In reality, relationships identified explicitly or implicitly as 'cohabitation' could refer to a range of circumstances, including master-servant, or servant-servant living arrangements.[44] Relationships, such as the one between Richard Walter of Wrexham and his servant, Jane, or Richard Pugh, a farmer in Llanwnog, and his servant, Margaret Jenkyn, which both produced illegitimate children can be interpreted as cohabitation because they likely lived in the same dwelling, but further details about the nature of their relationships are entirely lacking.[45] Likewise, David Williams and Lydia Evans could be labelled as cohabiting as they were both servants at Wainwen in the parish of Gladestry when they bore an illegitimate child together in 1781, despite the fact that their living arrangements were a result of their employment rather than their relationship.[46] Furthermore, in Garthbeibio in 1799 Mary Rees was identified as both the servant and concubine of David Pugh in the baptism entry for their illegitimate son, David.[47] In these cases, the couples were co-residing, but there is nothing to suggesting they were cohabiting in established, stable relationships.[48] Furthermore, terms such as 'concubine' cannot be taken as evidence of a relationship in which a man kept a woman for the purposes of extramarital sex. Concubinage in this sense was, in fact, quite rare in early modern Britain.[49] The term 'concubine' probably denoted a sexual relationship between a man and a woman who were not married to each other. This usage of the term appears to have been applied with some regularity across all three counties during the century, and to all unmarried couples who bore illegitimate children in the parish of Glascwm, Radnorshire up until the mid-1720s when identified paternity began to drop.

The numerous bastardy bonds, examinations and filiation orders which survive go even further in illustrating the diversity of sexual encounters which resulted in the birth of an illegitimate child. Bonds served a specific purpose in the management of illegitimacy. These documents were drawn up shortly before or after the birth of an illegitimate child that was deemed to pose a financial risk to the parish. As such, they were typically only produced when an expectant or newly delivered mother was either impoverished, or at risk of becoming so. Parish records reveal the lengths to which some fathers would go to avoid taking responsibility for their illegitimate child. However few went as far as William Chandley who, according to the baptism entry, 'hanged himself on the occasion' of his illegitimate son's birth.[50] Such instances are extremely rare, and most fathers who wished to avoid taking financial responsibility for their illegitimate child likely fled, and, in many cases, they were pursued by officials. The lengths to which parish officials would go to ensure a father was bound for the maintenance of his child is evident in account books for overseers of the poor in most parishes. Frequently, officials would incur expenses for warrants, horses, accommodation and meals for journeys to other parishes to pursue putative fathers who lived in, or had fled to, different parishes. For example, in 1751 officials in Aberhafesp paid 18s. 6d. for a warrant and two journeys to Llanfyllin to pursue the father of one of Elizabeth Kinsey's illegitimate children.[51] In 1771, in the parish of Ceri, officials paid 10d. for a 'Journey to Mochdre to fetch Margaret Newel, for a horse to carry her to the Pentre, [a] journey, horse hire and expenses to the justice with her, the justice for her second examination and oath to keep the father in the house of correction.'[52] Officials from different parishes would cooperate with one another to ensure that fathers were held accountable. Overseers of the poor in Trefeglwys wrote to their counterparts in the parish of Llanwnog to inform them that one of their parishioners:

> Thomas Davies a settled inhabitant of our parish of Trefeglwys hath begotten with child a pauper girl of your said parish which if not rightly considered may be a trouble to both our parishes. Now we whose names are hereunto subscribed do request that you would be pleased to accept of such security as the said Thomas Davies can prevail with to be bound for him; and that he may be at freedom to come home to his family as he and his wife promise faithfully to take the said child when born to keep and maintain, pray take this to consideration as it may be a means to indemnifie both our parishes from further trouble and charge, which is from us your humble servants, parishioners of Trefeglwys.[53]

Evidence of parish officials cooperating to ensure fathers were held accountable is common, but surety such as this, from a married man's wife that his child born to another woman will be supported, is incredibly rare.[54] The fate of this child and her mother is unknown, but the relationship she had with Thomas Davies could not have been one of genuine courtship as he was already married.

Failure to support a child after a filiation order had been made could result in goal time for the father. If an illegitimate child was not perceived to be a financial risk to the parish a bond was not likely to have been made. The mother was to swear the identity of the father before one or more justices of the peace, and the father would then be legally bound for the financial maintenance of the child. In some instances, fathers voluntarily admitted their paternity and committed to providing financial support for their children. For example, a bond dated 1727 noted that Edward Mortan, a yeoman in Llandegley, had voluntarily admitted that he fathered an illegitimate child with Dorothy Evans.[55] In the same parish in 1778 another yeoman named Richard Jones also voluntarily admitted that he had fathered an illegitimate child with Elizabeth Mantle.[56] Poor law accounts do suggest that some fathers were involved in the care of their illegitimate children, as some men received money from the parish for the maintenance of a child, such as Thomas Reece of Berriew who, in 1789, received £6 6d. for the maintenance of his illegitimate child born to 'D Evans'.[57] In 1793 John Davies of Norton was paid £2 12d. for the maintenance of his illegitimate child.[58] However there is no indication that these men were involved in established relationships with the mothers of their children, or that the mothers were still alive. Nicholas Rogers has argued that bonds such as these may be indicative of irregular relationships such as cohabitation or courtship which had involved some level of commitment at the time of conception, but had subsequently broken down, thus causing official concern for the financial circumstances of the children born into these non-conforming unions.[59] However, Samantha Williams has since argued that these documents would have been drawn up for all cases of illegitimacy, whether cohabiting or not, where the financial circumstances of the mother were at risk, and cannot be seen as direct evidence of cohabitation or the breakdown of relationships.[60]

If a man was identified in a bond as the father of an illegitimate child the onus was on him to prove he was not the father, should he choose to do so.[61] Bastardy bonds reveal this mechanism in action, such as in Llandegley in 1748 when John Owen, a yeoman, was 'adjudged' to be the father of Elizabeth Meredith's illegitimate child, and in Holt in 1766 George Matthews could not 'show sufficient cause why he should not be adjudged the father' of Elizabeth Follyman's illegitimate child.[62] Similarly, in 1800, Richard Nutt, a husbandman, could not show officials in Bettws Cedewain sufficient evidence that he was not the father of Mary Pritchard's illegitimate son.[63] It is possible in these instances that these men were not the actual fathers, but instead were identified by mothers because of their financial circumstances, which might have been more advantageous than the actual father. Officials were apparently aware of this practice, but appear to have been more concerned with financial indemnity than accuracy.[64] This is evident in the extent to which, in some parishes, such as Llandegley, Radnorshire, more than one man could be held accountable as the father. In 1753 John Drew, a yeoman, and his son David Drew, were sworn to be the 'father or fathers' of Alice Lewis's illegitimate child.[65] Steven King has demonstrated that some pauper women in early nineteenth-century Lancashire were aware of their rights for support under the old poor law, and understood the legal mechanisms which would ensure they were financially provided for.[66] It is possible that impoverished, unmarried mothers in Wales also knew how to use the old poor law system to their advantage, and when they faced financial uncertainty they made decisions which were in the best interests of their child, or children, and themselves. Therefore, the identification of fathers, at least in some bastardy bonds, could be understood in part as an expression of female agency rather than as an expression of parish authority alone.

In the surviving documents from the Welsh parishes the identity of the father does not appear to have been as much of a priority as simply holding individuals financially accountable for the support of an illegitimate child. In some bonds as many as three individuals would be held bound for the maintenance of a child, and their relationship to the mother and the child was not always stated. For example, in the parish of Trefeglwys in 1788, two men and one woman agreed to provide support for the illegitimate daughter born to Elizabeth Rees, but neither man is identified as the father, and no baptism record exists to allow for a comparison.[67] In 1762, in the parish of Berriew, three men were bound for the maintenance of Ann Brees's illegitimate child, none of whom were listed in the bond as the father. The baptism record identifies Edward Rowton, one of the three bound men, as the father.[68] At least 30 of the surviving 85 bonds for the parish of Llandinam bind one or more individuals without explicitly naming the father. In other cases the person bound for financial maintenance of a child was a relative of the mother or father, such as in 1766 when Richard Brown, a blacksmith in Llandinam was bound for the maintenance of his daughter Mary's illegitimate son.[69] In Manafon in 1763, William Jones, a Tailor from Berriew was bound for the maintenance of his son John's illegitimate child born to Margaret James.[70] In Trefeglwys in the 1770s two widows, Elizabeth Rees and Elizabeth Woola, were bound for the maintenance of their unmarried sons' illegitimate children, and in 1783 Thomas Roberts was bound for the maintenance of his son's unborn illegitimate child.[71] The frequent provision of surety and maintenance by multiple people suggests complex networks of kinship and support which may have been available to unmarried mothers during times of adversity.[72] What these examples suggest is that establishing paternity in poor law records such as bastardy bonds was only important as a means of ensuring financial security for an illegitimate child, and was not concerned with establishing biological paternity. It is noteworthy that not a single man identified as a pauper was bound, which likely reflects the unlikelihood that a man in such economic circumstances could provide financial surety. If the parish could be indemnified by the swearing of maintenance by other people, parish officials were not likely to attempt to officially establish paternity.

Illicit and Non-Consensual Sex

Circumstances in which more than one man was bound as father, such as in the aforementioned example of Alice Lewis, raises the issues of sexual exploitation and rape. It is impossible to know if either or both of the men identified did engage in some sort of sexual encounter with her, but if the circumstances which led to the conception of Alice's child involved both men it was unlikely to have been a matter of courtship, and was quite possibly non-consensual, and even violent. Historians such as Adair have suggested that the stereotype of poor peasant or servant girls being sexually exploited by 'arrogant aristocrats or top-hatted Victorian capitalists' has little evidentiary basis as the primary cause of illegitimacy.[73] Adair does not argue that sexual exploitation of women did not happen, but uses this farcically extreme example to suggest that rape was likely to have only contributed to the overall illegitimacy ratio in a small way.[74] There is limited documentary evidence of rape in early modern England and Wales because it was a difficult crime to report and prove.[75] Attitudes towards sexuality and culpability meant that men who committed rape were rarely charged, and those who were charged were frequently acquitted.[76] Evidence of rape rarely appears in parish registers. During the eighteenth century and earlier rape was rarely prosecuted and, when it was, it seldom led to a conviction except in cases of extreme violence or extreme youth. Married women were more likely to be believed because their chastity less likely to be doubted than their unmarried counterparts.[77] If a woman found herself pregnant several months after being forced into sex against her will, she was unlikely to accuse the father if she had not done so already. This means that conceptions resulting from non-consensual sex are virtually impossible to quantify, but we should not assume, as Adair does, that statistical insignificance equals actual insignificance. Adair was searching for a primary cause of increasing levels of illegitimacy, however the search for a single leading cause has led to the construction of narratives which dismiss rape or coercion in favour of the much more pleasant hypothesis of courtship. In reality, rape would have been one of the many types of sexual experience which resulted in an illegitimate birth. None of the instances of rape, or attempted rape, found in the Court of Great Sessions *Gaol Files* database can be directly linked to any of the illegitimate baptisms found in the registers of the 45 parishes considered here.[78] Although there is no way to quantify its actual instance from parish records it is still worthwhile considering evidence that suggests non-consensual sexual encounters, which would have been a reality for many women.

The most obvious place to look for sexual assault is in court records, which do occasionally provide a link between rape and illegitimacy. For example, in Llangollen, Denbighshire in 1788 a single woman named Sarah Owen stood accused of murdering her newborn son.[79] A witness named Gwen Gabriel, in whose house Sarah gave birth, testified that Sarah had told her that a man had attempted to rape her, and had offered her half a crown.[80] The use of 'attempted' should not be taken to mean this man tried but failed to have non-consensual sex with Sarah. Rather, the evidence here indicates that he coerced Sarah into having sex with him, which at the time she did not consent to, and this resulted in her becoming pregnant. This narrative of events reflects eighteenth-century understandings of reproduction and consent. The boundaries between rape and seduction were frequently blurred, and 'forcible seduction' was a common feature in descriptions of sexual encounters between unmarried men and women.[81] Moreover, early modern and eighteenth-century understandings of reproduction held that both a man and woman needed to achieve orgasm in order to conceive, therefore, conception could be taken as evidence of consent, even if a woman had genuinely not consented.[82] The subsequent payment fits within this narrative, as assailants often paid a nominal fine to their victim.[83] The 'attempted' here then should be read as redefinition of Sarah's own experience of the encounter necessitated by her subsequent pregnancy, regardless of how she actually felt about it.[84] To a modern observer, what happened to Sarah would be interpreted as rape, but in the context of the eighteenth century, the distinction is not as clear cut. What is clear is that women could and did bear illegitimate children as a result of sexual assault.

Parish records also provide revealing glimpses of these encounters. Baptism registers provide little overt evidence of non-consensual or exploitative sexual relationships, with the exception of entries that identify relationships between parents of illegitimate children as incestuous. By early modern standards, 'incest' could include relationships between men and women who were closely related by marriage rather than by blood alone. The eight children born between 1695 and 1714 to Roger Edwards of Church Street in Oswestry, and Jane Roberts his wife's daughter, 'being his pretend wife' are examples of this.[85] It is possible that such relationships were genuine and consensual, but frowned upon by parish officials. However, given the potential for an exploitative power imbalance to exist between a man and his stepdaughter, and the unfortunate possibility that a man could sexually assault his own biological daughter, relationships of incest should not be overlooked. Moreover, these sexual encounters should not be categorised alongside relationships of courtship. Therefore, baptism entries such as the two children 'incestuously begotten' between Simon Rogers and Elizabeth Roberts in Llangollen in the 1720s, or Matthew Morris of Llansillin who in 1743 fathered an illegitimate child with his own daughter Elizabeth are plausible examples of illegitimacy resulting from coercive or exploitative sexual encounters.[86] Such instances are, fortunately, quite rare, but again serve as evidence that illegitimacy should not be examined in terms of thwarted courtships alone.

Although not explicit in accusations of rape and exploitation, bastardy papers can also provide evidence of sexual relationships the likely resulted from male abuses of power against women who were socially subordinate to them.[87] In 1761 a bond was drawn up against Edward Davies, a gentleman of the Maesmawr estate in Llandinam, who was identified as the father of an illegitimate daughter born to a single woman named Susan Morgan. The bond was signed both by Edward and by a widow named Elizabeth Davies, who was likely either Edward's mother or his wife.[88] Between December 1750 and January 1751 Richard Francis, a yeoman farmer of Maesmawr, and two of his sons, John and Morris all had bonds drawn against them for fathering illegitimate children with three different women, all of whom were identified as spinsters.[89] In Berriew in 1746 a bond named John Griffiths, a gentleman from the parish of Ceri, as the father of former servant Ursula Jones's unborn child.[90] In the same parish in 1751 Jerimiah Brown, a gentleman of Bishops Castle, Shropshire was named in a bond as the father of Sarah Luscott's unborn child. Sarah did not have legal settlement in Berriew, but she was listed as being from Chirbury, Shropshire, so Jerimiah probably paid parish officials enough to relocate Sarah and save his reputation at home.[91]

In each of the instances found in parish records it is impossible to ascertain the precise nature of the relationship between these men and women, and of course, to know with certainty that these men were the biological fathers of these children. But, if we take them at face value it seems unlikely that any of these sexual relationships were part of courtship, irregular marriage or even a casual, consensual encounter. Gentleman such as Edward Davies, John Griffiths and Jerimiah Brown were likely to court and marry a woman of similar social status who would not have been at risk of ending up dependent on parish poor relief. It is likely that Susan Morgan, Ursula Jones and Sarah Luscott were from lower social orders, and that their sexual encounters may have resulted from some sort of power imbalance and coercion. In the case of the Francis men, it is difficult to imagine a circumstance which would result in three male members of the same immediate family all conceiving children with women who were not their legal spouses at roughly the same time that is not in some way linked to sexual exploitation. Examples from nineteenth-century Welsh newspapers do indicate that family members could join together in the rape of young women who were subordinate to them in some way, such as servants within their household, and these bonds may be evidence of similar behaviour.[92]

Such encounters may not have resulted in accusations which led to official charges and a trial, but women may still have been able to exercise agency by naming the fathers of their children and holding them financially accountable. Similar manifestations of female agency may be at work when mothers chose to withhold a father's name, such as in Trefeglwys in 1718 when Margaret Smyth refused to identify the father of her illegitimate child. Instead, she and two other men were bound. It could be that one of the two men was the father, or that alternative arrangements were made to preserve the reputation and anonymity of the father by guaranteeing financial security for the mother. Such circumstances may be speculative, but could indicate that women had some control, however little, over their circumstances. These hypotheses are no more speculative, and are ultimately more plausible than those which suggest that these records are evidence of cohabitation and irregular marriage.

Another category of sexual encounter which warrants examination is prostitution. As in England, there is evidence that formal and informal prostitution existed across Wales to at least some degree. Although not well documented, it is probable that at least some illegitimate children were born as a result.[93] Across Britain and Europe, formalised prostitution tended to be located in larger centres such as ports and market towns, which had larger populations from which to draw clientele.[94] In Wales, the only charges relating to keeping a bawdy house in the eighteenth century come from the towns of Caernarfon and Cardigan, which both fit this description.[95] In Caernarfon in 1755 Mary Meredith was convicted, pilloried and imprisoned for keeping a bawdy house, thanks in large part to the damning evidence provided by many of her clients and neighbours. Meredith had in her employ at least three women: Gaynor, who was the wife of a farmer named Evan Jones, Ann Lloyd and a woman who went by the name of 'Martha Fawr', all of whom were named in witness depositions.[96] A second, more tragic, example can be found in Cardigan in 1788, when a sick and elderly woman named Elizabeth George, who was known to have previously kept a bawdy house in the town, was murdered.[97] The suspects were two men from Cheltenham who, according to witnesses, had called into the town's Black Lion pub and asked about her services. When told she had been very ill for some time and was no longer in business, the two men allegedly helped themselves to a bottle of brandy and made their way to her house. Neighbours reported hearing calls of distress from her home, and Elizabeth's body was found in 'a very indecent manner' the following morning.[98] The two men fled before they could be apprehended and charged.

This limited evidence does indicate that bawdy houses were a feature in some, if not all, Welsh towns, particularly those in or near ports. However, prostitution was not limited to such establishments. Across Wales, informal arrangements where women occasionally engaged in sex in exchange for money or goods could have occurred virtually anywhere. For example, in 1771, James Price, the excise officer in Carmarthen brought charges against a married woman named Elizabeth Lewis for stealing his watch. He alleged that she had agreed to have sex with him in the churchyard in exchange for six pence. However, just as she lifted her skirts someone walked through the churchyard, thus preventing them from proceeding. According to Price, Lewis took advantage of their close proximity to pick his pocket and steal his silver watch. No formal charges were laid.[99] Unfortunately, such evidence is rare, but what does exist does demonstrate that prostitution existed in Wales to at least some degree, and although its contribution to illegitimacy is impossible to qualify, it also should not be overlooked.

A final category of relationships which could result in the birth of an illegitimate child, but clearly cannot be described a courtship are those which one or both parents were already married to someone else. This appears frequently in parish records, as is evident in the correspondence between officials in Trefeglwys and Llanwnog regarding Thomas Davies, who fathered an illegitimate child that his wife agreed to take care of. Additional examples appear in baptism registers, where one parent is identified as single, and the other identified as married. For example, in Llangollen in 1791, married men named John Jones and Edward Humphreys both fathered illegitimate children with women identified as 'spinsters'.[100] Likewise, in Llanrhaeadr ym Mochnant in 1798 Mary Jones, married woman bore an illegitimate child whose father was identified as a bachelor.[101] These are a few examples of a situation that appears relatively frequently across parishes. It is possible that, as with the burglary case of Griffith Roberts discussed in Chapter 1, the married individual did not disclose to their sexual partner that they were not legally in a position to marry, and therefore any conjugal courtship practices were undertaken under false pretences.[102] It is also likely that in many of these instances, the individual identified as 'married' was no longer living with his or her spouse as a result of abandonment or relationship breakdown. During the eighteenth century divorce required a private act of parliament, and was therefore out of reach for the vast majority of unhappily married couples. Therefore it is possible that some of these couples were involved in serious relationships, but were prevented from marrying on the grounds of prior marriage. These instance would be more in line with irregular marriage or conjugal courtship. However, it is also possible that both parties in these relationships were willingly involved in extramarital sex. It is impossible to tell which of these circumstances applied in most instances. With the exception of those involving deception, such relationships would likely not have been coercive, but as with all other relationships considered here, they should also not be understood in terms of genuine courtship.

The notion that illegitimacy resulted almost exclusively from consensual sex as a step in the process of marriage is an appealing one, as it nicely accounts for otherwise inexplicable demographic changes linked to sexual activity which places premarital sex into a context of order, propriety, and community acceptance. This is evidence of what Barry Reay describes as 'our ignorance about sexual attitudes and behaviours of people in the past [which] is matched only by a desire to rush to generalisation.'[103] The available evidence for Wales does indicate that conjugal courtship was happening, and likely accounts for most instances of illegitimate baptisms. However, we should not then disregard the myriad other types of sexual encounters which produced illegitimate children. For most couples, all we have is a single baptism entry, with little or no additional information, no correlating marriage record and in most cases no further baptism records. Ultimately, we have no way of knowing for certain how many of these resulted from courtship, or from any number of other sexual encounters. The evidence from bastardy bonds, filiation orders, churchwardens and overseers of the poor accounts, and court records suggests a much broader range of sexual experience which cannot be confined neatly to a single custom or behaviour. Careful consideration of the different types of evidence available suggests a diverse tapestry of sexual experience which resulted in myriad forms of illegitimacy which cannot be attributed to a single pattern of sexual behaviour, and cannot be quantified and mapped as unified demographic phenomena. The problem lies not with our inability to identify a single, primary cause of illegitimacy, but rather with a desire to clearly demarcate, compartmentalise, and then explain legitimate/illicit and illegitimate/illicit sex. If we consider the contextual richness of sources, this endeavour appears impractical, if not impossible, and somewhat misguided.[104] Illegitimacy resulted from different types of sexual encounters, each of which deserves separate consideration.[105]

Illegitimate Identities: Parents

The diversity of illegitimacy and illegitimate paternity is further revealed through an analysis of the various occupations and social status of parents of illegitimate children. The naming of so many fathers in parish registers provides a unique opportunity to study the socioeconomic backgrounds of the men who fathered children outside of marriage. To a lesser degree, parish records can also provide some information about mothers, but this is considerably limited compared with evidence about fathers. Most studies of illegitimacy in early modern Britain have attempted to analyse the socioeconomic and moral background of mothers, which led to the development of theories such as the bastardy prone sub-society hypothesis. It has generally been assumed that women from poorer backgrounds were at greater risk of bearing an illegitimate child.[106] However, this risk factor could more usefully be understood as an effect rather than a cause because of the economic reality facing the vast majority of women in the eighteenth century. Women lacked the economic opportunities which would have provided financial independence, and therefore they were at greater risk of poverty.[107] This is evidenced by studies which have found that a greater proportion of women claimed parish poor relief than men during the eighteenth century.[108] Rather than poor, single women being at greater risk of conceiving and bearing illegitimate children than their better-off peers, a woman who bore an illegitimate child was at greater risk of poverty than her married or childless counterparts. Where there is evidence of a bastardy prone sub-society it does appear that the women who were involved in these networks were from the lower orders of society, but such evidence is limited, and it is impossible to determine if the state of poverty or illegitimacy came first. The reality is that single mothers from different backgrounds would have had few economic opportunities available to them which would have allowed them to support their child and themselves on their own, which meant they would have been reliant upon support from family and the community. If such support was not available, then they would invariably end up having to rely on poor relief. Therefore, it is more accurate to view illegitimacy as a contributing factor towards poverty for women, or, rather, that the prevailing social order created a state of disadvantage for women who bore children without being suitably married.

The restricted opportunities available to women are evident in the limited descriptive language used in parish registers and poor law documents. Britain in the eighteenth century was deeply patriarchal, and women's identities were tied to the dominant male figure in their lives, such as a father or husband, and in the absence of these, brothers, grandfathers, uncles and so on.[109] Although this can shed light on family structures, it makes it difficult to uncover details about the lives of women themselves, particularly women from the lower orders of society. In most baptism registers and poor law documents, when a description of a woman is given, it is typically in relation to her marital status, or parentage: terms are used such as 'single woman', 'spinster', 'widow', 'wife of' or 'daughter of'. Certain socioeconomic labels could be applied to women, but these were typically limited to servants and paupers, and, in some poor law accounts, midwives. In Llangollen in 1784 the mother of an illegitimate child was identified as a 'schoolmistress', and this is the only example of an occupation other than servant given to an unmarried mother in any of the baptism records considered here.[110] Although women in early modern Britain were actively employed in domestic, agricultural and commercial activities, this was seldom revealed in parish documents.[111] Moreover, the labels used for some women were heavily laden with moral judgement based on their perceived sexual deviance, particularly with regards to illegitimacy, which can be seen in labels such as 'whore' and 'concubine.' Because of this, and the absence of any ego documents written by women drawn from the middling and lower orders of society for the regions considered here, it is difficult to determine who the mothers of illegitimate children actually were. However, it cannot be assumed simply because impoverished unmarried women appear in poor law accounts that poor women bore more illegitimate children. With the exception of certain exploitative relationships, there is a high probability that consensual sex which resulted in the birth of an illegitimate child most likely occurred between men and women from similar socioeconomic backgrounds, such as Mr Rice and Mrs RG., who were very likely not poor.[112] This hypothesis cannot be explored using evidence pertaining to mothers alone, and therefore the details relating to fathers must be considered. If fathers of illegitimate children were drawn from the full spectrum of society it is highly probable that many of the mothers were as well.

Some earlier studies of illegitimacy have briefly focused on the occupational or socioeconomic backgrounds of the fathers of illegitimate children. In *Bastardy and its Comparative History*, Oosterveen, Smith and Stewart found that most illegitimate children in the parishes they studied were born to labourers, servants and paupers.[113] They based this on their observation that men identified as such appeared, numerically speaking, more often than men from the upper ranks. Evidence from other parishes, including the Welsh parishes studied here, supports this conclusion, but this analysis on its own is inadequate as it fails to take into consideration the proportional distribution of different social and economic groups. British society in the eighteenth century would have had far more labourers, yeomen and paupers than gentlemen, so numerically speaking, they would be likely to appear more frequently. More recently, however, John Black has analysed the occupational backgrounds of the fathers of illegitimate children in three London parishes, and, contrary to what Oosterveen et al, found, the proportional representation of fathers of illegitimate children broadly represented the occupational structures of the communities studied, with the majority of fathers in all three parishes working in manufacturing, which was the largest form of employment in these parishes.[114] Between 30 and 40 per cent of men were employed in manufacture in these areas, and a similar proportion of fathers of illegitimate children were as well. Although men who earned their living through agriculture, a profession, or through rents from property ownership, fathered fewer illegitimate children, they do appear in records in proportion to their local occupational distribution.[115]

Similar quantitative analysis cannot be applied to data from the Welsh parishes included in this study because the surviving documents do not consistently identify occupations for all fathers. However, qualitatitive analysis suggests that a similar proportional distribution of occupations existed in Denbighshire, Montgomeryshire, and Radnorshire. Overall, 92 different occupations or economic categories were given for fathers of illegitimate children listed in baptism registers, bastardy bonds or quarter sessions records (Table 2.1). The most frequent occupations which appear are yeoman, farmer/husbandman and labourer. In predominantly agricultural regions such as mid and northeast Wales these would make up the vast majority of occupations for adult men. The term 'yeoman' was applied loosely to a broad range of agricultural men of varying fortunes who were in possession of the land on which they farmed or reared livestock.[116] The

Table 2.1 Occupations of fathers of illegitimate children as listed in baptism registers, bastardy bonds and filiation orders, and quarter sessions records in Denbighshire, Montgomeryshire and Radnorshire.

Economic and Occupation or Social Status of Fathers

Apothecary	Gardner	Saddler
Attorney	Gentleman	Sailor
Baker	Glazier	Sawyer
Barber	Glover	Scotchman
Blacksmith	Groom	Servant
Bodice maker	Grocer	Ship's Carpenter
Brazier	Gunner	Shoemaker
Brewer	Hatter	(corvisor/
Bricklayer	Horse Courser	cordwainer)
Buckle maker	Innkeeper	Shopkeeper
Butcher	Innkeeper's Servant	Skinner
Cabinet maker	Joiner	Slater
Cardman	Labourer	Soap boiler
Carpenter	Lawyer	Sojourner
Carrier	Livery Man	Soldier
Chandler	Major	Stranger
Chimneysweep	Maltster	Surgeon
Clothier	Mason	Tailor
Coachman	Master of House of	Tanner
Collier	Corrections	Tinker
Cooper	Mercer	Traveller
Cotton Spinner	Militia Man	Turner
Currier	Miller	Usher
Drawer	Miner	Vagabond
Druggist	Nailor	Waggoner
Dyer	Officer of Excise	Walker
Esquire	Ostler	Watchmaker
Farmer/husbandman	Pauper	Weaver
Felt maker	Paper man	Wheelwright
Fiddler	Paver	Widower
Flax dresser	Plasterer	Yeoman
Furnaceman	Post boy	

designation therefore cannot be seen as an indication of wealth, although some yeomen would certainlly have enjoyed a degree of wealth. Trades such as bodice maker, tailor, watchmaker and hatter appear more frequently in towns and in more populated communities such as Wrexham, Llanfyllin and Machynlleth, while occupations which were relevant to both towns and rural areas, such as blacksmiths and carpenters, appear in all areas. Occupations such as miner and collier appear exclusively in areas in and around the coal seams in Denbighshire and, to a lesser extent, in parts of Montgomeryshire. Labels such as 'traveller' or 'stranger' cannot be taken as occupations per se, but do indicate someone lower down the social order, as does the label of 'pauper'. Titles such as 'gentleman' and 'esquire', and occupations such as 'excise officer', 'master of the house of corrections', 'attorney' and 'surgeon' demonstrate that men of all ranks could, and did, father illegitimate children. Overall, the occupations represented in parish illegitimacy records represent the broad range of occupations available to men in eighteenth-century Wales, and thus illegitimacy in Wales cannot be understood as the plight of the poor alone. Nor can illegitimacy in these parishes be understood as the remit of a small network or under-class of people prone to bearing children outside of marriage.

Further evidence of the broad socioeconomic spectrum from which fathers of illegitimate children were drawn can be found in the fact that many of the men bound through bastardy bonds for the maintenance of illegitimate children were able to sign their names with varying degrees of refinement. Men across the region from diverse occupations, such as Stephen Thomas, a Bricklayer, and Edward Evans, a yeoman, both of Berriew, and Richard Richards, an innkeeper, and Richard Stephens a shopkeeper, both of Llandinam, and three yeoman, two farmers and a husbandman from Holt were all able to clearly and legibly sign their own names to their respective bastardy bonds.[117] These are a few examples of various men from different trades and backgrounds who signed their own names. Many more men who were identified as fathers in bonds but had no occupational description also signed their names, such as William Williams and Evan Davies of Berriew.[118] Even though these men had no discernible profession, the ability to sign their names suggests that they were unlikely to have been from an impoverished background. Signatures are one of the few limited personal details we have about the socioeconomic background of men listed in illegitimacy documents. Although the ability to sign one's name is by no means an indicator of affluence, at the very least it can be taken as evidence to demonstrate that many of these men were not drawn from the lowest and poorest stratum of society, and therefore most likely to have been lacking in literacy, as has previously been assumed.[119] None of the men from occupations further down the economic spectrum, such as labourers and servants, signed their names, but instead marked with an 'X'.

In his study of London parishes, Black determined that the majority of mothers of illegitimate children were unmarried plebeian women of comparable socioeconomic status and occupations as the men who fathered their children.[120] Nicholas Rogers has argued that the mothers of illegitimate children in London came from less socioeconomically diverse backgrounds than fathers as many worked in service, although many were identified as the widows of tradesmen.[121] Furthermore, young, unmarried women from diverse backgrounds could work in service, and therefore service alone cannot be seen as an indicator of low economic standing, or a lack of economic diversity amongst mothers. Black's findings about male occupational diversity translate well to the Welsh sources; therefore, it is not implausible that female occupational diversity follows a similar pattern. When we consider that bastardy bonds were one of the many mechanisms available to parish officials under the poor law, it is likely that the women listed in bonds were deemed to be at risk of poverty to some degree. Given women's limited economic opportunities it is probable that women from both the lower and middling orders could be at risk of impoverishment if they bore an illegitimate child. Therefore, it cannot be assumed that all women who found their way into parish documents were necessarily financially destitute, and bonds cannot be taken as an indicator of actual female poverty. In 1768 an unmarried mother named Elizabeth Read signed her own bond, suggesting she may not have come from an impoverished background.[122] On the occasions when a gentleman was identified as the father, particularly in bastardy bonds, there is a high probability that the sexual encounter which led to the conception of an illegitimate child was not between social equals, as a woman of similar rank would not be likely to provoke the creation of such a document. It is possible, therefore, that such circumstances could have been the result of exploitative or non-consensual sexual relations. However, many of the sexual relationships that men lower down the social scale had with women who were not their wives are much harder to classify, but, as in London, when the relationships were consensual, they were likely to have been with women who were drawn from a similar background.

Illegitimate Identities: Children

Illegitimacy posed a clear risk of impoverishment to some mothers, and therefore their children would have faced similar risks. The extent to which this risk was manifested can be found by analysing the ways in which illegitimate children appear in parish records. If being born into a state of illegitimacy predicated a life of abject, long-term poverty, we would expect to see many of the illegitimate children who were baptised in parish registers or accounted for in bastardy bonds listed in parish poor law accounts on an ongoing basis. Furthermore, if the state of being illegitimate was one which brought its own set of risks or inherent shame it would be expected that the label of 'illegitimate' would be applied to a child throughout his or her life. A significant amount of poor relief was allocated to pauper children, including those born to parents who were not married.[123] Some of these children would have remained in their mother's care, while others would have been placed with family members or neighbours while mothers returned to employment.[124] Infants not cared for by their mothers could have been placed in the care of wet nurses, which carried notoriously poor outcomes for such children.[125] If they survived the first few precarious years of childhood, pauper children, both legitimate and illegitimate, would then be apprenticed, frequently from as young as seven years of age, but sometimes even earlier. The evidence from the Welsh parishes considered here does suggest that some illegitimate children were dependent on parish poor relief, but this was typically only for short periods of time.

Payments for lying-in, delivery, nursing and clothing of illegitimate pauper children can be found in all surviving account books for the parishes considered in this study. The range of care provided during birth and after birth will be examined further in Chapter 6, but it is apparent is that the majority of illegitimate children who were in receipt of parish poor law support were only supported for short periods of time. In some cases, this was only during the period immediately following birth, after which time they were probably supported by family members or neighbours. Brueton found that only a small percentage of illegitimate children in Glamorganshire and Carmarthenshire were supported by the parish, and this appears to be true for mid and northeast Wales as well.[126] For example, of the 450 illegitimate children baptised in Berriew between 1680 and 1799, only a handful appear as in receipt of parish support, and most appear to be one-off payments. Within each parish there are a few individuals who are repeatedly in receipt of poor law support, but these are by far the minority. Elizabeth, Mary, Margaret and Thomas Kinsey, two sets of illegitimate twins born to Elizabeth Kinsey in 1747 and 1752 are exceptions to the rule. Elizabeth and her children appear to be in regular receipt of poor relief throughout a 28-year period from 1748 onwards, and seem to be one of the single greatest expenses for the parish.[127] However, the vast majority of illegitimate children appear to have been cared for privately.

Parish officials were acutely concerned about the particular financial burden posed by illegitimate children, and therefore it would make sense for the label of 'illegitimate' to be attached as long as this risk was apparent. Baptism records for children identified as illegitimate who were as old as eight or nine do exist, such as an eight-year-old illegitimate child baptised in Llanbister in 1705, although they are rare. The label of illegitimate was frequently, but not always, applied whenever payments were made to children born to single mothers. In Berriew, throughout the 1780s, the illegitimate daughters of Judith Humphreys were in regular receipt of poor relief, and were consistently labelled as 'bastard' in each record of expenditure.[128] It would likewise be expected that older pauper children would be referred to as illegitimate in records relating to their support, such as in apprenticeship indentures. This is evident in a few apprenticeship documents, such as the indenture for Harry Lloyd, a 'base born child' in Llangyniew, Montgomeryshire who was apprenticed to a husbandman, or Samuel, the eight-year-old son of Anne Walters and Samuel Gittens who was apprenticed to a blacksmith in Meifod in 1783. The latter's indenture did not explicitly identify him as illegitimate, but he was identified as such in a supplementary document.[129] However, apprenticeship indentures from the parishes studied do not typically identify any child as legitimate or illegitimate, but the payments made by poor law officials for the cost of setting a child up as an apprentice, which were recorded in poor law account books, do sometimes record this detail. For example, when David Lewis, an illegitimate child in Meifod, was apprenticed in 1747, parish officials used the label of illegitimate in the entry for expenses incurred by the parish to prepare him for his apprenticeship.[130] Similarly, in 1746 the parish vestry of Llangyniew ordered that the parish pay for Harry Lloyd, who was identified as illegitimate, to be provided with two new sets of clothing to prepare him for his apprenticeship to Edward Evans, a local husbandman.[131] It is possible that the 9s. 10d. paid by officials in Gresford for a 'coat, waistcoat and breeches for a bastard of Jane Gabrielle' in 1751 were intended to prepare him for an apprenticeship as well.[132]

It is evident that an illegitimate identity could follow children beyond the first and most precarious years of life. However, the label of illegitimate does not appear to have followed children into adulthood, and after the age of apprenticeship it was no longer applied to any children born to single mothers. This was the case for illegitimate children born to plebeian mothers across mid and northeast Wales. The circumstances for illegitimate children higher up the social ladder, where anxieties about illegitimacy were informed by concerns over inheritance, would have been different. However, it is noteworthy that in none of the parish records analysed, including marriage and burial registers, churchwarden, poor law accounts and court records are adults or older children referred to as illegitimate. As soon as illegitimate pauper children became economically active the label appears to have been shed. This suggests that illegitimacy was first and foremost an economic concern for parish officials, rather than a moral designation which was officially attached to a child throughout life. Once illegitimate pauper children were forced into the labour market, their potential dependence on parish relief diminished, and therefore the label of 'illegitimate' carried less significance.[133] Although illegitimacy could create disadvantage and lead to children becoming impoverished when they may otherwise not have been so, any officially documented discrimination associated with a state of illegitimacy waned over time. Given the economic motivation, impoverished illegitimate children would very likely have been given similar pauper apprenticeship opportunities to those available to poor children whose parents were married. The social and cultural significance of bearing an illegitimate identity, and the extent to which such labels endured over time is much more difficult to access, but, at least as far as official opinion was concerned, the label of 'illegitimate' could be shed once a child entered the labour market.

Conclusion

Welsh parish records provide a unique perspective on illegitimacy in eighteenth-century Britain because they so frequently identify fathers of illegitimate children. The significance of this is that it allows for a detailed examination of the diverse sexual experiences which could result in the birth of illegitimate children in the eighteenth century. The presence of fathers from diverse backgrounds also presents an alternative to the traditional search for a single, primary cause of illegitimacy. The only common feature these men shared with one another was that they engaged in penetrative sex with women who were not their wives; their socioeconomic backgrounds, customs, values, motivations and relationships varied far too much to be understood as a unified demographic trend. Analysis of paternal identities helps to reveal the different relationships, and the multiplicity of sexual experiences of a broad range of people, which resulted in diverse kinds of illegitimacies. Although courtship practices which involved sex certainly contributed to some of the elevated levels found in Wales, this evidence demonstrates that we should not consider illegitimacy in terms of courtship alone. This has also revealed a great deal about the nature of the sexual encounters these men had, and the women they had them with, both within a specifically Welsh context and with regards to the broader British perspective. Thus, the evidence of sexual encounters found in Welsh sources does much to contribute to our understanding of the sexual lives of men and women in eighteenth-century Britain more broadly.

The identification of fathers in parish registers and poor law documents such as bastardy bonds also provides convincing evidence that communities were aware, to at least some degree, of the relationships and sexual activities of their neighbours. This is not to suggest that such behaviour was condoned or broadly accepted, but that it was acknowledged and managed within communities. It is difficult to determine what attitudes were held in particular communities or more broadly in Welsh society about those who were involved in illegitimacy, but it is clear that being illegitimate or bearing an illegitimate child was concerning for parish officials. Official anxieties were based primarily on financial concerns, but illegitimacy would have elicited moral rebuke as well, as revealed in

98 Prevalence and Causes

the language used to describe women who bore illegitimate children, if not for the men who sired them. This reservation of pejorative language for women alone is also indicative of the double standard for sexual behaviour that was prevalent at this time.[134] This double standard ultimately meant that unmarried mothers bore the brunt of the stigmatisation associated with sex ouside of marriage, especially if it resulted in the birth of an illegitimate child. The personal implications for mothers and children of bearing the stigmatised label of illegitimacy will be explored in the next chapter though an examination of the 'mortality penality' of illegitimacy for unmarried mothers and their children.

Notes

1. Macfarlane, 'Illegitimacy and Illegitimates', p. 81.
2. Black, 'Putative Fathers', p. 51.
3. Laslett, 'The Bastardy Prone Sub-Society', pp. 217–246.
4. Adair, *Courtship*, pp. 92–109.
5. Gillis, *For Better, for Worse*, pp. 128, 219; Adair, *Courtship*, p. 79.
6. Gillis, *For Better, for Worse*, pp. 128, 219.
7. Rosemary O'Day, *Women's Agency in Early Modern Britain and the American Colonies: Patriarchy, Partnership and Patronage* (Harlow and New York: Pearson Longman, 2007), p. 43.
8. 26 George II, c. 33, *An Act for the Better Preventing of Clandestine Marriage* (1753); Peter Laslett, *The World We Have Lost: Further Explored*, 3rd edn (Abington: Routledge, 2000), pp. 169–170; Gillis, *For Better, for Worse*, p. 6; Martin Ingram, *Church Courts, Sex and Marriage in England, 1570–1640* (Cambridge: Cambridge University Press, 1987), p. 189; GR Quaife, *Wanton Wenches and Wayward Wives* (London: Croom Helm, 1979), p. 45; Muir, 'Illegitimate in Eighteenth-Century Wales', pp. 374–375; Howell, *Rural Poor*, p. 146.
9. Rebecca Probert, 'Chinese Whispers and Welsh Weddings', *Continuity and Change*, 20 (2005), 211–228; Gillis, *For Better, for Worse*; Gwenith Gwynn, 'Besom Weddings in the Ceiriog Valley', *Folklore*, 39 (1928), 149–166.
10. Probert, 'Chinese Whispers'; Gillis, *For Better, for Worse*, pp. 222–224.
11. PCA (Kerry) M/EP/8/O/RT/9 (1796); PCA (Tregynon) M/EP/51/O/RT/3 (1796).
12. Stone, 'Kinship and Forced Marriage', p. 356.
13. MGS (Machynlleth) MGY/MR/C/37 (1765).
14. MGS (Llangadfan) MGY/MR/PR/38 (1768); MGS (Llangadfan) MGY/MR/PR/39 (1768).
15. MGS (Llangadfan) MGY/MR/PR/39 (1774).
16. MGS (Llangadfan) MGY/MR/PR/39 (1774).
17. FRO (Hawarden) D/BJ/326 (1748).
18. PFHS (New Radnor), POW/PR16CD (1698–1699).
19. PFHS (New Radnor), POW/PR16CD (1701).
20. PCA (Llandegley) R/EP/1/O/BB/31 (1761).
21. CFHS (Wrexham), CLD-22703 (1682).
22. MGS MGY/MR/PR/93, 1780, 1782.
23. MGS (Llanfair Caereinion) MGY/MR/PR/68 (1788, 1790), MGS (Llanfair Caereinion) MGY/MR/C/21, (1785, 1787, 1788, 1789).
24. CFHS (Wrexham) CLD-22707 (1766–1767, 1773–1782).

25. PFHS (New Radnor), POW/PR16CD (1756).
26. PFHS (Glascwm) POW/PR01CD (1699, 1704, 1708, 1710, 1716, 1718, 1720).
27. DAO (Holt) PD/39/1/62 (1771).
28. CFHS (Holt) CLD-21010 (1771).
29. DAO (Holt) PD/39/1/62 (1772).
30. CFHS (Holt) CLD-21011 (1773).
31. PCA (Trefeglwys) M/EP/50/O/BB 4 & 6 (1752).
32. King, 'The Bastardy Prone Sub-Society', p. 54.
33. Black, 'Putative Fathers', p. 51; Andrew Blaikie, *Illegitimacy*, p. 144.
34. MGS (Llanfyllin) MGY/MR/PR/58 (1759, 1762, 1769, 1781, 1782, 1784).
35. MGS (Llanfyllin) MGY/PR/57 (1747, 1751).
36. Amy Louise Erickson, 'Mistress and Marriage: Or, a Short History of the Mrs', *History Workshop Journal*, 78 (2014), 39–57 (pp. 39, 44–49).
37. Erickson, 'Mistress and Marriage', p. 46.
38. Erickson, 'Mistress and Marriage', pp. 39, 44–49.
39. PFHS (Glascwm) POW/PR01CD (1752, 1753).
40. PFHS (Llanfihangel Nant Melan) POW/PR15CD (1791, 1794, 1797, 1803).
41. Reay, *Microhistories*, p. 197.
42. Brueton, 'Illegitimacy in South Wales', p. 73.
43. Rebecca Probert, *The Changing Legal Regulation of Cohabitation: From Fornicators to Family, 1600–2000* (Cambridge: Cambridge University Press, 2012), p. 24.
44. Williams, 'They Lived Together', p. 66.
45. CFHS (Wrexham) CLD-22702 (1680); MGS (Llanwnog) MGY/MR/C/55 (1756).
46. PFHS (Gladestry) POW/PR17CD (1781).
47. MGS (Garthbeibio) MGY/MR/PR/26 (1799).
48. Probert, *Changing Legal Regulation*, p. 24.
49. Probert, *Changing Legal Regulation*, p. 34 citing Ingram, *Church Courts*, p. 265.
50. CFHS (Gresford) CLD-20701 (1769).
51. PCA (Aberhafesp) M/EP/2/O/RT/1 (1751).
52. PCA (Ceri) M/EP/8/O/RT/5 (1771).
53. PCA (Llanwnog) M/EP/38/O/BB/1 (no date, eighteenth-century).
54. See Shepard, 'Brokering Fatherhood', pp. 58–59 for a discussion of some of the circumstances which could motivate wives to take in their husbands' illegitimate children.
55. PCA (Llandegley) R/EP/1/O/BB/39 (1727).
56. PCA (Llandegley) R/EP/1/O/BB/36 (1778).
57. PCA (Berriew) M/EP/3/V/VM/4 (1789).
58. PCA (Norton) R/EP/47/W/AC/2 (1793).
59. Rogers, 'Carnal Knowledge', p. 368.
60. Williams, 'They Lived Together', p. 73.
61. Nutt, 'Paradox and Problems', p. 109.
62. PCA (Llandegley) R/EP/1/O/BB/38 (1748); DAO (Holt) PD/39/1/61 (1766).
63. PCA (Bettws Cedewain) M/EP/4/O/BB/14 (1800).
64. Gowing, 'Ordering the Body', pp. 56–57; Black, 'Putative Fathers', pp. 102–103.
65. PCA (Llandegley) R/EP/1/O/BB/44 (1753).
66. King, 'Bastardy Prone Sub-Society', pp. 66–68.
67. PCA (Trefeglwys) M/EP/50/O/BB/9 (1788).
68. PCA (Berriew) M/EP/3/O/BB/3 (1762); MGS (Berriew) MGY/MR/PR/44 (1762).

69. PCA (Llandinam) M/EP/15/O/BB/43 (1766).
70. PCA (Manafon) M/EP/40/O/BB/3/3 (1763).
71. PCA (Trefeglwys) M/EP/50/O/BB/11 (1776) 12 (1778), 18 (1783).
72. Brueton, 'Illegitimacy in South Wales', pp. 156–175; Barry Reay, 'Kinship and the Neighbourhood in Nineteenth-Century Rural England: The Myth of the Autonomous Nuclear Family', *Journal of Family History*, 21 (1996), 87–104.
73. Adair, *Courtship*, p. 5.
74. Adair, *Courtship*, pp. 5–6.
75. A search of the NLW Gaol Files database for the years 1730 to 1799 yields only 40 results rape (including aiding and abetting), and 87 attempted rape or assault with attempt to ravish, although several are cases with multiple individuals accused and/or indicted. Of these, only a fraction resulted in conviction <https://crimeandpunishment.library.wales> [accessed 23/8/2019].
76. Walker, 'Rape, Acquittal and Culpability', pp. 116–117; Garthine Walker, 'Sexual Violence and Rape in Europe, 1500–1750', in *Routledge History of Sex and the Body*, ed. by Toulalan and Fisher, pp. 429–443 (pp. 431–435).
77. Walker, 'Sexual Violence', p. 435.
78. NLW *Crime and Punishment Database* <https://crimeandpunishment.library.wales> [accessed 23/8/2019].
79. NLW 4/62/1 (Denbighshire, Sarah Owen, 1788).
80. NLW 4/62/1 (Denbighshire, Sarah Owen, 1788).
81. Julie Gammon, 'Researching Sexual Violence, 1660–1800: A Critical Analysis', in *Interpreting Sexual Violence, 1660–1800*, ed. by Anne Greenfield (Abington: Routledge, 2015), pp. 13–22 (p. 15).
82. Gammon, 'Researching', p. 15.
83. Such fines are evident in Court of Great Sessions and quarter sessions. For example, in 1751 Harry Thomas John paid a fine for 'assault with intent to ravish' (NLW 4/615/5, Glamorgan, Harry Thomas John, 1751), and in 1752 Richard Davies was discharged after paying a fine for 'assault with intent to ravish' (NLW 4/616/2, Glamorgan, Richard Davies, 1752). In 1777 Edward Davies was discharged after, 'submitting to a small fine' of 6d. for the 'assault with an intent to commit rape' of Mary Probert (See PCA M/QS/1770–1779 (Session Rolls) items M/QS/77/: T7; T43; M/SO/2/147v). See also, Watson, 'Women, Violent Crime', pp. 253–255.
84. Garthine Walker, 'Rereading Rape and Sexual Violence in Early Modern England', *Gender & History*, 10 (1998), 1–25; Thomas Laqueur, *Making Sex: Body and Gender from the Greeks to Freud* (Cambridge, MA: Harvard University Press, 1990), pp. 161–162.
85. ANG (Oswestry), ANG/ARA/398 (1695–1714).
86. CFHS (Llangollen) CLD-21616 (1724, 1726); CFHS (Llansilin) CLD-21917 (1743).
87. Crawford, *Blood, Bodies and Families*, p. 125.
88. PCA (Llandinam) M/EP/15/O/BB/36 (1761).
89. PCA (Llandinam M/EP/15/O/BB/20, 21, 22 (1750).
90. PCA (Ceri) M/EP/3/O/BB/39 (1746).
91. PCA (Ceri) M/EP/3/O/BB/35 (1751).
92. Jill Barber, '"Stolen Goods": The Sexual Harassment of Female Servants in West Wales During the Nineteenth Century', *Rural History*, 4 (1993), 123–136 (p. 132).
93. Sharpe, *Crime in Seventeenth-Century England*, p. 58.
94. Marion Pluskota, *Prostitution and Social Control in Eighteenth-Century Ports* (Abington: Routledge, 2015); Lizbeth Johnson, 'Sex and the Single

Welshwoman: Prostitution and Concubinage in Late Medieval Wales', *Welsh History Review*, 27 (2014), 253–281 (p. 256).
95. NLW 2/272/4 (Caernarfon, 4/272/4, Mary Meredith) NLW 4/904/2 (Cardiganshire, Samuel Mann and Ephraim Wells, 1788).
96. NLW 2/272/4 (Caernarfon, 4/272/4, Mary Meredith), Fawr being a soft mutation of the Welsh word 'mawr', meaning, big or large.
97. NLW 4/904/2 (Cardiganshire, Samuel Mann and Ephraim Wells, 1788).
98. NLW 4/904/2 (Cardiganshire, Samuel Mann and Ephraim Wells, 1788).
99. NLW 4/740/4 (Carmarthenshire, Elizabeth Lewis, 1771).
100. CFHS (Llanarmon Dyffryn Ceiriog) CLD-21302 (1791).
101. CFHS (Llanrhaeadr ym Mochnant) CLD-21808 (1798).
102. NLW 4/259/5 (Anglesey, Griffith Roberts, 1824).
103. Reay, *Microhistories*, p. 179.
104. Reay, *Microhistories*, p. 212.
105. Adair, *Courtship*, p. 8.
106. Oosterveen, et al, 'Family Reconstitution', p. 113.
107. Connors, 'Poor Women', p. 127.
108. Connors, 'Poor Women', p. 127.
109. O'Day, *Women's Agency*, pp. 152–153.
110. CFHS (Llangollen) CLD-21619 (1784).
111. Bridget Hill, *Women, Work & Sexual Politics in Eighteenth-Century England* (London: UCL Press, 1994), pp. 148–173.
112. MGS (Llanfyllin) PR/57 (1747).
113. Oosterveen, et al, 'Family Reconstitution', p. 112.
114. Black, 'Putative Fathers', pp. 51–54.
115. Black, 'Putative Fathers', pp. 54–58.
116. Lesley Davison, 'Spinsters Were Doing It for Themselves: Independence and the Single Woman in Early Eighteenth-Century Rural Wales', in *Women and Gender in Early Modern Wales*, ed. by Michael Roberts and Simone Clarke (Cardiff: University of Wales Press, 2000), pp. 186–209 (pp. 190–191).
117. PCA (Berriew) M/EP/3/O/BB/47 (1740); 34 (1751); PCA (Llandinam) M/EP/15/O/BB/66 (1789), 70 (1794); DAO (Holt) PD/39/1/61 (1772), DAO (Holt) PD/39/1/62 (1767).
118. PCA (Berriew) M/EP/3/O/BB/13 (1760); 36 (1750).
119. David Cressy, *Literacy and the Social Order: Reading and Writing in Tudor and Stuart England* (Cambridge: Cambridge University Press, 1980), p. 54; Rogers, 'Carnal Knowledge', p. 358.
120. Black, 'Putative Fathers', pp. 60–61.
121. Rogers, 'Carnal Knowledge', p. 357.
122. DAO (Holt) PD/39/1/61(1768).
123. Howell, *Rural Poor*, p. 102.
124. Howell, *Rural Poor*, p. 102; Brueton, 'Illegitimacy in South Wales', p. 80.
125. Howell, *Rural Poor*, p. 102.
126. Brueton, 'Illegitimacy in South Wales', p. 246.
127. PCA (Aberhafesp) M/EP/2/O/RT/2 (1748–1774).
128. PCA (Berriew) M/EP/3/V/VM/4 (1780–1789).
129. PCA (Llangyniew)M/EP27/V/VM/1 (1746); PCA (Meifod) M/EP/41/O/AP/79 (1783).
130. PCA (Meifod) M/EP/41/O/RT/1 (1747).
131. PCA (Llangyniew) M/EP/27/V/VM/1 (1746).
132. DAO (Gresford) PD-34-1-320 (1751).
133. Lisa Zunshine, *Bastards and Foundlings: Illegitimacy in Eighteenth-Century England* (Columbus: Ohio State University Press, 2005), p. 3.

134. See: Keith Thomas, 'The Double Standard', *Journal of the History of Ideas*, 20 (1959), 195–216; Lawrence Stone, *The Family, Sex, and Marriage in England, 1500–1800* (New York: Harper & Row, 1977), part 5; Laura Gowing, *Domestic Dangers: Women, Words and Sex in Early Modern London* (Oxford: Clarendon Press, 1996); Bernard Capp, 'The Double Standard Revisited: Plebeian Women and Male Sexual Reputation in Early Modern England', *Past & Present*, 162 (1999), 70–101.

Part II
The Mortality Penalty

3 Illegitimate Infant and Maternal Mortality

This chapter will examine the survival prospects for children whose parents were not married at the time of their baptism. The purpose here is not to conduct a detailed demographic analysis of infant mortality in eighteenth-century Wales, but rather to analyse comparatively the frequency with which legitimate and illegitimate infants in certain parishes died. In so doing, this analysis will further interrogate the hypothesis that the presence of unmarried fathers in baptism registers is indicative of the widespread prevalence of acceptable conjugal courtship customs, or established non-marital unions. This will be done by comparing the mortality levels of illegitimate children whose fathers were identified at baptism with those whose fathers were not. The focus will then shift to consider the perinatal survival of unmarried parturient women, as documented in the detailed burial register of one sample parish. Illegitimate maternal mortality in early modern Britain has not been considered in any detail by historians. Childbirth at this time was a potentially precarious experience for all women, and, if illegitimate infant survival chances were poorer, then it is also worth considering whether or not their mothers' prospects were negatively affected as well, particularly during, and in the days and weeks following, parturition.

Counting Infant Mortality

Although this chapter begins with a quantitative analysis of illegitimate infant and maternal mortality, it does so cautiously and with a specific purpose. The numerical study of significant life events, such as birth and death, can be seen as reductive and dehumanising.[1] This process of counting live births and dead bodies in aggregate replaces the lived experience and all its meaning with impersonal rates and ratios.[2] This becomes even more problematic when these methods are used to draw conclusions about otherwise invisible populations, such as individuals from the past who left no written accounts of their own experiences. Mortality rates deal with the end of a life, and in the cases of infant and maternal mortality, this means the death of a child or a mother. The trauma of these experiences cannot be included in any demographic equation, so through the process of translating these events into a numerator the lived experience becomes eclipsed.[3]

Biopower, which Foucault argued emerged in the late eighteenth century, and which generated concerns for population, so turning birth outside marriage into a social problem, can also be seen operating in the attempt to quantify death.[4] Deaths, or more appropriately Mortality Rates (MR), are often not used to represent actual deaths, but function as proxies for factors such as social conditions, maternal wellbeing, ethnic and socioeconomic background and life choices, such as alcohol consumption and cigarette smoking. Knowledge about these bodies can then be used to inform and reinforce the social practices and institutions which seek to regulate and normalise these bodies.[5] Infant Mortality Rates (IMR) rarely consider paternal agency or influence, which inevitably bolsters gendered assumptions about appropriate or inappropriate motherhood, and can be used to support moral and political agendas which seek to further stigmatise, regulate and control women's reproductive bodies.[6] Evidence that suggests more children born to single women die than those born into nuclear families can be used as evidence not of deep, structural inequalities, but of the dangers of single motherhood, and measures can then be taken to regulate the bodies of single women.[7] Temporal distance from the present does not create neutrality; historical data can be used in this process to help those who wish to control populations by providing evidence that these are centuries-old problems, and comparisons can be made between the past and developing countries.[8] Statistical analysis is not inherently unjust, as it can be used to effect positive change for underprivileged communities.[9] However, because data collection and analysis is usually a process undertaken by those in positions of power, data can be seen as an instrument of power. It is the ways in which the data is used that is crucial, and for this reason, context is vital. As with the statistical analysis of illegitimate births, the act of considering statistical data about illegitimate deaths without considering the individual lived experiences and the broader social context can help to reinforce particular biases and agendas. My purpose in applying a statistical analysis of illegitimate death here is not to calculate and predict marital and illegitimate IMRs. Rather, the aim here is to apply the methodology which has led some historians to make broad assumptions and generalisations about the nature of non-marital sexual experiences as a means of challenging those very assumptions and generalisations.

The principle questions which will be addressed in this section are twofold. First, did children who were born as a result of pre- and extramarital sex die more frequently in their first year of life than children whose parents were married? And, if so, is the identification of the unmarried fathers in their children's baptism records indicative of the non-traditional yet stable unions about which historians such as Gillis and

Adair hypothesised?[10] More specifically, do the survival rates of illegitimate children whose fathers were identified correspond enough to the survival rates of children whose parents were married to suggest that non-marital relationships were normative enough to counteract the socioeconomic disadvantage associated with single motherhood? Interrogating the significance of fathers not only sheds further light on the nature of reproductive sexual experiences which resulted in conception and birth outside of wedlock, but also considers the all too often overlooked impact of unmarried fathers on the survival chances of their children. For as long as statistics on infant death have been collected the emphasis has typically been on maternal influence, placing varying levels of responsibility and accountability on mothers, but rarely measuring the same for fathers.[11] In many ways it is easier to blame women, particularly disadvantaged women, for what is perceived as their deviant behaviours and unregulated bodies which, in reality, reflect deep structural inequalities.[12] Assessing the relevance of the presence or absence of unmarried fathers is one small way of making use of the available evidence to shift the gendered imbalance to include, as much as is possible, both parents.

Illegitimate Infant Mortality

Before interrogating the significance of identified unmarried paternity on infant survival chances, it must first be established whether or not children whose parents were unmarried faced a greater mortality risk. It is widely accepted that, before the twentieth century, the risk of dying in early childhood from prenatal, perinatal or postnatal complications, genetic abnormalities, infectious diseases, malnutrition, accidents and many other problems was great. Thanks to a number of sensationalised cases in the nineteenth century, the mortality penalty of illegitimate birth also conjures up images of the negligent wet nurse who starved, drugged or otherwise murdered poor, unwanted children left in her care.[13] This undoubtedly happened, but not necessarily to the dramatic extent which has been assumed.[14] In reality, there were innumerable threats to young lives in early modern Britain. The most common of those identified by contemporaries were fevers, infectious diseases such as smallpox or whooping cough and disorders which affected breathing or swallowing.[15] However, death within the first year of life was so commonplace that the burial registers that routinely listed causes of death frequently did not do so for infants.[16] Parish officials in Llanrhaeadr ym Mochnant, which sits on the border between Montgomeryshire and Denbighshire, left the cause of death blank for over 30 per cent of infants under one year of age who died between 1759 and 1799.[17] In this parish, this age group was the only one for which cause of death was so frequently omitted. The simple state of being very young and vulnerable could sufficiently explain why an infant died. This harsh reality led early historians of childhood to suggest that parents in earlier centuries avoided forming emotional bonds with their children, lest they experience the grief of losing a child.[18] Such theories have since been rejected.[19]

Small glimpses of these tragedies can be witnessed in parish registers. For example, in Glascwm, Radnorshire in February 1705 Thomas Matthews and his wife Johan buried their three-week-old son James, and in September the following year they buried their five-month-old son Henry.[20] In the same parish, three of the seven children born to Thomas Parry and his 'concubine' Elizabeth died within three months of birth.[21] The fate of twins in particular appears to have been quite bleak. In Llanfihangel Nant Melan, Radnorshire on 3 May 1761 Peter and Mary Thomas baptised their twin children Peter and Susannah. Five days later Peter was buried, and five days after that Susannah was buried. The couple had another child who was baptised on 27 November 1762; he was buried the next day.[22] Every set of twins baptised in Glascwm between 1680 and 1740 experienced the death of one, if not both, children within days or weeks of birth, such as the twin sons of David Bowen baptised on 15 October 1681 and buried on 25 and 31 October, or James and Catherine the twin children of John and Catherine Gwyn baptised on 29 June 1710 and buried on 15 and 16 July, respectively.[23] Twins born to unmarried mothers also fared as badly, such as Elizabeth and Jane, the twin daughters born to Jane Probert, who were baptised on 2 August 1733, and buried on 19 and 23 August respectively. For these parents, and for the mothers in particular, the experience of enduring a full-term pregnancy and labour, and then losing their child within days, weeks or months of birth, only to be reminded of the loss by the changes to, and processes of, their bodies, such postnatal bleeding, lactation, stretchmarks, uterine prolapse, perineal tears, incontinence and so on, must have been tremendously difficult. Many women, such as Johan and Elizabeth, experienced this on multiple occasions.

For other families, their tragedies played out over a period of months or years rather than days and weeks. For example, in the parish of Marchwiel in Denbighshire in April 1699 a sixteen-month-old child named Elizabeth Clark was buried and later that month her young brothers Frances, Jacob and Peter were also buried. Jacob and Peter were buried on the same day. The Clark children were the only burial entries for the month of April that year.[24] Poignantly, the tragedy experienced by the Tonmans, who were landed aristocracy in Llanfihangel Nant Melan, Radnorshire, demonstrates that childbirth carried risks at all levels of society.[25] In May 1708 Roger Tonman and his wife Theodosia baptised their infant daughter, who was given her mother's name. She was buried less than one month later. In March 1711, they again had a daughter who they again christened Theodosia. She too did not live to see her first birthday, having died in November of that year, aged only eight months. Finally, in December 1713, a third daughter was born, yet again named Theodosia, who appears to have survived the precarious first year of life. However, her mother was not so lucky, as she succumbed to the physical perils of childbirth three days after giving birth. It is impossible to know the precise circumstances surrounding these deaths, how they were experienced by surviving family members, or whether the pregnancies were welcomed in the first place, but it cannot be said that any of these events were insignificant for those who experienced them. It is experiences such as these which must be borne in mind when assessing aggregate mortality figures. Each of these numbers represents an actual birth and actual death. Their significance lies not only in the broad patterns which counting them may reveal, but also in their individual lived experience.

Although infant mortality in general was high in Britain during the early modern period, historians have long suggested that illegitimate children in early modern Britain faced an even greater risk of dying within the first year of life than their marital counterparts.[26] Greater vulnerability for illegitimate infants is typically attributed to the greater level of poverty experienced by unmarried mothers and a lack of traditional social supports.[27] This hypothesis has not been thoroughly tested for the parish registration period in Britain, although studies have been carried out for Scotland during the nineteenth century.[28] A recent study by the Cambridge Group used census data to investigate some of the possible causes of increased vulnerability of early death amongst illegitimate children on the Isle of Skye, and found that illegitimate infants were at a disadvantage in terms of mortality only during periods of economic crisis. During these periods, it was more likely for unmarried mothers, who would otherwise care for their own children, to move elsewhere in search of employment, leaving children in the care of family or neighbours whose resources were already stretched. The authors conclude that this sporadic increase in illegitimate infant mortality linked to periods of economic crisis suggests that there was little stigma associated with childbirth outside of marriage in this region, but that illegitimate infants were still amongst the community's most vulnerable.[29]

As with illegitimacy, evidence of infant mortality in Britain prior to civil registration can be gleaned through analysis of parish burial registers. These records can be problematic for a variety of reasons, many of which have already been outlined, such as under-registration, which affects baptisms as well. There are additional problems when it comes to accounting for deaths, such as if an infant died and was buried in a parish other than the one in which he or she was baptised, making it virtually impossible to trace. Furthermore, many infants who perished soon after birth may have died unbaptised or without having been formally baptised in the church, and therefore would be almost completely absent from the historical record.[30] Such children may still be recorded in burial registers, but details of such burials are frequently vague, and simply list 'child of' without providing the given name. It is therefore apparent that many stillborn infants and neonates who died shortly after birth cannot be accounted for statistically. However, parish registers are one of the only sources of information available relating to mortality prior to the nineteenth century. As with baptisms, any challenges relating to these records must be mitigated through the use of large samples of the high-quality data and, more importantly, must be balanced out and contextualised through the thorough use of qualitative analysis of available records.

Infant mortality here has been calculated by linking the burials of all children which took place within one year of baptism.[31] For the purposes here, this method considers only the burials which can be linked as a proportion of baptisms without any correction for errors, and will therefore be presented as percentages rather than traditional IMR, which is represented as a rate per 1,000 live births. Age at death is seldom given, and many entries list 'infant', which was a label not restricted to the very young but which was also frequently used for older children and adolescents. It is not assumed therefore that this data is reflective of actual infant mortality, as it is likely that the results are far too low. Rather, the data is used to compare the survival rates of legitimate and illegitimate children who were baptised and buried within the same parish, and to test the significance of identified, unmarried fathers. The linking of burials to baptisms is not possible for all parishes nor for the entirety of the study period. For this analysis, the data from eight parishes which have more complete data have been used, six of which are in Montgomeryshire, and two in Radnorshire.[32] Data from Denbighshire has not been included. The evidence considered here accounts for 11,729 baptisms and 950 burials between 1750 and 1799. Each linked burial will be considered in relation to its specific category of baptisms. For example, total burials are considered in relation to total baptisms, and then broken down into subcategories based on marital and paternal statuses as indicated in baptism registers. Legitimate burials are considered against legitimate baptisms, illegitimate burials as a proportion of illegitimate baptisms, and so on. What these equations are asking is this: of those baptised legitimate, or illegitimate, what percentage died within the first year of life? And, of those baptised illegitimate whose fathers were identified (and were not), what proportion died within the first year of life? Because levels of illegitimate baptism and identification varied widely across these counties this method allows for a more proportional comparison. Given these differences, and the disproportionate sample sizes, the data from each county will be presented separately.

In Montgomeryshire, between 1750 and 1799, 8.4 per cent of all baptised infants were buried within one year (Figure 3.1). This appears low when compared with demographic estimates of the IMR for this period, which calculate rates ranging between 9.8 and 14 per cent.[33] This is more likely the result of the under-recording of infant burials than of improved

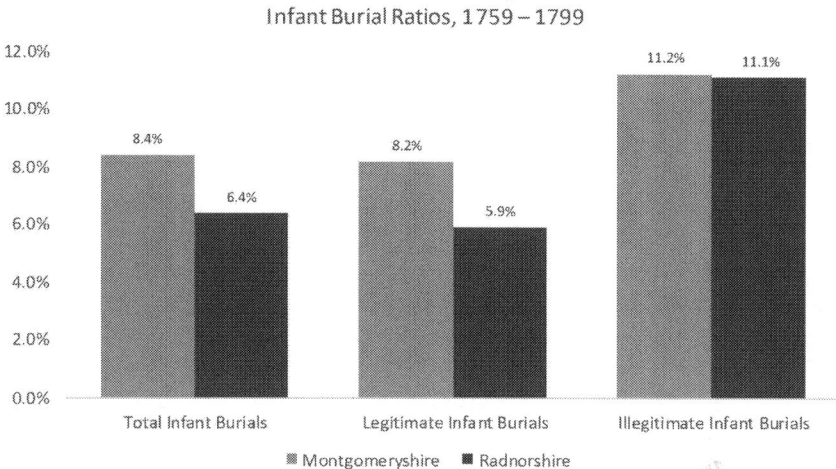

Figure 3.1 Percentage of legitimate and illegitimate infants buried within one year of baptism, c. 1759–1799.

survival chances for infants in mid-Wales. Therefore, as with all demographic data from this period, these results must be used with caution. If we take these figures at face value, it appears that, of those infants in Montgomeryshire whose parents were married, 8.2 per cent were buried, and of those whose parents were not married, 11.2 per cent were buried within one year. During the same 50-year period in Radnorshire, 6.4 per cent of all children baptised were buried within one year. Again, this low figure is likely the result of under-recording rather than lower levels of infant mortality. Of those whose parents were married, 5.9 per cent died within 12 months, and 11.1 per cent of those whose parents were not married died. Although overall these levels are low, the variation between categories of baptisms does support the hypothesis that children born outside of wedlock in the latter half of the eighteenth century were, at least to some degree, more likely to pay a mortality penalty for being born to parents who were not married to each other. In Montgomeryshire, infants born outside of wedlock were approximately one-third more likely to die than their legitimate counterparts, however in Radnorshire illegitimate infants were almost twice as likely to die in the first year of life. Intriguingly, there does not appear to be a correlation between the prevalence of illegitimate baptisms and the severity of the mortality penalty. Despite Radnorshire having significantly higher levels of illegitimacy than many parts of Montgomeryshire, roughly the same proportion of illegitimate infants died in both counties.

However, when illegitimate infant burials are disaggregated into those whose fathers were identified at baptism, and those whose were not, differences do appear (Figure 3.2). These differences provide further evidence of the complexity and variation in regional experiences of illegitimacy. The hypothesis being tested here is as follows: if unmarried fathers who were identified in baptism registers are actually indicative of acceptable, conjugal courtship customs, or stable yet formally unrecognised non-marital unions, then the survival rates of the children born into these unions should more closely resemble those of children whose parents were married. This appears to be somewhat the case in Montgomeryshire, where the difference in burials ratios between legitimate and illegitimate with fathers identified at baptism is only 1.5 per cent, whereas illegitimate infants whose fathers were not identified fared considerably worse, with 14 per cent of this category of infants dying over the 50-year period. Therefore, in Montgomeryshire, which consistently had elevated levels of paternal identification, it would appear that the identification of a father indicated improved survival chance. However, in Radnorshire, which had overall low levels of paternal identification, illegitimate infants whose fathers were named at baptism fared marginally (1.1 per cent) worse than those whose fathers were not identified, and fared twice as bad as their legitimate counterparts. Therefore, in Radnorshire, the identification of unmarried fathers was possibly indicative of a very slight increased risk for their infants, although the significance of this this should not be overstated.

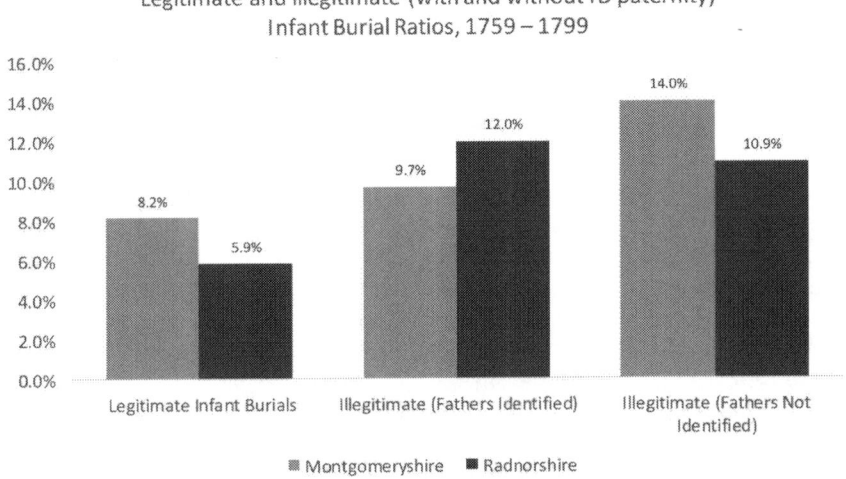

Figure 3.2 Percentage of legitimate infants and illegitimate infants (with and without identified fathers) buried within one year of baptism, c. 1759–1799.

What does this mean in terms of the relationship hypothesis? In Radnorshire, they hypothesis does not hold up. In the parishes considered here it would appear that identified fathers were not indicative of parental relationships which were normative and conforming enough to reduce the mortality risk for illegitimate infants in their first year of life. On the other hand, the evidence from Montgomeryshire could, at least initially, be taken as support for the relationship hypothesis. Although children in Montgomeryshire born to unmarried mothers whose fathers were identified still had a slightly higher risk of dying than infants whose parents were married, their prospects appear to have been considerably better than those without a father named at baptism. Overall, the mortality penalty paid by illegitimate children in Montgomeryshire who had named fathers does more closely resemble that of legitimate children than illegitimate children with no father named. However, there is still one significant problem with this hypothesis, which is the lack of significant qualitative evidence which can convincingly link this correlation to the relationship hypothesis. It is quite likely that some non-conforming relationships did exist, but in the face of considerable evidence to the contrary, which will be examined in the next chapter, a more plausible hypothesis for this correlation must be pursued.

As discussed in the first chapter, the identification of fathers was likely used by some parish officials as a means of ensuring that financial maintenance would be provided for children born outside of wedlock, and their unmarried mothers, without the parish and its ratepayers incurring additional costs. Levels and patterns of reported illegitimate birth and identified paternity in Montgomeryshire and Radnorshire varied considerably throughout the latter decades of the eighteenth century. Therefore, it is not surprising that illegitimate infant burial levels also varied in proportionate ways. What may, however, be at work with regards to levels of illegitimate infant burial levels are two different manifestations of the same mechanism of social control, which sought to indemnify the parish. As Melvin Humphreys has argued, Montgomeryshire had tightly knit networks of neighbourly observation, which probably resulted in the higher proportion of named fathers, regardless of relationship between the unmarried parents of an infant.[34] In communities such as these, parish officials would likely have been far more successful at extracting payment from reputed fathers. As such, these children and their mothers were more likely to receive the financial support needed to prevent them from the negative consequences to their health of the worst levels of poverty. Conversely, parishes in Radnorshire did not share this custom of recording the names of unmarried fathers in baptism registers, which is most likely due to the persistent poverty of many fathers, as noted in the responses to *Town Queries*.[35] It is therefore possible that the naming of fathers in Radnorshire was only practised when the parents, or at least the mother and her child, were more likely to face extreme poverty, and thus face a greater risk of dying. In other words, the naming of fathers in Radnorshire may, in some cases, actually be an indicator of increased maternal and infant disadvantage.

Maternal Mortality

If infants born to unmarried mothers faced an increased risk of dying as a result of the disadvantage caused by being born outside of wedlock, does it follow that their mothers also faced an increased risk of dying? There were many concomitant causes of infant and maternal mortality, particularly those which occurred during labour and delivery. However, mothers were also at risk of additional potentially fatal complications in the hours, days and weeks which followed. Causes of maternal mortality fall into two categories: haemorrhage or accidents of childbirth, such as pelvic obstructions, which in the eighteenth century could commonly be caused by bone deformations resulting from nutritional deficiencies such as rickets, and puerperal infections which could lead to fatal sepsis or toxaemia.[36] With the exception of complications such as haemorrhaging, accidents of childbirth could frequently affect both mothers and children, whereas puerperal infections primarily affected mothers. It is therefore important to consider maternal mortality as a separate, yet related, phenomenon. Differences or similarities between marital and non-marital maternal mortality may be indicative of the level of care and support available to unmarried parturient women whose pregnancies were not necessarily welcomed by their communities, and therefore may have lacked potentially life-saving support during and after childbirth. Analysis and comparison of illegitimate infant and maternal burial ratios is yet one more method of assessing the complexities of the experience of illegitimacy in the eighteenth century.

Regardless of marital or socioeconomic status, in the eighteenth century there was little that could be done to save women suffering from some of the more serious complications associated with childbirth, such as severe haemorrhaging, puerperal infections and sepsis. But during delivery and lying-in, most women would have been supported by midwives, married female neighbours and family members, which could mitigate many other risks.[37] However, there is evidence which suggests that some unmarried women did not have access to this type of support. The stigma and disadvantage associated with illegitimate birth could limit support during the later stages of pregnancy, delivery, and the following lying-in period, which could carry potentially grave consequences. If a woman who was pregnant and unmarried was found to be living in a parish other than her parish of legal settlement she could be the subject of a removal order, sometimes at the behest of parishioners, which could see her physically moved outside of the parish boundaries.[38] Overseers' records document costs incurred during this process, and often such women were escorted back to their last known place of settlement. In Montgomeryshire in 1764 Elizabeth Evans, an unmarried pregnant woman living in the parish of Llanwnog, was removed to the parish of Aberhafesp at the expense of the parish which removed her. Elizabeth died as an unfortunate consequence of her pregnancy before her child was born.[39] In 1792 a pregnant servant named Mary Powell was removed from the parish of Clyro in Radnorshire to Llanhamlach. She later delivered, alone and without assistance, in a cowshed.[40] As will be discussed in the next chapter, these women were perceived to be liabilities, economic or otherwise, and the actions taken against them jeopardised their health and the health of their unborn children.

Maternal mortality is commonly defined as deaths during pregnancy, or for a period following delivery ranging from 30 to 60 days, depending on the study.[41] However, for the purposes here, maternal mortality refers to the death of a woman which can be identified as a direct result of complications due to labour and delivery. Deaths in childbed are exceedingly difficult to identify, and the nature of parish registers prevents the linking of the majority of mothers' burials to a birth event. Such linking is only possible if a child had been born alive and was then baptised. Burial registers very rarely recorded stillborn children, and if a woman and her child both died during delivery there would be no way of identifying this in parish registers, unless the cause of death was explicitly stated. Without evidence of an infant it is impossible to differentiate the deaths of a woman of childbearing age who died as the result of complications during childbirth from those who died from any other cause. For this reason, this analysis will only use the exceptionally detailed burial records of one parish, Llanrhaeadr ym Mochnant (henceforth Llanrhaeadr), as a case study to compare the mortality levels of married and unmarried parturient women.

From 1759 onwards parish officials in Llanrhaeadr recorded a cause of death for every burial in their registers. Similar records exist for London, Norwich and parts of south east England, but in Wales it was exceedingly rare to record the cause of death with such frequency.[42] Unique in both detail and consistency, each of the burial entries in this register lists the name of the deceased, date of death and of burial, age, place of residence and in most instances a cause of death. The occupation or status of adult men, the marital status and affiliation of women, and the parental affiliation of children was also listed. If a child had been identified as illegitimate this information was also typically given as well. Overall, deaths in childbed account for a very small proportion of the 1,491 burials recorded over this 40-year period. Only 18 women, or 1.2 per cent of all burials, were listed as related to parturition. For the purposes here, only entries which list the cause of death as 'childbed' or 'childbirth' have been counted (see Table 3.1). This does present the possibility of excluding women who died of a puerperal fever and were recorded as

116 *The Mortality Penalty*

Table 3.1 Recorded instances of maternal mortality in Llanrhaeadr ym Mochnant when the cause of death is identified as 'childbed' or 'childbirth', 1759–1799.

Mother's Name	Age	Date of Death	Corresponding birth details	Interval between birth and death	Child burial within 1 year
Catherine Humphrey	31	12 Apr 1759	Mary, born 3 Mar	40 days	No
Jane Roberts	30	21 Mar 1762	Anne, born 2 Mar	13 days	No
Margaret Owen	29	21 Mar 1762	Elizabeth, born 25 Mar	4 days	No
Mary Pierce	27	7 Sept 1765	Sinah, born 3 Sept	4 days	9 Sept 1765
Ursula Roberts	25	18 Jan 1769	No	N/A	N/A
Mary Parry (single woman)	27	22 Feb 1769	Griffith (Morris), born 11 Feb	11 days	No
Elizabeth Vaughan	20	26 Feb 1769	No	N/A	N/A
Catherine Jones	42	24 Mar 1769	No	N/A	N/A
Jane Evans	32	9 Jan 1771	No	N/A	N/A
Anne Davies	23	20 May 1775	No	N/A	N/A
Jane Arthur	28	28 Sept 1776	No	N/A	N/A
Catherine Lloyd	34	10 Aug 1779	No	N/A	N/A
Elizabeth Nichols	34	10 Aug 1782	No	N/A	N/A
Mary Evans	44	13 Nov 1784	No	N/A	N/A
Catherine Jones	33	12 Apr 1792	No	N/A	N/A
Anne Edwards	28	24 Sept 1792	Anne, born 16 Sept	8 days	No
Margaret Jones	26	14 Jan 1795	No	N/A	N/A

dying of fever rather than childbed. However, if women who died of fever within 40 days of the birth of a child listed in the corresponding baptism register are also included, only one additional woman would be counted. During this same period 2,031 children were entered in the parish's baptism register. The ratio of maternal deaths to infant baptisms may appear surprisingly small considering that, prior to the advent of antibiotics in the twentieth century, childbirth was one of the leading causes of death for women of childbearing age.[43] However Roger Schofield has demonstrated that, statistically speaking, women were at no greater risk of dying during childbirth as they were of dying from a common infectious disease.[44] This apparent statistical reality does not necessarily mean that pregnant women were not acutely aware of the potential risks they faced, but rather that the historical records analysed to date suggest the mortality penalty of parturition was not as great as previously thought, and the evidence for Llanrhaeadr supports this.[45]

No corresponding baptism record exists for 12 of the 18 women who were listed as having died in during childbirth, which suggests that their children were either stillborn, were not successfully delivered before the mother died, or perished shortly after. These 12 women most likely died as a result of accidents of childbirth. For the maternal deaths in childbed which can be linked to a baptism record, the interval between birth and death ranged from 4 to 40 days, making it likely that these women died as a result of infection. Five of the six infants who lived long enough to be baptised survived their first year of life. The fact that out of 18 childbirth events, only 6 resulted in a baptism record demonstrates the large number of birth events which may be missing from baptism registers overall, and reveals how potentially unrepresentative these records are. In the case of Llanrhaeadr, two thirds of birth events related to maternal death were missing from the baptism register. This further highlights the problems inherent in using these sources, and the perils of depending too heavily on them for statistical analysis.

However, most significantly for our purposes here, a 27-year-old-woman named Mary Parry was the only individual amongst the 18 women who died due to complications of labour to have been identified as unmarried. Mary died 11 days after giving birth to her son, Griffith, who was among the five infants who lived to see their first birthdays. In the last four decades of the eighteenth century the illegitimate baptism ratio in Llanrhaeadr was slightly higher than the aggregate for Montgomeryshire, with a 40-year average of 5.6 per cent, whereas the county average for the same period was 5.2 per cent. This equated to 119 baptisms of illegitimate children. Translated into a statistic, less than 1 per cent of unmarried women who gave birth to a child who was baptised died as a result of childbirth. This is a tiny sample size and cannot be seen as representative of wider patterns, but does appear to indicate that bearing a child outside of wedlock, at least in Llanrhaeadr, did not necessarily put an unmarried woman at greater risk. This is likely due to the care provided to unmarried parturient women, which will be discussed further in Chapter 5.

Conclusion

Crucially, the records used here to calculate maternal mortality only account for the women whose labours and deliveries were known, and documented by, parish officials. Not all unmarried pregnant women made their pregnancies known, and some even went as far as to conceal their labour and delivery. What makes the aforementioned examples of Elizabeth Evans and Mary Powell significant is that we are aware of their experiences because they were recorded in entirely different records. Both appear in the records of the Court of Great Sessions, which heard the most serious criminal cases in Wales. After delivering her illegitimate child in a cowshed in Radnorshire, Mary Powell stood accused of strangling and killing her newborn child.[46] Not long after returning to Llanwnog Elizabeth Evans disappeared and was later found in a field with a handkerchief around her neck, which the supposed father of her unborn child had used to strangle her.[47] These women were in the minority, but their cases are not unique. The experience of pregnancy and childbirth for women such as Elizabeth and Mary was entirely different to many of the single and married women and their children recorded in registers as having died in childbed. The latter were those individuals whose pregnancies and births occurred within the context of the parish community and conformed to at least some degree to acceptable childbirth practice. As will be discussed in the final chapter, even the poorest, unmarried mothers were still provided with support in childbirth if they found themselves in their parish of settlement at the time of their delivery. Poor law records for Llanrhaeadr only survive for the final few years of the eighteenth century, so it is not possible to know how many expectant pregnant women were removed to another parish prior to delivery, or how many were provided for by the parish during their delivery and lying-in. However, what this brief analysis does suggest is that, if an unmarried woman gave birth with the knowledge and support of the parish community, her odds of surviving may have been similar to those of married women in receipt of similar support.

However flawed, statistical analysis does indicate that illegitimate children did appear to pay a greater mortality penalty than their legitimate counterparts, and this penalty was connected, in varying degrees, to reproductive sex outside of marriage. Children whose mothers were not married stood a greater risk of dying within the first year of life, and the presence of their father did not necessarily indicate better survival prospects. The correlation between identified illegitimate paternity and increased maternal disadvantage is only one possible hypothesis based on available data. Analysis such as this has its limitations in that it can only provide numerical answers to the specific questions asked of it, and therefore leaves much room for interpretation and speculation, and raises more questions than it answers. It cannot, for example, reveal the extent to which any pregnancies resulting in the births and baptisms of these children were wanted, which would likely have been related to the circumstances surrounding conception, and would have played a significant role in their survival chances. Analysis which seeks to address questions such as these is far more telling of the lived experience of illegitimacy for both parents and children. What this analysis has demonstrated is that, overall, children who were born to unmarried parents in mid-Wales during the latter half of the eighteenth century appear to have paid a penalty for being born outside of wedlock, and many of them paid that penalty with their lives. For many, but certainly not all, the higher risk of death was likely a result of economic hardship which resulted in poorer maternal and infant health.[48] However diverse and complicated, the causes behind the mortality penalty cannot be explained simply through quantitative means. Detailed qualitative analysis of the records which relate to the circumstances surrounding their deaths is therefore necessary. The narratives surrounding some of these deaths will be explored in the following chapter.

Notes

1. Monica J Casper and Lisa Jean Moore, *Missing Bodies: The Politics of Visibility* (New York: New York University Press, 2009), p. 9.
2. Casper and Moore, *Missing Bodies*, p. 9.
3. Furthermore, as custodians of the past with a vested interest in the social problems of the present, historians have an ethical responsibility to do more than simply count dead bodies. As sociologists Monica Casper and Lisa Moore argue, dead babies and women must be, 'seen in situ and on their own terms. The act of seeing them, of focusing on them in a critical way, is an ethical responsibility.' This is no less important when analysing dead bodies in the past as it is those in the present. Adding a qualitative analysis of individual and idiosyncratic historical experiences can help to synthesise and individualise quantitative modes of demographic analysis, which allows the subjects of historical analysis to become more than simply generators of raw data. See also Casper and Moore, *Missing Bodies*, p. 15; Trent MacNamara and Yuliya Hilevych, 'Living in the Demos: Qualitative Approaches to Demographic Questions', *The History of the Family*, 20 (2015), 1–8 (p. 2).
4. Foucault, *History of Sexuality*, pp. 140–141; Casper and Moore, *Missing Bodies*, p. 6.
5. Casper and Moore, *Missing Bodies*, pp. 6–7, 61–62; Andrew Blaikie, 'Infant Survival Chances, Unmarried Motherhood and Domestic Arrangements in Rural Scotland, 1845–1945', *Local Population Studies*, 60 (1998), 34–46 (p. 34); Susan Scott and CJ Duncan, 'Malnutrition, Pregnancy and Infant Mortality: A Biometric Model', *Journal of Interdisciplinary History*, 30 (1999), 37–60 (pp. 39–40).
6. Casper and Moore, *Missing Bodies*, pp. 6, 61–62; Reekie, *Measuring Immorality*, p. 106.
7. Reekie, *Measuring Immorality*, p. 104.
8. Vincent de Brouwere, René Tonglet and Wim Van Lerberghe, 'Strategies for Reducing Maternal Mortality in Developing Countries: What Can We Learn from the History of the Industrialized West?' *Tropical Medicine and International Health*, 3 (1998), 771–782 is a positive an example of the use of mortality in the past to help understand modern manifestations of the problem, but such methods can also be deeply moralising; see Reekie, *Measuring Immorality*, p. 105.
9. de Brouwere, et al, 'Strategies for Reducing Maternal Mortality', pp. 771–782.
10. Gillis, *For Better, for Worse*, pp. 128, 219; Adair, *Courtship*, p. 79.
11. Casper and Moore, *Missing Bodies*, pp. 6, 61–62.
12. Casper and Moore, *Missing Bodies*, p. 77.
13. See Cossins, *Female Criminality*.
14. Valerie Fildes, 'Maternal Feelings Re-Assessed: Child Abandonment and Neglect in London and Westminster, 1550–1800', in *Women as Mothers*, ed. by Fildes, pp. 139–170; Wrightson, 'Infanticide in Earlier

Seventeenth-Century England', p. 16; Shirley Ann Smith, '"A Crying Sin": Infanticide in South-West Wales, 1870–1922' (unpublished doctoral thesis, Aberystwyth, 2015).

15. Mary J Dobson, *Contours of Death and Disease in Early Modern England* (Cambridge: Cambridge University Press, 1997), p. 242.
16. Dobson, *Contours of Death*, pp. 242–243; Angela Joy Muir, 'Death and the Parish: Mortality in Eighteenth-Century Wales', *Postgraduate Journal of Medical Humanities*, 4 (2017), 101–133 (pp. 110–114).
17. CFHS (Llanrhaeadr ym Mochnant) CLD-21809; Muir, 'Death and the Parish', pp. 111–112.
18. Philippe Ariès, *Centuries of Childhood: A Social History of the Family*, trans. by Robert Bladick (London: Cape, 1962); Stone, *Family, Sex and Marriage*; Edward Shorter, *The Making of the Modern Family* (New York: Basic, 1975).
19. For example, Rosemary O'Day, *The Family and Family Relationships, 1500–1900: England, France and the United States* (Basingstoke: Palgrave Macmillan, 1994); Hannah Newton, *The Sick Child in Early Modern England, 1580–1720* (Oxford: Oxford University Press, 2012); Linda Pollock, *Forgotten Children: Parent-Child Relations from 1500–1900* (Cambridge: Cambridge University Press, 1983); Linda Pollock, *A Lasting Relationship: Parents and Children Over Three Centuries* (Hanover: University Press of New England, 1987).
20. PFHS (Glascwm) POW/PR01CD (1705, 1706).
21. PFHS (Glascwm) POW/PR01CD (1711, 1716, 1720).
22. PFHS (Llanfihangel Nant Melan) POW/PR15CD, 1761, 1762.
23. PFHS (Glascwm)POW/PR01CD, 1681 (2), 1683 (2), 1684 (2), 1696 (1), 1710 (2), 1719 (1), 1723 (1), 1733 (2).
24. CFHS (Marchwiel) CLD-22101 (1699).
25. PFHS (Llanfihangel Nant Melan) POWPR15CD (1708, 1711, 1713).
26. Adair, *Courtship*, p. 33; EA Wrigley, RS Davies, JE Oeppen and RS Schofield, *English Population History from Family Reconstitution 1580–1837* (Cambridge: Cambridge University Press, 1997), p. 95; Blaikie, 'Infant Survival Chances', p. 37; Crawford, *Blood, Bodies and Families*, p. 82; RI Woods, PA Watterson and JA Woodward, 'The Causes of Rapid Infant Mortality Decline in England and Wales, 1861–1921, Part I', *Population Studies*, 42 (1988), 343–366.
27. Alice Reid, 'The Influences on the Health and Mortality of Illegitimate Children in Derbyshire, 1917–1922', in *Illegitimacy*, ed. by Levene, et al, pp. 168–189.
28. Blaikie, 'Infant Survival Chances', pp. 34–46; Alice Reid, Ros Davies, Eilidh Garrett and Andrew Blaikie, 'Vulnerability Among Illegitimate Children in Nineteenth Century Scotland', *Annales de Démographie Historique*, 1 (2006), 89–113.
29. Reid, et al, 'Vulnerability', pp. 89–113.
30. Wrigley and Schofield, *Population History of England*, p. 96.
31. Jones, 'Infant Mortality', pp. 305–317.
32. Montgomeryshire: Berriew, Bettws Cedewain, Llangadfan, Llanrhaeadr ym Mochnant, Llanwrin, and Trefeglwys. Radnorshire: Llanfihangel Nant Melan, and Llanbister.
33. Wrigley and Schofield, *Population History of England*, p. 249; Jones, 'Infant Mortality', p. 313 (i.e. per 1,000 live births for this period).
34. Humphreys, *Crisis of Community*, p. 218.
35. As discussed in Chapter 1, 'Town Queries', p. 662e.

36. Schofield, 'Did the Mothers Really Die?' pp. 231–232; Loudon, 'Deaths in Childbed', pp. 22–24.
37. Patricia Crawford, 'The Construction and Experience of Maternity in Seventeenth-Century England', in *Women as Mothers*, ed. by Fildes, pp. 3–38 (p. 21).
38. Gowing, 'Ordering the Body', pp. 43–62.
39. PCA (Llanwnog) M/EP/38/O/RT/12 (1764).
40. Woodward, 'Infanticide in Wales', p. 110; NLW 4/530/6 (Radnorshire, Mary Powell, 1792).
41. Schofield, 'Did the Mothers Really Die?' pp. 231–233; Wrigley, et al, *English Population History*, p. 309.
42. Dobson, *Contours of Death*, p. 2.
43. Louden, 'Deaths in Childbed', p. 6.
44. Schofield, 'Did the Mothers Really Die?' p. 260; Louden, 'Deaths in Childbed', p. 6.
45. Schofield, 'Did the Mothers Really Die?' p. 260; Linda A Pollock, 'Embarking on a Rough Passage: The Experience of Pregnancy in Early Modern Society', in *Women as Mothers*, ed. by Fildes, pp. 39–67 (p. 49).
46. NLW 4/530/6 (Radnorshire, Mary Powell, 1792).
47. NLW 4/188/1 (Montgomeryshire, Evan Jenkins, 1764).
48. Reid, et al, 'Vulnerability', p. 90.

4 Fatal Violence Against Illegitimate Children and Unmarried Pregnant Women

The mortality penalty should not only be understood as the unfortunate yet indirect consequence of socioeconomic hardship and marginalisation as demonstrated in broad, statistical terms; many unmarried women and their children met far more violent ends as a result of hostility towards the perceived threat of their unmarried status. Depositions and examinations relating to murder trials in the Court of Great Sessions reveal intriguing and tragic narratives of violence against unmarried women and their children. Newborn child murder, also known as infanticide, in eighteenth-century Wales is one of the few subjects directly related to illegitimacy which has received attention from academic historians. However, as with illegitimacy, the most detailed studies to date have focused on quantifying and statistically analysing the phenomena, as well as drawing out the similarities with other parts of Britain, with brief examples of individual cases woven throughout. In the process, the complex diversity of individual experience is overlooked in the larger goal of seeking patterns, thus resulting in overgeneralisation. This chapter will first analyse the narratives and discourse of individual cases in which mothers were charged with the murder of their newly born infants. In so doing, the focus will shift away from the legal processes onto the experiences of unmarried women, their children and their communities, and the social and cultural contexts and mind-sets which informed, and made sense of, their actions. The second section of this chapter will address the killing of unmarried pregnant women. Analysis of court depositions related to these crimes reveals a considerable amount about complex, popular and often conflicting perceptions surrounding the dangers and consequences of the deviant female reproductive body.

Fatal Violence Against Children

The most graphic and well documented of the mortality penalties paid by illegitimate children was when, as newborns, they were intentionally killed by their parents. This phenomenon is typically referred to as infanticide. However, as a distinctive legal concept infanticide is modern, and carries with it particular understandings of maternal mental health issues which result in women killing their infant children in the days, weeks and even months after giving birth. This differentiates it from the motives for, and experience of, killing one's own child in past centuries.[1] In the eighteenth century the act of killing or concealing the birth of a newborn infant was referred to simply as murder, but was understood as a specific type of murder which could only be committed by unmarried women for social, economic and, in contemporary terms, moral reasons. It typically occurred immediately after birth.[2] Many women in earlier centuries likely did suffer from what we might now identify as postpartum depression or psychosis, which could carry catastrophic consequences for them and their children. However, narratives which capture these experiences are exceedingly rare. The narratives of infanticide which do exist consistently reveal the complex negotiation between social, economic and moral anxieties and priorities surrounding the birth of children outside of wedlock. The mortality penalty of illegitimacy in this context needs to be understood not only in terms of the actions of certain women within broader social and economic contexts but in terms of the influence and agency of these women's families and communities as well.

The killing of newborn infants in Britain by their unmarried mothers in the seventeenth and eighteenth centuries has received considerable attention from historians.[3] To a greater or lesser degree, the studies of this period have been framed around the broad changes which occurred between the passing of the 1624 'Act to prevent the Destroying and Murthering of Bastard Children' and its repeal in 1803, and consist primarily of different readings of the extensive legal records which exist for most high courts across England and Wales. Broadsides, ballads and newspapers have also provided historians with popular representations of these crimes.[4] Some studies, such as those carried out by Keith Wrightson and Nick Woodward, have attempted to quantify the phenomenon and identify broad trends and patterns, whereas historians such as Mark Jackson, Laura Gowing and Anne-Marie Kilday have sought to delve into the complex social, medical and legal experiences and understandings of infanticide. The purpose of this study is to focus more closely on the narratives conveyed in detailed pre-trial accounts of infanticide in eighteenth-century Wales to draw out the complicated and often paradoxical processes of stigmatisation and social control which operated against unmarried mothers, and which ultimately cost some of their children their lives. These documents provide glimpses of how this manifestation of the mortality penalty operated, and how this type of violence was understood by Welsh communities.

The most detailed source of evidence relating to infanticide in eighteenth-century Wales are the records from the Court of Great Sessions, which was the highest criminal court in Wales, and similar to the English Assizes.[5] Historians who have studied these records to date have identified certain broad patterns which are congruous with patterns observed in England, including the predominance of unmarried mothers as suspects, many of whom were servants; the concealing of pregnancy, labour and delivery and the hiding, and eventual finding, of the infant's body.[6] Parallels have also been found in the ways in which these crimes were investigated and prosecuted by communities. The alarm would be raised following the discovery of an infant's body, or on the suspicion that a woman had secretly given birth and disposed of her infant. At that point, local authorities would become involved, such as constables, magistrates, coroners, surgeons or other medical practitioners, as well as groups of married women, some of whom would be midwives. Evidence and witness testimony would be collected and passed either to the coroner's jury or grand jury. Not all cases went to trial however.[7] Of the 190 cases which appear in the records of the Court of Great Sessions for the years 1730 to 1830, only 101 resulted in indictments which were heard by juries.[8] The majority of indictments resulted in acquittal; only a small proportion resulted in convictions. The remaining cases were dismissed as no true bill. Indictments and convictions reduced considerably over the eighteenth century, which is evident in both Welsh and English sources. Of those cases that went to trial, only a small minority resulted in a conviction, which carried a mandatory death penalty. However, only half of all Welsh sentences were carried out. Of the six women convicted between 1730 and 1805, only three were hanged, two of whom were hanged in the 1730s, and the third was hanged in 1805 after the law had changed.[9] Not a single suspect was convicted in Wales in the 20 years between 1770 and 1790.[10]

Overall, historians who have quantified infanticide in Wales have argued that it closely resembled the English context, and have noted that there is little convincing evidence to indicate a positive correlation between high levels of illegitimate birth and a higher prevalence of infanticide.[11] In other words, levels of newborn infant murder do not appear to increase proportionally with levels of illegitimacy. Across Britain, only a small proportion of unmarried women, and occasionally men, ever resorted to the extreme measure of killing their newborn infant. It has been suggested that, in the regions with higher levels of illegitimacy, lower indictment and conviction rates for infanticide may indicate the presence of conjugal courtship practices that resulted in greater acceptance of children born outside of marriage.[12] However there is little evidence to support this. Furthermore, using levels of infanticide as a measure of acceptable non-marital sex is another consequence of overgeneralisation about non-marital sex. It creates a false 'either-or' dichotomy which assumes that all non-marital conceptions must either be associated with courtship, which means infants are allowed to live, or marital nonconformity, resulting in extreme destitution, which means infants are killed. It does not account for the fact that many of those who conceived children out of wedlock came from diverse socioeconomic backgrounds, and therefore did not feel compelled by poverty and desperation to take extreme measures. It further assumes that all unmarried parents who were not in established courtships or stable unions must have wanted to kill their children. It cannot be said that the degree of relationship between parents determined their level of affection towards their children, even if their conception was unplanned and unwanted. Evidence of low levels of infanticide across Britain is evidence only of how uncommon the compulsion to kill one's offspring actually was.

Studies that analyse broad patterns of newborn infant murder are intriguing and reveal a great deal about the nature of infanticide in the eighteenth century. However, they fail to capture the nuances of the individual lived experiences of these women and their communities. Few crimes attracted as much popular interest and outcry as when a woman stood accused of killing her own child. These crimes fundamentally challenged contemporary understandings of womanhood in two key, interrelated ways: they defied heavily gendered understandings of violence which assumed women were far less likely to be perpetrators of violent crimes; and that such crimes went against the natural, nurturing feelings all mothers should feel towards their young.[13] Women who committed infanticide were routinely portrayed in Welsh and English popular literature as deviant, unnatural and violent. However, narratives such as these are not apparent in depositions.[14] Before examining the narratives found in depositions it is worth exploring some specific examples of how these crimes were portrayed in popular literature such as ballads.

At least six Welsh ballads appear to respond to real cases of infanticide in Wales during the eighteenth century.[15] Like English ballads, many Welsh ballads carried warnings and advice to unmarried women, cautioning against the economic and social consequences of illegitimacy, often using quite bawdy language.[16] However, ballads which responded to infanticide took a more severe, condemnatory tone which portrayed the mother's actions as evil and violent. As Siwan Rosser argues, these ballads were written with the explicit desire to provoke feelings of hatred and disgust towards these women and their crimes.[17] Accused women in ballads about infanticide (*babanladdiad*) were frequently portrayed as evil and vicious:

Mae calon drŵg gan ferched,
A laddo eu plant trwy chwerw chwant,
A hyn o dost ddihenydd,
Sydd yn cuddio cerydd cant[18]

[Evil-hearted women,
Who kill their children through bitter lust,
And these cruel deaths,
Hide the chastisement of a hundred][19]

Ballads were uncompromisingly critical of mothers, who were viewed not only as culpable, but unnatural and evil.[20] Condemnatory narratives such as these are absent from most witness depositions from Wales during the eighteenth century. As will be explored later, witnesses did view these deaths as horrendous, but the lived experiences of them were far more complicated.

A ballad written by Ellis Roberts (Elis y Cowper) in 1784, which appears to respond to the trial of Mary Owen of Llansantffraid Glan Cownway, serves as an excellent example of unequivocal censure of infanticidal mothers found in ballads.[21] Mary was accused of delivering her infant son in secret, and then strangling him. The details of how the crime was discovered are not given in any of the surviving records. The preamble to the coroner's inquest states that information was recorded, 'on view of a part of the body of the said bastard child then and there lying dead,' suggesting the infant's body was not immediately found.[22] Mary was charged, but not indicted, of strangling her infant son.[23] Several neighbours informed the coroner that they had suspected Mary of being pregnant, and had made repeated attempts to convince her parents of this. At the inquest, her mother and stepfather deposed that late one February evening, Mary complained of feeling unwell, and 'very much troubled with the worms.'[24] She left their shared bedchamber to sit by the fire in the kitchen. Her mother deposed that, 'she heard something squeaking like a child', and got out of bed to find Mary sat by the fire in the kitchen.[25] Mary told her mother that she felt better, and they returned to bed. Despite having heard what she thought might be the cry of an infant, Mary's mother stated that she did not see a baby, nor any sign of one. Not a single witness commented on Mary's behaviour or character other than to say they suspected she was pregnant. The coroner declared that the infant died as a result of 'choking, strangling and suffocating.'[26] Elis y Cowper's 112-line ballad is decidedly more graphic in details of the crime, and is unambiguously condemnatory.

> *Fo gadd yn lle bedydd enwaediad anedwydd,*
> *A thori yno beunydd ei ben,*
> *Yn le gwlanen wen gyfa I gario ir cae nesa,*
> *Ir eira naws oera blin senn,*
> *Ar hwn ar hin rewlyd,*
> *Ymborthe'r cŵn gwangclyd,*
> *Ar Cigfrain anhyfryd oedd hyn,*
> *Ow ddynes ddi-fuchedd,*
> *Am wneuthyd ei ddiwedd,*
> *Mor gîedd a sadwedd fodd synn,*
> *Pen y bath gwirion a garie'r cŵn creulon,*
>
> *A gafwd ar finion ffordd fawr,*
> *Hi fedrodd ei simio a hir edrych arno,*
> *Heb altro na gwyro mo'I gwawr*[27]

[Instead of a baptism he was given a wretched circumcision,
And his head severed,
Instead of a white woollen cloth he was carried to the next field,
Into the cold, angry snow
And this little one froze,
The hungry dogs feasted,
And the horrible ravens,
Oh, immoral woman,
For causing his death,
In such a savage, senseless way,
The dogs carried the innocent one's head,
Where it was found by the highway,
She was able to look upon him for some time,
Without showing any loss or mourning][28]

Although he did not name Mary directly, several features such as the location, year and season, as well as the detail of only parts of the infant's body remaining, make it highly probable that he was writing about her case.

Elis's version also contains vivid descriptions not present in any of the existing trial documents, which are probably the product of artistic embellishment and exaggerated word-of-mouth accounts. Rather than being strangled or suffocated, the infant in Elis's account has his throat slit, allowing for juxtaposition with the ritual cutting involved in circumcision.[29] Elis contrasts Mary's apparent coldness and lack of shame with the brutality of the infant's body being devoured by wild animals. He went on to lament the loss of the life of the child who should be suckling her breast (*Ow'r plenty a fase yn sugno ei gwythena*), and declares women such as Mary are 'worse than snakes' (*yn waeth nag iw neidr*).[30] Finally, he closed with a biblical analogy of the judgement of Solomon by stating, 'but it is a pity that old Solomon did not have the chance/to run her through with his horrifying, sharp sword' (*Ond grefynna chawfe'r hen Solomon ynte/Roi drwyddi hi gledde llym glas*).[31] As a creative expression with both moral and commercial objectives, it is not surprising that ballad writers such as Elis y Cowper portrayed events in more dramatic, condemnatory terms. However, it is noteworthy that similar attitudes towards these crimes are absent in the narratives found in witness depositions.

Despite many infants, whose mothers stood accused of their murder, having met violent ends through being stabbed, strangled, smothered or beaten, witnesses in Welsh depositions rarely describe suspected mothers in terms of violence. Rather, once confronted with evidence of their crimes, many women were portrayed as docile and implicitly remorseful, albeit somewhat uncooperative. For example, in 1768 in the parish of Trefeglwys, Montgomeryshire, Mary Davies and Anne Thomas, two married women of the parish, confronted Margaret Jenkin about the allegations that she had killed her infant and disposed of his body in a nearby wood. In the weeks which preceded the discovery of his body, rumours circulated that Margaret, who lived alone in a small one-bedroom house with a garden that was adjacent to her landlord's dwelling, was pregnant. Anne and Mary testified that they had examined Margaret's breasts and found milk in one of them, which was understood to be a sign of a woman having recently given birth. They then asked her if she had been 'brought to bed of a child, to which she at first gave no answer, but on frequently repeating the question she at last said she did not know what to say and then laying down her head gave no further answer.'[32] In Machynlleth in 1791 a servant woman was accused of murdering her newborn daughter with some sort of 'instrument', and throwing the infant's body into the river Dyfi. When Anne's master and mistress were informed that an infant's body had been found and that the child was rumoured to have been Anne's they questioned her, to which the only reply she would give was, 'God knows.'[33] These are two of the many examples in which witnesses described the actions of accused women in terms of silence or tacit remorse. Some women, such as Margaret hung their heads and said nothing, whereas others make reference to an awareness of the stain on their mortal soul. Such descriptions can be read as more than simply expressions of the accused's guilt, but rather as important character descriptions whereby witnesses emphasised their meekness, submissiveness and remorsefulness in an effort to mitigate the severity of the crime. This in turn could help influence juries and magistrates to take pity on these women and their unfortunate circumstances, rather than condemn them.[34]

Similar themes of meekness and submission can be found in confessions and testimonies woven amongst the evidence of criminal acts of concealment, death and burial. These serve to veil or soften the graphic nature of the crimes, and to portray mothers as gentle and nurturing, despite their actions. In Llanbedr-Goch on the island of Anglesey in 1737 Elizabeth Morris was passing by the house of her neighbour, Arabella Williams, when she heard the cry of a newborn infant.[35] Elizabeth called to Arabella through the locked front door, and eventually Arabella let her in, whereupon Elizabeth asked Arabella if she was 'indisposed or no?' Elizabeth testified that Arabella replied, 'I shall beg of thee, Betty Bach, to fetch a little water' to put on the fire, which Elizabeth did, and then Arabella subsequently confessed that she 'was much out of order and . . . had a little child in bed.'[36] The two women then washed and clothed the infant boy, who at that point was still alive. Elizabeth returned later that evening to find Arabella sat with her father by the fire, with the child nowhere in sight. She told Elizabeth that a hat maker and his wife, who allegedly knew the father of the child, took him away to be nursed. Two other witnesses, Margaret Williams and her daughter Jane, then testified that they urged Arabella to tell them what she had done with the child.

The two testified that Arabella confessed to them that they could find her dead son buried near a hawthorn bush, where they indeed found him wrapped in a piece of linen. Elizabeth, Margaret and Jane all make it clear in their depositions that Arabella concealed the birth and death of her child, but put far more emphasis on details such as where and how the body was carefully laid out, Arabella's desire to wash and cloth the child, and her obedient, if not reluctant, cooperation when questioned. These actions are not those of a monster, but of a woman who, despite her actions, still conformed to certain expectations of appropriate female, and even maternal, behaviour. Had these women wanted Arabella to be viewed as guilty or evil by the jury, they could have resorted to much different language. Instead, despite the fact that she concealed the death of her child, her female neighbours portrayed her in terms of the behaviour which was understood to be more appropriate for her gender.[37] Arabella was found not guilty.

Laura Gowing has argued that narratives such as these, which suppress details about the birth and death of infants, and rarely mention women actively harming their children, is evidence of the lack of language available to describe female violence.[38] As Garthine Walker has also suggested, understandings of women's honour were incongruent with acts of extreme, fatal violence.[39] Outside the literary tropes found in ballads, there was, therefore, a shortage of narrative modes that could be used to describe women who had committed homicidal violence.[40] This is very much apparent in Welsh court cases. However, these records go further in that they portray many of these women either as victims or in neutral terms. Despite the lack of vocabulary of violence available to describe women's actions, witnesses would still have had access to a vocabulary of deviance, which can be seen in parish registers and church court defamation cases.[41] However, with the exception of a couple of cases, most mothers were not portrayed as deviant or immoral. This is not to say that such cases are evidence of Thomas Laqueur's 'humanitarian narrative', as witnesses do not appear to go out of their way to portray the extreme details of suffering which could elicit compassion.[42] Rather, these records subtly portray the demeanour of these women, who were suspected of having committed horrific acts, as implicitly normative. Other than the fact that all of these women had either concealed the death of their children, or had actually killed their infants, most of them were described as behaving as women were expected to behave.

Details of each recorded case vary slightly in terms of where and how women delivered and disposed of their infant, but one key characteristic apparent in each of the depositions considered is that the sexual morality of these mothers was never called into question. Although all of the newborn murders which appear in the Great Sessions were tied to non- or extramarital sexual encounters, the language of sexual deviancy—including morally and sexually charged words such as whore and concubine, which can be found in parish baptism registers—are absent from witness depositions. In very few cases was the character of a woman who stood accused called into question, and even then, it was a woman's general character and demeanour, rather than specifically her sexual propriety, that was doubted. Sarah Owen, whose circumstances were discussed in Chapter 2, was supposed by one witness to be a 'wicked woman', but only in so far as he feared that she might abandon her newborn infant.[43] It was not because she was perceived to be lewd or lascivious. The most detailed and noteworthy case in which a woman's character was portrayed negatively took place in 1735 in Glascwm, Radnorshire. Neighbours accused a servant named Margaret Thomas Preece of being the mother of a newborn infant whose decomposing body was found by her master, Evan Prees, buried in a dunghill on his property.[44] Margaret was suspected of having been pregnant some months earlier, and her master's wife even found 'blood and the filth like that which came from a woman at the birth of a child' in her bedchamber. However, it was not until the body of an infant was found that she was confronted about it. Evan testified that when he found the body he was reluctant to approach Margaret about it, and instead told some neighbours he was 'afraid to take her up, she being of a dangerous and wicked family.' Thomas Prees, another witness, further testified that when Margaret had previously worked for him she had 'offered to swear for him whatever he pleased' against another man, and he further believed her to be a 'scandalous, woman and might be bribed to swear anything.' A neighbour who did confront Margaret about their suspicions testified that when he asked her 'who buried the child in the dunghill', she replied, '"My arse", in the Welsh tongue.'[45] The details around Margaret's conception, her sexual history or any suspected licentious relationships were never mentioned. Deponents clearly did not want to portray Margaret as meek and submissive, and they perceived her behaviour as dangerous and inappropriate, but their attacks were on her general character and family's reputation rather than on her sexual morality. Margaret was never indicted for the crime.

Furthermore, the unlawfulness of the sexual encounter which resulted in non-marital conception is rarely mentioned, and the fathers of these children and the relationships they had with the mothers are seldom discussed. With the exception of a few passing mentions fathers are only typically discussed when they are in some way implicated in the concealment of the birth or death of the child, the concealment of the infant body or when the nature of the relationship could serve as a mitigating circumstance.[46] When fathers are mentioned they are seldom, if ever, portrayed in a positive manner.[47] In Brecon in 1755 a servant named Mary Harris was charged with the murder and concealment of her newborn infant.[48] She testified that the father of her child was William Powell, a blacksmith who worked for her master. She confessed that she had repeatedly informed him of her pregnancy, and that he wanted her to swear their child to another man, which she refused to do. He further ignored her when she informed him she was in labour. When she told him that their son had been stillborn, and she had hidden the child in the bog house, he went and pushed it in deeper, so as to conceal it further. Mary was found not guilty, and William was never indicted. Three years later, in Forden, Montgomeryshire, Mary Barret testified that she was on the road to Guilsfield with William Davies, who was the father of her child, when she went into labour and gave birth. Mary stated that William took the child from her, and she had not seen William or the child since.[49] In the parish of Halkyn, Flintshire in 1797 Joseph Emerson and Margaret Jones were accused of delivering their daughter in a barn, suffocating her, and then concealing her body in a piece of linen.[50] Margaret was found not guilty, and Joseph was never indicted. In other cases, the details of fathers may have helped sway prosecutors and juries and encouraged them to feel compassion towards a woman's situation. Sarah Owen, whose son was born alive and was christened John Jones before being found murdered, told a witness that her pregnancy resulted from 'attempted' rape, which may have garnered her some degree sympathy, and therefore leniency.[51]

Overall, the absence of morally charged language and details about how these children were conceived suggests that infanticide was perceived not as a crime linked to sexual immorality but to other more complicated circumstances. Many of these narratives reveal tensions between sympathy for these women and their circumstances, and an understanding of the economic reality of bearing a child out of wedlock on the one hand, and the value placed on the lives of innocent young children, regardless of non-marital status, on the other.[52] This is never explicitly stated, but is revealed through certain witness depositions. The very real financial risk for women of bearing a child outside of wedlock, and the potential burden it presented to families and communities, compelled some women with unwanted pregnancies to resort to drastic measures. This is evident in many records in a variety of ways. For example, it is widely known that pregnant servants risked being dismissed from employment.[53] Mary Jones's employer testified that he told his son he wanted a new servant because his was with child, but did not want to send her away until he could find a replacement.[54] His priorities demonstrate a widespread disregard for what many unmarried mothers faced. It cannot be said that Mary's employer wished her or her child harm, but that he nevertheless did not want to be burdened by her circumstances. Many other women's narratives, as told by them and by witnesses, also reveal how they lacked any support whatsoever. When Mary Harris found herself pregnant, the child's father refused to acknowledge her circumstances and provide support, even when she was in labour.[55] In 1746 Jane Williams concealed her pregnancy because the father of her child was a married man, and she therefore felt she had no other options.[56] For some, the financial burden was combined with the traumatic experience surrounding conception, such as rape.[57]

Other narratives suggest that a key motivating factor was the desire to not implicate, or be a liability to, others. Ann Owen, whose child was found in the river Dyfi in 1791, testified that she fell into a violent passion because she did not want to deliver in someone's house, suggesting she did not want the burden of responsibility to fall to her employers, or bring shame upon them.[58] Narratives such as these were not only conveyed in women's confessions. Thomas Gabriel, in whose house Sarah Owen gave birth, said he saw Sarah with her child walking down the high road 'and being afraid of incurring the parishioners displeasure on account of her lying-in at his house' he went after her and saw her out of the parish.[59] Most poignantly, Paul Barnes, the churchwarden of the parish of St Asaph, Flintshire, testified that when rumours of the unmarried Jane Griffith's pregnancy reached him he went to her house to enquire, and when she denied being pregnant he unequivocally expressed how unwelcome her suspected pregnancy was.[60] Both she and her sister had already bore children out of wedlock, and Paul deposed that he

> told her that the parish had been at a vast trouble and expense about her sister upon the like account, and that it would be such another trouble to the parish upon her score if she would not discover and give them light in the matter in due time, to which she replied that the parish or parishioners should be at no charge or trouble upon her account.[61]

If Jane had any doubts about how the parish felt about her pregnancy, this conversation would have confirmed them, and this encounter may have been one of the many factors which compelled her to take extreme measures, as the body of her newborn child was later found in a cheese vat in her pantry. In all of these examples the details were provided in depositions by both suspects or by witnesses, and can be read either explicitly or implicitly as motives for these women's acts. These reasons demonstrate the ways in which communities and authorities understood these crimes. For many unmarried pregnant women, the only alternative to financial destitution was to destroy their newborn infants. That many of these details were conveyed by witnesses demonstrates how communities understood why some women took these actions, even if they condemned them.

This broader community understanding about the complex burden of unwanted, non-marital pregnancies can also be seen in certain actions taken by some of those in close proximity to suspects, and can be understood as complicity with these women's actions. Some women, such as Jane Williams, whose mother was indicted along with her, did not act alone, and the direct involvement of friends, family members and fathers has been discussed in depth by other historians.[62] However, what is noteworthy in many of these records is the ways in which some witnesses passively implicate themselves. Anne Owen's employers sent her away to run an errand on their behalf on the very day she fell into labour.[63] Margaret Thomas Preece's employers both testified that they believed Margaret went into labour on a particular Saturday and Sunday, but that they both then left for a short trip to the nearby town of Builth. When they returned they found evidence of a woman having delivered a child, and Margaret appeared smaller around the waist.[64] In both cases, enough physical distance was created between witnesses and the accused to make it clear that they did not want to be involved in any way. However, in so doing they also created the circumstances in which women could conceal their labour and deliveries, as well as bodies of their dead infants. Upon the return of those who went away, no questions were asked. Their absence at the crucial moment of parturition enabled women and their households to pretend these unwanted pregnancies never happened. In these cases, it was only when the body of the infant was discovered that the women's actions were scrutinised. In another example, Margaret Lewis testified that when she went into labour and cried out to her mother to fetch help from the nearby midwife, her mother replied, 'what do you want with her, thow [sic] has nothing but the spleen.'[65] Margaret testified that she made repeated pleas to her mother for help, which were denied, frequently along with verbal abuse. It was only through the suspicion of neighbours that Margaret's delivery, and the death of her child, were revealed. Leaving the scene, sending the parturient woman away, or denying support can be read not only as these witnesses attempting to remove any suspicion that they might have been accessories, but also as wilful ignorance. These individuals were either parents or employers who would have been well aware of these women's situation, but rather than providing necessary support for the parturient women in their care they chose to avoid taking any responsibility. As will be discussed in the next chapter, many unmarried women who were suspected of being pregnant were confronted by family and neighbours, but not all were. In many cases confrontation and exposure were replaced with strategies of detached collusion, and therefore culpability can, in many cases, be directly extended to a woman's kin and community networks.[66]

However, despite evidence of reluctant understanding of women's circumstances, and even complicity with their actions, there was still a certain value placed on the lives of infants born to unmarried women. Regardless of low indictment and conviction rates, the simple fact that the murder of newborn infants by their unmarried mothers was processed through legal channels does demonstrate that these deaths were more than simply a form of birth control.[67] However, the laws surrounding newborn child murder operated as a punitive mechanism which aimed to either punish or discourage, but provided no form of practical intervention.

The law relating to the killing of newborn children only pertained to unmarried women, which served more to codify official anxieties about non-marital reproduction rather than to protect infant life.[68] Far more nuanced evidence of the tension between the problems posed by children born to unmarried mothers and the intrinsic value of these infants' lives is revealed in some women's testimonies. Women, and midwives in particular, repeatedly testified that they lamented the loss of life caused by the act of delivering in secrecy. Mary Evans, who was called to the home of Margaret Lewis and her mother, was reported to have exclaimed 'for shame, you had not got some assistance and help.'[69] A midwife named Martha Roberts and another woman named Elinor Bollin both asked Mary Dell, who in 1750 was acquitted of murdering her infant daughter, why 'she had not applied to Martha in time for proper assistance.'[70] Jane Griffiths asked Elinor Pugh, who was accused of murdering her infant son in 1730, why she had not called for help, as Elinor stated she was certain she could have saved the child's life.[71] To at least some degree, these witnesses clearly felt that the lives of these infants could, and should, be preserved. In all these depositions, however, these few examples represent the only voices that expressed what appears to be an actual sense of loss over the death of these infants. This may be attributed, at least in part, to the official oath which some midwives took which required them to endeavour to preserve the lives of infants at almost any cost.[72]

However, this testimony should not simply be read as a display of official duty, as not all of those who made such statements were identified as midwives. Rather, these lamentations may be evidence of positionality on a complex spectrum of conflicting priorities. As women and mothers who were peripheral to the lives of the women in question, these witnesses may have had a particular understanding and expectation of the unmarried mother's circumstances which prioritised infant life above all other concerns. Conversely, sexual partners, family, employers and parish officials may have prioritised the various types of burden these infants represented.

Narratives in which the loss of infant life caused by maternal violence sit alongside others which sympathise with mothers' circumstances demonstrate the deeply complex and conflicting structures which operated against unmarried pregnant women. Their reproductive bodies were performing in an expected manner, but under unacceptable circumstances. Their bodies, therefore, were carrying lives which were, paradoxically, both valued and unwanted. Infanticide as a mortality penalty for illegitimate birth should therefore not simply be understood in terms of unmarried pregnant women reacting in an extreme manner against harsh economic circumstances, but as a complex struggle between conflicting personal and community priorities, of which, to varying degrees, those around them were implicitly aware, and often complicit.

Fatal Violence Against Unmarried Pregnant Women

Infants born to unmarried women were not the only victims of this tension over women's unregulated reproductive bodies. This conflict could also be manifested in violence towards women's bodies. Although statistically uncommon, the records of the Court of Great Sessions do contain examples of unmarried pregnant women who died as a result of violence which contemporaries associated with their unmarried and pregnant state. Most historical studies of gender and homicide have focused on men who kill other men, husbands who kill their wives, and on women who kill their own infants, their partners or occasionally other women.[73] The history of intimate partner violence as a distinct, complex social and cultural phenomenon is still very much in its infancy, and has focused almost exclusively on the use of physical force by husbands as a means of disciplining wives.[74] To date, very little research has been carried out on violence against unmarried women in early modern Britain. This may be due in part to a lack of evidence of cases found in online digital archives such as the records of the Old Bailey.[75] However, cases can be found in unpublished records from other regions of Britain. This lacuna is both unfortunate and surprising when the persistence and prevalence of violence against pregnant women is considered in a modern and global context. In the UK, for the year ending March 2017, official statistics reveal that half of all adult female murder victims were killed by a current or ex-partner.[76] This number dropped to 33 per cent for the following year, but this was because of the number of female victims killed in terrorist attacks such as the Manchester bombing and the London Bridge attack, rather than a decrease in domestic homicide. The World Health Organisation has indicated that, worldwide, being pregnant significantly increases a woman's risk of being murdered.[77] When pregnant women are murdered, they are almost always killed by the father of their child.[78] This risk appears to be even greater when a pregnancy is unintended.[79] In Britain at present, the number of pregnant women killed by their partners is relatively low, but the period of, and immediately following, pregnancy is still understood to put women at higher risk of violence.[80] However, a regional study in the United States found homicide to be the leading cause of death amongst pregnant women, whereas it was the fifth leading cause of death for women who were not pregnant.[81] In other words, in some parts of the world, pregnant women are more likely to die as a result of homicide than from another cause. Moreover, marginalised women are also known to be at an increased risk of fatal violence.[82] Many of these risk factors are evident in non-marital intimate partner homicide cases from eighteenth-century Wales.

Of over 350 cases of murder recorded in the Court of Great Sessions between 1750 and 1800 only seven involve unmarried pregnant women. This number may appear statistically insignificant. The details of these cases, however, are revealing not only of the experience of non-marital childbirth, but also of yet another way in which the mortality penalty might become visible. Just as infanticide cases cannot be seen as representative of the actual incidence of infanticide, the records of the killing of only seven unmarried pregnant women are not representative of the extent of actual violence directed towards woman in these circumstances. The killing of women is not a crime of concealment in the same way infanticide is understood to be, but it can still be understood as an invisible crime. It is likely that many more acts of violence were directed towards unmarried pregnant women which were never recorded. The scarcity of records pertaining to non-fatal violence against unmarried pregnant women may be more reflective of attitudes towards such crimes, which resulted in a reluctance to prosecute, than of their actual instance.[83] Moreover, it is possible that some unmarried pregnant women were killed by their partners well before they showed any observable signs of pregnancy that would have alerted family and neighbours to their condition. Even today violence against women, and intimate partner violence in particular, is incredibly difficult to identify, and those who work closely with at-risk women are trained in how to detect the various signs of violence.[84] The small number of cases does not mean this type of violence should be overlooked, but rather serves as tragic and tantalising evidence of yet another form of gender-based violence, and another way in which the mortality penalty of illegitimacy was manifested.

The details of each case vary, but all share key similarities. In all cases, the suspected perpetrator of violence was also known or believed to be the father of the unborn child. In each case, the depositions of various witnesses clearly implicate the father, provide no other plausible explanation for the women's violent deaths and suggest no alternative suspects, with the exception of an accessory in one case. When the alleged perpetrators were married men, the methods of violence used appear to have been directed at their unborn child. The death of these women may not have been the intended outcome, but were the consequence of extreme attempts to terminate a pregnancy. However, the fatal violence inflicted on women by unmarried partners was deliberately and unequivocally directed at the women themselves. Finally, in all but one case, the men were charged with murder and were acquitted of their alleged crimes. The actual guilt or innocence of these men cannot be determined, nor is it the most relevant feature. What is important, as will be seen, is that communities clearly believed these men were guilty, and for reasons not documented, judges and juries did not. In cases where women were physically assaulted, the last person seen with each victim was almost always the father of her child. The narratives contained in these examinations demonstrate that witnesses could see no other reason for these women to have died other than their state of pregnancy outside of marriage, and their tenuous and conflicted relationship with their children's fathers.

The unmarried pregnant women who were killed died by one of two means: they were either fatally poisoned in an attempt to procure an abortion, or their bodies were acted upon through direct physical violence, such as strangulation, beating, drowning or stabbing. Two women died by consuming poison given to them in an attempt to cause them to miscarry. In 1752, William Berwick allegedly forced Rachel Whittingham, his servant, to consume yellow arsenic in the hope that it would induce an abortion, despite the fact that Rachel was seven months pregnant.[85] A local doctor named Thomas Vaughan was also charged with allegedly supplying the poison. Williams's wife Susan was one of the witnesses who provided evidence. She deposed that William had recently told her that Rachel was pregnant by him, but she did not appear to believe William's actions caused Rachel's death. She deposed that her husband had gone seeking something to make the heavily pregnant Rachel miscarry. However, Susan also deposed that William had not prepared the mixture himself, and was assured that it would not cause Rachel any harm. Several male witnesses within William's network in the community also deposed that he had gone to them on different occasions seeking something to make his servant miscarry. He had been seen in the town of Montgomery buying items from an apothecary, such as savin, rue (both of which were believed to be abortifacient botanicals) and a half penny's worth of yellow arsenic.[86] William attempted to give Rachel a drink containing the arsenic one evening, but she refused, stating she would drink it the following morning, which she did. A fellow servant saw her go milking that morning, and she soon fell ill. Rachel's mother Elizabeth deposed that she heard her daughter cry out 'mother, mother, I am just gone,' before being carried to the house where she died a few hours later. Edward Bright, the surgeon who examined Rachel's body after she died, deposed that she died from a 'mortification of the stomach' caused by the consumption of yellow arsenic. Both William and Thomas were found not guilty. In a similar case in Narbeth, Pembrokeshire in 1780 an unmarried woman named Sarah Powell was given a mixture containing ground glass, iron rust and treacle by George Williams, a married man by whom she was pregnant, with the intention of inducing an abortion. After languishing with a 'great distemper' for four days, Sarah died as a result of the poisoning.[87] George was found not guilty.[88]

In both of these cases, and in a similar case from 1823, when poison was administered to unmarried pregnant women, the men who fathered their children and provided the poison were married.[89] This is too small a sample to identify a broader trend, but it is possible that through being married these men acquired limited knowledge of what measures, however extreme, could be taken to terminate an unwanted pregnancy. It is also possible that by administering poisons that cause symptoms that mimicked natural illnesses, such as gastrointestinal ailments and spontaneous miscarriages, these men hoped to conceal the shame associated with their adultery and preserve their honour and standing within their communities. That they were all able to coerce their lovers into taking toxic substances against their will demonstrates how much power they were able to exert over these women and their bodies. We cannot know if these men genuinely wished the women any serious harm, but the fact that they sought to remedy their situations by forcing their extramarital sexual partners to consume known toxins suggests that they were more concerned about their own reputations than about the lives of these women.

The reasons for the acquittal of these men is not clear, but it could be because the women appeared to have willingly or knowingly consumed the substance which killed them. These deaths were not deemed suicide, but it is possible that juries viewed the women as accessories to their own murders. However, this does not mean that these women willingly consumed toxic substances, but rather that they felt they had no other option. In an English case heard before the Northern Circuit Assizes in 1774, witnesses testified that Hannah Stocks, a pregnant single woman, had fallen violently ill shortly after John Scott, the father of her unborn child and an older son, paid her a visit.[90] Lydia Barstore, with whom Hannah and her son lived, and a neighbour both stated that Hannah told them she had consumed a substance off the end of a knife, which John had offered her. John had told her the substance would induce an abortion and destroy their unborn child. When witnesses asked Hannah if she had taken the substance willingly she said she had, because John had 'made her take it, and said he would run his knife into her if she did not take it.'[91] Given the choice to either die by the knife of her lover, or to consume an unknown substance, Hannah opted to take the poison, which ultimately resulted in her death.[92] However, in this case, John was convicted for Hannah's murder and was sentenced to death.

The remaining cases of murder against unmarried pregnant women found in Great Sessions' records involved targeted, external violence against the woman's body. These cases cannot be read as attempts to procure abortions which then go too far, but instead appear to be active attempts to end each woman's life. The only case which resulted in a conviction and execution was one such act of violence. In October 1764 in the parish of Llanwnog, Montgomeryshire, a servant named Evan Jenkins stood accused of strangling Elizabeth Evans, a single woman, with a handkerchief and leaving her body in a field near her mother's home.[93] Elizabeth's mother, Anne, deposed before a coroner that her daughter had left her house in good health carrying a basket and some yarn and went to meet Evan. Elizabeth was to bring Evan home with her that night to dine with them, and they had been preparing meat for the occasion. However, Elizabeth did not return, and the following morning Anne was informed that her daughter was dead. Elizabeth was found in a nearby field with extensive bruising on her chest and neck. Catherine Davies, a neighbour and friend of Elizabeth, further deposed that the deceased had also been at her home the previous day, but had left in a hurry as she was on her way to meet her 'sweetheart' and show him the way to her mother's house. Catherine stated that Elizabeth had been wearing a handkerchief around her head. Both Anne and Catherine deposed that Elizabeth was pregnant and that Evan was the father. Anne also revealed that Evan had offered her daughter a guinea to swear the child to someone else. In July 1764 Elizabeth was removed by parish officials to the nearby parish of Aberhafesp, her parish of settlement, and officially swore her unborn child to Evan. She was maintained at the expense of the parish for three days before returning to Llanwnog.[94]

Evan's employer, Edward Stephens, deposed that Evan had left his service temporarily due to a warrant against him relating to Elizabeth's pregnancy, but he believed Evan intended to marry Elizabeth as banns had been published. On the evening Elizabeth was murdered, Evan finished his work ploughing, returned to his master's house, ate dinner and then left shortly after nightfall, stating he was going to the home of another man in the village and would be back in a matter of hours. He returned shortly before midnight. The following morning, several neighbours found Elizabeth lying dead in a field. Her body had several marks of violence on it, including bruises to her face, and a handkerchief tied tightly around her neck which had left severe bruising. Thomas Rogers, the petty constable, arrested Evan once Elizabeth's body was found. It was what he did while in custody that sealed his fate. Thomas testified that Evan 'took him for a friend' and confided in him that 'he would rot in iron before he would marry the deceased,' and then confessed to strangling her with a handkerchief. Evan was the only suspect to admit to having killed the woman he had impregnated, and it was this confession that led to his conviction and consequent sentence of death.

Although none of the other men admitted to killing the women with whom they fathered children, many witnesses described the men as having acted suspiciously. In Breconshire in 1797, William Walter, a 30-year-old labourer, was suspected of having murdered Ann Watkin, who was pregnant with his child.[95] The night before Ann went missing, she and William stayed at the house of William's mother, Anne, along with Anne's daughter and William's sister Gwenllyan. The elder Anne deposed that the following morning she offered the pregnant Ann some old clothes for her to make into baby linens. Ann then left to make her way to her parish of settlement, and William accompanied her. William returned to his mother's house about three quarters of an hour later, saying he escorted Ann to the edge of a field and left her. She was never seen alive again. Her body was found five months later in the river Usk. During the period between her disappearance and the discovery of her body, several witnesses deposed that they had asked William if he knew where Ann was. William's mother deposed that he had told her he did not know Ann's whereabouts. However, some witnesses reported William telling them that Ann was with her cousin Alice in Glamorganshire, and others stated that he had heard from a Thomas Price that she was working in another parish. Both Alice and Thomas deposed that neither of these explanations were true. William's sister Gwenllyan also deposed that she had asked William several times where Ann was, and he variously replied that Ann was in different locations across the county or over 100 miles away in Crewe. Another witness deposed that he had asked William if he knew where Ann was, and if she was with child or free, to which William ominously replied, 'she was free enough.'[96] Prior to her disappearance Ann had been working for a short time in spinning, however she left her employment to return to her parish. Rachel Williams, her employer, deposed that when Ann left she paid her the full amount due to her. Two weeks after Ann had disappeared, William went to Rachel saying that Ann was in the workhouse in Talgarth and he was there on Ann's behalf to collect her outstanding wages, of which there were none. When Ann's body was finally discovered witnesses reported finding various marks of violence on her, including bruises on her neck and arm, and two holes in the lower part of her abdomen. She was also visibly very pregnant. William went on trial for the murder, but, despite the fact that his community and his own family clearly believed he had acted suspiciously, he was found not guilty.

The murder of Margaret Mathews in the parish of Old Radnor 40 years earlier bears striking similarities to both Ann Watkin and Elizabeth Evan's murders.[97] Margaret was known to be pregnant with Edward Pugh's child, and one witness deposed that the two were believed to be courting. Two witnesses, Jane Edwards and Elizabeth Price, both stated that on the last day Margaret was seen alive she told each of them separately that she had arranged to see Edward, a yeoman, that evening. Both women's depositions suggest that the planned meeting was likely to be a difficult one, if they met at all. According to both witnesses, Margaret had tried on several previous occasions to have Edward acknowledge that she was pregnant with his child, which he refused to do. Edward had also recently failed to meet Margaret as previously agreed, leaving her to wait several hours for him in the rain. On the evening Margaret disappeared, she intended to push the matter further and 'to know his answer . . . whether he would have her or take care of her and her child.' When Margaret failed to return home, her neighbours quickly grew suspicious and searched for her. Jane deposed that a small group of neighbours searched Edward's field, and the other places where Edward and Margaret usually met. Margaret's body was found in a field adjacent to Edward's property with bruises on her head, breast and arms. Two of the witnesses who viewed her body stated that they believed Margaret 'did not dye [sic] a natural death, but by some act of violence.' However, Edward was acquitted, and Margaret was deemed to have been murdered 'by person or persons unknown.'[98]

In a similar case in Ystradfellte, Brecon in 1788, the body of Margaret Thomas, a servant, was found in a river.[99] Margaret's employers and neighbours deposed that they knew Margaret was pregnant by William Williams, a fellow servant, and that she intended to return to her parish to swear the child to him. Margaret's employer, Evan Jones, deposed that on a Sunday in late September Margaret left his household to return to her home parish. Shortly after Margaret departed, William returned from collecting nuts in a nearby wood along with Evan's wife and children, and Evan informed William that Margaret had left to return to her parish of settlement. William and the family then went to another wood to continue collecting nuts. While there, William told his employer that he had spotted horses trespassing in a field and asked leave to move them on. He returned approximately one hour later, and then asked leave again to go with another servant to a nearby village, returning around dusk. Two different witnesses deposed that on the same evening, around dusk, Williams ran to them separately with some urgency asking them if they had seen the pregnant Margaret. The following day, William asked for leave to attend the swearing of Margaret's child, which he was prevented from doing because of poor weather, however he did leave his master's home on an errand that afternoon. Evan then spotted William in the woods near the river with a horse and sled, which William said he was using to collect wood. Margaret's body was found in the river with bruises on her neck the following morning. Evan deposed that he saw fresh sled marks in the mud going down to the river near where Margaret's body was found. According to Evan, 'the sled had been taken considerably further through the wood than necessary to fetch any wood and that the sled could not be turned at the extremity where the track was without taking the horses out of it.'[100] Evan then accused William of the murder, and of implicating him in it by using his sled, which William denied. One of the witnesses William ran to on the Sunday evening deposed that she had been working alongside William and Margaret when she heard William tell Margaret he wanted to be present when she swore her child, as he suspected another man was the father. He also told Margaret that if she refrained from swearing her child to him he would maintain it, but insisted that if he was legally bound to maintain the child he would end up in gaol because he did not have the means to provide formal support. Evan's wife, Catherine, was the one witness who did not cast doubt on William, as she believed he did not have the opportunity to chase after Margaret and kill her. Furthermore, she deposed that she had overheard William asking Margaret to publish marriage banns. However, a friend of Margaret's deposed that Margaret had told her that on several occasions that she 'had been obliged to leave her bed in the night and go and lie in the hay loft for fear of . . . William.'[101] William was indicted, but an inquest determined that Margaret drowned, and William was found not guilty.

The final, and arguably most unsettling, case is the murder of Mary Jones in Erbistock, Denbighshire in January 1762.[102] As with the other women who had met violent ends, Mary was known to be pregnant and the father of her child, Samuel Rogers, was suspected to have killed her. Mary, who worked as a domestic servant, had informed her master and mistress that she was with child. As previously mentioned, Mary's master, Robert Payton, told his son that he intended to dismiss her once he found a suitable replacement. Mary's mistress, Eleanor, deposed that Mary had recently appeared before the local justice of the peace to swear her unborn child to Samuel Rogers, who was also a servant. According to Eleanor, around eight o'clock in the evening on the day Mary died, she had been at work washing dishes in the kitchen when her mistress sent her outside to perform a task. A quarter of an hour later she returned and stated that Samuel was outside waiting for her, and had been since approximately six o'clock that evening, and he was nearly frozen as a result. Eleanor deposed that Mary seemed pleased to see Samuel, and took her hat and 'cheerfully' went outside to see him. Mary was never seen alive again. Other servants in the household, including Rachel Taylor, deposed that following her disappearance Samuel, accompanied by his mother, came to the house in a violent rage stating that the Paytons had brought a scandal on him by telling others Mary had last been seen with him. His alleged alibi was that he had decided to go to Overton to buy himself a waistcoat, but returned before reaching his destination because in one account he said he had forgotten money, and, in another, because he had taken leave without permission and feared being reprimanded. Mary was missing for at least two days before her body was found partially submerged in a water-filled gravel pit. Rachel deposed that, in the interim, she heard Samuel say, 'god send she has not made away with herself or some bad thing happened to her for that she had foreswear herself by laying the child to him, which was not true.'[103] As with most of the other cases, Samuel Rogers was indicted, tried and was subsequently acquitted. Despite her mistress describing Mary's demeanour as cheerful, and despite there being no other mention of her displaying melancholic or hysterical behaviour, an inquest deemed her death a suicide, and labelled Mary a 'lunatic and of insane mind.'[104]

In one of the only studies to consider this particular type of violence against unmarried pregnant women, Dana Rabin suggests that the men who perpetrated these crimes were attempting to 'restore patriarchal discourse.'[105] She argues that maintenance payments from fathers granted women a level of financial independence, which threatened the male position as patriarch and provider in a family.[106] However, I would argue that this understanding of motive is far too abstract. Although women bearing children outside of wedlock challenged the patriarchal ordering of society in which the male-headed household served as a microcosm of the broader social order, it does not follow that this deviation from the norm therefore motivated men to kill unmarried pregnant women. Witness statements recorded in Welsh depositions suggest that the men suspected of murdering these women were motivated to kill because they did not want their reputation damaged, or did not want the burden of maintaining their child and the mother. Despite a very low conviction rate, a compelling motive is still apparent. Again, what is significant is not whether these men actually committed these crimes, but that witnesses consistently constructed narratives that identified the suspect and motive in particular ways. In most of these cases the unmarried mothers had attempted to hold their suspected murderers accountable for their children. A similar motive can be seen in the murder of some older children as well. In 1741 James John was convicted of murdering his two-year-old daughter, Sarah Powell, by throwing her in the river Usk after he had requested that her mother bring Sarah to him rather than ask the vestry to ensure he made maintenance payments.[107] He met the mother on a bridge, took Sarah from her, and threw her in the river, where she died. These crimes were understood to have been motivated by men's reluctance to take financial responsibility for their children. The alleged actions of these men were understood by witnesses as violently self-serving and should not therefore be interpreted as abstract attempts to restore social order.

Unlike the cases of married men poisoning their pregnant lovers, these more overt examples of intimate partner homicide cannot be understood as attempts at abortion-gone-wrong by means of what Sara Butler has called 'abortion by assault.'[108] These suspects did not simply want to terminate the women's pregnancies, but wanted to cause significant harm to the women themselves. The signs of violence found on these women's bodies were not directed towards their bellies and foetuses, but towards the women's bodies. In every case, the women's bodies bore bruises and wounds on their heads, necks, chests or arms: Elizabeth Evans was beaten around the head and chest, and was strangled; Margaret Mathews was found with bruises on her head, chest and arms; Margaret Thomas was found strangled and left in a river; and Mary Jones was found drowned in a gravel pit. Ann Watkin did have two possible stab wounds on her belly, but her body also bore several other marks of violence that could have proven fatal, and her body was disposed of in the river. The fatal violence carried out on these women's bodies was not accidental nor was it random; it can only be read as evidence of direct and deliberate violence.

The reluctance of juries to convict without a confession may be evidence of a tension between the perceived gravity of the crime committed against these women, and the hostility felt towards their active, deviant and unregulated reproductive bodies. In this conflict, the values upholding the social order may have taken precedence over the lives of women whose bodies and actions officials perceived as deviant. Most witnesses clearly viewed the fathers of these women's unborn children as guilty, but those charged with deciding verdicts disagreed. In a patriarchal system that necessitates the presence of a male head of household, the absence of such a figure creates a problem for the community. Under such circumstances, women who bear children outside of marriage are inevitably marginalised, and their behaviour stigmatised to at least some degree. This also leads to a sexual double standard whereby a man's sexual deviance is more forgivable than that of a woman. It is possible that the act of women swearing, or threatening to swear, their unborn child to the accused was seen as a threat to a man's honour and reputation, which elicited an excessive but excusable aggressive response.[109] Such persistence on the part of an expectant mother could constitute provocation, or what is now called 'victim precipitation', which justified men's alleged actions and provided just enough mitigating circumstances to result in acquittals.[110]

In her analysis of records from the Court of Great Sessions, Sharon Howard has argued that in cases of wife killing, male jurors and justices did tend to subject prosecution evidence to very high levels of scrutiny, but also accepted any mitigating circumstance as justification for acquittal.[111] Furthermore, Howard has also noted that it was rare for a person to be indicted for physical assault or murder if the attack was on someone of the opposite sex.[112] The same is likely true in the killing of unmarried pregnant women. Moreover, Peter King has demonstrated that when certain marginalised groups in London, such as Irish migrants, were murdered their assailants were less likely to receive full convictions due, in part, to prejudice against victims.[113] Judicial prejudices against the single pregnant women may have operated in similar ways. The extremely low conviction rates found in the murder of pregnant single women may simply be in line with overall conviction rates, but in the absence of any significant studies on non-marital intimate partner homicide in early modern Britain alternative gendered hypotheses should not be ruled out.[114]

Evidence of the gendered nature of indictment and conviction is evident in other crimes as well.[115] Male judges and juries heard these cases, and their own personal values and opinions about a woman's sexual history could have worked against female homicide victims. As Cynthia Herrup has argued, legal decisions reflect the values of local men of middling status, the gentry and the legal elite.[116] These men may have had hostile attitudes toward women who were pregnant outside of marriage. Feminist critics of the criminal justice system have observed that in modern murder trials where men stand accused of killing women it is not uncommon for the victim, her relationship with the accused and her personal and sexual history to be put on trial as well.[117] Furthermore, when marginalised female bodies are victimised they are more likely to be neglected by the criminal justice system.[118] The violent death of unmarried women in eighteenth-century Britain was certainly not encouraged by authorities, but preliminary analysis would suggest that their loss of life did not justify the loss of another life, because had their sexual partners been convicted of murder they would have faced the death penalty. Historians of infanticide agree that low conviction rates reflect a reluctance to mete out what was viewed as disproportionally harsh justice for crimes with which judges and juries could empathise.[119] It is possible that when unmarried pregnant women were killed, judges and juries either felt a similar empathy towards the men who would have been burdened with the care of their children, or they viewed the woman's own role in her pregnancy as a form of personal culpability that exonerated their partners enough for them to be acquitted, especially when the evidence was circumstantial. Because of their state of pregnancy outside of marriage, these women's bodies were not seen as innocent, and, as such, violence against them was harder to condemn.[120]

Fatal violence against unmarried pregnant women serves as further evidence that women ultimately bore the brunt of the consequences of sex outside of marriage in early modern Britain.[121] Witness narratives reveal that communities and authorities understood that the threat to honour and the financial expense of supporting a child outside of wedlock were burdens that some men may have sought to avoid through violent means. Most observers would not have wanted to see children born outside of wedlock, but not all would have wanted to see unmarried mothers or their unborn children come to harm. It is, however, noteworthy that in all of these cases the women were in advanced stages of pregnancy when they died, yet none of the depositions, inquests or verdicts refer to the corresponding loss of the unborn life. Those charged with providing financial support to impoverished mothers and children may have felt some degree of relief when problems seemingly took care of themselves, and those charged with upholding the social and moral order may have felt that the 'immoral' behaviour of these women justified their fate. However, those who had personal bonds with the unmarried female victims of intimate partner homicide would have felt a deeper sense of loss and a need for justice.

Conclusion

The aim of this section has been to demonstrate the various manifestations of the mortality penalty of non-marital childbirth for both children and their mothers. Evidence of the extent of this penalty is apparent in a range of parish and legal documents. However, to a lesser degree, evidence of care and compassion towards unmarried mothers and their children is also evident. In light of the overwhelming evidence of violence, neglect and disadvantage it is important to note that not all infants and their unmarried mothers were treated harshly.[122] Some children born to unmarried women were cared for in various ways which went beyond the provision of the basic necessities of food, clothing and shelter. In 1758 parish officials in Meifod paid to clothe and send a boy named David, identified as base, to the infirmary in Shrewsbury to be cured of a 'Rupture.'[123] In the following decade, officials in the same parish also paid a woman of the parish to take a pauper boy named Richard, also identified as base, to the sea because he was, 'in a mizerable condition with a sort of leprosy, which might want for a cure'. This chronic condition had apparently made Richard an expensive burden to the parish for his entire life; nevertheless, care was still provided.[124] These are examples of care given by the parish for poor children born to unmarried mothers. Many unmarried mothers, and even fathers, would have loved their children as well, and would have provided for them to the best of their ability.[125] For example, the will of James Thomas of Talley in Carmarthenshire in 1662 details bequests of his leases, livestock and possessions to his 'supposed wife,' Margarett Morgan, their children Thomas, John and Elizabeth, all of whom were variously referred to as 'supposed' and 'reputed,' and their spouses and children.[126] Not all unmarried fathers may have been in such a position, but this does demonstrate that some men undoubtedly did care for children they bore outside of wedlock.

These are examples of care provided to maintain children when they lived, but compassion was also shown to many others in death. There is compelling evidence to suggest that the lives of children who were identified by parish officials as 'illegitimate' were mourned as much as children born to parents who were married. Numerous poor law entries detail the costs incurred for infant burials, and many of these are for infants born to unmarried mothers. Between 1773 and 1775 parish officials in Castell Caereinion paid for shrouds and coffins for at least three infants born to single women.[127] In 1792 parish officials in Berriew not only provided a shroud and coffin for the burial of Catharin Parry's child, they also spent 12d. on alcohol to be consumed at the funeral.[128] This small gesture indicates that these infants were still deemed to be worthy of the customs surrounding death afforded to 'legitimate' members of the community. It is impossible to know if these pregnancies were unplanned or unwanted, but it does appear that the deaths of these children did not go unnoticed or un-mourned.

This chapter has again demonstrated that experience of non-marital childbirth in the eighteenth century was diverse and complicated, as was the mortality penalty. For unmarried mothers and their children, it was manifested in a variety of ways ranging from the fatal consequences of elevated levels of poverty and disadvantage to outright hostility and violence. In most cases it is difficult, if not impossible, to determine how each woman and child paid the price. It appears that if a mother was not the victim of some form of violence before giving birth, and if she delivered with the knowledge of the community and with access to support, she stood no greater risk of dying than married parturient women. This will be explored further in the final chapter. We cannot know how many unmarried women had access to such support, but it is clear that the prognosis for unmarried mothers who did not seek, or were denied support, and their children was potentially poor. If infants survived birth without being fatally harmed in some way they could, in many cases, receive support from the parish or from their mother's or father's extended networks of kin, which could help to preserve their lives. Furthermore, the role of fathers is also central to our understanding to the mortality penalty of illegitimacy. By acknowledging and providing support for their children, unmarried fathers could significantly improve their children's prospects. However, if they rejected their paternity it could have dire consequences, particularly if they were predisposed to violence.

We also cannot know how the loss of these lives was received by communities, but what court and parish burial records do indicate is that non-marital deaths were just as complicated as non-marital births. Each woman and child's experience was different, and would have depended a great deal upon the nature of the relationship between the mother and father, the mother's own socioeconomic circumstances, and whether or not the father could, or did, provide financial support. Each death was likewise viewed differently by different members of the community. Most observers would not have wanted to see children born outside of wedlock, but not all would have wanted to see unmarried mothers or their children suffer and die. When mothers and/or their infants did die, those charged with providing financial support may have felt some degree of relief, and those charged with upholding the social and moral order may have felt that these women and children got what they deserved, whereas those who may have had a personal bond with the woman or child, or who had a professional interest in preserving maternal and infant life, may have felt a sense of loss more deeply. The experience of losing a child, even if the loss was at the hands of the mother, must have been traumatic for many. Simply because a child was conceived and born into less than ideal circumstances it cannot be assumed that anyone wanted to see these children come to any harm. The loss of mothers, however, is perhaps more complex. Ultimately, fatal violence against women and children was rare. The murder of children is far better documented, perhaps because it occurred more frequently, or perhaps because the perceived innocence of the victim resulted in more attention being paid to their deaths than to the deaths of unmarried women who were known to have conceived outside of wedlock. Fatal violence against unmarried women has received virtually no attention from historians, but what this small study has hopefully demonstrated is that it is a subject which deserves to be analysed in far greater detail, especially given the gendered context of indictment and conviction rates. It is likely that at some point most unmarried mothers and their children experienced some degree of hostility, directly or indirectly, towards them because they represented the deviant female reproductive body, and, for an unfortunate few, this had fatal consequences. Analysis of responses to the mortality penalty of non-marital childbirth further reveals a complex negotiation between conflicting forces of anxiety, hostility and compassion towards reproductive sex outside of marriage.

Notes

1. Gowing, 'Secret Births', p. 88; Kilday, *History of Infanticide*, pp. 183–217; Woodward, 'Infanticide in Wales', p. 94.
2. Gowing, 'Secret Births', p. 88.
3. See: Hoffer and Hull, *Murdering Mothers*; Gowing, 'Secret Births'; Grigg, 'Getting Away with Murder'; Jackson, *New-Born Child Murder*; Jackson, *Infanticide*; Kilday, *History of Infanticide*; Walker, *Crime, Gender and Social Order*; Malcolmson, 'Infanticide in the Eighteenth Century'.
4. Thorn, *Writing British Infanticide*.
5. Jackson, *Infanticide*, p. 37; Watson, 'Women, Violent Crime', p. 249.
6. Muir, 'Illegitimate in Eighteenth-Century Wales'; Malcolmson, 'Infanticide in the Eighteenth Century', pp. 192–193.
7. Woodward, 'Infanticide in Wales', p. 96.
8. Woodward, 'Infanticide in Wales', p. 101.
9. Watson, 'Women, Violent Crime', p. 260.
10. Woodward, 'Infanticide in Wales', p. 122.
11. Woodward, 'Infanticide in Wales', p. 124.
12. Muir, 'Illegitimate in Eighteenth-Century Wales', pp. 385–387; Woodward, 'Infanticide in Wales', pp. 102–103.
13. Kilday, *History of Infanticide*, p. 98; Walker, *Crime, Gender and Social Order*, pp. 157–158; Jackson, *New-Born Child Murder*, p. 72.
14. Kilday, *History of Infanticide*, p. 41; Miriam Jones, 'Fractured Narratives of Infanticide in the Crime and Execution Broadside; in Britain, 1780–1850', in *Writing British Infanticide*, ed. by Thorn, pp. 112–142 (p. 112).
15. As listed in Davies, *Bibliography of Welsh Ballads*. My thanks to Dr Siwan Rosser for her identifying these cases for me, and to Rhian Richards and Ian Rees for their help in translating these ballads. See also Rosser, *Y Ferch ym Myd y Faled*, p. 90.
16. Rosser, *Y Ferch ym Myd y Faled*, pp. 78–119.
17. Rosser, *Y Ferch ym Myd y Faled*, p. 98.
18. Thomas Edwards (Twm o'Nant BOWB 243), as discussed in Rosser, *Y Ferch ym Myd y Faled*, p. 98–99.
19. Many thanks to Rhian Richards for her help with this translation.
20. Rosser, *Y Ferch ym Myd y Faled*, p. 97.
21. NLW 4/60/5 and 4/61/1 (Denbighshire, Mary Owen, 1784).
22. NLW 4/60/5 (Denbighshire, Mary Owen, 1784).
23. NLW 4/60/5 and 4/61/1 (Denbighshire, Mary Owen, 1784).
24. NLW 4/60/5 (Denbighshire, Mary Owen, 1784).
25. NLW 4/60/5 (Denbighshire, Mary Owen, 1784).
26. NLW 4/60/5 (Denbighshire, Mary Owen, 1784).
27. Elis Roberts (BOWB 357) Many thanks to Rhian Richards for her help with this translation, and to Siwan for sharing much of this interpretation with me, which she discusses in detail in her book.
28. Many thanks to Rhian Richards for her help with this translation, and to Siwan for sharing much of this interpretation with me, which she discusses in detail in her book.

29. Rosser, *Y Ferch ym Myd y Faled*, p. 98.
30. Elis Roberts BOWB 357.
31. Elis Roberts BOWB 357; 1 Kings 3:16–3:28 is the biblical story of two women who fight over which of them is the rightful mother of a child. Solomon resolves the dispute by threatening to slice the infant in two so both can have half. One woman insists he give the child to the other woman, thus allowing the child to live. The other woman insists he cut the child in two. Solomon takes the former woman's desire to save the child's life as a sign of her maternal love, and declares her the rightful mother.
32. NLW 4/189/1 (Montgomeryshire, Margaret Jenkin, 1768).
33. NLW 4/194/7 (Montgomeryshire, Ann Owen, 1791).
34. Kilday, *History of Infanticide*, p. 43.
35. Bach being a colloquial term of endearment in Welsh, literally meaning little or small.
36. NLW 4/250/6 (Anglesey, Arabella Williams, 1737).
37. Walker, *Crime, Gender and Social Order*, p. 157.
38. Gowing, 'Secret Births', p. 105.
39. Walker, *Crime, Gender and Social Order*, p. 157.
40. Gowing, 'Secret Births', p. 105.
41. Ingram, *Church Courts*, pp. 292–320.
42. Thomas Laqueur, 'Bodies, Details, and the Humanitarian Narrative', in *The New Cultural History*, ed. by Lynn Hunt (Berkeley: University of California Press, 1989), pp. 176–204 (pp. 176–177, 185–187).
43. NLW 4/62/1 (Denbighshire, Sarah Owen, 1788).
44. NLW 4/518/2 (Radnorshire, Margaret Th Prees, 1735).
45. NLW 4/518/2 (Radnorshire, Margaret Th Prees, 2735).
46. Walker, *Crime, Gender and Social Order*, p. 156.
47. Grigg, 'Getting Away with Murder?' pp. 115–133 (p. 129).
48. NLW 4/381/2 (Breconshire, Mary Harris, 1755).
49. NLW 4/186/1 (Montgomeryshire, Mary Barret, 1758).
50. NLW 4/1013/9 (Flintshire, Joseph Emerson, 1796).
51. NLW 4/62/1 (Denbighshire, Sarah Owen, 1788).
52. Reekie, *Measuring Immorality*, p. 113.
53. Barber, 'Stolen Goods', p. 127.
54. NLW 4/53/3 (Denbighshire, Samuel Rogers, 1762).
55. NLW 4/381/2 (Breconshire, Mary Harris, 1755).
56. NLW 4/49/2 (Denbighshire, Jane Williams, 1746).
57. NLW 4/62/1 (Denbigshire, Sarah Owen, 1788).
58. NLW 4/194/7 (Montgomeryshire, Ann Owen, 1791).
59. NLW 4/62/1 (Denbigshire, Sarah Owen, 1788).
60. NLW 4/1002/4 (Flintshire, Jane Griffith, 1739).
61. NLW 4/1002/4 (Flintshire, Jane Griffith, 1739).
62. Kilday, *History of Infanticide*, pp. 65–66; NLW 4/49/2 (Denbighshire, Jane Williams, 1746).
63. NLW 4/194/7 (Montgomeryshire, Ann Owen, 1791).
64. NLW 4/518//2 (Radnorshire, Margaret Th Prees, 1735).
65. NLW 4/188/6 (Montgomeryshire, Margaret Lewis the Younger, Margaret Lewis the Elder, 1767).
66. Gowing, 'Secret Births', p. 115.
67. Angus McLaren, *Reproductive Rituals: The Perception of Fertility in England from the Sixteenth to the Nineteenth Century* (London: Methuen, 1984), p. 7; Catherine Ward, 'Desperate Remedies': A Historical Overview of Women's Methods of Procuring Abortion' (unpublished MA dissertation, Wellcome Institute for the History of Medicine, 1996), pp. 1–2.

68. 21 James I c. 27.
69. NLW 4/188/6 (Montgomeryshire, Margaret Lewis the Younger, Margaret Lewis the Elder, 1767).
70. NLW 4/183/5 (Montgomeryshire, Mary Dell, 1750).
71. NLW 4/177/7 (Montgomeryshire, Elinor Pugh, 1730).
72. Doreen Evenden, *The Midwives of Seventeenth-Century London* (Cambridge: Cambridge University Press, 2000), pp. 27–30.
73. See: Beattie, *Crime and the Courts*; Cossins, *Female Criminality*; Foyster, *Manhood in Early Modern England*; Foyster, *Marital Violence*; Kilday and Nash, eds, *Histories of Crime*; Sharpe, *Crime in Seventeenth-Century England*; Walker, *Crime, Gender and Social Order*; Kesselring, 'Bodies of Evidence'.
74. See: Roth, 'Gender, Sex and Intimate-Partner Violence'; Bailey, 'I Dye by Inches'; Leneman, 'A Tyrant and Tormentor'; Foyster, 'Male Honour'; Hunt, 'Great Danger'.
75. A search of the Old Bailey Online found no comparable cases www.oldbaileyonline.org [accessed 26/8/2019].
76. Office of National Statistics (ONS), 'Homicide in England and Wales: Year Ending March 2017' [accessed 18/3/2019].
77. World Health Organisation, 'Intimate Partner Violence During Pregnancy Information Sheet' (2011) (WHO/RHR/11.35).
78. Knight, Marian, Kathryn Bunch, Derek Tuffnell, Hemali Jayakody, Judy Shakespeare, Rohit Kotnis, Sara Kenyon, Jennifer J Kurinczuk, eds, on Behalf of MBRRACE-UK, 'Lessons Learned to Inform Maternity Care from the UK and Ireland Confidential Enquiries into Maternal Deaths and Morbidity 2014–16' (Oxford: National Perinatal Epidemiology Unity, University of Oxford, 2018), p. 63; (WHO/RHR/11.35).
79. Christina C Pallitto, Jacquelyn C Campbell and Patricia O'Campo, 'Is Intimate Partner Violence Associated with Unintended Pregnancy?' *Trauma, Violence & Abuse*, 6 (2005), 217–235.
80. Knight, et al, 'Lessons Learned', pp. 73–74.
81. Isabelle L Horon and Diana Cheng, 'Enhanced Surveillance for Pregnancy-Associated Mortality—Maryland, 1993–1998', *Journal of the American Medical Association*, 285 (2001), 1455–1459.
82. World Health Organisation, 'Understanding and Addressing Violence Against Women: Femicide' (WHO/RHR/12.38), p. 3.
83. Sharon Howard, *Law and Disorder in Early Modern Wales: Crime and Authority in the Denbighshire Courts, c 1660–1730* (Cardiff: University of Wales Press, 2008), p. 92.
84. Susan Bewley and Jan Welch, *ABC of Domestic and Sexual Violence* (Chichester: John Wiley & Sons, 2014), pp. 30–36.
85. NLW 4/184/2 (Montgomeryshire, William Berwick and Thomas Vaughan, 1752).
86. Anon. (William Salmon), *Aristotle's Compleat and Experience'd Midwife* (London, 1740), p. 28, 521; James Copland, *Practical Medicine: Comprising General Pathology, the Nature and Treatment of Diseases, Morbid Structures, and the Disorders Especially Incidental to Climates, to the Sex, and to the Different Epochs of Life* (New York, 1845), vol. 1, p. 14.
87. NLW 4/821/5 (Pembrokeshire, George Williams, 1780).
88. NLW 4/821/5 (Pembrokeshire, George Williams, 1780).
89. NLW 4/537/1 (Radnorshire, Edward Evans, 1823).
90. Dana Rabin, 'Beyond "Lewd Women" and "Wanton Wenches": Infanticide and Child-Murder in the Long Eighteenth Century', in *Writing British Infanticide*, ed. by Thorn, pp. 45–69 (pp. 48–49).

91. Rabin, 'Lewd Women', p. 49.
92. Rabin, 'Lewd Women', p. 49.
93. NLW 4/188/1 (Montgomeryshire, Evan Jenkins, 1764).
94. PCA (Llanwnog) M/EP/38/O/RO/12 (1764); M/EP/38/O/RT/1 (1764).
95. NLW 4/390/4 (Breconshire, William Walter, 1797).
96. NLW 4/390/4 (Breconshire, William Walter, 1797).
97. NLW 4/523/4 (Radnorshire, Edward Pugh, 1756).
98. NLW 4/523/4 (Radnorshire, Edward Pugh, 1756).
99. NLW 4/388/5 (Breconshire, William Williams, 1797).
100. NLW 4/388/5 (Breconshire, William Williams, 1797).
101. NLW 4/388/5 (Breconshire, William Williams, 1797).
102. NLW 4/53/3 (Denbighshire, Samuel Rogers, 1762).
103. NLW 4/53/3 (Denbighshire, Samuel Rogers, 1762).
104. NLW 4/53/3 (Denbighshire, Samuel Rogers, 1762).
105. Rabin, 'Lewd Women', pp. 60–61.
106. Rabin, 'Lewd Women', p. 59.
107. NLW 4/377/2 (Breconshire, James John, 1741).
108. Sara M Butler, 'Abortion Medieval Style? Assaults on Pregnant Women in Later Medieval England', *Women's Studies, an Inter-Disciplinary Journal*, 40 (2011), 778–799.
109. Robert Shoemaker, 'Male Honour and the Decline of Public Violence in Eighteenth-Century London', *Social History*, 26 (2001), 190–208 (p. 197) cited in Bailey, 'I Dye by Inches', p. 275; Alexandra Shepard, *Meanings of Manhood in Early Modern England* (Oxford: Oxford University Press, 2006), pp. 168–170. Oxford Scholarship Online.
110. Sue Lees, 'Naggers, Whores, and Libbers: Provoking Men to Kill', in *Femicide: The Politics of Women Killing*, ed. by Jill Radford and Diana EH Russell (Buckingham: Open University Press, 1992), pp. 267–288.
111. Howard, *Law and Disorder*, p. 94.
112. Sharon Howard, 'Crime, Communities and Authority in Early Modern Wales: Denbighshire, 1660–1730' (unpublished doctoral thesis, Aberystwyth, 2003), p. 83.
113. Peter King, 'Ethnicity, Prejudice, and Justice: The Treatment of the Irish at the Old Bailey, 1750–1825', *Journal of British Studies*, 52 (2013), 390–414 (pp. 396–397).
114. Howard, 'Crime, Communities and Authority', p. 63.
115. Howard, 'Crime, Communities and Authority', p. 96.
116. Cynthia B Herrup, 'Law and Morality in Seventeenth-Century England', *Past & Present*, 106 (1985), 102–123 cited in Howard, 'Crime, Communities and Authority', pp. 102–123 (p. 97).
117. See: Part 5, 'Femicide and Travesties of Justice': Jill Radford, 'Retrospect on a Trial', pp. 227–232; Lucy Bland, 'The Case of the Yorkshire Ripper: Mad, Bad, Beast, or Male?' pp. 233–252; Radford, 'Womanslaughter: A License to Kill? The Killing of Jane Asher', pp. 253–266; Lees, 'Naggers, Whores, and Libbers', pp. 267–288; Russell, 'Fay Stender and the Politics of Murder', pp. 289–302, in *Femicide*, ed. by Radford and Russell.
118. Carolyn Strange, 'Masculinities, Intimate Femicide and the Death Penalty in Australia, 1890–1920', *The British Journal of Criminology*, 43 (2003), 310–339. For a recent example of the neglect of marginalised women by a criminal justice system see Jason Gratl, ' "Wouldn't Piss on Them If They Were on Fire" How Discrimination Against Sex Workers, Drug Users and Aboriginal Women Enabled a Serial Killer' (Report of Independent Counsel to the Commissioner of the Missing Women Commission of Inquiry, 2012).

119. Mark Jackson, 'Infant Deaths: The Statues of 1624 and Medical Evidence at Coroners' Inquests', in *Legal Medicine in History*, ed. by Michael Clark and Catherine Crawford (Cambridge: Cambridge University Press, 1994), p. 74; Wrightson, 'Infanticide in Earlier Seventeenth-Century England', p. 17; Allyson N May, 'She at First Denied It: Infanticide Trials at the Old Bailey', in *Women and History: Voices of Early Modern England*, ed. by Valerie Frith (Concord: Irwin, 1997), pp. 19–49 (p. 23).
120. Casper and Moore, *Missing Bodies*, p. 21.
121. Evans, *Unfortunate Objects*, p. 46.
122. Evans, *Unfortunate Objects*, p. 25.
123. PCA (Meifod) M/EP/41/V/VM/1 (1758).
124. PCA (Meifod) M/EP/41/W/AC/4 (1769).
125. Evans, *Unfortunate Objects*, p. 131; Crawford, *Blood, Bodies and Families*, p. 130.
126. NLW *Edwinsford Estate Records*, Probate of the Will of James Thomas Late of the Parish of Talley, Co. Carmarthen, Deceased, Edwinsford Estate Records (1662).
127. PCA (Castell Caereinion) M/EP/7/O/RT/2 (1773–1775).
128. PCA (Berriew) M/EP/3/V/VM/4 (1792).

Part III
The Experience of Pregnancy and Childbirth for Unmarried Mothers

5 Reading and Regulating Reproductive Bodies

This examinant sayth that she often heard that Catherine Roberts of Abergele aforeseaid was great with child in the last Christmas Holydays and that she told her about the same time, that the first time her menses appeared was about the time her father dyed, which was about October 1733. And that she had not seen them since, to the time she spoke to her.

Notwithstanding this the said Catherine Roberts own'd at another time to this examinant that some little time before the last Christmas being with child she miscarried at [Llanrwst] and buried the embryo in a garden there. This examinant further deposeth, that her mother confronted her at a certain merry night when company was merrily disposed at her house that her daughter slipt out of company, and was found by her in the cellar indisposed, where upon she asked her the reason of her indisposition, and she replied that she had reason rather to be merry in hopes of enjoying her health better hearafter, because she was freed from the occasion of it, and then took up her petticoats to show her some bloody symptoms upon her shift.[1]

The examinant in this deposition was Mary Williams, a widow and practising midwife, who in March 1736 provided evidence to a justice of the peace for the county of Denbighshire regarding the murder of an infant whose body was found in a local pond. Catherine Roberts was the young single woman who stood accused of concealing her pregnancy and delivery, murdering her child and disposing of the body three months earlier. Other witnesses include Catherine's mother, a jury of midwives, churchwardens, neighbours, family members and patrons of the inn run by Catherine's family. Central to each witness narrative was Catherine's reproductive body.

Every witness who provided evidence about Catherine described in some way the physical signs on her body, which they read as different indicators of pregnancy, childbirth, menstrual disorder or miscarriage. Robert Evans, whose relationship to Catherine is not clear, deposed that on Christmas Eve Catherine accompanied him on a journey from Llanrwst back to Abergele some 30 miles away. Catherine was apparently unable to walk quickly, which Robert attributed to her heavily pregnant condition, which he observed himself and had been informed of by others in Llanrwst. Robert stated that he then grabbed Catherine by the neck, choking her, and told her of the rumours he had heard about her and her condition. He then 'made bold to feel her belly, and found the same hard as his own wife's belly used to be when she was with child,' which Catherine denied.[2] Another witness deposed that Catherine's sister had told her that Catherine's menses 'flowed extraordinarily' around the time of Hilarytide (13 January) and that their mother had washed five petticoats within a 24-hour period as a result.[3] Elizabeth Edwards, a patron of the public house run by Catherine's family, testified that around 11 January she witnessed Catherine uncorseted, wearing a loose gown, and 'looking as if she had been in labour.'[4] When asked what ailed her, Catherine replied that she simply had a pain in her eye and in her foot.[5] However, Elizabeth also testified that she too knew of the rumours about Catherine's mother washing out five petticoats over the following days. Catherine's mother deposed that her daughter had never actually been with child, but did have menses that 'flowed something extraordinarily once of late,' the reason for which was a stoppage of her menses, which had caused Catherine's swollen belly.[6] When questioned by neighbours, churchwardens, the local vicar and the justice of the peace, Catherine fervently denied being pregnant. It was only after the body of an infant was found that Catherine was physically examined and 'discovered' by five midwives who all swore she had recently been pregnant and delivered of a full-term child. Only then did Catherine stop denying that she had been with child.[7] She did not, however, confess to the crime of which she was accused. Rather, she told one of the midwives, Mary Smith, as she had told Mary Williams, that she had miscarried around Christmas, and that she had only been 'quarter gone.'[8] Despite officials 'vehemently' suspecting Catherine guilty of the crime, and despite considerable testimony against her, she was found not guilty.[9]

Infanticide trial records from the Court of Great Sessions such as these demonstrate the extent to which women's bodies served as a locus of broader social anxieties about unregulated reproduction in the eighteenth century. By their very nature, legal documents represent acts of regulation, intervention and surveillance, and thus offer vital clues to the social and cultural priorities and perceptions that inform them.[10] Witness depositions, confessions and inquests all reveal diverse interpretations, negotiations and confrontations between uncertainty, secrecy, and authority that are all directly related to early modern understandings of the reproductive body. This chapter explores the complex ways in which the bodies of unmarried women who were suspected of being pregnant, or of having given birth in secrecy, and the infants they were accused of killing, were read, interrogated and regulated by families, communities, authorities and by the women themselves. Any unmarried woman of reproductive age was at risk of bearing a child outside acceptable, normative patriarchal family structures.[11] This posed a significant threat, not only to the established social order, but also to the parish economy. Communities were therefore compelled to maintain the social order by surveying and regulating the bodies which posed the greatest threats. Paradoxically, pregnancy was a highly visible state that was shrouded in mystery. This mystery was rooted in the ambiguities surrounding the identification of pregnancy, which could not be revealed through a single, definitive test, but which was rather discovered gradually, first to the mother through her own physical symptoms, and eventually to those around her.[12] Reading and interpreting these signs, and attempting to either conceal or reveal them offered different means of regulating bodies and mitigating perceived risks.[13] However, the physical symptoms experienced by women, such as the cessation of menses and 'the quickening', could only be interpreted as pregnancy if a woman was equipped with the knowledge, experience, and desire to identify them as such.[14] The physical signs available to most external observers, such as a swollen belly, even at advanced stages, were ambiguous and potentially concealable, thus making single women's bodies dangerous. The mystery and unreadability of female reproduction meant single women's bodies represented a risk of sin, disorder and murder.[15]

By examining the various ways in which the bodies of unmarried women, and the children born to them, were interpreted and interrogated we can better understand the significance and experience of bearing a child outside of wedlock. The previous chapter analysed narratives of fatal violence found in court records as a means of better understanding the social and cultural context which both informed and made sense of crimes such as infanticide. This chapter will examine narratives of pregnant, parturient, and infant bodies found in 39 infanticide trial records between 1730 and 1799, which reveal the ways in which women, their families, communities and authorities attempted to regulate and make sense of reproduction outside of wedlock, its risks, and its consequences.[16] These cases are undeniably exceptional, and the ultimate outcome of these incidents is not representative of the experience of non-marital childbirth in general. However, the narratives and discourses within depositions and inquests are revealing of contemporary social, cultural, medical and legal understandings of reproduction and the body, which played out within complex hierarchical social and legal structures. Many of the negotiations and confrontations described in witness depositions would have been experienced in very similar ways by unmarried women whose pregnancies and deliveries were not concealed.

The ways in which pregnant bodies, parturient bodies and infant bodies were read and regulated will be examined separately. Although each intersects, the nature of interventions and interpretations in each category reveals different aspects of these tensions. Anxieties surrounding deviant, unregulated reproduction meant that unmarried women's bodies were highly visible and open to public scrutiny; however not all single women's bodies were interrogated in the same way. Access to women's bodies, including who had the authority to read and touch them, and how intrusive these interventions could be, was restricted by numerous variables including a woman's age, socioeconomic circumstances and the level of perceived threat that a crime might be committed. If pregnancy was suspected but not confirmed, the level of surveillance would be great, but interventions would be limited. If parturition was suspected, interrogation strategies changed, but the level of intervention did not always increase. At the most extreme, the discovery of an infant body sanctioned much greater degrees of interrogation of women's bodies from a much broader range of individuals. Moreover, murdered or stillborn infants whose births had been concealed also presented authorities with an additional body which could be read for signs of deviant reproduction in entirely different ways. These bodies were the products of, and potentially bore the signs of, sin whilst retaining their own innocence. Surgeons, midwives, neighbours, families and the accused women all had their own ways of reading, interacting with and describing these bodies.

The correlations between reproductive knowledge and the authority to read bodies is an important factor in how women's bodies were read, and by whom. Women's bodies were highly visible, and the suspicion of an illegitimate pregnancy blurred the lines between a woman's private body and broader community priorities.[17] Knowledge and experience authorised access and validated individual interpretations of physical signs, but knowledge and authority were manifest in diverse and complex ways. The ways in which female bodies were read for the signs of pregnancy, both by unmarried pregnant women, and by their families, employers, neighbours and by authorities is revealed in the evidence provided by them in witness depositions and women's own confessions. These depositions and confessions of suspects indicate the extent of unmarried women's knowledge about their reproductive bodies—although they may be shaped by women's perception of the acceptable limits of such knowledge. Similarly, witness depositions reveal complex and often fraught hierarchies of knowledge about reproduction, and authority to access, read and diagnose the bodies of women suspected of being pregnant. The ways in which the signs of labour and delivery were read on the bodies of women suspected of delivering a child in secrecy reveal significant differences between witnesses according to both gender and social status. Depositions reveal diverse and intriguing ways of interpreting and describing the evidence of parturition which reflect conflicting accounts of experiences, different hierarchies of medical knowledge and understandings of reproduction. Evidence in these narratives demonstrates just how equivocal certain physical signs of childbirth could be. Although many of the explanations and descriptions seem implausible to a modern reader, these narratives were within the realm of possibility to eighteenth-century minds: these experiences were all phenomena that could, and did, happen.[18] Finally, the different ways that mothers, families, neighbours and authorities read the bodies of infants who were either stillborn or murdered and then disposed of reveal yet other kinds of knowledge and assumptions that were interpreted as indicative of innocence or guilt. Whereas women's bodies were read for signs of deviance, infant bodies were read for evidence of healthy gestation and parturition as well as malicious intent. Differing interpretations of infant bodies reveal not only diverse types of authority over and knowledge about reproduction, but also the underlying uncertainties and precariousness of pregnancy and childbirth in early modern Britain.

Sexual Knowledge and Authority

Central to the ways in which the bodies of women and infants were read was knowledge about reproduction and childbirth, and with such knowledge came the authority to access, interrogate and diagnose. Most people living in early modern Wales would have been exposed to the 'facts of life' to at least some degree.[19] The majority of the population lived in small homes in nucleated, rural communities with limited privacy and surrounded by breeding farm animals. Witnessing copulation and birth would have been a common experience in these circumstances.[20] However, peripheral exposure to these lifecycle events did not necessarily provide in-depth understandings of the processes involved. Sexual knowledge was ultimately restricted to those deemed worthy and able enough by society to safeguard and administer it responsibly. Reproductive knowledge was acquired either through the knowledge and experience shared by matrons and midwives in the woman-only space of the birthing chamber, or through the education and experience obtained by male medical practitioners.[21] Specialist knowledge gave midwives and surgeons official, and often legally sanctioned, authority to access and read the bodies of single women and infants, but in very different ways. Married women's access to reproductive knowledge was not as specialised or extensive as midwives', but it nonetheless imbued them with legally recognised authority to interrogate single women's bodies which was drawn from their own experiences of conception, pregnancy and childbirth. Although husbands and fathers typically did not witness or participate in the births of their children, married men were still exposed to pregnancy and childbirth through the experiences of their wives. Such observation gave many married men the ability to read and identify common signs of pregnancy and childbirth.[22] However, young, unmarried people were largely excluded from these situations, which meant most only came across fragments of reproductive knowledge, either by chance or through conversations with peers.[23] The consequence of such inexperience meant that many young, unmarried pregnant women were not only ill-equipped to decipher their symptoms, but were also denied personal autonomy over their own bodies, and were thus exposed to the physical authority of their community.[24]

Reproductive knowledge directly influenced who had authority to access and interrogate deviant bodies, and those with the greatest knowledge had the greatest authority. However, intimate access to the bodies of women suspected of having committed infanticide, and the bodies of their infants, was complicated by the conflicting priorities of sexual propriety and public interest.[25] This meant that different 'experts' accessed the bodies of women and infants in different ways. The most marked differences were in the ways female midwives and medical men interacted with women's bodies, which at times resulted in conflicting conclusions. For example, in Flintshire in 1797, Margaret Jones, who stood accused of murdering her infant, was examined separately by a surgeon named Mr Hughes and a midwife named Catherine Owen. Mr Hughes concluded that Margaret had not been delivered of a child, but Catherine Owen determined that she had.[26] Although both the surgeon and the midwife examined Margaret, they did not necessarily examine her in the same ways. Examinations were not always physical searches of the body, and were often verbal interrogations performed under oath. The methods of examination employed by the surgeon and the midwife in this case are not described in their respective depositions, but following the midwife's examination, Margaret confessed to having been delivered of a stillborn infant. It is likely that the midwife's examination was far more intimate and physically intrusive than the surgeon's, and thus revealed more conclusive evidence of childbirth, which Margaret was unable to deny. Margaret was indicted and tried for the crime, but was found not guilty. Although midwives and surgeons did not always disagree in their assessments of women's bodies, this case serves to illustrate the deeply gendered patterns of access to women's bodies found in infanticide records.[27]

Overall, the evidence from the Court of Great Sessions suggests that surgeons and man-midwives seldom utilised their medical authority to examine intimately the bodies of unmarried women. Male practitioners were occasionally called upon to examine the bodies of women and to provide expert opinions about the signs of childbirth, but this was exceedingly rare. Rarer still were expert male examinations of the bodies of women who were suspected of being pregnant. In 1759 William Taylor was asked by the justices of the peace in Flintshire to examine the breasts of Mary Davies, who was suspected of abandoning her infant in a ditch. In 1774 William Lloyd and Raleigh Colborne were similarly ordered by justices of the peace in Denbighshire to examine Elizabeth Bellis for signs of childbirth.[28] In 1794 William Williams and John Williams, both surgeons and man-midwives in Cardiganshire examined Sarah David's body and determined she had 'lately been delivered of a child.'[29] These are three of only a handful of instances where male practitioners physically examined women's bodies. Such access was only permissible because of the authority of the medical gaze, which throughout the eighteenth century in Wales remained subordinate to the authority of experienced female knowledge in the examination of infanticide suspects. As childbirth became increasingly medicalised and the influence of man-midwives grew in the latter half of the eighteenth century we might expect that cases in which male medical practitioners examined women's bodies would occur with increasing frequency. Mark Jackson in his study of Northern Circuit Assizes, and Sheena Sommers in her study of Old Bailey Proceedings, have both identified a shift from female midwives to male medical practitioners as the voices of authority in infanticide trials.[30] However, Welsh records do not reflect a similar shift in authority over unmarried women's bodies. Throughout the century, the intimate interrogation of single women's bodies remained almost exclusively the remit of female midwives and matrons. The jury of midwives who examined Catherine Roberts's body is just one of many examples of this continuing practice. Moreover, there is evidence that male medical practitioners could, at times, rely on female midwives because of their unique female authority. In 1799, Carmarthenshire surgeon William Jones was summoned by Hannah John's parents to determine if she had delivered a child. However, William, 'objected to go without having one Margaret Williams, a midwife' accompany him.[31] It is impossible to know if his objection was because he felt it necessary to have additional specialist witnesses present, or because of a desire to maintain respectability and sexual modesty, but this does suggest that female midwives in Wales retained a distinctive type of gender-based authority over reproductive knowledge to at least some degree. In other cases where female midwives and male surgeons gave evidence, midwives often examined suspected mothers, and surgeons examined infant bodies. In Flintshire in 1789 midwife Mary Tattum examined the body of Eleanor Jones to determine if she had recently been in labour, while surgeon William Denman examined the body of her suspected child for signs of violence that could have caused his death.[32] This gendered division of expertise is further epitomised in the 1765 infanticide trial of Elizabeth Williams, where surgeons and man-midwives John Kerry and Honoratus Leigh Thomas examined the body of Elizabeth's child, but the examination of Elizabeth's body was performed by Alice Kerry, who was John's wife.[33] Therefore, in 1784 when several neighbours urged Mary Owen's parents to have her examined by a 'proper person' to have her cleared of the suspicion that she was pregnant, that proper person was likely to have been a midwife.[34] The professional relationship between female midwives and male medical practitioners will be explored further in the next chapter.

Where Welsh records do reveal an increase in the involvement of male medical practitioners was in the examination of infant bodies. Both male and female practitioners were called upon to examine the bodies of infants to determine whether a child had been stillborn or had been born alive and succumbed to an act of perinatal or postnatal violence. The depositions of expert witnesses who examined infant bodies were frequently framed in terms of their experience and knowledge, such as Dorothy ferch Edwards, who in 1739 could say with certainty because she had been a midwife for 54 years that the infant Jane Griffith stood accused of murdering was born alive.[35] Similarly, in 1734 the surgeon Edward Neals, determined that the child Jane Williams was accused of killing, 'was born alive according to the best of [his] experience and knowledge.'[36] However, female midwives' and male surgeons' access to infant bodies was significantly different. Male medical practitioners, such as surgeons, apothecaries and man-midwives, were granted greater authority to interrogate the bodies of infants in more intrusive, anatomical and scientific ways, especially in the later decades of the eighteenth century.[37] Their expertise in this regard was not so much associated with reproductive knowledge, but with contemporary medical knowledge. Such knowledge granted male medical practitioners authority to examine the bodies of infants both externally and internally. As with English infanticide trial records, increases in the number of dissections are apparent in Welsh records from the 1750s onwards.[38] The earliest example of this was in Brecon in 1755, when an infant body was retrieved from a bog house, cleaned by two matrons, and then turned over to an apothecary named George Williams. Williams opened the chest cavity, removed the lungs and placed them in a pail of water.[39] Lung tests, such as this, were used to determine if a child was born alive or dead. It was believed that if a child had taken a breath the lungs would have filled with oxygen, thus making the lung tissue float. Lungs that had never taken air were believed to sink, thus proving the child had been stillborn.[40] Similar examples increase in frequency in the last three decades of the century. In 1776 Chester-based surgeon David Parry examined the lungs of an infant suspected of having been murdered.[41] In 1789 surgeon Richard Lloyd was called by the coroner to dissect an infant and its placenta, the latter of which he preserved in a quart of brandy.[42] In 1796 surgeon Thomas Simon examined the lungs, windpipe and brain of an infant believed to have been murdered.[43] Male medical practitioners such as these were granted access to anatomise infants' bodies only because of their specialist knowledge and medical authority. Female midwives, whose expertise came not from medical training but from experiences in the birthing room, were never involved in the dissections of infant bodies. Rather, their authority lay in their ability to identify and interpret external signs of premature births, stillbirths, full-term healthy births and postnatal violence.

Authority to read and interrogate unmarried women's bodies was not limited to those who possessed formal medical knowledge. Many others could—and did—claim authority to read women's bodies, and even demanded access to them.[44] Such access was justified by an individual's own personal experiences of pregnancy and birth. Marital status provided sufficient authority for neighbours to interrogate the bodies of unmarried women when suspicion of a concealed pregnancy or childbirth had been raised.[45] The policing of women's bodies in this way was almost exclusively the remit of women.[46] However, men also knew the outward signs of pregnancy. Robert Evans, who physically constrained and forcefully touched Catherine Roberts's belly, is one of the more extreme examples of this. His implicit justification for his actions was his prior experience of seeing and touching his wife's pregnant body. However, in Wales as in England, men rarely claimed authority over unmarried women's bodies, and physical confrontations and searches instigated by men were not common.[47] It was much more common for married women to intervene, and their readings of unmarried women's bodies were based on their own personal experience of pregnancy and childbirth within marriage. Women played an essential role in maintaining the patriarchal order of society, which involved interventions to expose and monitor childbirth out of wedlock. For example, in 1755, Rachel Lewis, a married woman, deposed that she had confronted Mary Harris, who was accused of murdering her infant son, and told her 'was in the same state as she had been in when she had been delivered of a child.'[48] Rachel's authority to examine and interpret Mary's body was defined by her status as both lawful wife and mother.[49] In 1768 a surgeon named Anthony Poole accompanied two matrons to the home of Margaret Jenkin so the matrons could examine Margaret's breasts on his behalf.[50] Women's authority in all of these cases was based on marital status, and is replicated across Welsh infanticide records. All the women who interrogated the bodies of unmarried suspects were themselves either married or widowed. Adrian Wilson has gone so far as to suggest that the role of matrons in assessing pregnant women's bodies was more essential than that of midwives, and that midwives only played a minor part.[51] However Welsh records do not necessarily support this hypothesis. As authorities on reading the signs of pregnancy, both midwives and matrons were central to infanticide investigations. Ultimately, all women who were in possession of legitimately acquired reproductive knowledge could exercise their authority and interrogate the bodies of unmarried women.

Unmarried women who were suspected of being pregnant, or of having given birth secretly to a child, were thus subjected to acts of surveillance and confrontation from their community. As Laura Gowing has argued, the state of pregnancy, or suspected pregnancy, reinforced single women's subordination to the physical authority of their community.[52] However, even within this rigid social code some single women were still able to retain some agency over their bodies. Older women and those with more socioeconomic independence were less subjected to physical confrontation than younger single women, or single women who lived with their families or employers.[53] Margaret Jenkin, whose examination by two matrons was observed by a surgeon, was widely suspected of being pregnant, but, despite their suspicions, most witnesses reported that they did not confront her until after the body of an infant had been found. Mary, her landlord's wife, deposed that she checked on Margaret several times over the course of the week when she was suspected of having delivered, observing that she seemed unwell, at one point found her as she undressed for bed.[54] Mary also observed some blood on Margaret's bed sheets, but did not enquire about it, nor did she confront Margaret about the possibility that she may have been in labour or recently delivered of a child. Mary's surveillance seems somewhat intrusive, but, by the standards of early modern communities, it could be interpreted as neighbourly care for a sick member of the community.[55] Margaret was surveilled by her community but from a distance. At no point during Margaret's suspected pregnancy or delivery did any of her neighbours interrogate her or touch her body. Trial records do not reveal Margaret's age, but several deponents described her as living alone in a small one-room house adjacent to her landlord's property. This may have given Margaret enough independence to ward off physically intrusive confrontations. Even if neighbours did not actively confront suspects, their depositions reveal that they were closely monitoring single women's bodies for signs of pregnancy. Numerous witnesses deposed that they had observed either a change in physical appearance, which motivated them to pay close attention over the following weeks and months, or they had been informed through neighbourhood gossip that a single woman was rumoured to be pregnant, and thus took more notice of her.[56]

However, Catherine Roberts was subjected to physical interrogation. As with Margaret Jenkin, Catherine's age was not given, but details in witness depositions suggest she was relatively young. Mary Williams, whose deposition opened this chapter, stated that Catherine had experienced menarche two and a half years previously, and other deponents mention her grandmother, who was still alive.[57] This evidence helps to place Catherine's age as under 20 years.[58] Catherine's youth may have been a contributing factor in Robert Evans's physical confrontation of her. However, with the help of her mother, Catherine retained a certain amount of authority over her own pregnant body. Two churchwardens deposed that they were sent to find out from Catherine who was the father of her child. Not only did Catherine refuse to disclose a name, she also refused to admit she was pregnant, and went so far as to threaten 'a lawsuit against any person who defamed her,' which was enough to dissuade further interrogation.[59] Catherine's ability to assert herself in such a way was bolstered by her mother's own authority as a matron herself. Single women's authority, or their lack thereof, was not based on access to reproductive knowledge, but on their precarious, subordinate position within the patriarchal order.[60] However, single women's reproductive knowledge was central to the ways in which they read, understood and accounted for the signs of pregnancy on their own bodies, which often differed considerably to the ways in which families, neighbours and authorities read pregnant bodies.

Reading the Signs of Pregnancy

Pregnancy in the early modern period was notoriously difficult to detect. Even for experienced midwives, surgeons and mothers who bore multiple children, the signs of pregnancy could be uncertain.[61] Common signs, such as the cessation of menses or changes in bodily appearance could be interpreted as numerous other medical ailments or conditions.[62] This was especially true for young, single women who may have lacked the knowledge or experience to recognise many of the signs of conception. Authors of midwifery manuals, such as Jane Sharp, noted that, 'young women especially of their first child are so ignorant commonly, that they cannot tell whether they have conceived or not.'[63] Although some of the Welsh women who stood accused of murdering their infants were older, married or widowed, a significant portion were younger and had never been married.[64] Within consummate marriage, pregnancy would have been anticipated, and thus married women would have actively looked out for the signs of pregnancy on their bodies. However, many unmarried pregnant women would have been ignorant, or afraid of, any changes that may have indicated they had conceived, and therefore their pregnancies could be journeys of denial.[65] Not all unmarried pregnant women denied their pregnancies entirely, as is evident in the many voluntary examinations of single women found in bastardy bonds. Unfortunately, we know very little about how these women experienced and interpreted their pregnancies because such details were never recorded. However, because the ultimate consequence of denying pregnancy was the unlawful loss of a child's life, which often resulted in the production of detailed legal records, we do have accounts of the ways in which some single women read and made sense of their pregnant bodies.[66]

The voices of women who were accused of concealing their pregnancies are captured, to at least some degree, in the sworn confessions and second-hand witness depositions given to justices of the peace as part of the pre-trial process. As discussed previously, these third-person accounts are not without their problems, which include the mitigating processes of translation and transcription, which inevitably altered and edited statements to some degree. However, even if not verbatim accounts, these narratives are still revealing of widely held beliefs surrounding women's knowledge about their own reproductive bodies. As such, included here are not only women's own depositions and confessions, but also the accounts of conversations accused women had with other witnesses, as these too reflect the limited ways in which unmarried women were expected to know and discuss their reproductive bodies. However, simply because a woman displayed a lack of knowledge about her body does not necessarily mean she was entirely ignorant of her pregnancy, as ignorance could just as easily have been deployed as a defence strategy. Narratives in which women did not recognise the signs of pregnancy could have been constructed in their defence based on cultural assumptions about what sexual and reproductive knowledge unmarried women should have.[67] It is impossible to know if these women's narratives reflect real or feigned ignorance of reproductive processes. What these legal records do reveal are the types of sexual knowledge unmarried women could have. Moreover, the various alternative explanations they give for their symptoms and experiences are reflective of popular understandings of the female body more broadly. Female defendants were able to employ these descriptions because, to eighteenth-century minds, these were all plausible phenomena.[68]

One of the first and most widely acknowledged signs of pregnancy is the cessation of menses. For centuries menses were recognised as essential to women's reproductive health, and menarche represented the beginning of a woman's fertile years.[69] However, historians are divided over the significance of the cessation of menses as an indicator of pregnancy in early modern Britain. Using evidence from medical textbooks, Patricia Crawford has argued that early modern women viewed the cessation of menses as the most usual sign of pregnancy.[70] Sara Read has also suggested that missed periods were regularly recognised as a sign of potential pregnancy.[71] However, both Laura Gowing and Lisa Forman Cody have brought into question the importance of menses as confirmation of conception. By taking into consideration factors such as malnutrition, which may lead to irregular menstruation or amenorrhoea, Gowing has argued that the absence of menses was likely not the first sign of pregnancy for many women.[72] Furthermore, Cody has suggested that amenorrhoea was one of the last scrutable signs of pregnancy in the early modern period.[73] As Mark Jackson, Daniel Grey and numerous other historians including Gowing and Cody have demonstrated, the cessation of menses was likely to have been one of many potential symptoms of pregnancy, which also included a swollen belly or breasts, food cravings, nausea, vomiting, back pain and weight gain.[74] These same symptoms were also common indicators of other early modern reproductive ailments, such as the 'green sickness' or 'white fever', which Jane Sharp described as 'most common in maids of ripe years when they are in love and desirous to keep company with a man,' the symptoms of which were 'stoppage of the terms, headache, disgust and loathing of good nutriment . . . swelling of the legs, belly and vomit.'[75] The presence or absence of menses was therefore as much an indicator of overall female health as it was a signifier of pregnancy.[76]

Given the inherent inconclusiveness of what the absence of menstruation meant, it is not surprising that evidence of menses is only infrequently cited in discussions about women's reproductive bodies in Welsh infanticide records. Of the 39 cases considered here, menstruation was only mentioned by witnesses in five cases, and was only central to the narrative in one case. The first and most significant reference to menses as evidence was in Catherine Roberts's 1736 trial in which Mary Williams, the midwife, discussed the timing of Catherine's menarche, followed by the cessation of her menses, and their sudden, unusually heavy, reappearance.[77] According to Mary, Catherine interpreted this heavy bleeding as a welcome indication that she had been 'freed' of a complaint that had been causing her ill health.[78] Catherine's mother described her daughter's ailment as a menstrual stoppage, which, when it cleared, caused her menses to flow, 'something extraordinarily.'[79] We cannot know if Catherine and her mother genuinely believed that her menstrual irregularities were caused by blockage, or if they were intentionally passing Catherine's symptoms of pregnancy and labour off as a menstrual disturbance.[80] What is significant is that eighteenth-century understandings of the female reproductive body offered a plausible alternative explanation for Catherine's symptoms, and this cast doubt on the allegations that she had possibly been pregnant. Two other cases refer to the absence of menses as evidence of a menstrual disorder. In 1756 Margaret Lewis had told her mistress that the reason she appeared ill was because her 'monthly courses' did not flow regularly, and later informed her that she was 'much better after her natural courses were broken.'[81] In 1774 Margaret, the mother of Elizabeth Bellis, deposed that her daughter's menses had ceased 12 months earlier, but attributed the cause of this to a cold that Elizabeth had caught at that time.[82]

In the remaining cases where menstruation was mentioned, it accounted for the discovery of large amounts of blood. In 1732, when Mary Williams discovered blood on the floor of Elizabeth Morris's bedchamber, Elizabeth explained that she had experienced the same phenomena two months earlier, which Mary 'took to be that the custom of woman was upon her after a violent manner.'[83] In 1789, when accused of having delivered a child secretly in her bed, Anne John replied that 'she was not guilt[y] of the charge laid against her for she was not nor had not been then lately with child, but that she was only afflicted with the monthly complaint of women.'[84] Other than these cases, none of the other female suspects provided defences or gave confessions which included descriptions of their menses. Moreover, as depositions may represent answers recorded in response to specific questions asked by justices of the peace, it is highly likely that, in addition to not offering information about menstruation as evidence, women were not asked about the presence or absence of their menses either.[85] Therefore, the dearth of evidence relating to menstruation may reflect its perceived limited significance more broadly.[86] The cessation of menses was certainly one of many possible signs of pregnancy which women could read and interpret, but Welsh records demonstrate that it was by no means the most important.

A more commonly recognised confirmation of pregnancy in early modern Britain was the quickening. Occurring roughly between the fourth and fifth months of gestation, this was the point at which a woman felt the foetus move within her for the first time, and was understood to occur at the moment when an infant was imbued with a soul, and thus became a live human being.[87] This immensely significant event was readable only to the mother, and as such contributed to anxieties about the uncertainty of identifying pregnancy, especially in unmarried women.[88] In order to recognise the quickening a woman would have to be open to the possibility that she might be pregnant, and therefore be willing to acknowledge it. For women who did not want to be pregnant, such a discrete symptom could be ignored or misinterpreted.[89] The quickening was more than simply an important gestational milestone for pregnant women, as it carried crucial legal significance as well. Harm caused to a foetus after the quickening could carry similar legal ramifications as causing harm to a child.[90] Many court records describe heavily pregnant women as being 'quick with child', such as Sarah Lumley, who in 1742 was in labour with a 'quick child' when she was allegedly attacked by Richard Pryce in the parish of Berriew, Montgomeryshire.[91] The onset of foetal movement signified the beginning of an infant's life, and movement continued to represent foetal development and health. Therefore, if movement ceased, it was commonly believed that the infant had died in the womb. As will be explored more later, determining if a child was born alive was central to the examination of infant bodies, but it was also central in some women's defences.

Many of the Welsh women accused of murdering their infants assiduously denied having been pregnant at all, and therefore the discussion of infant movement in the womb would be out of place in their legal examinations. However, in the few cases where the quickening was mentioned it was always in the form of accused women describing *in utero* foetal death and stillbirth. As a sign that was only revealed to a pregnant woman the quickening gave single women a means of accounting for the crime they were accused of committing which was difficult for legal and medical authorities to challenge conclusively. Only a pregnant woman could know when her infant started moving, and only she could know if and when it stopped. The most detailed example of foetal movement used in a woman's defence was in the trial of Jane Griffith, whose case was discussed briefly in the previous chapter. In 1739, Jane was accused of murdering her infant son immediately after delivering him, and hiding his body in a cheese vat in her pantry.[92] Jane deposed that she had been 'frightened by the noise of drums & guns and the other marks of rejoicings . . . on the king's birthday last past which caused her to have pains from the child in her womb.'[93] These pains continued until she delivered a stillborn child. She further deposed that she did not seek assistance from a midwife or from neighbours because she did not believe she was near the time of her delivery. A witness named Ellen deposed that Jane had visited her house the following day, and noticing Jane in pain, asked if she was in labour. Jane replied that she was not, and told Ellen the child had been delivered the previous day and had been born dead. Ellen asked Jane when she had last felt her child move in her, 'and know it quick,' to which Jane replied that it was on the King's birthday, but 'had not perceived the said child alive within her since she had heard the bash of a drum on the king's birthday then last past.'[94] Having previously felt her child move within her, Jane could pinpoint the moment he stopped moving, and correlate it with a plausible cause of his death, which eliminated her culpability.

Jane's defence was constructed around the common, long-held belief that foetuses were incredibly vulnerable to external stimuli and maternal distress, so that loud, sudden noises that startled the mother could fatally harm the infant she was carrying. Ideas such as this can be traced at least as far back as Ambroise Paré in the sixteenth century. According to Paré, 'thundering, the noise of the shooting of great ordnance, the sound, and vehement noise of the ringing Bells constrain women to fall into travail before their time.'[95] Seventy years prior to Jane's trial, Jane Sharp had written that loud noises such as thunder could cause spontaneous miscarriage.[96] In 1718 a similar defence had been successfully used in London by an accused single woman named Francis Bolanson, who testified that she had been frightened by thunder and lightning, which caused her to miscarry.[97] Single women also attributed the loss of foetal movement to illness, accidents and sudden physical injuries as well. In 1788 Elizabeth Williams, whose mistress found her infant's body hidden in her bed, explained that 'she had not found the child move after she met an accident in the lower kitchen.'[98] In 1789 Anne John told Sabaoth, the father of her child, that she had felt it quick, but that, 'in trying to raise a load of firewood on her shoulder the load slipped on her belly and gave her some pain, that she did not find the child alive ever since that.'[99] In 1795 Ann Parry confessed to delivering a stillborn, which she believed had died in the womb, 'owing to a fall she had by bringing a bunch of wood.'[100] In the same year a servant named Elizabeth Jones was found in her bed with the body of her infant lying dead in the bedclothes with her. Her mistress called for female neighbours to attend and assess the scene. One neighbour asked Elizabeth why she had not called for assistance, and also enquired about whether the child was born alive, and if she 'had done something wrong to it.'[101] Elizabeth replied that she had not, 'for I have felt no life in it since I had a fall upon the ice which happened to me six weeks ago.'[102] In 1799 Hannah John told the servant who found her infant's body stuffed in a feather-filled bag that, 'she felt the child alive some time back, but some time afterwards she . . . though[t] that she was not with child, but something else caused her illness.'[103]

All these women had recognised the signs of pregnancy on their own bodies, which were confirmed for them by the movement of their infants in their wombs. However, they all also denied being pregnant right up until the discovery of their infant's dead body. Elizabeth's mistress deposed that on the morning of her delivery, Elizabeth had told her she had hit her head, which was the reason she had not attended to her duties or come when beckoned.[104] Jane's neighbour Ellen deposed that Jane told her she kept her pregnancy a secret for fear of being hanged should the child be stillborn.[105] However, after their infants' bodies were found in their possession, these women used defences which were dependent not only upon them acknowledging they had been pregnant, but were contingent upon them having the knowledge to be able to correctly identify the quickening and its subsequent absence. Ultimately, these defences were difficult, if not impossible, to contest: with the exception of one case where the records have not survived, all of the women were either never indicted, or were found not guilty.[106]

Menstrual changes and foetal movements were unlikely to elicit much response from all but those closest to a pregnant single woman. In most cases, when a woman was confronted about suspicions she was pregnant it was because those around her observed significant changes on her body, which will be discussed in more detail later. By the time such changes were noticeable to others, a woman was likely to be in the later stages of pregnancy and nearing her time of delivery. Throughout the duration of her pregnancy, a single woman would experience many bodily changes and feelings which she would have understood in various ways based on her own understandings of reproduction and the strength of her conviction as to whether or not she was pregnant. Most of these experiences would have been private reflections, or intimate discussions with trusted friends and family, and therefore have left no historical trace. Infanticide court records only reveal the ways in which single women read and accounted for the most obvious, outwardly visible signs of advanced pregnancy and the onset of labour, which were larger than normal bellies and symptoms of physical distress.

General physical ailments, such as those affecting the bowels, stomach, womb, breasts, joints and head, were the most common alternative explanations given by unmarried women who were suspected of being pregnant to account for observable symptoms of pregnancy and labour. Common complaints affecting the stomach, such as colic or gripes, or systemic ailments such as ague, were potentially plausible alternatives to women's labour pains.[107] In 1765 Elizabeth Williams's fellow servant and bedmate, Ann, deposed that one night as they lay in bed Elizabeth complained to her of being restless and 'troubled with the gripes.'[108] Elizabeth was accused of strangling her newborn daughter. In 1774 Jannet John told her fellow servant and bedmate that she was feeling better, and when 'asked what her complaint was . . . she sayd it was the ague.'[109] She was also accused of strangling her infant daughter. In 1793 surgeon Richard Baxter of Berriew was called on by Margaret Evans who complained of an inflammation of the bowels brought on by gamboge extract (a purgative and abortifacient believed to 'excite pelvic circulation') which he had sent to her the previous day.[110] Margaret had previously complained to a married neighbour, also named Margaret, about a discomfort in her breast, which she believed was caused by sleeping in a damp bed.[111] The married Margaret recommended the single Margaret take gamboge to help cure her breast.[112] Richard Baxter deposed that, if Margaret had been pregnant, the gamboge may have induced an abortion.[113] As a result, when questioned about her labour pains and the death of her infant, Margaret had recourse to multiple physical complaints which were known to other members of her community. Single women also explained their symptoms of pregnancy and labour in terms of broader bodily ailments, such as gout or 'rheumatick pains.'[114] As we have already seen, Elizabeth Jones attempted to excuse her absence from her duties by claiming she had hit her head.[115] Catherine Roberts told a suspicious guest at her family's inn that she was simply suffering from a pain in her eye and in her foot.[116] When Mary, the wife of her landlord, found Margaret Jenkin in bed and asked her what the matter was, Margaret replied that she was suffering from 'a pain in her limbs.'[117] How convinced neighbours were of these alternative explanations is debatable, especially in the face of other evidence, such as the discovery of blood or the body of dead infant. Some witnesses were unequivocal in their scepticism in suspects' stories. In 1734 Margaret Davies deposed that she had seen Jane Williams, who appeared heavily pregnant, moving about the community under the 'pretence' of her being sick with a distemper.[118] In 1756 Jennet John deposed that she believed Gwenllian David was 'very big and like a woman near her time of delivery.'[119] Not long after, Jennet observed that Gwenllian appeared much smaller, which Gwenllian explained as because 'a disorder or swelling she had in her belly was gone off.'[120] However Jennet deposed that she firmly believed Gwenllian had been pregnant. Ultimately, all these single women eventually ended up in front of magistrates accused of murdering their infants, and therefore their personal accounts had done little to allay neighbourly suspicions.

Alternative explanations for the observable signs of pregnancy and labour on unmarried women's bodies may have been knowingly contrived by suspects as defences, but it cannot be assumed that all such descriptions were wilfully deceitful.[121] Laura Gowing has noted that infanticide cases across Europe feature pregnant single women who, like their friends, insisted they had not known they were pregnant, and who had confused their symptoms with other common ailments.[122] It is fully plausible that single women who knew very little about reproduction were unable to correctly identify their bodily changes. So it is possible that Jane Williams was telling the truth in 1746 when she swore 'that she found herself out of order . . . but did not then imagine herself to be with child nor did [she] at any time since believe or confess to any person or persons whatsoever that she was with child, but saith that she found herself sick . . . with a gripeing pain in her womb.'[123] Likewise, when Elizabeth Morris swore in 1732 that she did not know 'the occasion of her disorder of her being sick with the throws of pains of labour of childbirth but that her distemper must have been occasioned by cold or by her labouring hard in the cold country,' she could have genuinely not realised she was pregnant and in labour.[124] If unmarried women were excluded from the reproductive knowledge which would have enabled them to identify the signs of pregnancy within their own bodies they may have known very little about what pregnancy actually felt like.[125] In the eighteenth century, women were presumed to be the best judges of their own pregnant body, and the experience of pregnancy was thus entirely subjective.[126] If a woman was not equipped with the knowledge to decipher accurately the signs of pregnancy in and on her body, she could easily get it wrong. Symptoms which married pregnant women may have read as normal female processes may just as easily have been read by unmarried women as symptoms of disease.[127]

Despite the inherent ambiguities of the pregnant body, the one sign of pregnancy which ultimately made pregnant bodies highly visible and open to public scrutiny were swollen bellies.[128] In both England and Wales, the single most commonly observed feature of single women's bodies described in infanticide court records were their bellies.[129] Slowly growing bellies were often the first indicator for a community that a woman might be pregnant, and as soon as suspicion was raised, a single woman's stomach became the focus of neighbourly surveillance. In the overwhelming majority of cases, if a witness discussed the physical appearance of a woman they suspected of being pregnant, they described the size of her stomach. However, once a swollen belly was noticed, the responses of neighbours could vary. Rumours that a single woman might be pregnant would cause neighbours to pay closer attention to her shape. In 1759 a fellow lodger reported that Mary Davies appeared to have a noticeably big belly and was 'seemingly with child.'[130] A husband and wife who lived near Elizabeth Bellis deposed in 1774 that, 'of late she had the appearance of being big with child and it was generally reported that she was.'[131] In Cardiganshire in 1776 Jane Brewster deposed that her household and community suspected her fellow servant, Ann Hughes, to be pregnant, and so she took more notice of her as she dressed in the morning and undressed before bed. Jane stated that she 'observed her large about the waste which increased from time to time.'[132] In 1783, Sarah Bithell deposed that rumours had spread that her father's servant, Mary Jones, was pregnant. Sarah believed these rumours to be true because during the short time Mary was in service her waist 'was very big and bulky'.[133] In 1795, neighbours deposed that they began paying closer attention to Margaret Evans's stomach when they heard she might be pregnant, and described her as seeming 'bigger around the waste than usual.'[134] David Evans, a yeoman further deposed that Margaret had lived as a servant under the same roof as him, and that one evening while his family was at dinner some family members began laughing at Margaret. When David enquired as to why, they told him it was because 'there was an alteration in her waste, and . . . after that time he himself thought there was an alteration in her.'[135] In many cases, a swollen stomach would prompt neighbours to question single women, such as Robert Evans who forcefully grabbed Catherine Roberts's belly and challenged her about the rumours of her pregnancy.[136] However, surveillance did not always lead to confrontation, or to confirmation that a woman was indeed pregnant. Margaret Evans was reported to look bigger, but a neighbour named Mary Powell deposed that despite this, she could not tell for certain if Margaret was actually pregnant.[137] Several of Margaret Jenkin's neighbours deposed they believed she was pregnant because of the size of her stomach, but none of those examined by the justices of the peace described questioning Margaret. Furthermore, Margaret's landlord Thomas, and his wife Mary, were both uncertain about how far along Margaret may have been, as Thomas deposed: 'she looke'd pretty big, but not so big . . . as to lye in about three weeks' time.'[138] Mary also 'believed she was then with child, but not very near her time.'[139]

Many women whose bellies aroused suspicion dismissed their appearance by asserting that their bodies had been misread. In 1794 Martha Valentine dismissed Mary Morgan from her service because she refused to acknowledge her pregnancy and swear the identity of the father. Mary instead insisted that her appearance of pregnancy 'arose from the mismanagement of the midwife who had attended her on her delivery of a bastard child about five years before.'[140] When, in 1732, a neighbour asked Elizabeth David, who was accused of abandoning her infant son in a ditch, why her waist looked so big, Elizabeth responded that it was because her coats were wrapped up around her waist.[141] The nature of female dress in the eighteenth century, with multiple layers of skirts and petticoats, allowed pregnant single women more easily to conceal their growing bellies; similar accounts of clothing concealing pregnant bellies can be found in English court records.[142] A contemporary case from London further demonstrates another way in which pregnant women could attempt to justify a large stomach. In 1732 the Old Bailey heard how Hannah Butler, who was accused of murdering her newborn daughter, told her mistress that she was not pregnant but 'only Pot-belly'd, all our Family are Pot-belly'd,—and what a Disgrace it is to be Potbelly'd!'[143] Pregnant single women's increasing waistlines could also be attributed to a range of other physical causes. Catherine Roberts's mother defended her daughter's swollen belly by arguing it had been caused by a menstrual blockage.[144] When Jane Williams was asked in 1734 why she looked so big, she answered that it was because of a 'distemper of her bowels,' which also caused her to not leave her house.[145] It is interesting that none of the women whose swollen bellies raised suspicions claimed they were simply gaining weight. As most were servants or lower status-women, the combination of poor diets and physical labour might have made such claims implausible. However, this could also be because the observed changes were restricted to the women's stomachs, making generalised weight gain an improbable cause.

Just as a woman's swollen belly could denote pregnancy, its rapid reduction in size could signify that childbirth had taken place, and if this change in size did not coincide with the appearance of a mother with her child, such a reduction could be read as a sign of murder. Numerous witnesses deposed observing an accused woman's belly as appearing significantly smaller in a very short period of time. Sarah Bithell deposed that Mary Jones left the house one evening, and the following morning her belly, which had previously seemed 'big and bulky,' appeared much smaller.[146] Jane Brewster deposed that she looked on Ann Hughes with 'great amazement' one morning because she looked so much smaller around the waist than she had the previous night, when she had become ill and left their shared room.[147] Elizabeth Jones, who lived under the same roof as Margaret Evans, deposed that Margaret 'seemed to be in the shape like a woman with child,' and then about a month ago did not appear at home for two or three days, then on her return she seemed smaller.[148] When Mary, the wife of Margaret Jenkin's landlord was examined she deposed that, 'Margaret appears now much smaller than she was the beginning of this month.'[149] Margaret Davies, who was sceptical about Jane Williams's 'distemper,' deposed that she had seen Jane walking to a neighbour's house, and that she had appeared much smaller in size.[150] A sudden reduction in the size of a suspected pregnant woman could provoke a search of her body and of her residence for signs of childbirth. For example, in Carmarthenshire in 1795 several female members of a dissenting meeting house were chastised for not examining Anne Abel, who had been suspected of being pregnant. Hannah David deposed that she and several other female congregants went to Anne and demanded to physically examine her, which Anne refused. However, Hannah further deposed that at that time Anne appeared much smaller in size than she previously had been.[151] Sixty years earlier, in 1735, Anne Stephens was prompted to search the home of a single woman named Hannah Morris after her stomach, which had grown big enough for neighbours to suspect she was pregnant, suddenly became smaller. The subsequent search uncovered a newly born infant's body buried in Hannah's garden.[152] The discovery of an infant's dead body, or the mere suspicion that a secret birth had taken place, compelled neighbours and authorities to search for physical evidence of parturition. Such searches centred primarily on women's bodies.

Reading the Signs of Childbirth

Denial and concealment of pregnancy could raise suspicions and disapproval from a single woman's community because if a woman was capable of hiding her pregnancy, then it was assumed she was also capable of murdering her child.[153] However, as Mark Jackson has argued, concealing pregnancy and childbirth was not a capital offence on its own.[154] Under the 1624 infanticide legislation, it was the concealment of a child's death that was considered an offence, so if a concealed pregnancy and delivery resulted in a living infant, a woman would not be charged with a capital crime. However, if a concealed pregnancy and delivery resulted in a dead infant, the mother was presumed to have killed it.[155] In order to corroborate that a child had died of natural causes in the womb or shortly after birth, a woman needed witnesses, otherwise she could be accused of causing her infant's death. Thus, childbirth needed to be monitored and regulated. Childbirth for both married and unmarried women was a private, physical experience that carried great social significance, and therefore required witnesses.[156] If a community suspected that a woman had secretly given birth but was not then seen with a living newborn infant, it followed that the child had likely died unlawfully, regardless of whether an infant's body had been found. Under such circumstances, neighbours turned to women's bodies to determine if a crime had taken place. Once concealed delivery was suspected the surveillance of single women's bodies and the spaces they occupied intensified significantly.

The signs of childbirth were considerably harder to conceal than the signs of pregnancy. Searches for evidence of concealed childbirth typically focused on bellies, breasts and blood, as well as on a woman's overall health, and, depending on who was reading them, some signs could still be somewhat ambiguous. Numerous witness statements describe women as appearing to be unwell, which was interpreted as the onset of, or recent after-effects of, the strains of labour.[157] In 1730 Elizabeth Powell suspected Gwenllian Powell, who was a widow and daughter-in-law to Elizabeth's master, of being in labour because she appeared unwell. When Elizabeth asked Gwenllian what her ailment was she replied, 'nothing ailed her but a stitch or pain in her side.'[158] In 1734 Elizabeth David told a witness who asked how she was that she had a bellyache.[159] In 1783 Sarah Bithell deposed that Mary Jones not only appeared smaller in the waist the morning after she was suspected of having delivered in private, but also looked 'extremely ill in the face.'[160] Another witness described Mary as looking 'pale and sickly.'[161] Elizabeth, a guest at Catherine Roberts's family's inn deposed that Catherine had looked unwell, and 'seemed if she had been in labour.'[162] However, the general appearance of a woman who looked sickly was not concrete evidence that she had delivered a child, and many women continued to offer alternative explanations, or to simply deny that they had been with child. When asked by a neighbour where her child was, because she looked slimmer and unwell, Mary Jones replied, 'hold your noise, I had no child.'[163] Ann Owen told her master and mistress that she had been 'struck with a weakness and fainting.'[164] Those who were with a single woman at the time of her delivery could also misread the signs of labour. Margaret Lewis deposed that when she went into labour and implored her mother to call for a midwife her mother replied, 'what will you do with her, thou has nothing but the spleen.'[165]

Not all corporeal signs that a woman had gone through labour could so easily be denied. However, the most obvious signs of birth were located on intimate parts of women's bodies, which were hidden from sight and made them difficult to access. In Welsh records, it was only once a single woman was believed to have been delivered secretly that she was subjected to intrusive physical searches. At that point, communal focus shifted from watching a woman's stomach to physically interrogating her body. A woman's breasts were most often examined for signs, such as lactation, which could reveal if she had recently been delivered of a child.[166] The presence of milk in the breasts was almost always seen as an unequivocal sign that a woman had, at the very least, been pregnant and had experienced the quickening.[167] It did not, however, confirm if the child had been born alive, and therefore was only one of many signs for which neighbours and communities sought. Margaret Jenkin was confronted in her own home by two matrons and a surgeon who requested to see and examine Margaret's breasts. She acquiesced, first by exposing her right breast, which appeared to not be producing milk, and then by exposing her left breast, which had 'milk in it and . . . it was pretty full.'[168] Alice Kerry examined the breasts of Elizabeth Williams and found 'milk in her breasts and verily believes [Elizabeth] lately delivered of a child.'[169] In 1774, Raleigh Colborne, a surgeon and man-midwife, and one of the few men to examine a woman's breasts, deposed that he found milk in Elizabeth Bellis's breasts and determined her to 'have the appearance of a woman who has lain in within a few months.'[170] In the same year, Margaret Powell examined one of Jannet John's breasts, and deposed that, 'on viewing it sayd she never saw such a breast of any honest girl.'[171] Evidence of lactation, or lack thereof, could be used as a defence at trial. In 1746, Jane William's mother Margaret deposed that she did not believe her daughter had been pregnant and that she had no milk in her breasts to the best of her knowledge.[172]

Women's breasts could also be surveilled from a distance. A neighbour deposed that she believed Mary Davies had been pregnant, and when her belly suddenly appeared smaller, she peered into Mary's house to observe her. The witness stated that she 'saw Mary sitting on the side of her bed with a wooden bowl and that with the other hand she was there milking one of her breasts into the bowl.'[173] She further stated that she saw a spoonful of milk come out of the breast, but she 'saw no young sucking child.' However, a surgeon named William Taylor examined Mary's breasts and found milk in them, and concluded that she 'very probably' had delivered a child. However, 'as the symptoms are equivocal and might have proceeded from other causes,' he could not be positive that she actually had done so.[174] The surgeon who examined Anne Abel's breasts found a small amount of milk in them, however, he also discovered that during the time she was alleged to have delivered, 'she had not lost one hour's work, which being the case renders the case rather dubious.'[175] Even the signs that were considered to be the most conclusive could also, at times, be ambiguous. Lactation was the most obvious sign searched for, but it was not the only one. Physiological changes to breasts that took place before or after birth could also indicate that a woman had delivered a child. In 1747 constables in Swansea sent for Mary Smith, a local midwife, to examine the breasts of Joan David. However, instead of finding milk in Joan's breasts Mary found they 'were very hard and black', and she attested that she had 'never seen nor heard of any woman [having] such breasts but when they have been very big with a child.'[176] Another witness deposed that she had examined Mary's breasts and found them to be 'similar to the breasts of a woman who had had a child'.[177]

Breasts were not the only parts of a woman's body which could be searched for evidence of childbirth. Although such examinations appear to have been carried out less frequently, women's abdomens and pubic areas could also be searched for signs of pregnancy. Descriptions of these physical examinations captured in depositions are far less detailed, and were frequently referred to in vague terms. Midwife Margaret Williams and several other women examined the body of Mary Philips in 1742, and by the appearance of 'other signs' determined she had been with child.[178] In 1759 surgeon William Taylor examined Mary Davies' breasts, and 'other signs', which he read as possible indications she may have given birth.[179] Alice Kerry determined from milk in Elizabeth William's breasts, and 'other reasons' relating to a woman's lying-in, that she had delivered.[180] Likewise, midwife Mary MacGibbon found milk in Margaret Williams's breasts, and 'fresh tokens of a lying-in.'[181] Presumably the signs midwives, matrons and occasionally surgeons looked for were evidence of swollen, stretched and hard bellies, and stretched, torn and bruised skin in and around the vulva, and possibly inside the vagina, as well as the presence of the lochia, or postpartum bleeding. Sarah Toulalan has demonstrated that intimate physical examinations of genitals were carried out on adolescent girls in attempts to find evidence of penetration in rape trials in early modern England.[182] It is therefore plausible that similar intimate examinations of women's bodies were conducted in attempts to establish whether a woman had recently delivered. In 1732 midwife Lucy Jones searched the body of Elizabeth David and, 'saw symptoms which only appear upon the body of women who bear children.'[183] In 1750 midwife Martha Roberts examined the body of Mary Dell and found on her belly, 'marks that a woman had been just before delivered of a child.'[184] Likewise, the absence of such marks could also be used in a woman's defence. In 1735 a widow named Lea Price examined the body of Hannah Morris and deposed that she had no signs of having been lately delivered.'[185]

The contrast between the oblique language used to describe women's post-parturient genitals and the detailed descriptions of lactating breasts is striking, and further reveals the complex hierarchy of secrecy surrounding knowledge about the female reproductive body. Although breasts and vaginas were both essential parts of the female reproductive body, they carried different cultural significances. Lactating breasts were associated with nourishment and motherhood. Breastmilk was seen as a wholesome substance for young children, and was imbued with healing properties that could serve broader medical purposes.[186] Moreover, nursing women would have been a common sight within many homes, and lactating breasts would have been normalised to at least some degree. The normalisation of lactation enabled witnesses to describe the specific physical symptoms found on women's breasts. However, the cultural significance of the vagina was much more fraught. Although understandings of the female reproductive body were beginning to change in the eighteenth century, throughout the early modern period the part of the female body we now identify as the vagina was understood medically and culturally to be dangerous in that it compelled women's lustfulness and could entice and trap men.[187] Moreover, the mouth of the womb was the site where anxieties surrounding childbirth and reproductive sex intersected. It therefore carried an immense amount of symbolic power, to the extent that it was difficult to describe. Early modern medical descriptions of the vagina were veiled in ambiguous language which avoided naming it in anything other than euphemistic terms, such as 'privy parts' or 'sheath,' although in popular culture it was described in bawdy, colloquial terms, such as, 'cunt,' 'placket hole,' 'tuzzy-muzzy' or even 'wide-mouthed, greedy monster.'[188] Therefore, parts of women's bodies such as the vulva, vagina and cervix lacked a suitable vernacular which would allow detailed descriptions of them, and the post-parturient signs found on them, to be recorded in formal court documents. The nearest any of the records considered here come to naming the vagina is when Elizabeth Bellis's mother deposed that her daughter had 'passed a substance from within her private parts.'[189] One record from the early nineteenth century does mention a suspect's vagina, but for entirely different reasons.[190]

Another commonly described sign of childbirth that was slightly more conclusive, but also open to different interpretations, was blood. Witnesses in both England and Wales vividly describe finding blood on floors or other part of rooms, on bedsheets, in privies or on women's clothes.[191] As a product of childbirth, blood was often interpreted as evidence that a woman had recently delivered.[192] In 1734, several women examined the underskirts and coats of Jane Williams, and determined from the appearance of blood on them that she must have been delivered of a child.[193] In 1735 Evan Prees and his wife Jane returned to their home and found blood in the bed, on the floor around the bed, and on the latch of the door of their servant Margaret's room, which Jane described as 'filth like that which came from a woman at the birth of a child.'[194] In 1786 Anne Hugh deposed that her six-year-old nephew came running for her saying, 'aunt there is a woman and her blood has run till she is dead.'[195] She followed the boy to a neighbour's house and found Jane Thomas sitting on a stool near the fire with blood on the floor around her. When asked where the blood came from Jane said, 'send the children out . . . and I will inform you.'[196] In 1796 Dorothy Jones observed Margaret Parker, a servant, sat on the edge of her bed with blood beneath her on the floor. Margaret told Dorothy, 'I am a little out of order,' to which Dorothy replied, 'I am afraid something worse,' and proceeded to call for her mistress and a surgeon.[197] If blood alone was found, it could be interpreted as some form of menstrual disorder, or alternatively, as a miscarriage. A witness named Jane deposed that she had discussed the blood found around the bed of Eleanor Jones with another witness named Mary. According to Jane, Mary told her that Eleanor had miscarried, to which Jane replied, 'don't say that or else you will be laughed at for by her appearance it could not be a miscarriage.'[198] Two other women, named Elizabeth and Margaret, also observed Eleanor in her bedroom with blood smeared on the floor and discussed the possible causes. Margaret deposed that she told Elizabeth she believed the blood could possibly mean either a miscarriage or a birth. However, Elizabeth deposed that she told Margaret, 'I am afraid it can be no miscarriage for here is too much reason to suppose that there is a child.'[199] What exactly Jane and Elizabeth were referring to is not entirely clear, but it was likely either the sheer quantity of blood found, such as with Sarah Bithell, who deposed that she had examined Mary Jones's bedsheets and found them 'to be more bloody than anything else except labour would occasion them to be.'[200] Alternatively, it could have been the presence of other by-products of childbirth, such as the placenta, amniotic fluid, or faeces, which convinced these women that Eleanor had not simply miscarried. However, what a woman may have interpreted as a miscarriage, others may have interpreted as a full-term, live birth.

Reading Infant Bodies

Single women's bodies could be read for signs of concealed pregnancy and childbirth, which were indicative of deviance, but only infant bodies could reveal evidence of murder. As such, the bodies of dead newborn infants were therefore central to infanticide trials, and grew increasingly so as the eighteenth century progressed.[201] The discovery of a dead infant body automatically signalled that a particular type of crime had taken place: it was not simply that an infant had been murdered, but an infant who was born to an unmarried woman. The assumption, which was enshrined in the 1624 'An Act to Prevent the Destroying and Murthering of Bastard Children,' was that, motivated by shame and a fear of punishment, only unmarried mothers would conceal their deliveries and dispose of their infants.[202] Therefore, any infant body that was found improperly disposed of was assumed to have been a child conceived and born outside of wedlock, regardless of whether the mother's identity was known. For example, in the examination of John Parry in 1742, authorities described the female newborn's body he had found in a well as a 'female bastard child,' despite not yet having established the identity of the child's parents.[203] The discovery of an infant body served as evidence that a woman's sexual deviance had taken a felonious turn, and officials looked to infant bodies to determine the nature of the crime. In Wales, as in England, courts were concerned with determining whether a child had been carried near enough to full-term to have been viable, and, if so, whether the child was stillborn, or was born alive and then killed.[204]

The first challenge was therefore to read infant bodies to determine if they had been carried to full-term. Much has been written about the various subtle indicators of full-term delivery for which midwives and surgeons searched on infant bodies, such as an infant's size, or the presence or absence of fully formed fingernails and toenails on an infant's hands and feet.[205] Such evidence is common in witness depositions from the Court of Great Sessions. The male infant Margaret Jenkin was accused of killing was described as having fingernails and hair, and therefore the surgeon, Anthony Poole, determined he had been delivered full-term.[206] A midwife who examined the body of Jane Griffith's child, who was found in a cheese vat, described the male infant as having hair on his head, and so she believed he was full-term.[207] Mary Hunt's child, who was found buried under the floor near the head of her bed, was described as having nails on both hands and feet.[208]

However, Welsh records are also revealing of more considerable discrepancies in the various readings of suspected infanticide victim bodies. Most notable are the cases in which women described as miscarriage or spontaneous abortion what other witnesses interpreted as full-term deliveries. Examples include Mary Hunt, who, when pressed by authorities, confessed to having buried her infant near her bed, but insisted that the child was miscarried, not delivered.[209] Jane Thomas, who a neighbouring boy believed had bled to death, told Anne Hughes and the other female neighbours who had gathered that she had miscarried. Anne asked Jane if anything other than blood had came from her, to which Jane replied there was, and that she had placed it in a pudding pan. Anne fetched the pan and found what appeared to be a full-term infant boy inside, which everyone believed to be dead until he began to cry. However, the infant died shortly thereafter.[210] When surgeon and man-midwife John Thomas found 'clotted blood and other matters' on the floor of Maria Morris's bedchamber he suspected she had given birth.[211] Maria eventually confessed to having miscarried, saying she 'had three months to come of her time'. However, after viewing the body, John believed the child was full-term.[212] Women's explanations that they miscarried or spontaneously aborted were not uncommon. Discrepancies between interpretations of miscarriage and birth demonstrate that, even in its later stages, pregnancy was both precarious and ambiguous.[213] Moreover, such descriptions could have been fabricated as defences, for, by insisting she had come before her time, a suspect could account for why she was alone and unprepared when the child came, and also deter accusations of premeditation.[214] However, such accounts could also reflect genuine unawareness of how far along in her pregnancy a woman believed herself to be, especially if she was young, unmarried and pregnant for the first time, and therefore lacking in the knowledge and support which could help her predict her due date. In her discussion about young women's ignorance, Jane Sharp stated that not only could they not accurately recognise conception, but also, with reference to the recurrence of her menstruation, 'not one of twenty almost keeps just account, else they would be better provided against the time of their lying-in, and not so suddenly be surprized as many of them are.'[215]

Much more intriguing are the cases in which women described the bodies of their allegedly murdered infants in terms which denied that the birth was a fully formed infant. In 1746, Jane Williams was accused of burying the body of her infant in a forested hillside near her home. When examined, she described experiencing pain in her womb and was 'delivered in her mother's presence of some filthy matter of blood or false conception, but denies that such filthy matter had any resemblance of any human shape.'[216] Jane's mother Margaret, who also stood accused of murdering Jane's child, further explained that one evening Jane suddenly cried out, 'oh god what is this,' stood up, and, 'there dropped from her womb some filthy matter of blood', which Margaret insisted bore no resemblance to a child.[217] However, both Jane and Margaret later confessed to Jane delivering a stillborn child whose body they buried near their home. Similarly, Elizabeth Bellis's mother deposed that her daughter had previously suffered from a menstrual disorder, and during that time, 'she passed a substance from within her private parts as big as her two fists.'[218] Laura Gowing has noted that, in defending themselves, women frequently avoided descriptions of 'child', and instead used vague descriptions, such as those used by Elizabeth, Jane and their mothers.[219] It is impossible to know if descriptions such as these were entirely constructed as defences by single women and the mothers, who may have had previous experiences of miscarriages, or if they were dissociative reactions to unwanted pregnancies.[220] However, as Cathy McClive has argued, it was only possible for these women to utilise narratives of 'lumps and stillbirths' or 'false conceptions' because such things were within the realm of possibility.[221]

Court of Great Sessions' records also reveal the different ways in which witnesses attempted to determine if an infant had been born living or dead. Both midwives and male medical practitioners were called upon to examine the bodies of infants for signs of life, and the methods used by male and female practitioners differed significantly. When midwives and matrons examined the bodies of suspected infanticide victims, they typically described the presence or absence of signs that signified life and health which they would have recognised from their own experiences, all of which were on the outside of the body. Barbara Williams described the infant Mary Richards was accused of killing as 'a fine, stout, healthy looking child' which she and several other women believed had been born alive.[222] The four midwives who examined Jane Griffith's infant's body all described external indicators of life. Dorothy verch Edwards deposed that the infant's body had 'plump, full parts.'[223] Elizabeth Foulkes deposed that she 'never saw a fatter or better grown child in her life, she being a midwife.'[224] Ellen Weyman deposed that the child had long hair, and although the infant's eyes were closed, one of the eyelids could be easily lifted.[225] Mary Bryan also described the ease with which one of the infant's eyes could be opened, and also deposed that the infant's hands were almost, but not entirely, closed. Mary viewed the body while it was still in the cheese vat, and also described how he was still attached to the placenta, on which he lay.[226] All these signs were taken as indicators that the child could have been born alive, although not all of the midwives were willing to state definitively that it had been. Midwives and matrons also interpreted various signs of violence they found on the outside of infant bodies. Ellen Weyman deposed that the reason she believed Jane Griffith's child's other eye could not be opened was because it was swollen shut, and that the child's forehead, nose and lips were discoloured, and looked as though they had been crushed.[227] In 1744 a matron examined the child Barbara David was accused of murdering, and described bruising on the child's neck and under his chin.[228] Martha Roberts, who examined Mary Dell's body for signs of childbirth, also examined the body of her child and deposed that it was 'much bruised.'[229] None of these women suggested that the injuries they found on infants' bodies could have occurred during childbirth.

Although midwives and matrons played an important role in reading unmarried women's bodies throughout the eighteenth century in Wales, their role in examining infant bodies decreased as the century progressed. Increasingly, their role in providing expert testimony about the possible health of an infant at the time of delivery, and the potentially fatal signs of violence, was replaced by the expert opinion of male medical practitioners. As in England, depositions and inquests reveal the changing significance of medical evidence in the criminal process during this period.[230] Male medical practitioners played an occasional role in Welsh infanticide cases at least as early as the 1730s, and appeared with greater frequency in the last three decades of the century. In 1734 surgeon Edward Neals deposed that the body of Jane William's infant appeared to have marks of violence on her neck, and open hands and clenched fingers, from which signs he determined that the child had been born alive.[231] Similar to the examinations carried out by midwives and matrons, his deposition describes observable signs on the outside of the body. In 1738 Evan David 'found contusions and bruises on the chin' of the infant Ann Williams stood accused of killing, which he supposed might have been the cause of death.[232] However, from the 1750s onwards, medical men began searching for evidence of an unnatural death on the inside of infant bodies. Surgeons such as George Williams in 1755, David Parry and David Williams Hopkins in 1776, Richard Lloyd in 1789, Thomas Simon in 1796 and William Jones in 1799 all described dissecting, examining and experimenting on the bodies of infants who were believed to have been murdered.[233] Male medical practitioners examined infant bones, analysed and measured organs and performed experiments such as the lung test.[234] Richard Lloyd deposed that, prior to preserving an infant's placenta in a quart of brandy, he had washed it in cold water, measured the umbilical cord, and determined it to be from a fully developed foetus.[235]

Medical men in Wales dissected infant bodies for the same reasons midwives and matrons examined their outward appearance: to determine whether a child had been born alive, and to establish if the child had succumbed to an obvious act of violence. Despite their access to additional evidence, Welsh medical practitioners did no more speculating about the circumstances surrounding an infant's death than did midwives and matrons. Thomas Simon deposed that the lungs of the infant he examined appeared healthy, and he found no marks of violence on the body.[236] Richard Lloyd's account of the infant he dissected was that 'the throat had marks of great violence as had the whole skull with much exhausted blood part of the lungs was taken and thrown in cold water and kept suspended,' and hence deposed that he believed the infant was murdered.[237] None of the medical men who appear in Welsh infanticide depositions use evidence found in or on infant bodies to draw conclusions about the mental state of the women suspected of murdering them. In her analysis of Old Bailey proceedings from the eighteenth century, Sheena Sommers has argued that the increasing emphasis on infant bodies as the object of medical testing resulted in attempts on the part of male medical practitioners to determine the 'internal mental and emotional state of the accused at the time of delivery.'[238] Sommers suggests that Old Bailey infanticide records are evidence of what Thomas Laqueur called the 'humanitarian narrative', whereby those in positions of authority constructed narratives of suffering which absolved offenders of their crimes.[239] In the Old Bailey cases Sommers analysed, she found male medical practitioners who, without being prompted, offered sympathetic explanations for how various marks of violence could have occurred, such as a woman having been in a great deal of distress during an unexpected, solitary labour and accidentally harming her child in the process.[240] Sommers suggests that these narratives reflected the increasing reluctance to condemn women to death, and contributed to the lower conviction rates for infanticide in the late eighteenth century.[241] Eighteenth-century Welsh infanticide records do not reveal any similar narratives from male medical practitioners. Although their readings of infant bodies were highly detailed, they were not then used as a means of assessing single women's mental states. Despite this, conviction rates for infanticide in Wales remained remarkably low.[242] Of the 39 cases examined here only one resulted in the conviction of an unmarried woman for murdering her newborn infant. Jane Williams, a widow who was convicted and sentenced to be hanged in 1734, was one of the only cases where the infant's body bore extreme marks of violence, including a dislocated and deeply lacerated neck.[243] These details might have been what compelled a jury to convict her. The remaining suspects were either not indicted or were acquitted. Central to all of these cases were the bodies of women and infants.

Conclusion

The ways in which women's and infants' bodies were interrogated reveals the complex tensions between different types of reproductive authority. Although family, neighbours, employers, and authorities all played a part in monitoring and confronting suspected pregnant women, and in locating and reading the bodies of dead infants, they did not do so in the same ways. Midwives, matrons and medical men were not granted equal access to, and authority over, the bodies of infants and unmarried women. Like their counterparts in London, Welsh medical men gained increasing authority to examine and to dissect infant bodies as the eighteenth century wore on, and as they did so, the role of women in these infant examinations declined. However, medical men did not usurp women's authority entirely. Throughout the century, Welsh midwives and matrons retained almost exclusive authority to read women's bodies. In this regard, the expertise of medical men remained subordinated to the knowledge and experience of skilled, married women, unlike in England where the role of midwives in the courtroom were gradually usurped by male practitioners.[244]

Ultimately, the bodies of unmarried women and their dead infants could only reveal so much. The only evidence that could confirm if a woman had actually been pregnant was the birth of a child, but even then, without witnesses to the birth, the evidence could still be equivocal.

For judges and juries, no single corporeal sign provided enough evidence to prove that a single woman had wilfully murdered her child. These bodies may not have been conclusive evidence of crime, but they still served as evidence of deviance. Unmarried pregnant bodies and the children they produced carried tremendous cultural significance. Discarded infant bodies that were inevitably interpreted as 'bastards', and marks of pregnancy on single women's bodies, informed a community that sex outside of the acceptable bounds of marriage had taken place. Evidence about the ways in which bodies were read and regulated is therefore revealing of the broader social anxieties surrounding deviant reproduction. Court of Great Sessions' records demonstrate how Welsh communities sought to negotiate control over unmarried women's reproductive capacities by restricting access to reproductive knowledge and by surveilling and interrogating bodies. The boundaries between single women's bodies and the community were variable, and were contingent upon a variety of factors including the perceived level of risk, social and cultural sensibilities surrounding women's bodies, the knowledge and authority of neighbours, and the women's own personal authority and agency. This complex dynamic resulted in a multiplicity of confrontations and interrogations which reveal a great deal about the ways in which eighteenth-century Welsh men and women understood reproduction, and their anxieties about the dangers of childbirth out of wedlock.

The cases analysed in this chapter reveal one of the most extreme outcomes of extramarital pregnancy in the eighteenth century. The conflicting accounts of childbirth and infant death are likely not representative of the experiences of most parturient single mothers, as the majority did not culminate in the concealment of birth or the death of an infant. Most unmarried pregnant women did not wholly conceal and deny their pregnancies, as evidenced by the numerous bastardy bonds and filiation orders which survive. The countless entries in poor law account books also provide evidence that many unmarried women were provided with care and assistance during childbirth. However, neighbourly surveillance and physical confrontations intended to reveal a state of pregnancy may have been a common experience for unmarried women. Most unmarried pregnant women undoubtedly did reveal their pregnancies, voluntarily or otherwise, and therefore would have been offered the services of the same skilled matrons and midwives who interrogated the bodies of women who kept their pregnancies concealed. The experiences of these women, and the nature of the care they received will be explored in the next chapter.

Notes

1. NLW 4/46/2 (Denbighshire, Catherine Roberts, 1736).
2. NLW 4/46/2 (Denbighshire, Catherine Roberts, 1736).

186 *Pregnancy and Childbirth*

3. NLW 4/46/2 (Denbighshire, Catherine Roberts, 1736).
4. NLW 4/46/2 (Denbighshire, Catherine Roberts, 1736).
5. NLW 4/46/2 (Denbighshire, Catherine Roberts, 1736).
6. NLW 4/46/2 (Denbighshire, Catherine Roberts, 1736).
7. NLW 4/46/2 (Denbighshire, Catherine Roberts, 1736).
8. NLW 4/46/2 (Denbighshire, Catherine Roberts, 1736).
9. NLW 4/46/2 (Denbighshire, Catherine Roberts, 1736).
10. Luttfring, *Bodies, Speech and Reproductive Knowledge*, p. 5.
11. Gowing, 'Ordering the Body', p. 45; Wilson, *Ritual and Conflict*, p. 8.
12. Laura Gowing, *Common Bodies: Women, Touch and Power in Seventeenth-Century England* (New Haven: Yale University Press, 2003), p. 113; Cathy McClive, 'The Hidden Truths of the Belly: Uncertainties of Pregnancy in Early Modern Europe', *Social History of Medicine*, 15 (2002), 209–227 (p. 211).
13. Gowing, 'Knowledge and Experience', p. 242.
14. Gowing, *Common Bodies*, pp. 113–114.
15. Gowing, *Common Bodies*, p. 147.
16. Records related to all cases of infanticide heard between 1730 and 1800 in Montgomeryshire, Radnorshire, Breconshire, Denbighshire, Flintshire, Glamorganshire and Anglesey for which witness examinations, depositions or confessions survive. All Court of Great Sessions records are held at the National Library of Wales, and are catalogued in the NLW *Crime and Punishment Database* <https://crimeandpunishment.library.wales> [accessed 23/8/2019].
17. Gowing, 'Secret Births', p. 115.
18. McClive, 'Hidden Truths', p. 211.
19. Gowing, 'Knowledge and Experience', p. 241.
20. Gowing, 'Knowledge and Experience', p. 241.
21. Gowing, 'Knowledge and Experience', p. 247; Gowing, 'Ordering the Body', p. 49; Williams, 'Experience of Pregnancy', p. 70.
22. Gowing, 'Secret Births', p. 93.
23. Gowing, 'Knowledge and Experience', p. 247.
24. Gowing, *Common Bodies*, p. 147.
25. Michael Stolberg, 'Examining the Body, c. 1500–1750', in *The Routledge History of Sex and the Body*, ed. by Toulalan and Fisher, pp. 91–105 (p. 98).
26. NLW 4/1013/9 (Flintshire, Margaret Jones, 1797).
27. Gowing, 'Secret Births', pp. 90–91.
28. NLW 4/1005/11 (Flintshire, Mary Davies, 1759); NLW 4/58/2 (Denbighshire, Elizabeth Bellis, 1744).
29. NLW 4/906/1 (Cardiganshire, Sarah David, 1794).
30. Jackson, *New-Born Child Murder*, pp. 20, 70; Sheena Sommers, 'Remapping Maternity in the Courtroom: Female Defences and Medical Witnesses in Eighteenth-Century Infanticide Proceedings', in *The Body in Medical Culture*, ed. by Elizabeth Klaver (Albany: SUNY Press, 2009), pp. 37–59 (p. 37).
31. NLW 4/752/4 (Carmarthenshire, Hannah John, 1799).
32. NLW 4/1012/2 (Flintshire, Eleanor Jones, 1789).
33. NLW 4/1007/1 (Flintshire, Elizabeth Williams, 1765).
34. NLW 4/60/5 (Denbighshire, Mary Owen, 1784).
35. NLW 4/1002/4 (Flintshire, Jane Griffith, 1739).
36. NLW 4/178/2 (Montgomeryshire, Jane Williams, 1734).
37. Jackson, *New-Born Child Murder*, p. 87; Sommers, 'Remapping Maternity', pp. 45–46.

38. Jackson, *New-Born Child Murder*, p. 87; Sommers, 'Remapping Maternity', p. 37.
39. NLW 4/381/2 (Breconshire, Mary Harris, 1755).
40. Jackson, *New-Born Child Murder*, pp. 93–100. The test was not always seen as conclusive evidence of live birth, and both medical and legal practitioners increasingly debated the effectiveness of the test.
41. NLW 4/1009/5 (Flintshire, Jane Griffith, 1739).
42. NLW 4/62/4 (Denbighshire, Catherine Davies, 1789).
43. NLW 4/62/4 (Denbighshire, Catherine Davies, 1789, 4/1013/6 (Flintshire, Elizabeth Jones, 1795).
44. Gowing, 'Secret Births', p. 90.
45. Gowing, 'Ordering the Body', pp. 48, 61.
46. Gowing, 'Ordering the Body', p. 47.
47. Gowing, 'Secret Births', p. 93.
48. NLW 4/381/2 (Breconshire, Mary Harris, 1755).
49. Gowing, 'Ordering the Body', p. 48.
50. NLW 4/189/1 (Montgomeryshire, Margaret Jenkin, 1768).
51. Wilson, *Ritual and Conflict*, pp. 164–165.
52. Gowing, *Common Bodies*, p. 138.
53. Gowing, 'Secret Births', p. 92.
54. NLW 4/189/1 (Montgomeryshire, Margaret Jenkin, 1768).
55. Withey, *Physick and the Family*, p. 174.
56. For example, NLW 4/517/6 (Radnorshire, Hannah Morris, 1735) deposition of John Rogers; NLW 4/189/1 (Montgomeryshire, Margaret Jenkin, 1768) deposition of Mary Davies and Thomas Williams; NLW 4/195/3 (Montgomeryshire, Margaret Evans, 1793) depositions of Elizabeth Jones and John Thomas, to name just a few.
57. NLW 4/46/2 (Denbighshire, Catherine Roberts, 1736).
58. Sara Read, *Maids, Wives, Widows: Exploring Early Modern Women's Lives 1540–1740* (Barnsley: Pen & Sword, 2015), p. 77.
59. NLW 4/46/2 (Denbighshire, Catherine Roberts, 1736).
60. Gowing, 'Ordering the Body', pp. 60–61.
61. Crawford, 'Construction and Experience of Maternity', p. 17.
62. Daniel JR Grey, 'Crimes Related to Sexuality and Reproduction', in *Oxford Handbook*, ed. by Gartner and McCarthy, pp. 225–241 (p. 233).
63. David Cressy, *Birth, Marriage and Death: Ritual, Religion and the Life-Cycle in Tudor and Stuart England* (Oxford: Oxford University Press, 1997), p. 43; Jane Sharp, *The Midwives Book, or the Whole Art of Midwifery Discovered*, ed. by Elaine Hobby (Oxford: Oxford University Press, 1999), p. 81.
64. Catherine E Horler-Underwood, 'Aspects of Female Criminality in Wales, c. 1730–1830: Evidence from the Court of Great Sessions' (unpublished doctoral thesis, Cardiff, 2014).
65. Gowing, *Common Bodies*, pp. 113–114; Williams, 'Experience of Pregnancy', p. 73.
66. Gowing, *Common Bodies*, p. 139.
67. For the ways in which the language of sexual knowledge could legally implicate women see Gowing, *Domestic Dangers*, p. 61; Walker, 'Rereading Rape', p. 5.
68. McClive, 'Hidden Truths', p. 211.
69. Crawford, 'Construction and Experience of Maternity', p. 6.
70. Crawford, *Blood, Bodies and Families*, p. 92.
71. Read, *Maids, Wives, Widows*, p. 90.

72. Gowing, *Common Bodies*, p. 119.
73. Cody, *Birthing the Nation*, p. 32.
74. Grey, 'Crimes Related to Sexuality', p. 233; Jackson, *New-Born Child Murder*, p. 61.
75. Sharp, *Midwives Book*, pp. 194–195.
76. See also, Cathy McClive, *Menstruation and Procreation in Early Modern France* (Abingdon: Routledge, 2015).
77. NLW 4/46/2 (Denbighshire, Catherine Roberts, 1736).
78. NLW 4/46/2 (Denbighshire, Catherine Roberts, 1736).
79. NLW 4/46/2 (Denbighshire, Catherine Roberts, 1736).
80. Williams, 'Experience of Pregnancy', p. 73.
81. NLW 4/617/2 (Glamorgan, Margaret Lewis, 1756).
82. NLW 4/58/2 (Denbighshire, Elizabeth Bellis, 1744).
83. NLW/374/5 (Breconshire, Elizabeth Morris, 1732).
84. NLW 4/748/3 (Carmarthenshire, Anne John, 1789).
85. Garthine Walker, 'Just Stories: Telling Tales of Infant Death in Early Modern England', in *Culture and Change: Attending to Women in Early Modern England*, ed. by Margaret Mikesell and Adele Seeff (Newark: University of Delaware Press, 2003), pp. 98–115 (pp. 100–101).
86. Walker, 'Just Stories', pp. 100–101.
87. McLaren, *Reproductive Rituals*, p. 108; Gowing, *Common Bodies*, p. 147; Read, *Maids, Wives, Widows*, p. 91.
88. Gowing, *Common Bodies*, p. 147; Jackson, *New-Born Child Murder*, p. 73.
89. Gowing, *Common Bodies*, pp. 113–114.
90. McLaren, *Reproductive Rituals*, p. 108.
91. NLW 4/193/5 (Montgomeryshire, Richard Pryce, 1742).
92. NLW 4/1002/4 (Flintshire, Jane Griffith, 1739).
93. NLW 4/1002/4 (Flintshire, Jane Griffith, 1739).
94. NLW 4/1002/4 (Flintshire, Jane Griffith, 1739).
95. Ambroise Paré, *Workes of That Famous Chirugion Ambrose Parey, Translated Out of Latine and Compared with the French by Thomas Johnson* (London, 1665), p. 615.
96. McClive, 'Hidden Truths', p. 255; Sharp, *Midwives Book*, pp. 135–136, 169–171.
97. Cody, *Birthing the Nation*, p. 33.
98. NLW 4/388/3 (Breconshire, Elizabeth Williams, 1788).
99. NLW 4/748/3 (Carmarthenshire, Anne John, 1789).
100. NLW 4/64/4 (Denbighshire, Ann Parry, 1795).
101. NLW 4/1013/3 (Flintshire, Elizabeth Jones, 1795).
102. NLW 4/1013/3 (Flintshire, Elizabeth Jones, 1795).
103. NLW 4/752/4 (Carmarthenshire, Hannah John, 1799).
104. NLW 4/1013/3 (Flintshire, Elizabeth Jones, 1795).
105. NLW 4/1002/4 (Flintshire, Jane Griffith, 1739).
106. Jane Griffith and Francis Bolanson were acquitted; Elizabeth Williams, Anne John and Anne Parry were not indicted; the outcome of Hannah John's case has does not appear in the surviving documents held by the National Library of Wales.
107. Jackson, *New-Born Child Murder*, p. 66; Gowing, 'Secret Births', p. 96.
108. NLW 4/1007/1 (Flintshire, Elizabeth Williams, 1765).
109. NLW 4/623/3 (Glamorgan, Jannet John, 1774).
110. NLW 4/195/3 (Montgomeryshire, Margaret Evans, 1793); Copland, *Practical Medicine*, p. 14.
111. NLW 4/195/3 (Montgomeryshire, Margaret Evans, 1793).
112. McLaren, *Reproductive Rituals*, p. 100; Copland, *Practical Medicine*, p. 14.

113. McLaren, *Reproductive Rituals*, p. 100; Copland, *Practical Medicine*, p. 14.
114. Jackson, *New-Born Child Murder*, p. 66; Gowing, 'Knowledge and Experience', p. 245.
115. NLW 4/1013/3 (Flintshire, Elizabeth Jones, 1795).
116. NLW 4/46/2 (Denbighshire, Catherine Roberts, 1736).
117. NLW 4/189/1 (Montgomeryshire, Margaret Jenkin, 1768).
118. NLW 4/178/2 (Montgomeryshire, Jane Williams, 1734).
119. NLW 4/380/6 (Breconshire, Gwenllian David, 1753).
120. NLW 4/380/6 (Breconshire, Gwenllian David, 1753).
121. Gowing, *Common Bodies*, pp. 120–121; McClive, 'Hidden Truths', p. 211.
122. Gowing, 'Knowledge and Experience', p. 245.
123. NLW 4/49/2 (Denbighshire, Jane Williams, 1746).
124. NLW 4/374/5 (Breconshire, Elizabeth Morris, 1732).
125. Gowing, 'Secret Births', pp. 96–97.
126. Cody, *Birthing the Nation*, p. 34.
127. Gowing, 'Secret Births', p. 96.
128. Gowing, *Common Bodies*, p. 122.
129. Williams, 'Experience of Pregnancy', p. 72; Gowing, 'Secret Births', p. 91; Grey, 'Crimes Related to Sexuality', p. 234; Jackson, *New-Born Child Murder*, p. 62.
130. NLW 4/1005/11 (Flintshire, Mary Davies, 1759).
131. NLW 4/58/2 (Denbighshire, Elizabeth Bellis, 1744).
132. NLW 4/900/3 (Cardiganshire, Ann Hughes, 1776).
133. NLW 4/1010/10 (Flintshire, Mary Jones, 1783).
134. NLW 4/195/3 (Montgomeryshire, Margaret Evans, 1793).
135. NLW 4/195/3 (Montgomeryshire, Margaret Evans, 1793).
136. NLW 4/46/2 (Denbighshire, Catherine Roberts, 1736).
137. NLW 4/195/3 (Montgomeryshire, Margaret Evans, 1793).
138. NLW 4/189/1 (Montgomeryshire, Margaret Jenkin, 1768).
139. NLW 4/189/1 (Montgomeryshire, Margaret Jenkin, 1768).
140. NLW 4/629/4 (Glamorgan, Mary Morgan, 1794).
141. NLW 4/374/6 (Breconshire, Elizabeth David, 1732).
142. Williams, 'Experience of Pregnancy', p. 72.
143. OBP t17361208-40 (Hannah Butler, 1736).
144. NLW 4/46/2 (Denbighshire, Catherine Roberts, 1736).
145. NLW 4/178/2 (Montgomeryshire, Jane Williams, 1734).
146. NLW 4/1010/10 (Flintshire, Mary Jones, 1783).
147. NLW 4/900/3 (Cardiganshire, Ann Hughes, 1776).
148. NLW 4/195/3 (Montgomeryshire, Margaret Evans, 1793).
149. NLW 4/189/1 (Montgomeryshire, Margaret Jenkin, 1768).
150. NLW 4/178/2 (Montgomeryshire, Jane Williams, 1734).
151. NLW 4/751/1 (Carmarthenshire, Anne Abel, 1795).
152. NLW 4/517/6 (Radnorshire, Hannah Morris, 1735).
153. Jackson, *New-Born Child Murder*, p. 3; Grigg, 'Getting Away with Murder?' p. 116.
154. Jackson, *New-Born Child Murder*, pp. 33–34.
155. Jackson, *New-Born Child Murder*, p. 33.
156. Williams, 'Experience of Pregnancy', p. 70; Wilson, 'Ceremony of Childbirth', p. 70; Cressy, *Birth, Marriage and Death*, p. 15.
157. Williams, 'Experience of Pregnancy', p. 70.
158. NLW 4/373/6 (Breconshire, Gwenllian Powell, 1730).
159. NLW 4/298/4 (Merioneth, Elizabeth Davies, 1734).
160. NLW 4/1010/10 (Flintshire, Mary Jones, 1783).
161. NLW 4/1010/10 (Flintshire, Mary Jones, 1783).

162. NLW 4/46/2 (Denbighshire, Catherine Roberts, 1736).
163. NLW 4/1010/10 (Flintshire, Mary Jones, 1783).
164. NLW 4/194/7 (Montgomeryshire, Ann Owen, 1791).
165. NLW 4/188/6 (Montgomeryshire, Margaret Lewis the Younger, Margaret Lewis the Elder, 1767).
166. Gowing, 'Secret Births', p. 91.
167. Gowing, *Common Bodies*, p. 144.
168. NLW 4/189/1 (Montgomeryshire, Margaret Jenkin, 1768).
169. NLW 4/1007/1 (Flintshire, Elizabeth Williams, 1765).
170. NLW 4/58/2 (Denbighshire, Elizabeth Bellis, 1744).
171. NLW 4/623/3 (Glamorgan, Jannet John, 1774).
172. NLW 4/49/2 (Denbighshire, Jane Williams, 1746).
173. NLW 4/1005/11 (Flintshire, Mary Davies, 1759).
174. NLW 4/1005/11 (Flintshire, Mary Davies, 1759).
175. NLW 4/751/1 (Carmarthenshire, Anne Abel, 1795).
176. NLW 4/1005/11 (Flintshire, Mary Davies, 1759).
177. NLW 4/1005/11 (Flintshire, Mary Davies, 1759).
178. NLW 4/47/7 (Denbighshire, Mary Philips, 1742).
179. NLW 4/1005/11 (Flintshire, Mary Davies, 1759).
180. NLW 4/1007/1 (Flintshire, Elizabeth Williams, 1765).
181. NLW 4/380/7 (Breconshire, Margaret Williams, 1753).
182. Sarah Toulalan, ' "Is He a Licentious Lewd Sort of Person?" Constructing the Child Rapist in Early Modern England', *Journal of the History of Sexuality*, 23 (2014), 21–52.
183. NLW 4/374/6 (Breconshire, Elizabeth David, 1732).
184. NLW 4/183/5 (Montgomeryshire, Mary Dell, 1750).
185. NLW 4/517/6 (Radnorshire, Hannah Morris, 1735).
186. Marylynn Salmon, 'The Cultural Significance of Breastfeeding and Infant Care in Early Modern England and America', *Journal of Social History*, 28 (1994), 247–269.
187. Gowing, *Common Bodies*, pp. 27–29; Gowing, 'Knowledge and Experience', p. 248; Mary Fissell, *Vernacular Bodies: The Politics of Reproduction in Early Modern England* (Oxford: Oxford University Press, 2006), pp. 185–186.
188. Gowing, *Common Bodies*, pp. 27–28; Fissell, *Vernacular Bodies*, pp. 185–186; Emma LE Rees, *The Vagina: A Literary and Cultural History* (New York: Bloomsbury, 2013), p. 20.
189. NLW 4/58/2 (Denbighshire, Elizabeth Bellis, 1744).
190. In 1809 an older woman named Anne Jones, who was reported to be well past her reproductive years, was suspected of feigning pregnancy by disinterring the body of a recently deceased infant. The man-midwife who attended her discovered 'a parcel of child's bones crammed in the vagina.' NLW 4/757/2 (Carmarthenshire, Anne Jones, 1809).
191. Williams, 'Experience of Pregnancy', pp. 70, 76.
192. Jackson, *New-Born Child Murder*, pp. 66–67.
193. NLW 4/178/2 (Montgomeryshire, Jane Williams, 1734).
194. NLW 4/518/2 (Radnorshire, Margaret Th Prees).
195. NLW 4/746/3 (Carmarthenshire, Jane Thomas, 1786).
196. NLW 4/746/3 (Carmarthenshire, Jane Thomas, 1786).
197. NLW 4/1013/6 (Flintshire, Margaret Parker, 1796).
198. NLW 4/1012/2 (Flintshire, Eleanor Jones, 1789).
199. NLW 4/1012/2 (Flintshire, Eleanor Jones, 1789).
200. NLW 4/1010/10 (Flintshire, Mary Jones, 1783).
201. Sharon Howard, 'Communities Policing "Criminal" Bodies in Early Modern Wales' <http://sharonhoward.org/archive/controlling-bodies.pdf> [accessed

27/8/2019], 3; Sommers, 'Remapping Maternity', pp. 45–46; Kilday, *History of Infanticide*, p. 78.
202. Jackson, *New-Born Child Murder*, p. 40; 21 James I c. 27.
203. NLW 4/47/7 (Denbighshire, Mary Philips, 1742).
204. Jackson, *New-Born Child Murder*, pp. 104–105.
205. Jackson, *New-Born Child Murder*, pp. 84–109; Kilday, *History of Infanticide*, pp. 74–75; Sommers, 'Remapping Maternity', pp. 47–48.
206. NLW 4/189/1 (Montgomeryshire, Margaret Jenkin, 1768).
207. NLW 4/1002/4 (Flintshire, Jane Griffith, 1739).
208. NLW 4/1003/11 (Flintshire, Mary Hunt, 1746).
209. NLW 4/1003/11 (Flintshire, Mary Hunt, 1746).
210. NLW 4/746/3 (Carmarthenshire, Jane Thomas, 1786).
211. NLW 4/906/4 (Cardiganshire, Maria Morris, 1795).
212. NLW 4/906/4 (Cardiganshire, Maria Morris, 1795).
213. Gowing, *Common Bodies*, p. 121.
214. Sommers, 'Remapping Maternity', p. 42.
215. Sharp, *Midwives Book*, pp. 81–82.
216. NLW 4/49/2 (Denbighshire, Jane Williams, 1746).
217. NLW 4/49/2 (Denbighshire, Jane Williams, 1746).
218. NLW 4/58/2 (Denbighshire, Elizabeth Bellis, 1744).
219. Gowing, *Common Bodies*, p. 141.
220. Gowing, *Common Bodies*, p. 141.
221. McClive, 'Hidden Truths', pp. 211, 221.
222. NLW 4/626/4 (Glamorgan, Mary Richard, 1786).
223. NLW 4/1002/4 (Flintshire, Jane Griffith, 1739).
224. NLW 4/1002/4 (Flintshire, Jane Griffith, 1739).
225. NLW 4/1002/4 (Flintshire, Jane Griffith, 1739).
226. NLW 4/1002/4 (Flintshire, Jane Griffith, 1739).
227. NLW 4/1002/4 (Flintshire, Jane Griffith, 1739).
228. NLW 4/613/6 (Glamorgan, Barbara David, 1744).
229. NLW 4/183/5 (Montgomeryshire, Mary Dell, 1750).
230. Jackson, *New-Born Child Murder*, p. 20.
231. NLW 4/178/2 (Montgomeryshire, Jane Williams, 1734).
232. NLW 4/298/5 (Merioneth, Ann Williams, 1738).
233. NLW 4/381/2 (Breconshire, Mary Harris, 1755); NLW 4/1009/5 (Flintshire, Catherine Roberts, 1776); NLW 4/900/3 (Cardiganshire, Ann Hughes, 1776); NLW 4/62/4 (Denbighshire, Catherine Davies, 1789); NLW 4/1013/6 (Flintshire, Elizabeth Jones, 1795); NLW 4/752/4 (Carmarthenshire, Hannah John, 1799).
234. Jackson, *New-Born Child Murder*, pp. 93–100.
235. NLW 4/62/4 (Denbighshire, Catherine Davies, 1789).
236. NLW 4/1013/6 (Flintshire, Margaret Parker, 1796).
237. NLW 4/62/4 (Denbighshire, Catherine Davies, 1789).
238. Sommers, 'Remapping Maternity', p. 46.
239. Laqueur, 'Humanitarian Narrative', pp. 176–204; Sommers, 'Remapping Maternity', pp. 50.
240. Sommers, 'Remapping Maternity', p. 46.
241. Sommers, 'Remapping Maternity', pp. 37–60.
242. Watson, 'Women, Violent Crime', p. 260; Woodward, 'Infanticide in Wales', p. 122.
243. Jane Williams was sentenced to be hanged NLW 4/178/2 (Montgomeryshire, Jane Williams, 1734).
244. Sommers, 'Remapping Maternity', p. 37.

6 The Provision of Care for Unmarried Mothers[1]

The previous chapter examined the circumstances that arose when unmarried pregnant women attempted to conceal their pregnancies and deliveries. Although well documented, these experiences were rare. Most pregnancies that occurred outside of wedlock would have been known to families, communities and authorities, at least in the later stages when signs such as swollen bellies were most observable. When these pregnancies went full term, they would have resulted in labour and delivery, and would have required care and support for both mothers and infants. This chapter will explore the nature of care provided to unmarried pregnant women before, during and after parturition. Evidence about the lived experience of childbirth for most early modern women from the lower orders, both married and unmarried, is scarce. However, parish poor law records, court depositions and examinations, and applications for licences to practise midwifery do provide enough evidence to reveal the nature of care available to the poorest women in eighteenth-century Welsh society. These documents also allow for a comparison to be made between the care provided to impoverished married mothers, and their unmarried counterparts. Parish resources were limited, and the support provided under the poor law often covered only what was considered absolutely necessary. Analysis of what officials and communities deemed essential for the safe delivery of illegitimate infants is yet another means of assessing the underlying priorities and anxieties surrounding deviant reproduction in eighteenth-century Britain. Moreover, analysis of the care provided to unmarried mothers under different circumstances further reveals the diversity of experiences of childbirth outside of marriage.

Before any meaningful analysis of the care provided to unmarried parturient mothers can be undertaken, the overall availability of skilled midwives' services in eighteenth-century Wales must first be considered. Childbirth in early modern and eighteenth-century England has received considerable attention from historians but no similar studies of childbirth or midwifery in early modern Wales exist.[2] This chapter will therefore begin with an overview of midwifery in Wales within the context of eighteenth-century British childbirth practice. Many of the Welsh communities included in this study were remote and scattered, which raises questions about who was available to attend to parturient women. As we have seen in the previous chapter, Court of Great Sessions infanticide trial records demonstrate that midwives were present in some parishes, and could be called upon in more extreme circumstances. This chapter will cast the net more widely and examine evidence of those who provided maternity care in more routine situations, and will consider the socioeconomic backgrounds, skills and experience of those who delivered Welsh infants. As the eighteenth century was a period of significant change in childbirth practices associated with developments in obstetrics and the correlative rise of the man-midwife, the influence of these developments on maternity care for poorer women in Wales will also be considered.

After assessing the availability of midwifery services more broadly, and examining the identities of those who attended to poor parturient women, the actual process and rituals surrounding childbirth for poorer, unmarried women will be explored. The birth of a child was a biological event bearing immense social significance, and thus had established rituals and ceremonies which surrounded it.[3] The ceremony of childbirth has been written about in detail, most notably by Adrian Wilson, although his analysis primarily considers the experience of married women of the middling and upper classes. His assessment also portrays birth as a period of communal female celebration. However, as Laura Gowing has argued, the experience for poorer, single mothers was likely different.[4] Parish poor law accounts and quarter sessions records reveal that, for some unmarried women, labour could be a time of conflict and displacement. The experience for all single parturient women was not universal. When care was provided to poorer unmarried women it could range from limited support, offered only during the brief period of labour, to extended support for days or weeks before and after the birth event. These differences, and the reasons behind them, will be explored, as will the broader roles and responsibilities of midwives and other birth attendants beyond the safe delivery of infants. As Chapter 2 argued, not all unmarried mothers were destitute, and many were supported during labour by family, friends and even employers. Unfortunately, their experiences are all but lost to us. The records considered here only reveal the care provided to the poorest women who had no other means of support. Although limited, this evidence does provide a compelling glimpse of the complex and often, but not always, fraught experience of bearing a child outside of wedlock in the eighteenth century.

Midwifery in Wales

The eighteenth century saw some of the most significant changes to childbirth care in Britain before the twentieth century, and included the emergent popularity of the man-midwife, formal training in obstetrics for surgeons, and the establishment of lying-in hospitals in urban areas, particularly in London.[5] Despite these changes, the vast majority of women of the lower orders of society were attended by female midwives during labour and delivery throughout the century.[6] Skilled midwives were thus undoubtedly ubiquitous in early modern British society. Their presence can be found in a range of archival sources, and social, cultural, and medical historians of early modern England have utilised these for diverse histories of childbirth. Welsh sources have not been considered in any of these studies, and therefore the nature of childbirth in early modern Wales remains largely unknown. The predominantly rural, scattered nature of Welsh settlements raises questions about the availability of the services of skilled midwives and medical practitioners in many communities. The number of medical men trained in the new art of obstetrics was rapidly increasing over the eighteenth century in centres such as London, provincial cities and market towns.[7] Therefore, the persistence of a largely agrarian, rural economy in the region covered by this study also raises questions about the influences of advances in obstetric care on childbirth practice in Wales.

Evidence of midwives in Wales can be found in a wide range of documents, including applications for licences to practise midwifery, Court of Great Sessions and quarter sessions records, parish churchwarden and vestry accounts, as well as burial records, and wills. Only 11 applications for licences to practise midwifery have survived in the Welsh ecclesiastical records held by the National Library of Wales found in the collections for the diocese of Bangor, Llandaff and St Asaph, most of which date from the mid to late eighteenth century.[8] Many more licences were likely produced, however the survival rate for documents such as these in Wales is relatively poor. As the previous chapter demonstrated, midwives also appear frequently as witnesses in Great Sessions infanticide trial records between 1730 and 1800. Twelve of these cases have been examined here.[9] Quarter sessions records from across Wales have also survived to varying degrees and are held in county archives offices. The session rolls of the Montgomery quarter sessions from the 1750s to 1790s have been examined for this study.[10] Finally, parish overseers of the poor, churchwarden and vestry accounts, which survive with varying quality for parishes across all Welsh counties contain hundreds, if not thousands, of references of payments made to midwives for the delivery of pauper women. For this study, the accounts of 23 parishes across four Welsh counties from the eighteenth century have been analysed.[11]

The scope and variety of these sources provides ample evidence to suggest that the services of at least one woman experienced in delivering babies was readily available to most women across Wales, and that every parish appears to have had at least one woman on hand to deliver those in need. Given the shared ecclesiastical and legal systems, it is not surprising that the state of midwifery in Wales closely resembled midwifery in provincial England for much of the eighteenth century. By the 1760s, seven lying-in charities had been established in London, but throughout this period there were no formal institutions in Wales, or in most parts of rural England, dedicated to providing maternity care to either married or single women.[12] Women were attended by midwives in their own homes or within the community. The profiles of those who delivered infants in Wales resemble their English counterparts, and fall loosely into four categories: sworn midwives, midwives who practised without obtaining a formal licence, women who delivered infants but were not identified as 'midwife' and male practitioners, such as man-midwives and surgeons. Women who were simply identified as 'midwife' appear most frequently in available records, although it is not always possible to determine if they were formally sworn or not. Likewise, it is difficult to know what, if anything, was signified when a woman was paid for delivering infants without specifically being identified as a midwife. Very few oaths, licences and applications have survived, and it is highly probable that the distinction between those who paid for a licence and those who did not was somewhat arbitrary, as licences may simply have ratified decisions local women and officials had already made.[13] Therefore, for the purposes of this study, any woman identified as a midwife, or who was paid for providing the services of a midwife, will be considered as such.

Becoming a Midwife

Throughout the early modern period midwifery was not a formal trade for most practitioners, and the role of midwife was rarely a woman's only livelihood.[14] As David Harley has argued, for many, midwifery was a skill one possessed rather than a main social identity, especially for those who were not formally sworn.[15] In rural areas, early modern medical practice in general was typically a part-time occupation for most practitioners due to limited demand.[16] For female practitioners, the ability to successfully deliver infants and attend to women during labour was a skill learned entirely in the birth room. In London, experienced midwives would formally take on a 'deputy' who would learn their craft through what was essentially an apprenticeship. A similar system may have existed in some parts of Wales, although evidence is limited. From the sixteenth century the regulation of midwives was the remit of ecclesiastical authorities, and midwives, as well as physicians and surgeons, were expected to apply to their bishop to obtain a licence, and midwives were required to be formally sworn into office.[17] One clause found in several oaths from the diocese of Llandaff states that midwives 'will not make or assign any deputy or deputies to exercize or occupy under you ... but as you shall perfectly know to be of right honest and discrete behaviour.'[18] However, beyond this clause, there is no other evidence of how established or developed a practice of deputies was in Wales. Historians such as Doreen Evenden have suggested that the system of deputy midwives was unique to London, and therefore this clause may have reflected a formal route into gaining a licence which was unique to London, or was simply an administrative formality rather than an established practice.[19] Most midwives in Wales would have learned to deliver healthy babies through a less formalised system of assisting in deliveries, and after gaining sufficient experience, delivering infants on their own.[20]

In order to obtain a licence, an applicant was expected to provide written testimonies to prove her skills and abilities in the art of midwifery, and her sober and honest character.[21] Thus, paradoxically, midwives were expected to have successfully delivered numerous women before obtaining the licence that would allow them to legally carry out these duties. One application provides evidence of how this process may have operated in practise. The 1740 application of Rebecca Davies of Newtown, Montgomeryshire contained a testimonial of a Stafford Price, who stated that she, 'had practiced midwifery among her acquaintances with skill and success for some years and that [she is] duly qualified to receive a licence to practise the same publically for the future.'[22] It is therefore likely that women were allowed to provide the services of a midwife to their friends and family without a licence, but may have been expected to obtain one should they wish to offer their services beyond their extended networks. The cost of obtaining a licence varied, but could be as high as £2, which would have been a considerable and very likely prohibitive amount for many women.[23] Consequently, not all women who practised midwifery could obtain a license. Despite the potential risk of fines and presentments for not being licenced, it is highly probable that most women who delivered infants in early modern Britain were not licenced. In Wales, the risk of presentment was minimal, as there were few instances of unlicensed midwives, or any medical practitioners, being prosecuted.[24] With little chance of ever being called before ecclesiastical officials for practising without a licence, there would have been little incentive to obtain one. Despite this, some midwives did choose to go through the costly process to become licenced. Early modern British midwives should therefore not be considered as a homogeneous group who shared a common trade, status and experience, but rather should be understood as a diverse array of practitioners with varying skills, experiences, and responsibilities. The most detailed evidence of midwives comes from the testimonials accompanying their licencing applications. Despite the poor survival rate, the similarities between these documents and similar English records suggest comparable expectations and responsibilities for midwives. Of the 11 women whose oaths or applications survive, eight were described as the 'wife of' someone, and two midwives were described as widows.[25] The remaining midwife's marital status was not given, and therefore it is possible she was single. Unmarried midwives in England were not unheard of.[26] On rare occasions, single women gained experience in the birth room if they were an older daughter who had attended the labour of their mother, or if their mothers were practising midwives and they had assisted them in the birthing chamber.[27] However, this was not the norm, and although similar circumstances likely existed in Wales, there is little documented evidence of it. As in England, the majority of Welsh midwives appear to have been married women. The reasons for this were explored in detail in the previous chapter: reproductive knowledge was restricted, and it was through marriage that women were granted access to the knowledge about the female reproductive body that was central to becoming a successful, skilled midwife.

Midwives' Reputation

Marital status was not the only necessary requirement for admission into the office of midwife. Of equal, or perhaps more, importance was a woman's reputation, based on skill and character. Reputation was perhaps a midwife's, or any practitioner's, single most valuable trait.[28] Several of the surviving applications provide testimony attesting to a midwife's record in successfully attending to women during labour. In Wales, as in England, testimony about a woman's character and skills came from local officials, such as churchwardens and curates, and from the women she had previously delivered.[29] In 1740, Rebecca Davies of Newtown was described as 'a woman of grave and sober behaviour.'[30] In 1753, Wenllian Harry of Whitchurch in Glamorgan was certified to be a 'sober, modest person and very skilful in the art of midwifery.'[31] In 1774, Jane Morgan of Llantrisant in Glamorgan was certified by 11 of her neighbours to be 'a sober modest person of good life and conversation and very skilful in the art of midwifery, and . . . a proper woman to be licensed to practise the same.'[32] Descriptions of character were sometimes separated from descriptions of skill. In these cases, an applicant's character was vouched for by male officials from her parish, and her skills were verified by the women she had delivered. For example, in 1769, the vicar and portreeve (a higher-ranking administrative office in a town) of Llantrisant both certified that Elinor Ajax was 'a person of sober like & conversation,' while in a separate declaration three women stated that they had been delivered by Elinor, and certified that she was qualified to practise.[33] The 1753 application of Mary Winn of Cardiff provides details about the extent to which some midwives were considered skilled to manage difficult pregnancies and births. Winn's application contains two personal testimonials from women Winn had attended who had experienced complications as a result of less-skilled care. Jane Thomas stated that during a miscarriage at four months' gestation she was attended to by one Jennet Robert, who she described as an 'unskilful' midwife, who left her 'in a most deplorable condition so that [her] life was in the utmost danger.' However, her life was spared after being attended by Winn, who she described as 'a woman of great skill and knowledge in her profession.'[34] Similarly, Wenllian Watkins testified that she, too, had been left in 'a most deplorable condition' by the unskilled hand of a midwife named Ann Edward. Upon hearing of her 'melancholy condition,' Winn was sent for by 'Councillor Richard's Lady,' delivering Wenllian 'from the jaws of death.'[35]

The socioeconomic status of these midwives is difficult to ascertain, but there are indications to suggest they were of middling status. As the authority of the church courts waned in the eighteenth century, the system of ecclesiastical licencing, which was already weak in Wales, increasingly fell into disuse, particularly after 1750.[36] Therefore, any licence obtained in the latter half of the century may have been acquired for symbolic rather than practical reasons. Moreover, the fact that they were able to obtain an official licence indicates the means to afford one, and thus licences would have been restricted to the wives of yeoman, artisans and others of similar standing.[37] The occupation of only one applicant's husband was given. Elizabeth Anwyl's husband was described as an innkeeper, an occupation in line with many sworn midwives found in England.[38] Other indications of the status of these women can be found in the identities of those who vouched for them. All of the surviving testimonials bear the signatures of respected men from the communities, such as churchwardens, portreeves and curates. Many of the women whose names appear on testimonials were able to sign their own names as well, such as Margaret John, Magadalen Jones and Jane Morgan who provided evidence of Elinor Ajax's skills, Jane Jenkin who certified Margaret David's skills and Jane Thomas and Margaret Thomas who vouched for Mary Winn.[39] Their literacy indicates that these signatories were not of the lower orders of society. If witnesses were part of the midwives' immediate social networks, as Rebecca Davie's earlier testimonial suggests, they were likely to have been of similar social status. It is perhaps not coincidental that one of the only surviving presentments for a midwife accused of practising without a licence is included in a summons for a widow to appear for failing to properly administer her husband's estate.[40] In 1755, Elizabeth John Griffith of Anglesey was summoned to appear at the Bangor consistory court

> to answer to the articles which shall be objected against her touching the . . . administration of the goods, chattels, rights and credits of Owen Prichards Owen, taylor [sic], her late husband . . . and also for using or occupying the mistery or calling of a midwife without being thereunto lawfully authorized.[41]

The wife of a tailor would have been amongst those who could potentially have afforded a licence; however this may have gone unnoticed until the mismanagement of her late husbands' estate was brought to attention of the authorities. Her lack of licence despite her ability to afford one may have helped the ecclesiastical authorities to build a stronger case against her. This presentment was by no means evidence of Elizabeth Griffith's skills and experience as a midwife, but does provide further evidence of the correlation between licencing and socioeconomic status.

It is possible that many more practising midwives in Wales may have obtained licences, which may have long since been lost or destroyed. These include Margaret Davies who was identified as a 'sworn midwife' in her 1742 Court of Great Sessions deposition in the infanticide trial of Jane Harrington.[42] However, most midwives who appear in court and parish records were not identified as having been 'sworn', and there is no way of knowing if they were. Whether one was sworn does not appear to have been a significant detail, as it was seldom mentioned in court records when midwives were called upon to provide expert opinions. Court of Great Sessions infanticide records contain numerous examples of women who were called upon to examine the bodies of dead infants and their suspected mothers. These women were described as 'practising' or 'professional' midwives with no reference to having been formally sworn. In 1799, when surgeon William Jones was called to examine Hannah John for signs of childbirth, he objected to going without midwife Margaret Williams accompanying him.[43] In neither William's nor Margaret's depositions was she referred to as a 'sworn' midwife. Women such as Ellen Davies, who in 1734 was called upon to help 'ease' Elizabeth Davies of her afterbirth, was described as 'by profession a midwife.'[44] Lettice Lynstone and Anne Edwards, who examined the breasts of infanticide suspect Gwenllian David in 1753, were described as 'having for several years practised the profession of midwifery.'[45] Many others, such as Mary Williams and Margaret Williams were described simply as practising midwives.[46] In some cases, a quantifiable amount of experience appears to have been the most noteworthy credential, such as Dorothy verch Edwards, whose opinion of the body of Jane Griffith's dead infant was supported by her having practised midwifery for 54 years.[47] If these midwives were not sworn, it does not appear to have had any bearing on their credibility. Simply having this type of experience, which had been gained in the birthing chamber, but may not have been formally acknowledged by a bishop, may have been enough for a woman to be recognised and respected as a midwife.

It is impossible to determine if the ratio of sworn to unsworn midwives in Wales was comparable to England, but as in England, it is evident that a considerable number of midwives would not have taken the oath.[48] In reality, most would have lacked the means to pay for an official licence. The inability to obtain a licence would not have been a reflection of a midwife's reputation or capabilities, and the skills and reputations of most would have differed little from those who had licences.[49] What probably did differentiate sworn from unsworn midwives were individual economic circumstances. Women who worked as midwives came from across the social spectrum, including the lower orders. The aforementioned Anne Edwards, who examined Gwenllian Davies, was described as the wife of a labourer.[50] It is doubtful that a labourer's wife could have afforded the £1 to £2 needed to obtain a licence. Lacking means did not necessarily mean lacking reputation, standing and authority. Despite her lower status, Edwards' professional skills and opinions were valued highly enough to be sought by judicial officials as evidence in a murder trial. The same is likely true for all midwives who were called upon in legal proceedings. Countless other midwives were paid by parish officials to aid in the delivery of poorer inhabitants, and often the same women were called upon repeatedly over several years. Mrs Owens of Bettws Cedewain, Mary Goodwyn of Berriew, and Mrs Johnson of Hawarden all appear multiple times for deliveries over a span of several years.[51] In all instances, when a woman was referred to as a midwife, the English word was always used. The Welsh *bydwraig* never appears in official records; however, official ecclesiastical and secular records were kept in Latin until the 1730s, and English thereafter, so this is not surprising. The use of the title of 'midwife' outside of circumstances directly relating to the birth of a child may also indicate a certain level of respect attained after years of practise. The 1700 will of Frances Hughes of Haverfordwest, whose moveable goods were valued at a meagre £12, identified her as a midwife, although there is nothing in the inventory which relates in any way to her occupation.[52] Frustratingly, very few details are ever given about the status of these women and their backgrounds, but the fact that they were paid by parishes to perform specific duties, or identified as midwives in other official documents suggest that there was at least some level of recognition of their abilities. There is, of course, evidence of midwives whose skills were considered inferior. The two midwives who had initially attended to Mary Winn's clients are examples of this.[53] Additionally, in 1794, Mary Morgan, who was arrested on suspicion of infanticide, told a neighbour that the reason she looked pregnant when she was not was because a midwife who had previously attended to her had mismanaged her delivery, thus leaving her permanently disfigured.[54] The veracity of these accounts is debatable, but midwives' skills would certainly have varied considerably. However, it cannot be assumed that there was a direct correlation between holding a licence and having greater skills and experiences.

Fees for Midwives' Services

Sworn midwives and their unsworn counterparts from the lower orders would have been called upon most often to attend to poorer women in their parishes. The midwives' oath varied throughout the early modern period, and across regions, but one clause appears to have remained consistent: all sworn midwives were required to attend any woman in need, regardless of social status.[55] For example, Wenllian Harry's oath bound her to be, 'ready to help every woman labouring with child, as well the poor as the rich.'[56] This clause may have discouraged many higher-status midwives, who wanted to be more selective of their clientele, from obtaining a licence, as they could earn considerably more for their services by attending women higher up the social hierarchy than they could from serving poorer women.[57] Parish expenditure on maternity care will be explored further below, but a basic assessment of payments made to midwives by parishes may indicate why few midwives would have obtained licences. From the 1760s parish records in Montgomeryshire, Radnorshire, Denbighshire and Flintshire are full of entries for payments made to midwives for delivering the poor, and every parish for which detailed accounts exist made payments to midwives. These expenses show a clear need for the services of skilled midwives. A sample of 38 payments in seven parishes between 1765 and 1800, made specifically for the act of delivering an infant, demonstrates that most midwives employed by a parish were paid 2s. 6d. per delivery (Figure 6.1).[58] Although payments gradually increased over the period, with the highest payments made in 1797 (Castell Caereinion, 7s. 6d.), and 1800 (Bettws Cedewain, 7s.), payments for 2s. 6d. were made in all four decades. This is consistent with what midwives were paid for delivering pauper women in England.[59] Licences could cost as much as £2 so midwives, who were paid an average of 2s. 6d. per birth, would need to attend to at least 16 births before the cost of her licencing would have been fully amortised. If, as Adrian Wilson has suggested, most midwives had a low caseload of perhaps as few as ten deliveries per year, a licence could therefore represent roughly two years' wages. The caseload of most Welsh midwives is undeterminable, but one anecdotal reference from 1845 supports this figure. An epitaph for an

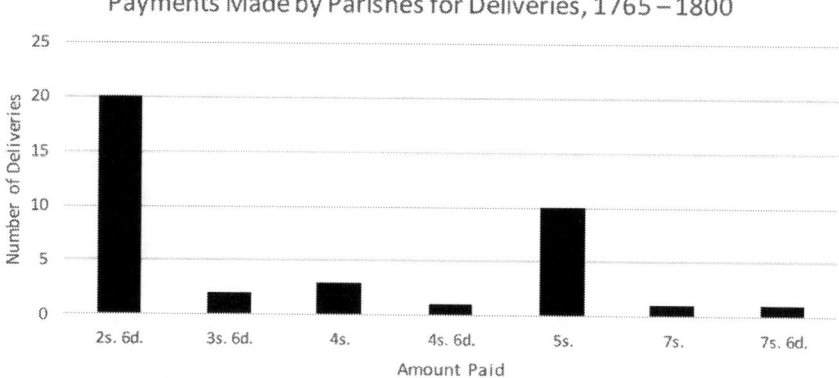

Figure 6.1 Sample of payments made by parish poor law officials for pauper births, 1765–1800.

'experienced and beloved' midwife named Elizabeth Davies, who died at the age of 81, proclaims that 'she received more than 300 babies into the world.'[60] If her career as a midwife spanned 30 years she would have averaged ten deliveries per year. It is likely that some midwives would have delivered significantly more, particularly in towns and larger settlements, but many others would have delivered much fewer. The effort and expense of obtaining a licence would not have been worthwhile for these women, particularly if women practised midwifery as a means of supplementing their household income.[61] Given the persistent need for the services of a skilled midwife, it would have been in the best interest of ecclesiastical authorities to disregard licencing requirements for those who could not realistically afford one, especially if they were suitably skilled.

For many midwives, the only evidence that they existed at all is when they are mentioned in churchwarden and vestry accounts, when their services were acquired by parish officials. The ambiguity of many entries makes it impossible to map the careers of these women, but most parishes probably had a reserve of two or three trusted women whose services could be called upon.[62] Very few details accompany entries made for payments to midwives, and often not even a name is given, as countless anonymous entries for 'paid the midwife' attest. For example, between 1765 and 1800 parish officials in Bettws Cedewain made payments for at least 19 pauper births, 12 of which specify payments made for a delivery. Seven of these payments either state 'paid the midwife' or 'paid for delivering' without identifying who provided these services. Three payments were made to a woman identified only as the wife of Robert Owen, and the remaining two were made to 'Edward Thomas's wife,' and to 'Margaret Thomas, midwife,'[63] It is possible that these distinctions between those identified as 'midwife' and those listed simply by name, or as 'wife of' may reflect different levels of experience, where a woman would only be referred to as 'midwife' after gaining a reputation for her skills, but there is little evidence to support this. In most cases, this variation appears to carry no overt significance, and may simply relate to the custom of referring to women first and foremost by their marital status. The payment made to an anonymous midwife in 1776 was identical to the payment made to the wife of Edward Thomas in 1781, which would suggest that the services provided by these women were deemed equal.[64] If midwifery was not considered a formal trade, and if a woman's main social identity was based on her marital status, the use of the title 'midwife' may not have been considered necessary. Moreover, if a woman was being paid to deliver a child, her status as a midwife for parish officials may have been axiomatic. The exception to this may have been instances where a pauper woman who was in receipt of parish support was paid to deliver other paupers. For example, in 1774 and 1779 the parish of Berriew paid for Mary Goodwyn, a single woman, to travel to nearby parishes to swear the paternity of her children. In 1777 and 1778 Mary Goodwyn was also paid by the same parish to deliver the wives of two other parish paupers.[65] It is possible that Goodwyn was expected to provide these services in exchange for the support she received. A further example can be found in 1791 in the parish of Castell Caereinon, where Elizabeth Oliver was paid 3s. 6d. to deliver Alice Roberts of her illegitimate child. Shortly thereafter, the parish paid 3s. 6d. to Elizabeth's mother to deliver Elizabeth of her illegitimate child.[66]

The differences in amounts parish officials paid to different midwives for their services therefore cannot be said to reflect whether a midwife held a licence, or the level of her skill and experience. Payments to midwives were not standardised, and varied considerably between parishes across Britain; however some patterns in Welsh parish records are evident.[67] Differing payments most likely reflect varying degrees of difficulties and birth complications, with a basic fee of 2s. 6d. for uncomplicated pauper births in Wales in the latter half of the eighteenth century. Adrian Wilson has argued that major complications such as obstructions, haemorrhaging, eclampsia and puerperal fever were relatively rare. Most births, therefore, would have been relatively uncomplicated, and manageable by most midwives.[68] The maternal mortality rate discussed in Chapter 3 supports Wilson's argument. However, complications did still occur, and midwives practising for any length of time were likely to encounter these, however infrequently. Higher payments for some pauper births can therefore be attributed to compensation for more difficult or protracted deliveries. In the eighteenth century, as in the present day, the progress of labour was determined by a variety of factors, including the size and shape of the mother's pelvis, as well as the position, or presentation, of the infant in the birth canal.[69] Most infants present head-first, which is the easiest presentation to deliver. Breech birth are less common but are not rare, and present increased, but not insurmountable, difficulties. Most experienced midwives would have been capable of successfully delivering these births.[70] The most rare and difficult presentations are those in which the infant lies transversely, presenting by the arm, shoulder, back or belly first.[71] These invariably resulted in an obstructed birth that required more aggressive intervention, and often resulted in the loss of infant life, and risked the mother's as well.[72] Other types of complicated births could challenge the skills of midwives. In Berriew in 1794 a midwife and attendant were paid 10s. for tending to Mary Rowlands for four days, presumably as a result of a complication which claimed her life, as the parish paid for her funeral three days after the baptism of her illegitimate daughter Ann.[73] The highest single amount paid to a midwife was in Castell Caereinion in 1797, where an unnamed midwife was paid 7s. 6d. to attend to Jane Rogers.[74] The parish spent a total of £9 6s. 7½d. on her care, maintenance and other related expenses, which included £1 1s. paid to a Dr Jones.[75] The corresponding baptism record provides evidence as to why this level of care was required, as Jane was delivered of twins.[76]

Jane Roger's lying-in is one of the few documented instances in which a male practitioner attended a pauper woman during her labour. In this case, the male attendant was identified as a doctor, but in other records, these men were identified with the additional label of 'man-midwife.' Although rare, instances such as this do provide limited evidence of the rise of the man-midwife in Wales. In England, from at least as early as the seventeenth century, male medical practitioners had been called upon to assist in difficult deliveries, but only as a last resort. Prior to the eighteenth century, men played no role in the management of normal childbirth.[77] This changed dramatically during the eighteenth century with the establishment of obstetrics as a medical specialisation, and its inclusion in formal medical training led by practitioners such as William Smellie, who taught over 900 male practitioners during the 1740s.[78] These developments emerged first in London, but soon spread to provincial centres and gradually into rural areas, but their inroads in Wales have never been examined. Historians have differed in their interpretations of the reasons behind the rise of the man-midwife. Adrian Wilson and Jean Donnison have argued that fashion played an important role, as upper and middle-class women opted for the more expensive and elite services of a man-midwife, who increasingly usurped the role of female practitioners.[79] However, others, such as Helen King, have suggested that the shift was supply-led, as medical men increasingly moved into midwifery as other medical fields became overcrowded, thus increasing the availability of their services.[80] The evidence for Wales unfortunately sheds no light on the tastes of middling and upper-class women, or on the numerical prevalence of man-midwives in the country as a whole. Most documented instances relate to practitioners who were called to attend to lower-status women, and only in exceptional circumstances. However limited, this evidence does demonstrate that man-midwives were making inroads into Welsh society to at least some degree.

Evidence of man-midwives in Wales is found in many of the same sources where female practitioners are found, such as court records and parish poor law accounts. The earliest mention of man-midwives in the Welsh sources examined here is from a Court of Great Sessions infanticide trial record. In 1765, two men identified as surgeons and man-midwives, named John Kerry of Chester and Honoratus Leigh Thomas of Hawarden, examined the body of a murdered infant.[81] Roughly ten years later, two other surgeons and man-midwives served as expert witnesses in infanticide trails in Cardiganshire and Denbighshire, and a third appears in a 1795 trial.[82] Midwifery was not these men's sole occupation, and like most man-midwives, obstetrics would have been incorporated into their routine practice.[83] As surgeons first and foremost, their fees for attending to parturient women were much higher than the fees paid to female midwives. For example, a Shropshire surgeon and man-midwife practising in the eighteenth century routinely charged between 10s. 6d. and £1 1s. per delivery.[84] The higher rates charged by man-midwives would, therefore, have been beyond the reach of many.[85] Man-midwives were therefore not a cost-effective choice for parish poor law officials, and thus only appear in exceptional circumstances. A petition to the overseers of the poor in the parish of Meifod demonstrates how the expense of having to call for a man-midwife could be ruinous. In February 1777, Samuel Ward wrote to officials asking them to support his tenant:

> This is to inform you as the bearer hereof David Thomas has been a tenant to me nine years and has always paid me. Only the last year and a half's rent will be due Lady Day Next. His wife has had a very bad time at her lying in, and David Thomas was obliged to have a man midwife in order to save his wife's life and the surgeon's bill is three guineas and will not stay any longer for it which has rendere'd him not able to pay me my rent if the doctor troubles him I must seize for my rent and by that means the children must come on the parish.[86]

That Thomas had to choose between paying his rent and paying for a man-midwife to attend to his wife shows how costly their services were. Man-midwives were therefore only called upon in the most complicated of circumstances. The delivery of Jane Rogers' twins is one example of this, as is the £1 15s. paid to an anonymous doctor by the parish of Llanfihangel-yng-Ngwynfa in 1797 for the delivery of Robert Ellis's wife. In this case, the parish also paid for a coffin, shroud, and ale for her funeral, which hints at a fatal complication such as an obstruction.[87]

Surgeons and man-midwives were traditionally called upon to perform the procedures female practitioners were not supposed to do. Despite their skills and experiences in the birth room, female midwives were expected to not use surgical instruments such as hooks, crochets or innovations such as forceps, which could have aided in certain situations such as foetal malpresentation.[88] As male practitioners were called upon only in emergency situations for pauper deliveries, they would have been sent for only after a woman had been labouring under the care of a midwife for some time, and thus it would have been the midwife who called for help. The midwife attending to Jane Rogers was likely the person who summoned Dr Jones when the severity of the situation became apparent, and the doctor who attended to Robert Ellis's wife would not have been her primary attendant. Thus, it was essential for surgeons and man-midwives to be known and respected by female midwives.[89] Evidence from infanticide trials suggests that this type of professional respect was reciprocated. Surgeon William Jones' insistence that he be accompanied by midwife Margaret Williams is indicative of their working relationship and his professional respect for her and her experience.[90] It does not follow that all midwives would have automatically respected all surgeons and man-midwives, or vice versa. However, a professional relationship clearly did exist between some of the male and female practitioners who attended to pauper deliveries.

This evidence only speaks to the care of the poorest women in Welsh society, as evidence of those who attended women higher up the socioeconomic ladder in Wales is scarce. It is likely that female midwives predominated throughout the eighteenth century, with the services of male practitioners gradually becoming more available as the century progressed. Man-midwives could have been increasingly hired to attend to the middling and upper classes not only for more complicated births, but also for those who preferred their services. The fact that they were available to attend to poorer women at all, and to provide testimony in Court of Great Sessions trials, shows that they did have a presence in Wales. It is therefore clear that a diverse range of skilled practitioners were available to at least some degree to attend to all parturient women in Wales. However, the treatment and care women received during childbirth, and in the periods immediately before and after, could vary considerably, especially for women who were poor, pregnant and unmarried.

The Ceremony of Childbirth for Unmarried Women

In eighteenth-century Britain, as in all periods, childbirth was more than just the physical act of delivering a child: it was a social event and rite of passage which carried immense social and cultural significance. Birth involved a series of prescribed rituals and participants: the birth room was to be prepared in particular ways, a mother was to be confined for the duration of her lying-in, which included the time leading up to and following delivery, certain individuals were to be excluded, and others expected to be in attendance.[91] These elements served the interests not only of the mother and the infant, but of the community as well. However, these interests could at times be conflicting, especially when mothers were poor and unmarried.[92] Moreover, women's access to each of the prescribed elements varied depending on a range of factors beyond marital status, including financial means and right of settlement in a parish. For married women of means, birth could be a period of celebration which conformed to prescribed expectations, and where a new life was welcomed into the wider community. However, if a child was born to a single mother who lacked the means to support herself and her child, the community could be far less welcoming, and in these circumstances, celebrations could be replaced with conflict and anxiety. Yet even for unmarried women, the experience of childbirth could vary immensely, and the evidence from Wales demonstrates that not all single mothers were treated with the same level of hostility.

Our understanding of the rituals surrounding the process of giving birth in early modern Britain are drawn almost exclusively from prescriptive literature and from autobiographical accounts from the middling sort and elites, such as the diary of seventeenth-century Essex vicar Ralph Josselin.[93] These accounts portray a frequently female-centred ritual with clearly defined rules, roles and expectations. Adrian Wilson's assessment of what he has dubbed, 'the ceremony of childbirth' portrays the rituals of childbirth as collective female celebrations and social occasions, where women of the community gathered to witness and support the delivery of one of their neighbours. This was a social occasion which also served to reinforce social relationships and hierarchies.[94] However, Laura Gowing has argued that the birthing chamber was not necessarily an entirely supportive space, and the social experience of childbirth for many women, married or single, could be characterised by tension and fear.[95] Unfortunately, available records from Wales do little to reveal the dynamics of the birth room in the eighteenth century. However, poor law and quarter sessions records do provide compelling evidence of the types of care provided to some poorer women, both married and unmarried, which hint at some of the tensions which could be present. Comparison of the care provided to poor unmarried parturient women with that of their married counterparts, and to the idealised ritual of childbirth in eighteenth-century Britain is revealing of the complex attitudes towards, and anxieties surrounding, childbirth outside of marriage.

In its most ideal form, the ceremony of childbirth in eighteenth-century Britain involved the confinement of a woman who was near her time of delivery in a chamber lit by candles, warmed by a fire, and sealed off from outside air and light.[96] All men, including the expectant baby's father, were to be excluded from this space, although this gradually changed with the rise of the man-midwife. The mother was to be attended by a midwife whose authority dominated the birth room, and a group of adult female family and neighbours known as the 'gossips' who provided assistance. After delivery, a woman's confinement would continue through the period known as 'lying-in' during which time she would stay in bed to rest and recover from labour, and she could remain there for up to one month. After her period of lying-in, the mother would be welcomed back into the community through the ritual of churching, which could correspond with the baptism of her child. The reality for many women would have come nowhere near this expectation. Not all women would have had access to a separate room where she could withdraw from the rest of the household, or have the means to acquire supplies such as candles and curtains, and many would not have been able to retire from their routine domestic tasks for an entire month.[97] However, it is likely that most women would have adapted many of these ritual elements as much as possible within their means.[98] Laura Gowing has argued that many of these elements would have been adapted even further for unmarried mothers. For example, the neighbourliness of gossips and the supportive role of midwives could be transformed into punishing interrogation.[99] However, many poor, unmarried women did receive basic elements of support nonetheless. By breaking the ceremony of childbirth down into its component parts and comparing recorded evidence of pauper experiences of the space and place of birth, the period of lying-in and its related rituals, and those who attended poor and unmarried women in Wales, it becomes clear that the experience of childbirth for unmarried mothers varied widely.

Where a woman gave birth was important in two ways: as set out earlier, the physical space, or birthing chamber, in which the birth took place was expected to conform to certain criteria which informed who and what should be included or excluded. However, the geographic location of the birth was also incredibly important, especially for poorer women. An Act from 1662 gave overseers of the poor and justices of the peace the authority to remove those who did not have the legal right of settlement from a parish to their last known place of settlement.[100] Prior to 1743, all children gained legal settlement in the parish in which they were born.[101] Thus, parish officials were highly motivated to remove unmarried pregnant women through legal channels to ensure that their infants did not become a financial burden on their rate payers. Poor law records demonstrate this procedure in action. In 1738, overseers in Trefeglwys presented an unmarried pregnant woman named Anne Bamford to a justice of the peace who ordered her to be removed to the parish of Newtown at a cost of 17s.[102] However, after 1743 illegitimate children gained legal settlement based on their mother's parish of settlement, regardless of where they were born, with the mother potentially facing whipping and imprisonment in the house of correction for up to six months.[103] Despite this, the numerous expenses incurred by parishes across Wales for the examination and removal of unmarried pregnant women suggest that parish officials were still keen to ensure single women did not deliver within their boundaries. In 1753 a pregnant woman named Estar Lowe was removed by order from the parish of Llandinam.[104] In 1770 the parish of Ceri spent 6s. 1d. to remove a 'vagrant girl that was with child' to the parish of Bettws Cedewain approximately seven miles away.[105] These women were removed because they were poor and pregnant, and therefore posed a long-term financial risk to parishes. Both married and unmarried pregnant paupers could be removed from a parish, although most entries in Welsh records relate to the removal of single pregnant women. Sympathetic parishioners did occasionally take pregnant strangers in, either because of a personal connection to them or simply out of charity. Harbouring an unmarried pregnant woman, however, was a punishable offence, and authorities did act against those who took women in.[106] In 1767 an overseer from Manafon travelled to the home of Adam Richard and ordered him to 'turn a woman that was big with child out of his house,' at a cost of 6d.[107] This practice meant that poor, pregnant women could be heavily stigmatised. An unmarried pregnant woman could find herself on the receiving end of hostility if she was visibly pregnant or found herself in labour in a parish where she did not officially belong.

For a poor, single woman who lacked settlement, going into labour was undoubtedly an anxious and distressing time. Fragments of evidence of what this experience may have been like can be found in quarter sessions and Great Sessions records. In 1750, a recently delivered single woman named Elizabeth Tomley was examined by the Montgomeryshire Quarters sessions regarding her settlement.[108] Her account of her delivery provides a rare glimpse of how harrowing some women's deliveries could be. Elizabeth had previously worked as a covenant servant in the parish of Llansanffraid-ym-Mechain, but after her period of employment ended, she 'wandered about the country following one Evan Rosser Russell a quack doctor chiefly residing in Llanfair,' and she became pregnant by him. Early one morning, Elizabeth found herself in labour in the parish of Llanfair. However, because she did not have legal settlement, 'the parishioners being alarmed thereat and fearing least the child should be born therein, and thereby gain a settlement, she could gain no admittance into any house but lay in that condition under the open air.' Elizabeth continued in that state, unaided, throughout the day until John Jones, who was a shopkeeper and high constable, came to her and 'used many threatening words to cause her to be gone.' Being in labour, Elizabeth was not able to make her own way out of the parish, and the constable ordered his servant to 'carry her by force on horseback towards the New bridges' in the neighbouring county of Meifod. Once there, she was set down and left to 'crawl with great difficulty and anguish' until she was finally taken in. That same evening she was delivered of a son by a midwife provided by parish overseers, and both Elizabeth and her child were then maintained for an undetermined period of time by the parish of Meifod. What happened to Elizabeth and her infant following this is evident, however given the fact that her case was heard by the quarter sessions under a charge of vagrancy it is possibly that she was publically whipped and confined in the house of corrections for up to six months.[109]

Elizabeth's experience bears striking resemblance to the treatment of poor, unmarried women in early modern England.[110] In her case, she was safely delivered by a midwife, but not all women were so lucky. Other single women, either by choice or necessity, did not or could not acquire similar support. In 1792, a pregnant servant named Mary Powell was removed from the parish of Clyro, Radnorshire to Llanhamlach, Breconshire 15 miles away. Soon after, she gave birth to an infant girl in a cowshed.[111] Unsurprisingly, Mary's child did not survive, and Mary was suspected of having murdered her daughter, although she was not indicted. The threat of this type of treatment could have motivated many poor, single pregnant women to conceal their pregnancies and take extreme measures, but could also put women in precarious circumstances that jeopardised their lives and the lives of their infants. Even if a woman without settlement was safely delivered of her child by a midwife, lying-in as a stranger could still carry consequences. When Sarah Owen fell into labour in Denbighshire in 1788 she sought help at the house of a blacksmith, where she was delivered of a son by a midwife. Fearing the repercussions from parish officials for having allowed an unmarried stranger to lay in at his house, the blacksmith escorted Sarah out of the parish. Her infant was later found dead and buried in a field.[112] Abandonment and murder represent the most desperate measures to which mothers resorted if they were unable to access any form of maternity support. However, the aggressive reluctance on the part of some parishes to provide care to unmarried parturient women can be seen as equally negligent or violent, and often resulted in identical outcomes. For example, after officials paid 15s. for the removal the aforementioned Estar Lowe from the parish of Llandiam, officials then paid an additional 1s. towards her infant's funeral.[113] How far the actions of Llandinam officials contributed to the death of her child is unclear, but her removal probably did not improve the infant's survival chances.

Not all unmarried pregnant women were moved about in this manner. Many other women went into labour in their parish of legal settlement, either because they were already present in their parish, or because they returned before going into labour. When this happened, officials had a legal requirement to provide care, and parish poor law accounts are full of examples of this in practise. Although far less tantalising and detailed than examinations and depositions of women who were displaced, this evidence is equally telling. It is also more abundant, which suggests that violent displacement was not the norm. As in the case of Elizabeth Tomley, removal could involve simply dumping an unwanted individual across parish boundaries, however it could also be a two-way process, where officials from one parish would remove, and officials in the parish of legal settlement would receive. This could come at a sizeable cost for the parish of settlement. When justices of the peace ordered Eliza Evans back to Trefeglwys, her parish of settlement, the overseers of Trefeglwys paid £1 5s. 4d. on her account, which included the cost of delivering her of her child.[114] It is difficult to imagine Eliza being warmly welcomed back to her home parish, but she was brought back and provided for during her time of need nonetheless.

The support Eliza was given during her delivery can be understood as a modified version of the ceremony of childbirth experienced by other women in her community.[115] If a single woman could not make her own arrangements, or did not have a family to return to, the parish would provide a suitable place in which to lie in.[116] Young single women could lie in at the home of her parents, such as the daughter of Thomas

Williams, whose father was paid 16s. for being delivered and maintained in his home.[117] Overseers frequently made payments to parishioners who lodged poorer married and unmarried pregnant women during their deliveries.[118] Frequently, unmarried women could be maintained in the home of a parish official, such as in Berriew in 1780, when an overseer received payment for lodging a single woman named Catherine Stokes in his house when she delivered her child.[119] In 1798, an overseer in Bettws Cedewain was paid 2s. 6d. for keeping Martha Morrice at his house for one week when she was delivered of her child.[120] Women could also be maintained in the homes of other neighbours, such as David Davies who kept Mary Calcot in his home in Llangadfan when she was brought to bed in 1788, or Anne Powell of Castell Caereinion who was paid 7s. for keeping Elizabeth Bayley when she was delivered of a daughter in 1773.[121] Women could also be lodged at the home of the midwife who delivered them, such as in Gresford in 1762, where a midwife was paid 10s. 'for houseroom and lying in William Hughes servant.'[122] Depending on the wealth of the person who took them in, unmarried women who gave birth in the home of a neighbour may not have had a separate room dedicated to her confinement. However, many married women who gave birth at home probably did not have a separate room at their disposal either.[123] What is significant, however, is that when under the care of the parish, women were provided with a safe space in which to give birth, and often this care closely resembled the care provided to married pauper women, evidenced by payments made to married women during lying which covered the costs of midwives and lodging.[124]

In these circumstances, single pregnant women were not being harboured, but were officially lodged and cared for by their parish. What single women experienced when they were tended to in the homes of neighbours or parish officials cannot be known, but it was possibly not entirely supportive or positive. The taking in of unmarried parturient women by parish officials could serve purposes that went beyond basic Christian charity, as this practice could have operated as an extension of the bodily surveillance of unmarried pregnant women examined in the previous chapter. The maintenance of unmarried parturient women could have been as much about the provision of care as it was about preventing further deviance in the form of concealment and infanticide.[125] The precariousness and uncertainty of childbirth for all women meant that witnesses were required, and, from the seventeenth century, women were legally prohibited from giving birth alone.[126] Birth attendants did support mothers and midwives, but could also provide vital evidence about what took place in the birthing chamber, such as witnessing that a stillborn child had indeed been born dead and was not a victim of infanticide.[127] A birth which took place without witnesses raised suspicions, especially if it resulted in a dead child, and infanticide trial records provide endless examples of this.[128] Birth attendants were therefore an essential part of the ceremony of childbirth in eighteenth-century Britain for all women, and Welsh officials ensured they were present for the deliveries of unmarried mothers. In 1787 the parish of Bettws Cedewain provided a midwife and other attendants for the delivery of Catharine Morris.[129] In 1797, Castell Caereinion officials paid a midwife 7s. 6d., and an attendant named Anne Evans a further 6d. to attend to Jane Rogers.[130] In the only example of the word in usage in the Welsh Records considered here, in 1769 officials in Guilsfield paid 1s. 'for the gossips' who attended the delivery of Jane Rowlands.[131] Gossips could be friends or family of a mother, but they also had a duty to the community.[132] When they were provided by the parish, it is possible that their loyalty lay in serving the interests of the community rather than the single mother, and they could have been expected to serve as witnesses and discuss publicly what took place in the birth room. Welsh parish records do not provide details about who these women were, what their relationship to the mother or role in the birth room was, but it is possible that these women provided support to the mother and midwife while also serving as witnesses in the interests of the wider community.

Historians have also argued that, for unmarried mothers, birth attendants served an additional purpose. As a respected member of the community, a midwife was required not only to safely deliver a woman, but also to uphold the interest of the parish.[133] It has been suggested by many historians that midwives would therefore threaten to withdraw their services during the most extreme moments of labour in order to force an unmarried mother to name the father of her child.[134] The female attendants present could assist in this punishing treatment, and then bear witness to any confessions that resulted. However, the extent of this practice across Britain is debatable. Evidence for it can be found in some areas. For example, filiation orders from Manchester in the 1730s contain the following clause:

> Jane Charnock of Manchester aforesaid widow examined upon her oath before us saith that she was present when the said Mary Gaskell was in extremity of labour of Phoebe Warburton the aforesaid bastard child and did officiate as midwife and that the said Mary Gaskell did then confess and declare that the above mentioned Charles Warburton is the only father thereof.[135]

However, this practice was not universal, and does not appear in filiation orders or bastardy bonds from eighteenth-century Wales.[136] The midwives' oath varied, and in some instances, did include a clause requiring midwives to extract information about paternity, but often this was not the case.[137] The surviving Welsh oaths that survive do contain a clause relating to paternal identification, but emphasised their duty to not extract a false confession. Sworn Welsh midwives were required not to force women 'to name or put any other person to be the father of her child, but only him who is the very father therefore.'[138] Thus, although sworn Welsh midwives were authorised to ascertain a father's identity, they were expected to take caution to not extract a false confession under duress and were not explicitly bound to obtain the identity of a father. Secular authorities had no statutory power to force midwives to extract information about paternity, and there is little evidence of midwives in Wales presenting evidence relating to paternity before Justices of the Peace.[139] Parish overseers regularly made payments to officials to take single women to swear the paternity of their child, but such payments rarely appear for midwives. In 1797 the parish of Castell Cereinion paid 3s. 6d. for a journey with a midwife to Bettws on account of Jane Rogers, which was possibly to provide evidence.[140] However, this is the only such example. Overall, Welsh records indicate that most unmarried mothers formally identified the fathers of the children prior to their birth, meaning there was little need for such punishment. A survey of 197 eighteenth-century bastardy bonds from six parishes in Montgomeryshire and Radnorshire shows that over half of all bonds were drawn up while a woman was still 'with child' rather than being 'lately delivered' or 'now delivered' (Figure 6.2).[141] It was therefore common practice in many parts of Wales for women to formally identify the father of her child before giving birth. Moreover, the exceptionally high rates of paternal identification discussed in Chapter 1 also suggests that there may have been no need for midwives and gossips to forcefully extract, or threaten to extract, information about paternity during a single woman's delivery, as the father's identity was usually already established by the time a woman went into labour. The midwives and gossips attending unmarried pregnant women would therefore have served the dual role of witnesses and carers, as they

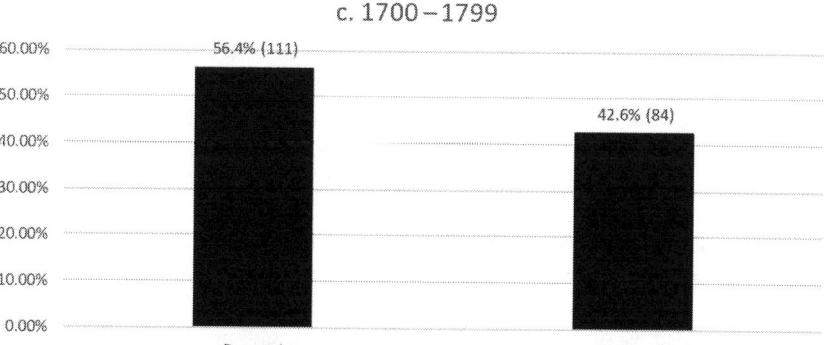

Figure 6.2 Comparison of bastardy bonds drawn up prior to vs after birth in Montgomeryshire and Radnorshire, c. 1700–1799.

would have for the birth of any other woman in the community. However, they would have attended to their duties with varying degrees of compassion or hostility depending on their relationship with the mother, and their opinions surrounding her circumstances.

One final way in which the provision of care towards unmarried parturient women can be explored is through their support during the lying-in period over the days and weeks following delivery. Under ideal circumstances, a woman would lie in for the period of one month following the birth of her child, and would then be welcomed back into the parish community through churching. There is limited evidence of churching in Welsh parish records. Across all parishes considered in this book, only two recorded the churching of women. Parish registers from Gladestry, Radnorshire recorded the churching of two married women in 1696, and the parish of Gresford, Denbighshire paid for the churching of several married and unmarried pauper women in the last three decades of the eighteenth century.[142] It is possible that churching was commonly practised throughout Wales, but too few records exist to allow for a meaningful analysis. However, there is evidence of married and unmarried pauper women being provided a lying-in period. During this time, it was expected that a new mother would remain confined to bed, and would refrain from work, going to church, and, for married women, engaging in sexual activities with her husband.[143] From 1733, unmarried mothers were excused from having to appear in front of a justice of the peace for the duration of the month following their delivery.[144] It would have been impractical for many women to remain confined for an entire month, and many single mothers in particular would have lacked the means to allow them to lie in for so long.[145] However, Welsh parish records do show that provisions were made for unmarried pauper women to have a lying-in period. Although it was not always for a month, it was often at least as long as the period provided to their married counterparts. In 1788 parish overseers in Llanarmon Dyffrin Ceiriog paid 2s. 6d. towards the lying-in expenses of Griffith Jones' wife, which was the same amount paid to unmarried women of the parish during their lying-in.[146] The duration of her lying-in period is not specified, but many unmarried women in other parishes lay in for anywhere from one week, such as Catherine Morris of Bettws Cedewain and Elinor Nicklas of Guilsfield, to several weeks or months.[147] At the furthest extreme is the 13-week lying-in period of Jane Jones of Castell Caereinion in 1795 when she was delivered of her second child outside of wedlock, at a cost of 16s. in total.[148] The reason for this extended lying-in period is not given, but the fact that parish officials supported her for this length of time is significant. In 1772, Elinor Jones of Llandrindod was similarly supported for a lying-in period of six weeks at a cost of 1s. per week, followed by an additional period of four weeks at 5s. per week.[149] Jane and Elinor likely both suffered complications that necessitated extended lying-in periods, and parishes supported them in this. Other single women, such as Gwen Thomas of Meifod, were allotted the prescribed lying-in month.[150] Like many Welsh single women, Gwen's child was put out to nurse, which meant she would not have been prevented by child care duties from returning to any employment she may have held before lying-in.[151] Despite this, Gwen was still allotted a full month's lying-in. What is significant is that single women were not only allotted a period of lying-in, but that parishes appear to have supported married and unmarried pauper women in similar ways.

Conclusion

It is difficult, if not impossible, to know if single women who were in receipt of parish support during their deliveries were treated with compassion or with contempt. For many unmarried women, the experience of the later stages of pregnancy, parturition and the period that immediately followed, may not have been a period of celebration, but neither was it inevitably a period characterised by conflict and hostility. Women's experiences would have varied depending on their reputations and standing in the community, and the circumstances surrounding the conception of their child. Many women likely did experience hostility from those who attended to them, but there is evidence of benevolence in the treatment of some unmarried mothers and infants as well. If an unmarried mother was in her parish of settlement during the later stages of her pregnancy, and if she conformed to expectations by making her pregnancy known, and cooperated with officials about the identity of her child's father, then she was likely afforded the same care provided to married pauper women. However, if she resisted the authority of her parish and her community, or if she fell into labour in a parish in which she did not belong, her experience was usually far more conflicted. Marital status was therefore one of several factors which influenced the care provided to women. Thus, there was no single experience of childbirth for unmarried mothers. This evidence necessitates a reconsideration of the role of communities in illegitimate childbirths to further examine the diverse, complex and nuanced relationships between neighbours, authorities and single women, as these encounters were not universally characterised by hostility and conflict.

The evidence examined here is exceptional in that it relates only to the poorest members of society who were in receipt of parish support. Moreover, most of these records relate to women who bore children outside of wedlock, which, again, were the exception rather than the norm. However, the management of illegitimacy and poverty in the eighteenth century has produced some of the only evidence of the experience of childbirth for women from the lower orders. Although this evidence relates only to the poorest women in eighteenth-century Welsh society, the fact that so many of the elements of the ceremony of childbirth were observed in unmarried pauper births strongly suggests that these

216 *Pregnancy and Childbirth*

experiences would have been replicated across Welsh society, and British society more broadly. The care provided to women was based upon what was considered necessary for a 'proper' birth experience. If even the poorest unmarried women were provided with the services of a midwife, and allowed a period of recovery afterwards, it is likely that all women in Welsh society had access to this type of care. Regardless of status, childbirth would have been an anxious and difficult time for all women in early modern Britain.[152] Welsh women, both married and unmarried, would have been tended to in similar ways to women in other parts of the British Isles. Despite its remoteness, most women in eighteenth-century Wales would have had access to the services of an experienced midwife and, as the century progressed, many would have been served by male practitioners as well. This analysis of the experiences of childbirth for unmarried mothers is revealing therefore not only of pauper women's experience, but of most women's experiences in the eighteenth century.

Notes

1. An earlier version of this chapter has been published as Angela Joy Muir, 'Midwifery and Maternity Care for Single Mothers in Eighteenth-Century Wales', *Social History of Medicine* (2018) <https://doi.org/10.1093/shm/hky092>. Oxford University Press.
2. Leah Astbury, 'Being Well, Looking Ill: Childbirth and the Return to Health in Seventeenth-Century England', *Social History of Medicine*, 20 (2017), 500–519; Cody, *Birthing the Nation*; Evenden, *Midwives of Seventeenth-Century London*; Fildes, *Women as Mothers*; Fissell, *Vernacular Bodies*; Gowing, *Common Bodies*; Williams, 'Experience of Pregnancy'.
3. Crawford, 'Construction and Experience of Maternity', p. 14.
4. Gowing, *Common Bodies*, p. 150.
5. Helen King, 'Midwifery, 1700–1800: The Man-Midwife as Competitor', in *Nursing & Midwifery in Britain Since 1700*, ed. by Anne Borsay and Billie Hunter (Basingstoke: Palgrave Macmillan, 2012), pp. 107–127; Jean Donnison, *Midwives and Medical Men: A History of the Struggle for the Control of Childbirth* (New Barnett: Historical Publications, 1988), p. 37; Evans, *Unfortunate Objects*, pp. 145–146; Adrian Wilson, *The Making of Man-Midwifery: Childbirth in England, 1660–1770* (London: UCL Press, 1995).
6. Lisa Forman Cody, 'The Body in Birth and Death', in *A Cultural History of the Human Body in the Enlightenment*, ed. by Carole Reeves (London: Bloomsbury Academic, 2014), pp. 13–31 (p. 15); Evans, *Unfortunate Objects*, p. 146.
7. Wilson, *Making of Man-Midwifery*, p. 2.
8. NLW (Llandaff) SD/LL/SM.2 (Elinor Ajax, 1769), 5 (Margaret David, 1761)), 8 (Wenllian Harry, 1753), 9 (Mary Hopkin, 1780), 11 (Jane Jones, 1754), 12 (Jane Lewelin, 1760), 15 (Jane Morgan, 1774), 17, 19; (Bangor) B/SM/1 (Elizabeth Annwyl, 1753); (St Asaph) SA/FB/1 (Rebecca Davies, 1740).
9. In the database, there are 142 records listed relating to infanticide cases, but some of these are cases have more than one accused, or are individuals who were indicted more than once. The records used here are as follows: NLW 4/46/2 (Denbighshire, Catherine Roberts, 1736),; NLW 4/47/7

(Denbighshire, Mary Philips, 1742); NLW 4/58/2 (Denbighshire, Elizabeth Bellis, 1744); NLW 4/62/1 (Denbighshire, Sarah Owen, 1788); NLW 4/298/4 (Merioneth, Elizabeth Davies, 1734); 4/380/6 (Breconshire, Gwenllian David, 1753); NLW 4/530/6 (Rednorshire, Mary Powell, 1792); 4/752/4 (Carmarthenshire, Hannah John, 1799); NLW 4/900/3 (Cardiganshire, Ann Hughes, 1776); 4/906/4 (Cardiganshire, Maria Morris, 1795); NLW 4/1002/4 (Flintshire, Jane Griffith, 1739); NLW 4/1007/1 (Flintshire, Elizabeth Williams, 1765).
10. PCA (Montgomeryshire) M/QS/SR 50–99.
11. FRO (Hawarden) D/BJ/324–328; DAO (Llanarmon Dyffrin Ceiriog) PD/41; (Llanarmon-yn-Ial) PD/43; (Llandegla) PD/45; PCA (Aberhafesp) M/EP/2; (Berriew) M/EP/3; (Bettws Cedwain) M/EP/4; (Carno) M/EP/6; (Castell Caereinion) M/EP/7; (Guilsfield) M/EP/19; (Kerry) M/EP/8; (Llandinam) M/EP/15; (Llanfihangel-yng-Ngwynfa) M/EP/21; (Llangadfan) M/EP/24; (Llangynyw) M/EP/27; (Llanllwchaearn) M/EP/30; (Llanwnog) M/EP/38; (Manafon) M/EP/40; (Meifod) M/EP/41; (Trefeglwys) M/EP/50; (Tregynon) M/EP/51; (Llanbister) R/EP/1; (Llandrindod) R/EP/47.
12. Evans, *Unfortunate Objects*, p. 145.
13. Samuel S Thomas, 'Early Modern Midwives: Splitting the Profession, Connecting the History', *Journal of Social History*, 43 (2009), 115–138 (p. 116).
14. David Harley, 'Provincial Midwives in England: Lancashire and Cheshire, 1660–1760', in *The Art of Midwifery: European Midwives in Europe*, ed. by Hilary Marland (Abingdon: Routledge, 1993), pp. 27–48 (p. 28).
15. Harley, 'Provincial Midwives', p. 28.
16. Margaret Pelling, *The Common Lot: Sickness, Medical Occupations and the Urban Poor in Early Modern England* (Abingdon: Routledge, 1998), pp. 203–229.
17. Wilson, *Ritual and Conflict*, p. 160.
18. NLW SD/LL/SM/8 (Wenllian Harry, 1753): O; SD/LL/SM/9:O (Mary Hopkin, 1780); SD/LL/SM/11:O (Jane Jones, 1754); SD/LL/SM/15:O (Jane Morgan, 1774); SD/LL/SM/19:O (Mary Winn, 1753).
19. Evenden, *Midwives of Seventeenth-Century London*, pp. 54–59.
20. Cody, *Birthing the Nation*, p. 35; Elaine Hobby, 'Introduction', in *Midwives Book*, ed. by Sharp, p. xiv.
21. Wilson, *Ritual and Conflict*, pp. 160–161; Thomas, 'Early Modern Midwives', p. 116.
22. NLW SA/FB/1 (Rebecca Davies, 1740).
23. Thomas, 'Early Modern Midwives', p. 116; Evenden, *Midwives of Seventeenth-Century London*, p. 38.
24. Withey, *Physick and the Family*, p. 153.
25. The married women were Elinor Ajax (NLW/SD/LL/SM/2); Margaret David (NLW/SD/LL/SM/5); Wenllian Harry (NLW/SD/LL/SM/8); Mary Hopkin (NLW/SD/LL/SM/9); Jane Llewellin (NLW/SD/LL/SM/12); Jane Morgan (NLW/SD/LL/SM/15); Jane Robert (NLW/SD/LL/SM/17); the widows were Mary Winn (NLW/SD/LL/SM/19) and Mrs Rebecca Davies (SA/FB/1); the midwife for whom no marital status was given: Jane Jones (NLW/SD/LL/SM/11).
26. Wilson, *Making of Man-Midwifery*, p. 30.
27. Cody, *Birthing the Nation*, p. 30; Williams, 'Experience of Pregnancy', pp. 67–86, endnote 33.
28. Withey, *Physick and the Family*, p. 158.
29. Thomas, 'Early Modern Midwives', p. 116.
30. NLW SA/FB/1 (Rebecca Davies, 1740).

218 *Pregnancy and Childbirth*

31. NLW/SD/LL/SM/8 (Wenllian Harry, 1753).
32. NLW/SD/LL/SM/15 (Jane Morgan, 1774).
33. NLW/SD/LL/SM/2 (Elinor Ajax, 1769).
34. NLW/SD/LL/SM/19 ii (Mary Winn, 1753).
35. NLW/SD/LL/SM/19 ii (Mary Winn, 1753).
36. Harley, 'Provincial Midwives', p. 39.
37. Wilson, *Making of Man-Midwifery*, p. 32.
38. NLW/B/SM/1 (Elizabeth Annwyl, 1753); Wilson, *Making of Man-Midwifery*, p. 30.
39. NLW/SD/LL/SM/2 (Elinor Ajax, 1769); NLW/SD/LL/SM/5 (Margaret David, 1761); NLW/SD/LL/SM/19 (Mary Wynn, 1753).
40. NLW B/CC/C(P)/39 (Elizabeth John Griffith of Newborough, widow, 1755).
41. NLW B/CC/C(P)/39 (Elizabeth John Griffith of Newborough, widow, 1755).
42. NLW/4/519/6 (Radnorshire, Jane Harrington, 1742).
43. NLW 4/752/4 (Carmarthenshire, Hannah John, 1799).
44. NLW 4/298/4 (Merioneth, Elizabeth Davies, 1734).
45. NLW 4/380/6 (Breconshire, Gwenllian David, 1753).
46. NLW 4/46/2 (Denbighshire, Catherine Roberts, 1736) & NLW 4/47/7 (Denbighshire, Mary Philips, 1742).
47. NLW 4/1002/4 (Flintshire, Jane Griffith, 1739).
48. Gowing, *Common Bodies*, p. 159.
49. David Harley, 'Historians as Demonologists: The Myth of the Midwife-Witch', *Social History of Medicine*, 3 (1990), 1–26 (pp. 11–12).
50. NLW 4/380/6 (Breconshire, Gwenllian David, 1753).
51. PCA (Bettws Cedewain) M/EP/4/O/RT/2 (Berriew); PCA M/EP/3/V/VM/3; FRO (Hawarden) D/BJ/326.
52. NLW SD/1700/56 (will of Frances Hughes, Midwife, 1700). At the time of her death she lived in a five-room house consisting of two bed chambers, a garret, a small parlour and a kitchen, but her goods were valued at £12. To put this in perspective, Lesley Davison's study of 56 spinster wills from the Diocese of St David's between 1700 and 1715 revealed a range of inventory values from as little as 2d. to as much as £322, with many under £20, and 18 with £10 or less. A large portion of these women were rural householders able to maintain themselves through subsistence farming, however most lived in much smaller houses. It would appear that Frances had a substantial house with a modest but comfortable level of wealth. See Davison, 'Spinsters'.
53. NLW SD/LL/SM/19 ii (Mary Winn, 1753).
54. NLW 6/629/2 (Glamorgan, Mary Morgan, 1794).
55. Wilson, *Ritual and Conflict*, p. 161.
56. NLW SD/LL/SM/8 (Wenllian Harry, 1753).
57. Gowing, *Common Bodies*, p. 159; Wilson, *Making of Man-Midwifery*, p. 26.
58. Source: PCA (Berriew) M/EP/3/V/VM/4; PCA (Bettws Cedewain) M/EP/4/O/RT/1 & 2; PCA (Castell Caereinion) M/EP/7/O/RT/2& 3; PCA (Ceri) M/EP/8/O/RT/3, 5, 6, & 9; PCA (Llanarmon Dyffrin Ceiriog), PD/41/1/6; PCA (Meifod M/EP/41/O/RT/3), PCA (Trefeglwys) M/EP/50/O/RT/3; PCA (Tregynon) M/EP/51/O/RT/3.
59. Wilson, 'Ceremony of Childbirth', pp. 72–73.
60. Frank T Jones, 'Notes on the Parish Registers of Merthyr Tydfil from AD 1703–1763', *Y Cymmrodor: The Magazine of the Honourable Society of Cymmrodorion*, 35 (1925), 157–186 (p. 164).
61. Wilson, *Making of Man-Midwifery*, p. 34.
62. Wilson, *Making of Man-Midwifery*, p. 34.

63. PCA (Berriew) M/EP/4/O/RT/1 & 2.
64. PCA(Berriew) M/EP/4/O/RT/1 & 2.
65. PCA (Bettws Cedewain) M/EP/3/V/VM/3 & 4.
66. PCA (Castell Caereinion) M/EP/7/O/RT/3.
67. Wilson, 'Ceremony of Childbirth', p. 72; Evenden, *Midwives of Seventeenth-Century London*, p. 127.
68. Wilson, *Making of Man-Midwifery*, p. 15.
69. Wilson, *Making of Man-Midwifery*, p. 11; Schofield, 'Did the Mothers Really Die?' pp. 231–232; Louden, 'Deaths in Childbed', pp. 22–24.
70. Wilson, *Making of Man-Midwifery*, pp. 11–12.
71. Wilson, *Making of Man-Midwifery*, pp. 11–12.
72. Wilson, *Making of Man-Midwifery*, pp. 11–12.
73. PCA (Berriew) M/EP/3/V/VM/4; MGS (Berriew) MR/C/27 (1794); MGS (Berriew) MR/PR/45 (1794).
74. PCA (Castell Caereinion) M/EP/7/O/RT/3.
75. PCA (Castell Caereinion) M/EP/7/O/RT/3.
76. MGS (Castell Caereinion) MR/C/15 (1797).
77. Wilson, *Making of Man-Midwifery*, p. 1.
78. Wilson, *Making of Man-Midwifery*, p. 2.
79. Donnison, *Midwives*, p. 38; Wilson, *Making of Man-Midwifery*.
80. King, 'Midwifery', p. 111.
81. NLW 4/1007/1 (Flintshire, Elizabeth Williams, 1765).
82. NLW 4/58/2 (Denbighshire, Elizabeth Bellis, 1744); NLW 4/900/3 (Cardiganshire, Ann Hughes, 1776); 4/906/4 (Cardiganshire, Maria Morris, 1795).
83. Penelope J Corfield, *Power and the Professions in Britain, 1700–1850* (London: Routledge, 1995), p. 146.
84. Alannah Tomkins, 'The Registers of a Provincial Man-Midwife, Thomas Higgins of Wem, 1781–1803', *Shropshire Historical Documents, a Miscellany*, 4 (2000), 65–148 (p. 74).
85. See Tomkins, 'Provincial Man-Midwife' for an example of an account book; Crawford, 'Construction and Experience of Maternity', p. 22.
86. PCA (Meifod) M/EP/41/W/AC/6 (1777).
87. PCA (Llanfihangel-yng-Ngwynfa) M/EP/21/O/RT/1 (1797).
88. Evenden, *Midwives of Seventeenth-Century London*, p. 101; Josephine M Lloyd, 'The "Languid Child" and the Eighteenth-Century Man-Midwife', *Bulletin of the History of Medicine*, 73 (2001), 641–679; Louden, 'Deaths in Childbed', p. 6.
89. King, 'Midwifery', p. 117.
90. NLW 4/752/4 (Carmarthenshire, Hannah John, 1799).
91. Wilson, 'Ceremony of Childbirth'; Gowing, *Common Bodies*, pp. 149–150.
92. Gowing, *Common Bodies*, p. 158.
93. Gowing, *Common Bodies*, p. 150; Alan Macfarlane, ed., *The Diary of Ralph Josselin 1616–1683* (British Academy Records of Social and Economic History, New Series, III, 1976) cited in Wilson, *Ritual and Conflict*, p. 1.
94. Wilson, *Ritual and Conflict*; Wilson, 'Ceremony of Childbirth'.
95. Gowing, *Common Bodies*, p. 176.
96. Wilson, 'Ceremony of Childbirth'; Gowing, *Common Bodies*, pp. 149–150.
97. Wilson, 'Ceremony of Childbirth', pp. 80–81.
98. Wilson, 'Ceremony of Childbirth', pp. 80–81; Wilson, *Ritual and Conflict*, p. 179.
99. Gowing, *Common Bodies*, pp. 156–176.
100. Snell, *Parish and Belonging*, p. 86; 17 George II c. 5.

101. Snell, *Parish and Belonging*, p. 85.
102. PCA (Newtown) M/EP/50/O/RT/1 (1738).
103. 17 George II c. 5.
104. PCA (Llandinam) M/EP/15/O/RT/1 (1753).
105. PCA (Ceri) M/EP/8/O/RT/6 1770.
106. Gowing, *Common Bodies*, p. 157.
107. PCA (Manafon) M/EP/40/O/RT/1 1767.
108. PCA M/QS/1750–1799 Session Rolls (SR 50E27).
109. 17 George II c. 5.
110. Laura Gowing, 'Ordering the Body', pp. 43–62.
111. Woodward, 'Infanticide in Wales', p. 110; NLW 4/530/6 (Radnorshire, Mary Powell, 1792).
112. NLW 4/62/1 (Denbighshire, Sarah Owen, 1788).
113. PCA (Llandinam) M/EP/15/O/RT/1 (1753).
114. PCA (Trefeglwys) M/EP/50/O/RT/2 (1753).
115. Wilson, *Ritual and Conflict*, p. 180.
116. Gowing, *Common Bodies*, p. 156.
117. PCA (Bettws Cedewain) M/EP/4/O/RT/2 (1789).
118. Wilson, 'Ceremony of Childbirth', pp. 80–81.
119. PCA (Berriew) M/EP/3/V/VM/3 (1780).
120. PCA (Bettws Cedewain) M/EP/4/O/RT/2 (1798).
121. PCA (Llangadfan) M/EP/24/O/RT/1 (1788); PCA (Castell Caereinion) M/EP/7/O/RT/2 (1773).
122. DAO (Gresford) PD/34/1/320 (1762).
123. 'Wilson, 'Ceremony of Childbirth', pp. 80–81.
124. PCA (Bettws Cedewain) M/EP/4/O/RT/1 (payment by officials in Bettws Cedewain for midwife and rent for the wife of William Jones, a soldier in 1762); PCA (Meifod) M/EP/41/O/RT/3 (payment by officials in Meifod for midwife and rent for wife of Thomas Jones in the 1780s).
125. Gowing, *Common Bodies*, p. 154.
126. Cody, *Birthing the Nation*, p. 36.
127. Abby Chandler, 'From Birthing Chamber to Court Room: The Medical and Legal Communities of the Colonial Essex County Midwife', *Early Modern Women: An Interdisciplinary Journal*, 9 (2015), 109–138 (p. 110); Crawford, 'Construction and Experience of Maternity', p. 21.
128. Gowing, *Common Bodies*, p. 153.
129. PCA (Bettws Cedewain) M/EP/4/O/RT/2 (1787).
130. PCA (Castell Caereinion) M/EP/7/O/RT/3 (1797).
131. PCA (Guilsfield) M/EP/19/O/RT/1 (1769).
132. Cody, *Birthing the Nation*, p. 36.
133. Gowing, *Common Bodies*, p. 159.
134. Gowing, *Common Bodies*, p. 160; Crawford, 'Construction and Experience of Maternity', p. 21.
135. Manchester, MRO (Manchester) GB124.E4/28/4/5 (1733). See also, documents 8, 9, 19, and 50 in the same folder.
136. Wilson, *Ritual and Conflict*, p. 26.
137. Wilson, *Ritual and Conflict*, p. 26.
138. NLW SD/LL/SM/8 (Wenllian Harry, 1753).
139. Wilson, *Ritual and Conflict*, p. 27.
140. PCA (Castell Caereinion) M/EP/7/O/RT/3 (1797).
141. Source: PCA (Llandegley) R/EP/1/O/BB/29/49; (Berriew) M/EP/3/O/BB/1/73; (Bettws Cedewain) M/EP/14/O/BB/4/12; (Llandinam) M/EP/15/O/BB 1/95 & M/EP/15/O/X/1; (Llangynyw) M/EP/27/O/BB/1/12 (Trefeglwys) M/EP/50/O/BB1/21.

142. PFHS (Gladestry) POW/PR17CD; DAO (Gresford) PD/34/1/320 (1770s–1790s).
143. Gowing, *Common Bodies*, p. 176; Wilson, 'Ceremony of Childbirth'; Williams, 'Experience of Pregnancy', p. 79.
144. Wilson, *Ritual and Conflict*, pp. 180–181.
145. Williams, 'Experience of Pregnancy', p. 69.
146. DAO (Llanarmon Dyffrin Ceiriog) PD/41/1/6 (1788).
147. PCA (Bettws Cedewain) M/EP/4/O/RT/7 (1787); PCA (Guilsfield) M/EP/19/O/RT/1 (1770).
148. PCA (Castell Caereinion) M/EP/7/O/RT/3 (1795).
149. PCA (Llandrindod) R/EP/47/W/AC/1 (1772).
150. PCA (Meifod) M/EP/41/V/VM/1 (1769).
151. PCA (Meifod) M/EP/41/V/VM/1 (1769).
152. Pollock, 'Embarking on a Rough Passage', pp. 39–67 (p. 49).

Conclusion

At the outset, the initial aims of this book were to investigate levels of illegitimacy in Wales, to examine the ways in which the Welsh context of illegitimacy differed to the English and to explore the 'traditional' courtship and marriage practices that influenced these patterns. However, during the course of research it became abundantly clear that there was no singular 'Welsh' experience of illegitimacy. Demographic analysis does indicate that aggregate levels of illegitimacy were significantly higher in Wales than in England by the end of the eighteenth century, but at the regional level, certain areas, such as northwestern Montgomeryshire and parts of Denbighshire, had levels lower than the overall English average. These variations reflect the complex and diverse nature of illegitimacy, not only in Wales, but across Britain. The distinctive patterns which emerged cannot be attributed to any uniquely Welsh circumstances, just as illegitimacy in England or Scotland cannot be attributed to any singular English or Scottish characteristics. To attribute the differences which did exist in Wales to idiosyncratic Welsh customs and culture alone would be essentialist. Although this book has argued that the elevated levels found in some parts of Wales can be attributed in part to courtship-led marriage practices, such as bundling, the presence or absence of bundling on its own cannot account for the varying levels found across Wales. As in London, it was the combination of courtship-led marriage practices and worsening economic circumstances that likely had the greatest influences on overall patterns in Wales. As this book has hopefully demonstrated, the prevalence of illegitimacy in eighteenth-century Wales was contingent upon a complicated combination of socioeconomic and cultural factors. Thus, by examining illegitimacy in its broader context, this study has also contributed to the historiography of gender, society and culture of Wales in the eighteenth century.

The underlying theme throughout this work has been that the individual experiences are as significant to our understanding of illegitimacy as the broader demographic trends. Mapping illegitimacy ratios was a necessary starting point given the lack of existing scholarship on illegitimacy in Wales, and allowed for meaningful comparisons with similar studies from elsewhere in Britain. Courtship-led marriage practices during periods of economic hardship can help to account for overall trends, but are by no means reflective of the diversity of lived experiences. The parish registers, poor law accounts, churchwarden accounts, and court records analysed in this study have demonstrated how varied, complicated, and often fraught the experience of conception, pregnancy and childbirth was for unmarried women. Ultimately, any unmarried woman of childbearing age was at risk of bearing a child outside of wedlock.[1] Equally, any man of reproductive age carried the potential to father an illegitimate child should he have penetrative sex—consensual or not—with any woman other than his wife. No social stratum was immune to this reality, as is reflected by the diverse identities revealed in parish registers and bastardy bonds. These documents also reveal the broader anxieties surrounding the perceived risk of illegitimacy to individuals, families, and communities in the responses, conflicts and negotiations they provoked.

What the varied responses to illegitimacy explored throughout this book demonstrate is that prevalence does not automatically reflect widespread acceptance. It is tempting to suggest, as some historians have, that high levels of reported illegitimacy brought greater leniency and acceptability and diminished negative stigma.[2] Evidence from Wales indicates that, regardless of its ubiquity, illegitimacy was interpreted as a problem which posed a risk of shame and hardship for individuals and communities, and needed to be managed accordingly. Unmarried pregnant women could, and did, resort to a range of survival strategies. At the furthest extreme, a small number concealed their pregnancies and deliveries, and ended their infants' lives through violence or neglect. Others sought financial security by holding the father, or a viable proxy, accountable through marriage or through the process of formal legal affiliation. Many more turned to the support of family, friends and their parish. Men also employed various strategies to manage their own individual experiences of illegitimate paternity. At the most extreme, they resorted to violence, which could be directed towards the foetus, and, with varying degrees of intent, the mother. In rare cases, this violence could also be directed towards their older illegitimate children. Other fathers simply fled, or attempted to lay the blame on someone else. However, many fathers would have chosen either to marry the mother, or at least provide support for their child. The strategies employed by families, neighbours and employers included confronting and interrogating single women suspected of concealing pregnancies or deliveries. When pregnancies were discovered, or when a woman made her circumstances known, the responses of those around her could range from chastising and punishing the woman, to turning a blind eye or simply providing her with support. Finally, authorities had at their disposal a range of legal tools which they used to manage illegitimacy. The ways in which parish officials went about this could vary from the extreme and harsh, where women could be removed from a parish by force, even during labour, to ensuring women were granted the proscribed period of lying-in and care afforded to married mothers. What these responses reveal is a diverse mosiac of illegitimate experiences which cannot be attributed to a single type of sexual encounter or cultural practice, or to a particular socioecoomic group, and which cannot adequately be quantified and mapped as an amalgamated demographic phenomenon.

This book is by no means a definitive study of illegitimacy in eighteenth-century Wales. The analysis of levels of illegitimacy in this study has focused on the predominantly agrarian rural parishes of Denbighshire, Montgomeryshire and Radnorshire, and to a limited degree several parishes across the border in England. However, Welsh counties further to the west and north have not yet been studied. Anna Brueton has made an important contribution in her study of south Wales, but much more research is still needed. The patterns, context and experience of illegitimacy in communities in coastal regions, such Aberystwyth and Caernarfon, or on the island of Anglesey in particular, could serve as compelling sources for comparison, as would parishes elsewhere in England and Scotland. Furthermore, this study has not explored the experiences of older illegitimate children, or of mothers beyond the period of lying-in. Although the label of 'illegitimate' does not appear to have followed illegitimate children in Wales beyond the first few years of life, it is still possible that the stigma associated with the circumstances into which they were born followed them later in life. This might be revealed in parish and court records if these children encounterd parish or secular authorities as adolescents or adults. The question of how illegitimate children in Wales were cared for, and by whom, has also not been explored. In addition to containing details about the care provided to poor, single parturient women, many poor law accounts contain information about payments made to unmarried mothers and fathers, as well as their families and neighbours for nursing and maintaining illegitimate children. Moreover, the response to *Rural and Town Queries* indicate that practices around care in Wales varied, with some parishes enabling unmarried mothers to nurse, clothe and rear their illegitimate children themselves, while other parishes put illegitimate children out to nurse.[3] The range of care provision, the impact this had on survival prospects, and the broader context of unmarried motherhood and fatherhood in Wales are promising areas for future research. However, as with the care provided to unmarried parturient women, the evidence of how illegitimate children were reared is limited to the poorest members of Welsh society, as it is drawn predominantly from poor law accounts. Unfortunately, few primary sources exist which can be used to access the experiences of those higher up the socioeconomic ladder. Nevertheless, there may be documents in existence which do yield more useful information concerning illegitimate children and their parents. Diaries and personal correspondence, for example, may be useful for providing incidental information about unmarried mothers and fathers, and illegitimate children, as well as attitudes towards them.[4] It may also be possible to locate some of the fathers listed in parish records in additional records, such as quarter sessions and Court of Great Sessions records. These could be used to build up a more detailed profile of the socioeconomic backgrounds of the men who fathered illegitimate children. This is not to say that illegitimacy is necessarily linked to criminality, as fathers could appear in these records as prosecutors or witnesses as well as defendants; however, these records are rich in detail, and are often some of the only evidence we have of individuals from the lower orders of society in earlier periods.

This study has also made a contribution to the histories sex, gender, the body and childbirth in Britain by considering evidence from eighteenth-century Wales. This demonstrates that such studies are not only possible, but necesssary. The conflicts and negotiations over unmarried pregnant women's bodies found in Court of Great Sessions records reveal eighteenth-century Welsh understandings of reproduction and the body. The evidence is remarkably similar to evidence found in English Assize records; however, subtle differences are evident. The signs sought, and often found, on the bodies of women suspected of committing infanticide, and on the bodies of their infants, are comparable across England and Wales. However, unlike in England, female midwives in Wales maintained almost exclusive authority to access and interrogate women's bodies. The continued authority of female midwives in the courtroom, despite the influx of male practitioners, is mirrored in the nature of care provided to poor parturient women. Man-midwives do appear with increasing frequency in Welsh court and parish records from the eighteenth century, but the evidence examined here suggests that the authority of female midwives nevertheless remained relatively intact at the end of the eighteenth century. Although evidence of midwifery and obstetric practice in Wales is limited, there is scope for further research nonetheless. The National Library of Wales holds a number diaries, recipe collections, and obstetrics manuals which were either written or collected by literate Welsh men and women in the eighteenth century, and may shed further light on contemporary understandings of reproduction and the body.[5] Analysis of responses to fatal violence against unmarried pregnant women found in Court of Great Sessions records also reveals a notable gap in the historiography of crime and gender in early modern and eighteenth-century Britain. Most studies of gender and homicide to date have neglected violence against unmarried women. This includes unmarried pregnant women, as well as women from diverse marginalised backgrounds, such as religious or ethnic minorities. In light of modern statistics about the prevalence and persistence of violence against marginalised women, the historical context of these crimes warrants further investigation.

Historians of illegitimacy have often focused either on broad trends which they have then endeavoured to explain, or they have examined certain facets in relative isolation, such as paternity, or pregnancy and parturition.[6] This book has drawn together many of these approaches for an examination of the prevalence, context and consequences of illegitimacy in eighteenth-century Wales. There is still much more Welsh evidence to be studied. Perhaps most importantly, more must also be done to integrate Welsh evidence into studies of Britain. Histories of illegitimacy do not need to be exclusively Welsh or English; studies can and should integrate evidence from across modern borders. This is as true for the history of illegitimacy as it is for the histories of sex, gender, the body and medicine in Britain. To understand these subjects more thoroughly, the reciprocal influences between Wales and England and the ways in which differences and similarities were regionally manifested must also be considered. As long as histories of 'Britain' exclude evidence from Wales, these studies will inevitably be incomplete.

Notes

1. Gowing, 'Ordering the Body', p. 45; Wilson, *Ritual and Conflict*, p. 8.
2. Woodward, 'Infanticide in Wales', p. 124.
3. 'Town Queries', p. 180a, Appendix B.2, part V.
4. For example, William Thomas, *The Diary of William Thomas of Michaelston-Super-Ely, Near St Fagans, Glamorgan, 1762–1795*, ed. by Roy Denning (Cardiff: South Wales Record Society, 1995).
5. For example, NLW, Bathafarn and Llanbedr Estate Records: *Volume of Lectures on the History and Practice of Midwifery, Bearing the Bookplate of Thomas White, MD* (1787); NLW MS 15193D, *Medical and culinary recipes by Mary* Owen (1712).
6. This is often because individual studies, although excellent, are limited to articles or chapters in edited collections, which preclude more varied approaches. Evans, *Unfortunate Objects* is evidence of the scope and depth that is possible in larger studies.

Bibliography

Primary Sources

Official UK Legislation

21 James I c. 27, *An Act to Prevent the Destroying and Murthering of Bastard Children* (1623/4).

14 Charles II c. 12, *An Act for the Better Relief of the Poor of This Kingdom* (1662).

6 George II c. 31, *An Act for the Relief of Parishes and Other Places from Such Charges as May Arise from Bastard Children Born Within the Same* (1732).

17 George II c. 5, *An Act to Amend and Make More Effectual the Laws Relating to Rogues, Vagabonds and Other Idle and Disorderly Persons, and to Houses of Correction* (1743).

26 George II, c. 33, *An Act for the Better Preventing of Clandestine Marriage* (1753).

43 George III c. 58, *An Act for the Further Prevention of Malicious Shooting, and Attempting to Discharge Loaded Fire-Arms, Stabbing, Cutting, Wounding, Poisoning, and the Malicious Using of Means to Procure the Miscarriage of Women; and also the Malicious Setting Fire to Buildings; and also for Repealing a Certain Act, Made in England in the Twenty-First Year of the Late King James the First, Intituled, an Act to Prevent the Destroying and Murthering of Bastard Children; and also an Act Made in Ireland in the Sixth Year of the Reign of the Late Queen Anne, also Intituled, an Act to Prevent the Destroying and Murthering of Bastard Children; and for Making Other Provisions in Lieu Thereof* (1803).

UK Parliamentary Reports (House of Commons)

Royal Commission of Inquiry into Administration and Practical Operation of Poor Laws (1834), Appendix B.1, Answers to Rural Queries, Appendix B.2, Answers to Town Queries.

Second Annual Report of the Poor Law Commissioners for England and Wales, Appendices A, B, C, D and E (19th Century House of Commons Sessional Papers, 1836), Appendix D.

Reports of the Commissioners of Inquiry into the State of Education in Wales (19th Century House of Commons Sessional Papers, 1847).

228   Bibliography

Parish Register Transcriptions

Denbighshire

CLWYD FAMILY HISTORY SOCIETY (CFHS)

Bryneglwys: CLD-20228.
Chirk: CLD-20315; CLD-20316; CLD-20317.
Gresford: CLD-20701; CLD-20702; CLD-20703; CLD-20704.
Holt: CLD-21007; CLD-21008; CLD-21010; CLD-21011.
Llanarmon Dyffryn Ceiriog: CLD-21301; CLD-21302.
Llangollen: CLD-21615; CLD-21616; CLD-21617; CLD-21618; CLD-21619; CLD-21620.
Llanrhaeadr ym Mochnant: CLD-21806; CLD-21807.
Llansilin: CLD-21917; CLD-21918; CLD-21919.
Marchwiel: CLD-22101; CLD-22102; CLD-22103.
Ruabon: CLD-22402; CLD-22403; CLD-22404.
Wrexham: CLD-22702; CLD-22703; CLD-22704; CLD-22705; CLD-22706; CLD-22707; CLD-22708.

Montgomeryshire

MONTGOMERYSHIRE GENEALOGICAL SOCIETY (MGS)

Aberhafesp: MR/PR/80; MR/PR/81.
Berriew: MR/C/27; MR/PR/42; MR/PR/43; MR/PR/44; MR/PR/45.
Bettws Cedewain: MR/PR/85; MR/PR/86; MR/PR/87.
Buttington: MR/PR/92; MR/PR/93; MR/PR/94.
Carno: MR/PR/114; MR/PR/115; MR/PR/116.
Castell Caereinion: MR/C/15; MR/PR/03; MR/PR/04.
Cemmaes: MR/C/39; MR/PR/99.
Darowen: MR/C/40; MR/PR/102; MR/PR/103.
Garthbeibio: MR/PR/25; MR/PR/26.
Guilsfield: MR/C/32; MR/PR/30; MR/PR/31; MR/PR/32; MR/PR/33; MR/PR/34; MR/PR/35.
Llandinam: MR/C/48; MR/C/49; MR/PR/107; MR/PR/108.
Llandrinio: MR/PR/61; MR/PR/62.
Llanfair Caereinion: MR/PR/65; MR/PR/66; MR/PR/67; MR/PR/68.
Llanfihangel-yng-Ngwynfa: MR/C/30; MR/PR/54.
Llanfyllin: MR/C/24; MR/PR/56; MR/PR/57; MR/PR/58; MR/PR/59.
Llangadfan: MR/PR/37; MR/PR/38; MR/PR/39.
Llangyniew: MR/C/21; MR/PR/18; MR/PR/19; MR/PR/20.
Llanwddyn: MR/PR/50; MR/PR/51.
Llanwnog: MR/C/55; MR/PR/141; MR/PR/142.
Llanwrin: MR/C/38; MR/PR/95.
Machynlleth: MR/C/36; MR/C/37; MR/PR/88; MR/PR/89; MR/PR/90.
Meifod: MR/C/16; MR/C/17; MR/PR/05; MR/PR/06; MR/PR/07.
Newtown: MR/C/23; MR/PR/28; MR/PR/29.
Trefeglwys: MR/C/43; MR/PR/10; MR/PR/104.
Welshpool: MR/C/08; MR/C/09; MR/C/10; MR/C/11.

Radnorshire

POWYS FAMILY HISTORY SOCIETY (PFHS)

Beguildy: POW/PR10aCD.
Gladestry: POW/PR17CD.
Glascwm: POW/PR01CD.
Llanbadarn Fawr: POW/PR08CD.
Llanbadarn Fynydd: POW/PR09CD.
Llanbister: POW/PR07CD.
Llanfihangel Nant Melan: POW/PR15CD.
Llansantffraed-in-Elwel: POW/PR02CD.
New Radnor: POW/PR16CD.
Norton: POW/PR06CD.

Shropshire

OPEN SHELVES, SHROPSHIRE RECORDS OFFICE

Bishops Castle, Kinnerley, Ludlow, Munslow

ANGULINE RESEARCH ARCHIVE (ARG)

Cardeston: ANG/ARA/615.
Hordley: ANG/ARA/471.
Onibury: ANG/ARA/373.
Oswestry: ANG/ARA/398.
Uffington: ANG/ARA/397.

Archival Records (National)

National Library of Wales (Aberystwyth)

BALLADS

Edwards, Thomas (Tw o'Nant) *Tair o gerddi newyddion*I. *Cerdd, neu ddychryn-dod gwraig yr hon a gafodd gorph plentyn bach ynghafn môch; gyda gweddi ar Dduw tros ferched: yr hon a genir ar,* Luseni mistress (BOWB 243).
Roberts, Elis, *Dwy o Gerddi Newyddion. 1. Yn rhoi byrr hanes Dynes a wnaeth weithred Ofnadwy Ymhlwy Llansantffraid glyn Conwy, sef diheunyddio ffrw-yth ei Biy ai ado fe rhwng Bwystsilod y Ddaear* (BOWB 357).

Bathafarn and Llanbedr Estate Records

Volume of Lectures on the History and Practice of Midwifery, Bearing the Book-plate of Thomas White, MD (1787).

Diocese of Bangor Ecclesiastical Records

B/CC/C(P)/39 Elizabeth John Griffith of Newborough, widow (1755).
B/SM/1 Elizabeth Annwyl (1753).

Bibliography

Diocese of St David's Ecclesiastical Records

SD/1700/56 Will of Frances Hughes, midwife (1700).
SD/LL/SM/2 Elinor Ajax (1769).
SD/LL/SM/5 Margaret David (1761).
SD/LL/SM/8 Wenllian Harry (1753).
SD/LL/SM/9 Mary Hopkin (1780).
SD/LL/SM/11 Jane Jones (1754).
SD/LL/SM/12 Oath of Jane Lewelin (1760).
SD/LL/SM/15 Jane Morgan (1774).
SD/LL/SM/17 Jane Robert (1753).
SD/LL/SM/19 Mary Winn (1753).

Diocese of St Asaph

SA/FB/1 Rebecca Davies (1740).

Edwinsford Estate Records

Probate of the Will of James Thomas Late of the Parish of Talley, Co. Carmarthen, Deceased, Edwinsford Estate Records (1662).

Gaol Files (Court of Great Sessions)

File number	Year	Accused	Offence	Victim (if murder)
ANGLESEY				
4/250/6	1737	Arabella Williams	Infanticide	
4/259/5	1824	Griffith Roberts	Burglary	
BRECONSHIRE				
4/373/6	1730	Gwenllian Powell	Infanticide	
4/374/5	1732	Elizabeth Morris	Infanticide	
4/374/6	1732	Elizabeth David	Infanticide	
4/377/2	1741	James John	Murder	Sarah Powell
4/380/6	1753	Gwenllian David	Infanticide	
4/380/7	1753	Margaret Williams	Infanticide	
4/381/2	1755	Mary Harris	Infanticide	
4/388/3	1788	Elizabeth Williams	Infanticide	
4/388/5	1788	William Williams	Murder	Margaret Thomas
4/390/4	1797	William Walter	Murder	Ann Watkin
CARDIGANSHIRE				
4/900/3	1776	Ann Hughes	Infanticide	
4/904/2	1788	Samuel Mann	Murder	Elizabeth George

File number	Year	Accused	Offence	Victim (if murder)
4/900/3	1776	Ann Hughes	Infanticide	
4/904/2	1788	Ephraim Wells	Murder	Elizabeth George
4/906/1	1794	Sarah David	Infanticide	
4/906/4	1795	Maria Morris	Infanticide	
CARMARTHENSHIRE				
4/740/4	1771	Elizabeth Lewis	Pickpocketing a silver watch	
4/746/3	1786	Jane Thomas	Infanticide	
4/748/3	1789	Anne John	Infanticide	
4/751/1	1795	Anne Abel	Infanticide	
4/752/4	1799	Hannah John	Infanticide	
4/757/2	1809	Anne Jones	Digging up the body dead infant	
4/760/4	1816	Rees Thomas Rees	Murder	Elizabeth Jones
CAERNARFON				
4/272/4	1755	Mary Meredith	Keeping a Bawdy House	
DENBIGHSHIRE				
4/46/2	1736	Catherine Roberts	Infanticide	
4/47/6	1742	Jane Edwards	Infanticide	
4/47/7	1742	Mary Philips	Infanticide	
4/49/2	1746	Jane Williams	Infanticide	
4/53/3	1762	Samuel Rogers	Murder	Mary Jones
4/58/2	1744	Elizabeth Bellis	Infanticide	
4/60/5	1784	Mary Owen	Infanticide	
4/61/1	1784	Mary Owen	Infanticide	
4/62/1	1788	Sarah Owen	Infanticide	
4/62/4	1789	Catherine Davies	Infanticide	
4/64/4	1795	Ann Parry	Infanticide	
FLINTSHIRE				
4/1000/8	1731	Mary Brown	Murder	Thomas Brown
4/1002/4	1739	Jane Griffith	Infanticide	
4/1003/11	1746	Mary Hunt	Infanticide	
4/1005/11	1759	Mary Davies	Infanticide	
4/1007/1	1765	Elizabeth Williams	Infanticide	
4/1009/5	1776	Catherine Roberts	Infanticide	
4/1010/10	1783	Mary Jones	Infanticide	
4/1012/2	1789	Eleanor Jones	Infanticide	
4/1013/3	1795	Elizabeth Jones	Infanticide	
4/1013/6	1796	Margaret Parker	Infanticide	
4/1013/9	1797	Joseph Emerson	Infanticide	
4/1013/9	1797	Margaret Jones	Infanticide	

(Continued)

(Continued)

File number	Year	Accused	Offence	Victim (if murder)
GLAMORGAN				
4/613/6	1744	Barbara David	Infanticide	
4/615/5	1751	Harry Thomas John	Assault with Intent to Ravish	
4/616/2	1752	Richard Davies	Assault with Intent to Ravish	
4/617/2	1756	Margaret Lewis	Infanticide	
4/623/3	1774	Jannet John	Infanticide	
4/626/4	1786	Mary Richard	Infanticide	
4/629/2	1794	Mary Morgan	Infanticide	
MERIONETH				
4/298/4	1734	Elizabeth Davies	Infanticide	
4/298/5	1738	Ann Williams	Infanticide	
4/298/5	1738	Gwen Ellis	Infanticide	
MONTGOMERYSHIRE				
4/177/7	1730	Elinor Pugh	Infanticide	
4/178/2	1734	Jane Williams	Infanticide	
4/183/5	1750	Mary Dell	Infanticide	
4/184/2	1752	William Berwick	Murder	Rachel Berwick
4/184/2	1752	Thomas Vaughan	Murder	Rachel Berwick
4/186/1	1758	Mary Barret	Infanticide	
4/188/1	1764	Evan Jenkins	Murder	Elizabeth Evans
4/188/6	1767	Margaret Lewis (jr)	Infanticide	
4/188/6	1767	Margaret Lewis (sr)	Infanticide	
4/189/1	1768	Margaret Jenkin	Infanticide	
4/193/5	1742	Richard Pryce	Assault	
4/194/7	1791	Ann Owen	Infanticide	
4/195/3	1793	Margaret Evans	Infanticide	
PEMBROKESHIRE				
4/821/5	1780	George Williams	Murder	Sarah Powell
RADNORSHIRE				
4/517/6	1735	Hannah Morris	Infanticide	
4/518/2	1735	Margaret Th Prees	Infanticide	
4/519/6	1742	Jane Harrington	Infanticide	
4/523/4	1756	Edward Pugh	Murder	Margaret Matthews
4/530/6	1792	Mary Powell	Infanticide	
4/537/1	1823	Edward Evans	Murder	Sophia Thomas

Bibliography 233

Miscellaneous Manuscripts

MS 15193D Medical and Culinary Recipes by Mary Owen (1712).
MS 20073A Anon., *Journal of a Tour of Wales and Parts of England*, 1793.

The National Archives (London)

MH 12/16543/316, Folio 449 (Llanfyllin Poor Law Union).

Archival Records (Local)

Denbighshire Archives Office (Ruthin)

Bryneglwys: PD/11/1/13; PD/11/1/22; PD/11/1/23.
Chirk: PD/24/1/58.
Gresford: PD/34/1/320.
Henllan: PD/38/1/68; PD/38/1/146; PD/38/1/148; PD/38/1/171; PD/38/1/174.
Holt: PD/39/1/53; PD/39/1/55; PD/39/1/61; PD/39/1/62.
Llanarmon Dyffrin Ceiriog: PD/41/1/5; PD/41/1/6.
Llanarmon-yn-Ial: PD/43/1/43; PD/43/1/44.
Llandegla: PD/45/1/14.
Llanfair Dyffryn Clwyd: PD/51/1/41; PD/51/1/42; PD/51/1/43.
Llangollen: PD/63/1/53; PD/63/1/54; PD/63/1/55; PD/63/1/58; PD/63/1/59; PD/63/1/66; PD/63/1/67; PD/63/1/70; PD/63/1/71; PD/63/1/72; PD/63/1/73; PD/63/1/74; PD/63/1/78.
Ruabon: PD/89/1/94; PD/89/1/95; PD/89/1/96; PD/89/1/102; PD/89/1/105; PD/89/1/124; PD/89/1/125; PD/89/1/128; PD/89/1/129; PD/89/1/130; PD/89/1/131; PD/89/1/132; PD/89/1/133; PD/89/1/134; PD/89/1/135.
Wrexham: PD/101/1/260; PD/101/1/263; PD/101/1/264; PD/101/1/265; PD/101/1/322; PD/101/1/323; PD/101/1/325.

Flintshire Records Office (Hawarden)

Hanmer: P/27/1/26; P/27/1/27; P/27/1/40.
Hawarden (Bell Jones Collection): D/BJ/324; D/BJ/325; D/BJ/326; D/BJ/327; D/BJ/328.

Powys County Archives (Llandrindod Wells)

Parish Record Collections

MONTGOMERYSHIRE

Aberhafesp: M/EP/2/O/RT/1; M/EP/2/O/RT/2; M/EP/2/V/VM/1.
Berriew: M/EP/3/O/BB/1-73; M/EP/3/V/VM/2; M/EP/3/V/VM/3; M/EP/3/V/VM/4.
Bettws Cedewain: M/EP/4/O/BB/1-35; M/EP/4/O/RT/1; M/EP/4/O/RT/2; M/EP/4/O/RT/3; M/EP/4/O/RT/4; M/EP/4/O/RT/5; M/EP/4/O/RT/6; M/EP/4/O/RT/7; M/EP/4/O/RT/8; M/EP/4/O/RT/9; M/EP/4/O/RT/10; M/EP/4/W/AC/1; M/EP/4/W/AC/2.

234 Bibliography

Carno: M/EP/6/O/RT/1.
Castell Caereinion: M/EP/7/O/RT/1; M/EP/7/O/RT/2; M/EP/7/O/RT/3.
Garthbeibio: M/EP/12/O/RT/1.
Guilsfield: M/EP/19/O/RT/1.
Hirnant: M/EP/14/O/RT/1.
Kerry (Ceri): M/EP/8/O/RT/1; M/EP/8/O/RT/3; M/EP/8/O/RT/5; M/EP/8/O/RT/6; M/EP/8/O/RT/7; M/EP/8/O/RT/9.
Llandinam: M/EP/15/O/BB/1-95; M/EP/15/O/RT/1; M/EP/15/O/RT/2; M/EP/15/O/RT/3; M/EP/15/O/X/1; M/EP/15/V/VM/1; M/EP/15/V/VM/2.
Llandysul: M/EP/18/O/RT/1.
Llanerfyl: M/EP/19/O/AP 1-4; M/EP/19/O/RT/1; M/EP/19/V/VM/1.
Llanfihangel-yng-Ngwynfa: M/EP/21/O/AP/1-16; M/EP/21/O/BB/1-12; M/EP/21/O/RT/1; M/EP/21/W/AC/1.
Llangadfan: M/EP/24/O/RT/1; M/EO/24/Z/MT/1.
Llangynyw: M/EP/27/O/BB/1-12; M/EP/27/V/VM/1; M/EP/27/V/VM/2.
Llanllwchaearn: M/EP/30/O/RT/1; M/EP/30/W/AC/1.
Llanrhaeadr ym Mocnant: M/EP/34/O/BB/1-31; M/EP/34/O/RT.
Llansanffraid-ym-Mechain: M/EP/35/W/AC/1; M/EP/35/W/AC/2.
Llanwnog: M/EP/38/O/BB/1-6; M/EP/38/O/X/6 18, 19; M/EP/38/O/RT/12; M/EP/38/O/RT/1.
Manafon: M/EP/40/O/BB/1-22; M/EP/40/O/RT/1.
Meifod: M/EP/41/O/RT/1; M/EP/41/O/RT/2; M/EP/41/O/RT/3; M/EP/41/O/RT/4.
M/EP/41/V/VM/1; M/EP/41/W/AC/1; M/EP/41/W/AC/2; M/EP/41/W/AC/3; M/EP/41/W/AC/4; M/EP/41/W/AC/5; M/EP/41/W/AC/6; M/EP/41/W/AC/7.
Newtown: M/EP/44/V/VM/1.
Trefeglwys: M/EP/50/O/BB 1-22; M/EP/50/O/RT/1; M/EP/50/O/RT/2; M/EP/50/O/RT/3; M/EP/50/O/RT/4; M/EP/50/W/AC/1; M/EP/50/W/AC/2.
Tregynon: M/EP/51/O/BB/1; M/EP/51/O/RT/1; M/EP/51/O/RT/2; M/EP/51/O/RT/3
Welshpool: M/EP/52/V/VM/1.

RADNORSHIRE

Llanbadarn Fynydd: R/EP/21/O/RT/1; R/EP/21/O/RT/2.
Llanbister: R/EP/30/O/BB/1; R/EP/30/O/RT/1.
Llandegley (Llandeglau): R/EP/1/O/BB/21-49; R/EP/1/W/AC/1; R/EP/1/W/AC/2.
Llandrindod: R/EP/34/O/RT/1.
Norton: R/EP/47 (Uncatalogued—Elinor Jones); R/EP/47/W/AC/1; R/EP/47/W/AC/2.

Quarter Sessions

MONTGOMERYSHIRE

Transcriptions
Order book and Session Rolls: QS/1707-1729.
Session Rolls: QS/1730-1739; QS/1740-1749; QS/1750-1759; QS/1760-1769; QS/1770-1779; QS/1780-1789; QS/1790-1799.

RADNORSHIRE

Session Rolls: QS/SR/3/2; QS/SR/3/3

Early Printed Materials

Anon (William Salmon), *Aristotle's Compleat and Experience'd Midwife* (London, 1740).
Bingley, William, *North Wales: Including Its Scenery, Antiquities, Customs, and Some Sketches of Its Natural History* (London, 1804).
Copland, James, *Practical Medicine: Comprising General Pathology, the Nature and Treatment of Diseases, Morbid Structures, and the Disorders Especially Incidental to Climates, to the Sex, and to the Different Epochs of Life* (New York, 1845).
Paré, Ambroise, *Workes of That Famous Chirugion Ambrose Parey, Translated Out of Latine and Compared with the French by Thomas Johnson* (London, 1665).
Mr. Pratt (Samuel Jackson), *Gleanings Through Wales, Holland and Westphalia* (London, 1797).
Sharp, Jane, *The Midwives Book, or the Whole Art of Midwifery Discovered*, ed. by Elaine Hobby (Oxford: Oxford University Press, 1999).
Thomas, William, *The Diary of William Thomas of Michaelston-Super-Ely, Near St Fagans, Glamorgan, 1762–1795*, ed. by Roy Denning (Cardiff: South Wales Record Society, 1995).

Websites

NLW *Crime and Punishment Database* <https://crimeandpunishment.library.wales> [accessed 23/8/2019].
Old Bailey Online <www.oldbaileyonline.org> [accessed 27/8/2019].
Samuel Lewis, *A Topographical Dictionary of Wales* (London, 1849) *British History Online* <www.british-history.ac.uk/topographical-dict/wales> [accessed 2019].

Secondary

Official Reports *(Modern)*

Gratl, Jason, ' "Wouldn't Piss on Them If They Were on Fire" How Discrimination Against Sex Workers, Drug Users and Aboriginal Women Enabled a Serial Killer' (Report of Independent Counsel to the Commissioner of the Missing Women Commission of Inquiry, 2012).
Knight, Marian, Kathryn Bunch, Derek Tuffnell, Hemali Jayakody, Judy Shakespeare, Rohit Kotnis, Sara Kenyon, Jennifer J Kurinczuk, eds, On Behalf of MBRRACE-UK, 'Lessons Learned to Inform Maternity Care from the UK and Ireland Confidential Enquiries into Maternal Deaths and Morbidity 2014–16' (Oxford: National Perinatal Epidemiology Unity, University of Oxford, 2018).
Office of National Statistics (ONS), 'Homicide in England and Wales: Year Ending March 2017' (18 March 2019).
World Health Organisation (WHO), 'Intimate Partner Violence During Pregnancy Information Sheet' (2011) (WHO/RHR/11.35).

World Health Organisation (WHO), 'Understanding and Addressing Violence Against Women: Femicide' (WHO/RHR/12.38).

Published Secondary Sources

Adair, Richard, *Courtship, Illegitimacy and Marriage in Early Modern England* (Manchester: Manchester University Press, 1996).

Anderson, Michael, ed., *British Population History: From the Black Death to the Present Day* (Cambridge: Cambridge University Press, 1996).

Ashton, OS, 'Eighteenth Century Radnorshire: A Population Survey', *Radnorshire Society Transactions*, 40 (1970), 40–55.

Astbury, Leah, 'Being Well, Looking Ill: Childbirth and the Return to Health in Seventeenth-Century England', *Social History of Medicine*, 20 (2017), 500–519.

Bailey, Joanne, '"I Dye [sic] by Inches": Locating Wife Beating in the Concept of a Privatization of Marriage and Violence in Eighteenth-Century England', *Social History*, 31 (2006), 273–294.

Barber, Jill, '"Stolen Goods": The Sexual Harassment of Female Servants in West Wales During the Nineteenth Century', *Rural History*, 4 (1993), 123–136 (p. 132).

Beattie, JM, *Crime and the Courts in England: 1660–1800* (Oxford: Oxford University Press, 1986).

Bewley, Susan and Jan Welch, *ABC of Domestic and Sexual Violence* (Chichester: John Wiley & Sons, 2014).

Binhammer, Katherine, 'The Sex Panic of the 1790s', *Journal of the History of Sexuality*, 6 (1996), 409–434.

Black, John, 'Who Were the Putative Fathers of Illegitimate Children in London?' in *Illegitimacy in Britain: 1700–1920*, ed. by Alysa Levene, Thomas Nutt and Samantha Williams (Basingstoke: Palgrave Macmillan, 2005), pp. 50–65.

Blaikie, Andrew, 'Infant Survival Chances, Unmarried Motherhood and Domestic Arrangements in Rural Scotland, 1845–1945', *Local Population Studies*, 60 (1998), 34–46.

Blaikie, Andrew, *Illegitimacy, Sex and Society in Northeast Scotland, 1750–1900* (Oxford: Clarendon Press, 1993).

Bland, Lucy, 'The Case of the Yorkshire Ripper: Mad, Bad, Beast, or Male?' in *Femicide: The Politics of Women Killing*, ed. by Jill Radford and Diana EH Russell (Buckingham: Open University Press, 1992), pp. 233–252.

Bonfield, Lloyd, Richard M Smith and Keith Wrightson, eds, *The World We Have Gained: Histories of Population and Social Structure* (Oxford: Blackwell, 1986).

Borsay, Anne and Billie Hunter, eds, *Nursing & Midwifery in Britain Since 1700* (Basingstoke: Palgrave Macmillan, 2012).

Braddick, Michael J and John Walter, eds, *Negotiating Power in Early Modern Society: Order, Hierarchy and Subordination in Britain and Ireland* (Cambridge: Cambridge University Press, 2001).

Burke, Peter, *Popular Culture in Early Modern Europe* (London: Temple Smith, 1978).

Butler, Sara M, 'Abortion Medieval Style? Assaults on Pregnant Women in Later Medieval England', *Women's Studies, an Inter-Disciplinary Journal*, 40 (2011), 778–799.

Capp, Bernard, 'The Double Standard Revisited: Plebeian Women and Male Sexual Reputation in Early Modern England', *Past & Present*, 162 (1999), 70–101.

Casper, Monica J and Lisa Jean Moore, *Missing Bodies: The Politics of Visibility* (New York: New York University Press, 2009).

Chandler, Abby, 'From Birthing Chamber to Court Room: The Medical and Legal Communities of the Colonial Essex County Midwife', *Early Modern Women: An Interdisciplinary Journal*, 9 (2015), 109–138.

Clark, Anna, 'Heterosexuality: Europe and North America', in *A Cultural History of Sexuality in the Enlightenment*, ed. by Julie Peakman (London: Bloomsbury, 2014), pp. 33–56.

Clark, Michael and Catherine Crawford, eds, *Legal Medicine in History* (Cambridge: Cambridge University Press, 1994).

Cockburn, JS, ed., *Crime in England 1550–1800* (Princeton: Princeton University Press, 1977).

Cody, Lisa Forman, 'The Body in Birth and Death', in *A Cultural History of the Human Body in the Enlightenment*, ed. by Carole Reeves (London: Bloomsbury Academic, 2014), pp. 13–31.

Cody, Lisa Forman, *Birthing the Nation: Sex, Science, and the Conception of Eighteenth-Century Britons* (Oxford: Oxford University Press, 2005).

Connors, Richard, 'Poor Women, the Parish and the Politics of Poverty', in *Gender in Eighteenth-Century England: Roles, Representations and Responsibilities*, ed. by Hannah Barker and Elaine Chalus (London and New York: Addison Wesley Longman, 1997), pp. 126–147.

Corfield, Penelope J, *Power and the Professions in Britain, 1700–1850* (London: Routledge, 1995).

Cossins, Annie, *Female Criminality: Infanticide, Moral Panic and the Female Body* (Basingstoke: Palgrave Macmillan, 2015).

Crawford, Patricia, 'The Construction and Experience of Maternity in Seventeenth-Century England', in *Women as Mothers in Pre-Industrial Britain*, ed. by Valerie Fildes (Abingdon: Routledge, 2013), pp. 3–38.

Crawford, Patricia, *Parents of Poor Children in England: 1580–1800* (Oxford: Oxford University Press, 2010).

Crawford, Patricia, *Blood, Bodies and Families in Early Modern England* (Harlow: Pearson Education, 2004).

Cressy, David, *Birth, Marriage and Death: Ritual, Religion and the Life-Cycle in Tudor and Stuart England* (Oxford: Oxford University Press, 1997).

Cressy, David, *Literacy and the Social Order: Reading and Writing in Tudor and Stuart England* (Cambridge: Cambridge University Press, 1980).

Dabhoiwala, Faramerz, *The Origins of Sex: A History of the First Sexual Revolution* (London: Allen Lane, 2012).

Davies, Janet, *The Welsh Language* (Cardiff: University of Wales Press, 1993).

Davies, John Humphrey, *A Bibliography of Welsh Ballads Printed in the Eighteenth Century* (London: Honourable Society of Cymmrodorion, 1911).

Davis, Natalie Zemon, *Fiction in the Archives: Pardon Tales and their Tellers in Sixteenth-Century France* (Stanford: Stanford University Press, 1987).

Davison, Lesley, 'Spinsters Were Doing It for Themselves: Independence and the Single Woman in Early Eighteenth-Century Rural Wales', in *Women and Gender in Early Modern Wales*, ed. by Michael Roberts and Simone Clarke (Cardiff: University of Wales Press, 2000), pp. 186–209.

de Brouwere, Vincent, René Tonglet and Wim Van Lerberghe, 'Strategies for Reducing Maternal Mortality in Developing Countries: What Can We Learn from the History of the Industrialized West?' *Tropical Medicine and International Health*, 3 (1998), 771–782.

Dobson, Mary J, *Contours of Death and Disease in Early Modern England* (Cambridge: Cambridge University Press, 1997).

Donnison, Jean, *Midwives and Medical Men: A History of the Struggle for the Control of Childbirth* (New Barnett: Historical Publications, 1988).

Erickson, Amy Louise, 'Mistress and Marriage: Or, a Short History of the Mrs', *History Workshop Journal*, 78 (2014), 39–57.

Evans, Tanya, *'Unfortunate Objects': Lone Mothers in Eighteenth-Century London* (Basingstoke: Palgrave Macmillan, 2005).

Evenden, Doreen, *The Midwives of Seventeenth-Century London* (Cambridge: Cambridge University Press, 2000).

Fildes, Valerie, 'Maternal Feelings Re-Assessed: Child Abandonment and Neglect in London and Westminster, 1550–1800', in *Women as Mothers in Pre-Industrial Britain*, ed. by Valerie Fildes (Abingdon: Routledge, 2013), pp. 139–170.

Fildes, Valerie, ed., *Women as Mothers in Pre-Industrial Britain*, ed. by Valerie Fildes (Abingdon: Routledge, 2013).

Fissell, Mary, *Vernacular Bodies: The Politics of Reproduction in Early Modern England* (Oxford: Oxford University Press, 2006).

Foucault, Michel, *The History of Sexuality Volume 1: An Introduction*, trans. by Robert Hurley (London: Penguin, 1990).

Foucault, Michel, *The Order of Things: An Archaeology of the Human Sciences* (New York: Vintage Books, 1973).

Foyster, Elizabeth A, *Marital Violence: An English Family History, 1660–1857* (Cambridge: Cambridge University Press, 2005).

Foyster, Elizabeth A, *Manhood in Early Modern England: Honour, Sex and Marriage* (London: Longman, 1999).

Foyster, Elizabeth A, 'Male Honour, Social Control and Wife Beating in Late Stuart England', *Transactions of the Royal Historical Society*, 6 (1996), 215–224.

Frith, Valerie, ed., *Women and History: Voices of Early Modern England* (Concord: Irwin, 1997).

Gammon, Julie, 'Researching Sexual Violence, 1660–1800: A Critical Analysis', in *Interpreting Sexual Violence, 1660–1800*, ed. by Anne Greenfield (Abington: Routledge, 2015), pp. 13–22.

Gartner, Rosemary and Bill McCarthy, eds, *The Oxford Handbook of Gender, Sex, and Crime* (Oxford: Oxford University Press, 2014).

Gaskill, Malcolm, 'Reporting Murder: Fiction in the Archives in Early Modern England', *Social History*, 23 (1998), 1–30.

Gillis, John R, *For Better, for Worse: British Marriages, 1600 to the Present* (Oxford: Oxford University Press, 1985).

Goose, Nigel, 'How Saucy Did It Make the Poor? The Straw Plait and Hat Trades, Illegitimate Fertility and the Family in Nineteenth-Century Hertfordshire', *History*, 91 (2006), 530–556.

Gowing, Laura, 'Knowledge and Experience, c. 1500–1750', in *The Routledge History of Sex and the Body: 1500 to the Present*, ed. by Sarah Toulalan and Kate Fisher (London: Routledge, 2013), pp. 239–255 (p. 242).

Gowing, Laura, 'Giving Birth at the Magistrate's Gate: Single Mothers in the Early Modern City', in *Women, Identities and Communities in Early Modern Europe*, ed. by Stephanie Tarbin and Susan Broomhall (Aldershot: Ashgate, 2008), pp. 137–150.

Gowing, Laura, *Common Bodies: Women, Touch and Power in Seventeenth-Century England* (New Haven: Yale University Press, 2003).

Gowing, Laura, 'Ordering the Body: Illegitimacy and Female Authority in Seventeenth-Century England', in *Negotiating Power in Early Modern Society: Order, Hierarchy and Subordination in Britain and Ireland*, ed. by Michael J Braddick and John Walter (Cambridge: Cambridge University Press, 2001), pp. 43–62.

Gowing, Laura, 'Secret Births and Infanticide in Seventeenth-Century England', *Past & Present*, 156 (1997), 87–115.

Gowing, Laura, *Domestic Dangers: Women, Words and Sex in Early Modern London* (Oxford: Clarendon Press, 1996).

Greenfield, Anne, ed., *Interpreting Sexual Violence, 1660–1800* (Abington: Routledge, 2015).

Grey, Daniel JR, 'Crimes Related to Sexuality and Reproduction', in *The Oxford Handbook of Gender, Sex and Crime*, ed. by Rosemary Gartner and Bill McCarthy (Oxford: Oxford University Press, 2014), pp. 225–241.

Griffin, Emma, 'Sex, Illegitimacy and Social Change in Industrializing Britain', *Social History*, 38 (2013), 139–161.

Grigg, Russell, 'Getting Away with Murder? Infanticide in Wales, 1730–1908', *Local Historian*, 44 (2014), 115–133.

Gwynn, Gwenith, 'Besom Weddings in the Ceiriog Valley', *Folklore*, 39 (1928), 149–166.

Harley, David, 'Provincial Midwives in England: Lancashire and Cheshire, 1660–1760', in *The Art of Midwifery: European Midwives in Europe*, ed. by Hilary Marland (Abingdon: Routledge, 1993), pp. 27–48.

Harley, David, 'Historians as Demonologists: The Myth of the Midwife-Witch', *Social History of Medicine*, 3 (1990), 1–26.

Herrup, Cynthia B, 'Law and Morality in Seventeenth-Century England', *Past & Present*, 106 (1985), 102–123.

Hill, Bridget, *Women, Work & Sexual Politics in Eighteenth-Century England* (London: UCL Press, 1994).

Hill, Bridget, 'The Marriage Age of Women and the Demographers', *History Workshop Journal*, 28 (1989), 129–147.

Hindle, Steve, Alexandra Shepard and John Walter, eds, *Remaking English Society: Social Relations and Social Change in Early Modern England* (Woodbridge: Boydell Press, 2013).

Hitchcock, Tim, 'Redefining Sex in Eighteenth-Century England', *History Workshop Journal*, 41 (1996), 72–90.

Hoffer, Peter C and NEH Hull, *Murdering Mothers: Infanticide in England and New England 1558–1803* (New York: New York University Press, 1981).

Horon, Isabelle L and Diana Cheng, 'Enhanced Surveillance for Pregnancy-Associated Mortality—Maryland, 1993–1998', *Journal of the American Medical Association*, 285 (2001), 1455–1459.

Howard, Sharon, 'Communities Policing "Criminal" Bodies in Early Modern Wales' <http://sharonhoward.org/archive/controlling-bodies.pdf> [accessed 27/8/2019].

Howard, Sharon, *Law and Disorder in Early Modern Wales: Crime and Authority in the Denbighshire Courts, c 1660–1730* (Cardiff: University of Wales Press, 2008).

Howard, Sharon, 'Imagining the Pain and Peril of Seventeenth-Century Childbirth: Travail and Deliverance in the Making of an Early Modern World', *Social History of Medicine*, 16 (2003), 367–382.

Howell, David, *The Rural Poor in Eighteenth-Century Wales* (Cardiff: University of Wales Press, 2000).

Hudson, Pat, *History by Numbers: An Introduction to Quantitative Approaches* (London: Arnold, 2000).

Humphreys, Melvin, *The Crisis of Community: Montgomeryshire, 1680–1815* (Cardiff: University of Wales Press, 1996).

Hunt, Alun, *Governing Morals: A Social History of Moral Regulation* (Cambridge: Cambridge University Press, 1999).

Hunt, Lynn, ed., *The New Cultural History* (Berkeley: University of California Press, 1989).

Hunt, Margaret R, '"Great Danger She Had Reason to Believe She Was in": Wife-Beating in the Eighteenth Century', in *Women & History: Voices of Early Modern England*, ed. by Valerie Frith (Toronto: Coach House, 1995), pp. 81–102.

Hurdsman, C Neville, *History of the Parish of Chirk* (Wrexham: Bridge, 1996).

Hurren, Elizabeth and Steven King, 'Courtship at the Corner's Court', *Social History*, 40 (2015), 185–207.

Ingram, Martin, *Church Courts, Sex and Marriage in England, 1570–1640* (Cambridge: Cambridge University Press, 1987).

Jackson, Mark, ed., *Infanticide: Historical Perspectives on Child Murder and Concealment, 1550–2000* (Aldershot: Ashgate, 2002).

Jackson, Mark, *New-Born Child Murder: Women, Illegitimacy and the Courts in Eighteenth-Century England* (Manchester: Manchester University Press, 1996).

Jackson, Mark, 'Infant Deaths: The Statues of 1624 and Medical Evidence at Coroners' Inquests', in *Legal Medicine in History*, ed. by Michael Clark and Catherine Crawford (Cambridge: Cambridge University Press, 1994).

Jenkins, Geraint H, *The Foundations of Modern Wales, 1642–1780* (Oxford: Oxford University Press, 1993).

Jenkins, J Geraint, 'The Welsh Woollen Industry', in *Wales in the Eighteenth Century*, ed. by Donald Moore (Swansea: C Davies, 1975), pp. 89–108.

Johnson, Lizbeth, 'Sex and the Single Welshwoman: Prostitution and Concubinage in Late Medieval Wales', *Welsh History Review*, 27 (2014), 253–281.

Jones, Frank T, 'Notes on the Parish Registers of Merthyr Tydfil from AD 1703–1763', *Y Cymmrodor: The Magazine of the Honourable Society of Cymmrodorion*, 35 (1925), 157–186.

Jones, Gareth Elwyn, *Modern Wales: A Concise History*, 2nd edn (Cambridge: Cambridge University Press, 1994).

Jones, Miriam, 'Fractured Narratives of Infanticide in the Crime and Execution Broadside; in Britain, 1780–1850', in *Writing British Infanticide: Childmurder, Gender and Print, 1722–1859*, ed. by Jennifer Thorn (Newark: University of Delaware Press, 2003), pp. 112–142.

Jones, RE, 'Infant Mortality in Rural North Shropshire, 1561–1810', *Population Studies*, 30 (1976), 305–317.

Kenyon, George T, *The Life of Lloyd, First Lord Kenyon, Lord Chief Justice of England* (London: Longmans, 1873).

Kesselring, KJ, 'Bodies of Evidence: Sex and Murder (or Gender and Homicide) in Early Modern England, c. 1500–1680', *Gender and History*, 27 (2015), 245–262.

Kilday, Anne-Marie, *A History of Infanticide in Britain, c. 1600 to the Present* (Basingstoke: Palgrave Macmillan, 2013).

Kilday, Anne-Marie and David S Nash, eds, *Histories of Crime: Britain 1600–2000* (Basingstoke: Palgrave Macmillan, 2010).

King, Helen, 'Midwifery, 1700–1800: The Man-Midwife as Competitor', in *Nursing & Midwifery in Britain Since 1700*, ed. by Anne Borsay and Billie Hunter (Basingstoke: Palgrave Macmillan, 2012), pp. 107–127.

King, Steven, 'The Bastardy Prone Sub-Society Again: Bastards and Their Fathers and Mothers in Lancashire, Wiltshire, and Somerset, 1800–1840', in *Illegitimacy in Britain: 1700–1920*, ed. by Alysa Levene, Thomas Nutt and Samantha Williams (Basingstoke: Palgrave Macmillan, 2005), pp. 66–85.

Klaver, Elizabeth, ed., *The Body in Medical Culture* (Albany: SUNY Press, 2009).

Laqueur, Thomas, 'Sex and Desire in the Industrial Revolution', in *The Industrial Revolution in British Society*, ed. by P O'Brien and R Quinault (Cambridge: Cambridge University Press, 1993), 100–123.

Laqueur, Thomas, *Making Sex: Body and Gender from the Greeks to Freud* (Cambridge, MA: Harvard University Press, 1990).

Laqueur, Thomas, 'Bodies, Details, and the Humanitarian Narrative', in *The New Cultural History*, ed. by Lynn Hunt (Berkeley: University of California Press, 1989), pp. 176–204.

Laslett, Peter, *The World We Have Lost: Further Explored*, 3rd edn (London: Routledge, 2000), pp. 169–170.

Laslett, Peter, 'The Bastardy Prone Sub-Society', in *Bastardy and Its Comparative History*, ed. by Peter Laslett, Karla Oosterveen and Richard M Smith (London: Arnold, 1980), pp. 217–246.

Laslett, Peter, *Family Life and Illicit, Love in Earlier Generations: Essays in Historical Sociology* (Cambridge: Cambridge University Press, 1977).

Laslett, Peter, Karla Oosterveen and Richard M Smith, eds, *Bastardy and Its Comparative History* (London: Arnold, 1980).

Lees, Sue, 'Naggers, Whores, and Libbers: Provoking Men to Kill', in *Femicide: The Politics of Women Killing*, ed. by Jill Radford and Diana EH Russell (Buckingham: Open University Press, 1992), pp. 267–288.

Leneman, Leah, ' "A Tyrant and Tormentor": Violence Against Wives in Eighteenth- and Early Nineteenth-Century Scotland', *Continuity and Change*, 12 (1997), 31–54.

Levene, Alysa, 'The Origins of the Children of the London Foundling Hospital, 1741–1760: A Reconsideration', *Continuity and Change*, 18 (2003), 201–235.

Levene, Alysa, Thomas Nutt and Samantha William, eds, *Illegitimacy in Britain: 1700–1920* (Basingstoke: Palgrave Macmillan, 2005).

Levine, David, *Family Formation in an Age of Nascent Capitalism* (New York: Academic Press, 1977).

Levine, David and Keith Wrightson, *The Making of an Industrial Society: Whickham, 1560–1765* (Oxford: Clarendon Press, 1991).

Lloyd, Josephine M, 'The "Languid Child" and the Eighteenth-Century Man-Midwife', *Bulletin of the History of Medicine*, 73 (2001), 641–679.

Loudon, Irvine, 'Deaths in Childbed from the Eighteenth Century to 1935', *Medical History*, 30 (1986), 1–41.

Luttfring, Sara D, *Bodies, Speech, and Reproductive Knowledge in Early Modern England* (London: Routledge, 2016).

Macfarlane, Alan, 'Illegitimacy and Illegitimates in English History', in *Bastardy and Its Comparative History*, ed. by Peter Laslett, Karla Oosterveen and Richard M Smith (London: Arnold, 1980), pp. 71–85.

MacNamara, Trent and Yuliya Hilevych, 'Living in the Demos: Qualitative Approaches to Demographic Questions', *The History of the Family*, 20 (2015), 1–8.

Malcolmson, RW, 'Infanticide in the Eighteenth Century', in *Crime in England 1550–1800*, ed. by JS Cockburn (Princeton: Princeton University Press, 1977), pp. 187–209.

Marland, Hilary, ed., *The Art of Midwifery: European Midwives in Europe* (Abingdon: Routledge, 1993).

May, Allyson N, 'She at First Denied It: Infanticide Trials at the Old Bailey', in *Women and History: Voices of Early Modern England*, ed. by Valerie Frith (Concord: Irwin, 1997), pp. 19–49.

McClive, Cathy, *Menstruation and Procreation in Early Modern France* (Abingdon: Routledge, 2015).

McClive, Cathy, 'The Hidden Truths of the Belly: Uncertainties of Pregnancy in Early Modern Europe', *Social History of Medicine*, 15 (2002), 209–227.

McDonald, RW, 'The Parish Registers of Wales', *National Library of Wales Journal*, 19 (1976), 399–429.

McLaren, Angus, *Reproductive Rituals: The Perception of Fertility in England from the Sixteenth to the Nineteenth Century* (London: Methuen, 1984).

Mikesell, Margaret and Adele Seeff, eds, *Culture and Change: Attending to Women in Early Modern England* (Newark: University of Delaware Press, 2003).

Mitchison, Rosalind and Leah Leneman, *Girls in Trouble: Sexuality and Social Control: Scotland 1660–1780* (Edinburgh: Scottish Cultural Press, 1998).

Mitchison, Rosalind and Leah Leneman, 'Girls in Trouble: The Social and Geographical Setting of Illegitimacy in Early Modern Scotland', *Journal of Social History*, 21 (1988), 483–497.

Mitchison, Rosalind and Leah Leneman, 'Scottish Illegitimacy Ratios in the Early Modern Period', *Economic History Review*, 2nd ser., 1 (1987), 41–63.

Moore, Donald, ed., *Wales in the Eighteenth Century* (Swansea: C Davies, 1975).

Muir, Angela Joy, 'Courtship, Sex and Poverty: Illegitimacy in Eighteenth-Century Wales', *Social History*, 43 (2018), 56–80.

Muir, Angela Joy, 'Midwifery and Maternity Care for Single Mothers in Eighteenth-Century Wales', *Social History of Medicine* (2018) <https://doi.org/10.1093/shm/hky092>.

Muir, Angela Joy, 'Death and the Parish: Mortality in Eighteenth-Century Wales', *Postgraduate Journal of Medical Humanities*, 4 (2017), 110–114.

Muir, Angela, 'Illegitimacy in Eighteenth-Century Wales', *Welsh History Review*, 26 (2013), 351–388.

Newman, Anthea, 'An Evaluation of Bastardy Recordings in an East Kent Parish', in *Bastardy and Its Comparative History*, ed. by Peter Laslett, Karla Oosterveen and Richard M Smith (London: Arnold, 1980), pp. 141–157.

Newton, Hannah, *The Sick Child in Early Modern England, 1580–1720* (Oxford: Oxford University Press, 2012).
Nutt, Thomas, 'Illegitimacy, Paternal Financial Responsibility, and the 1834 Poor Law Commission Report: The Myth of the Old Poor Law and the Making of the New', *Economic History Review*, 63 (2010), 335–361.
Nutt, Thomas, 'The Paradox and Problems of Illegitimate Paternity in Old Poor Law Essex', in *Illegitimacy in Britain: 1700–1920*, ed. by Alysa Levene, Thomas Nutt and Samantha Williams (Basingstoke: Palgrave Macmillan, 2005), pp. 102–121.
O'Brien, P and R Quinault, eds, *The Industrial Revolution in British Society* (Cambridge: Cambridge University Press, 1993).
O'Day, Rosemary, *Women's Agency in Early Modern Britain and the American Colonies: Patriarchy, Partnership and Patronage* (Harlow and New York: Pearson Longman, 2007).
O'Day, Rosemary, *The Family and Family Relationships, 1500–1900: England, France and the United States* (Basingstoke: Macmillan, 1994).
Oosterveen, Karen, Richard M Smith and Susan Stewart, 'Family Reconstitution and the Study of Bastardy', in *Bastardy and Its Comparative History*, ed. by Peter Laslett, Karla Oosterveen and Richard M Smith (London: Arnold, 1980), pp. 86–140.
Outhwaite, RB, *The Rise and Fall of English Ecclesiastical Courts 1500–1860* (Cambridge: Cambridge University Press, 2007).
Pallitto, Christina C, Jacquelyn C Campbell and Patricia O'Campo, 'Is Intimate Partner Violence Associated with Unintended Pregnancy?' *Trauma, Violence & Abuse*, 6 (2005), 217–235.
Peakman, Julie, ed., *A Cultural History of Sexuality in the Enlightenment* (London: Bloomsbury, 2015).
Pelling, Margaret, *The Common Lot: Sickness, Medical Occupations and the Urban Poor in Early Modern England* (Abingdon: Routledge, 1998).
Pluskota, Marion, *Prostitution and Social Control in Eighteenth-Century Ports* (London: Routledge, 2015).
Pollock, Linda, 'Embarking on a Rough Passage: The Experience of Pregnancy in Early Modern Society', in *Women as Mothers in Pre-Industrial Britain*, ed. by Valerie Fildes (Abingdon: Routledge, 2013), pp. 39–67.
Pollock, Linda, *A Lasting Relationship: Parents and Children Over Three Centuries* (Hanover: University Press of New England, 1987).
Pollock, Linda, *Forgotten Children: Parent-Child Relations from 1500–1900* (Cambridge: Cambridge University Press, 1983).
Porter, Roy, *English Society in the Eighteenth Century*, revised edn (Basingstoke: Palgrave Macmillan, 1990).
Probert, Rebecca, ed., *Cohabitation and Non-Marital Births in England and Wales, 1600–2012* (Basingstoke: Palgrave Macmillan, 2014).
Probert, Rebecca, *The Changing Legal Regulation of Cohabitation: From Fornicators to Family, 1600–2000* (Cambridge: Cambridge University Press, 2012).
Probert, Rebecca, 'Chinese Whispers and Welsh Weddings', *Continuity and Change*, 20 (2005), 211–228.
Pryce, WTR, 'Industrialism, Urbanization and the Maintenance of Culture Areas: North-East Wales in the Mid-Nineteenth Century', *Welsh History Review*, 7 (1975), 307–340.

Quaife, GR, *Wanton Wenches and Wayward Wives* (London: Croom Helm, 1979).

Rabin, Dana, 'Beyond "Lewd Women" and "Wanton Wenches"; Infanticide and Child-Murder in the Long Eighteenth Century", in *Writing British Infanticide: Child-Murder, Gender and Print, 1722–1859*, ed. by Jennifer Thorn (Newark: University of Delaware Press, 2003), pp. 45–69.

Radford, Jill, 'Retrospect on a Trial', in *Femicide: The Politics of Women Killing*, ed. by Jill Radford and Diana EH Russell (Buckingham: Open University Press, 1992), pp. 227–232.

Radford, Jill, 'Womanslaughter: A License to Kill? The Killing of Jane Asher', in *Femicide: The Politics of Women Killing*, ed. by Jill Radford and Diana EH Russell (Buckingham: Open University Press, 1992), pp. 253–266.

Radford, Jill and Diana EH Russell, eds, *Femicide: The Politics of Women Killing* (Buckingham: Open University Press, 1992).

Read, Sara, *Maids, Wives, Widows: Exploring Early Modern Women's Lives 1540–1740* (Barnsley: Pen & Sword, 2015).

Reay, Barry, 'Kinship and the Neighbourhood in Nineteenth-Century Rural England: The Myth of the Autonomous Nuclear Family', *Journal of Family History*, 21 (1996), 87–104.

Reay, Barry, *Microhistories: Demography, Society and Culture in Rural England, 1800–1930* (Cambridge: Cambridge University Press, 1996).

Reay, Barry, 'Sexuality in Nineteenth-Century England: The Social Context of Illegitimacy in Rural Kent', *Rural History*, 1 (1990), 219–247.

Reekie, Gail, *Measuring Immorality: Social Inquiry and the Problem of Illegitimacy* (Cambridge: Cambridge University Press, 1998).

Rees, Eiluned, *Libri Walliae: A Catalogue of Welsh Books and Books Printed in Wales 1546–1820* (Aberystwyth: National Library of Wales, 1987).

Rees, Eiluned, 'Developments in the Book Trade in Eighteenth-Century Wales', *Library*, 5th ser., 24 (1969), 33–43.

Rees, Emma LE, *The Vagina: A Literary and Cultural History* (New York: Bloomsbury, 2013).

Reeves, Carole, ed., *A Cultural History of the Human Body in the Enlightenment* (Oxford: Berg, 2010).

Reid, Alice, 'The Influences on the Health and Mortality of Illegitimate Children in Derbyshire, 1917–1922', in *Illegitimacy in Britain: 1700–1920*, ed. by Alysa Levene, Thomas Nutt and Samantha Williams (Basingstoke: Palgrave Macmillan, 2005), pp. 168–189.

Reid, Alice, Ros Davies, Eilidh Garrett and Andrew Blaikie, 'Vulnerability Among Illegitimate Children in Nineteenth Century Scotland', *Annales de Démographie Historique*, 1 (2006), 89–113.

Roberts, Gwyneth Tyson, *The Language of the Blue Books: The Perfect Instrument of Empire* (Cardiff: University of Wales Press, 1998).

Roberts, Michael and Simone Clarke, eds, *Women and Gender in Early Modern Wales* (Cardiff: Cardiff University Press, 2000).

Roberts, RO, 'Industrial Expansion in South Wales', in *Wales in the Eighteenth Century*, ed. by Donald Moore (Swansea: C Davies, 1975), pp. 109–126.

Rogers, Nicholas, 'Carnal Knowledge: Illegitimacy in Eighteenth-Century Westminster', *Journal of Social History*, 63 (1989), 355–375.

Rosser, Siwan M, *Y Ferch ym Myd y Faled: Delweddau o'r Ferch ym Maledi'r Ddeunawfed Ganrif* (Cardiff: University of Wales Press, 2005).

Roth, Randolph, 'Gender, Sex, and Intimate-Partner Violence in Historical Perspective', in *The Oxford Handbook of Gender, Sex, and Crime*, ed. by Rosemary Gartner and Bill McCarthy (Oxford: Oxford University Press, 2014).

Russell, Diana EH, 'Fay Stender and the Politics of Murder', in *Femicide: The Politics of Women Killing*, ed. by Jill Radford and Diana EH Russell (Buckingham: Open University Press, 1992), pp. 289–302.

Salmon, Marylynn, 'The Cultural Significance of Breastfeeding and Infant Care in Early Modern England and America', *Journal of Social History*, 28 (1994), 247–269.

Schofield, Roger, 'Did the Mothers Really Die? Three Centuries of Maternal Mortality in "The World We Have Lost"', in *The World We Have Gained: Histories of Population and Social Structure*, ed. by Lloyd Bonfield, Richard M Smith and Keith Wrightson (Oxford: Blackwell, 1986), pp. 231–260.

Scott, Susan and CJ Duncan, 'Malnutrition, Pregnancy and Infant Mortality: A Biometric Model', *Journal of Interdisciplinary History*, 30 (1999), 37–60.

Shapiro, Barbara J, 'Oaths, Credibility and the Legal Process in Early Modern England: Part Two', *Law and Humanities*, 7 (2013), 19–54.

Shapiro, Barbara J, 'Oaths, Credibility and the Legal Process in Early Modern England: Part One', *Law and Humanities*, 6 (2012), 145–178.

Sharpe, James A, *Crime in Seventeenth-Century England: A County Study* (Cambridge: Cambridge University Press, 1983).

Shepard, Alexandra, 'Brokering Fatherhood: Illegitimacy and Paternal Rights and Responsibilities in Early Modern England', in *Remaking English Society: Social Relations and Social Change in Early Modern England*, ed. by in Steve Hindle, Alexandra Shepard and John Walter (Woodbridge: Boydell Press, 2013), pp. 41–63.

Shoemaker, Robert, 'Male Honour and the Decline of Public Violence in Eighteenth-Century London', *Social History*, 26 (2001), 190–208.

Shorter, Edward, *The Making of the Modern Family* (New York: Basic, 1975).

Shorter, Edward, 'Illegitimacy, Sexual Revolution, and Social Change in Modern Europe', *The Journal of Interdisciplinary History*, 2 (1971), 237–272.

Snell, KDM, *Parish and Belonging: Community, Identity, and Welfare in England and Wales, 1700–1950* (Cambridge: Cambridge University Press, 2006).

Sommers, Sheena, 'Remapping Maternity in the Courtroom: Female Defences and Medical Witnesses in Eighteenth-Century Infanticide Proceedings', in *The Body in Medical Culture*, ed. by Elizabeth Klaver (Albany: SUNY Press, 2009), pp. 37–59.

Stevens, Catrin, *Welsh Courting Customs* (Llandysul: Gomer, 1993).

Stolberg, Michael, 'Examining the Body, c. 1500–1750', in *The Routledge History of Sex and the Body: 1500 to the Present*, ed. by Sarah Toulalan and Kate Fisher (London: Routledge, 2013), pp. 91–105.

Stone, Lawrence, 'Kinship and Forced Marriage in Early Eighteenth-Century Wales', *Welsh History Review*, 17 (1995), 356–364.

Stone, Lawrence, *Broken Lives: Separation and Divorce in England, 1660–1857* (Oxford: Oxford University Press, 1993).

Stone, Lawrence, *The Family, Sex, and Marriage in England, 1500–1800* (New York: Harper & Row, 1977).

Strange, Carolyn, 'Masculinities, Intimate Femicide and the Death Penalty in Australia, 1890–1920', *The British Journal of Criminology*, 43 (2003), 310–339.

Tarbin, Stephanie and Susan Broomhall, eds, *Women, Identities and Communities in Early Modern Europe* (Aldershot: Ashgate, 2008).

Teichman, Jenny, *Illegitimacy: A Philosophical Examination* (Oxford: Blackwell, 1982).

Thomas, Keith, 'The Double Standard', *Journal of the History of Ideas*, 20 (1959), 195–216.

Thomas, Samuel S, 'Early Modern Midwives: Splitting the Profession, Connecting the History', *Journal of Social History*, 43 (2009), 115–138.

Thorn, Jennifer, ed., *Writing British Infanticide: Child-Murder, Gender and Print, 1722–1859* (Newark: University of Delaware Press, 2003).

Tilley, Louise A, Joah W Scott and Miriam Cohen, 'Women's Work and European Fertility Patterns', *Journal of Interdisciplinary History*, 6 (1976), 447–476.

Tomkins, Alannah, 'The Registers of a Provincial Man-Midwife, Thomas Higgins of Wem, 1781–1803', *Shropshire Historical Documents, A Miscellany*, 4 (2000), 65–148.

Toulalan, Sarah, '"Is He a Licentious Lewd Sort of Person?" Constructing the Child Rapist in Early Modern England', *Journal of the History of Sexuality*, 23 (2014), 21–52.

Toulalan, Sarah, *Imagining Sex, Pornography and Bodies in Seventeenth-Century England* (Oxford: Oxford University Press, 2007).

Toulalan, Sarah and Kate Fisher, eds, *The Routledge History of Sex and the Body: 1500 to the Present* (Abingdon: Routledge, 2013).

Trumbach, Randolph, *Sex and the Gender Revolution, Vol 1: Heterosexuality and the Third Gender in Enlightenment London* (Chicago: University of Chicago Press, 1998).

Walker, Garthine, 'Rape, Acquittal and Culpability in Popular Crime Reports in England, c. 1670-c. 1750', *Past and Present*, 222 (2013), 115–142.

Walker, Garthine, 'Sexual Violence and Rape in Europe, 1500–1750', in *The Routledge History of Sex and the Body: 1500 to the Present*, ed. by Sarah Toulalan and Kate Fisher, (London: Routledge, 2013), pp. 429–443.

Walker, Garthine, *Crime, Gender and Social Order in Early Modern England* (Cambridge: Cambridge University Press, 2003).

Walker, Garthine, 'Just Stories: Telling Tales of Infant Death in Early Modern England', in *Culture and Change: Attending to Women in Early Modern England*, ed. by Margaret Mikesell and Adele Seeff (Newark: University of Delaware Press, 2003), pp. 98–115.

Walker, Garthine, 'Rereading Rape and Sexual Violence in Early Modern England', *Gender & History*, 10 (1998), 1–25.

Ware, Jean, 'How to Live in Wales: A Guide to Foreign Students, Including the English and Scots', *Wales*, 38 (1959), 57–61.

Watson, Katherine D, 'Women, Violent Crime and Criminal Justice in Georgian Wales', *Continuity and Change*, 28 (2013), 245–272.

White, Eryn M, *The Welsh Bible: A History* (Stroud: The History Press, 2007).

Williams, Samantha, *Unmarried Motherhood in the Metropolis, 1700–1850: Pregnancy, the Poor Law and Provision* (Basingstoke: Palgrave Macmillan, 2018).

Williams, Samantha, ' "They Lived Together as Man and Wife": Plebeian Cohabitation, Illegitimacy, and Broken Relationships in London, 1700–1840', in *Cohabitation and Non-Marital Births in England and Wales, 1600–2012*, ed. by Rebecca Probert (Basingstoke: Palgrave Macmillan, 2014), pp. 65–79.

Williams, Samantha, 'The Experience of Pregnancy and Childbirth for Unmarried Mothers in London, 1760–1866', *Women's History Review*, 20 (2011), 67–86.

Wilson, Adrian, 'The Ceremony of Childbirth and Its Interpretation', in *Women as Mothers in Pre-Industrial Britain*, ed. by Valerie Fildes (Abingdon: Routledge, 2013), pp. 68–107.

Wilson, Adrian, *Ritual and Conflict: The Social Relations of Childbirth in Early Modern England* (Farnham: Ashgate, 2013).

Wilson, Adrian, *The Making of Man-Midwifery: Childbirth in England, 1660–1770* (London: UCL Press, 1995).

Wilson, Adrian, 'Illegitimacy and Its Implications in Mid-18th Century London: The Evidence of the Foundling Hospital', *Continuity and Change*, 4 (1989), 103–164.

Withey, Alun, *Physick and the Family: Health, Medicine and Care in Wales, 1600–1750* (Manchester: Manchester University Press, 2011).

Woods, RI, PA Watterson and JA Woodward, 'The Causes of Rapid Infant Mortality Decline in England and Wales, 1861–1921, Part I', *Population Studies*, 42 (1988), 343–366.

Woodward, Nick, 'Infanticide in Wales, 1730–1830', *Welsh History Review*, 23 (2007), 94–125.

Wrightson, Keith, 'Infanticide in Earlier Seventeenth-Century England', *Local Population Studies*, 15 (1975), 10–22.

Wrigley, EA, and RS Schofield, *The Population History of England, 1541–1871: A Reconstruction* (London: Arnold, 1981).

Wrigley, EA, RS Davies, JE Oeppen and RS Schofield, *English Population History from Family Reconstitution 1580–1837* (Cambridge: Cambridge University Press, 1997).

Zunshine, Lisa, *Bastards and Foundlings: Illegitimacy in Eighteenth-Century England* (Columbus: Ohio State University Press, 2005).

Unpublished Theses and Dissertations

Brueton, Anna, 'Illegitimacy in South Wales, 1660–1870' (unpublished doctoral thesis, Leicester, 2015).

Horler-Underwood, Catherine E, 'Aspects of Female Criminality in Wales c. 1730–1830: Evidence from the Court of Great Sessions' (unpublished doctoral thesis, Cardiff, 2014).

Howard, Sharon, 'Crime, Communities and Authority in Early Modern Wales: Denbighshire, 1660–1730' (unpublished doctoral thesis, Aberystwyth, 2003).

Jones, Bethan Lloyd, 'Profile of a Welsh County Coalfield: The Denbighshire Coalfield, 1850–1914' (unpublished doctoral thesis, Cardiff, 2008).

Kitson, Peter, 'Differentials in Infant Survivorship Between Illegitimate and Legitimate Children: Case Studies of Two English Market Towns, ca. 1670–1830' (unpublished doctoral thesis, Cambridge, 2003).

Smith, Shirley Ann, ' "A Crying Sin": Infanticide in South-West Wales, 1870–1922' (unpublished doctoral thesis, Aberystwyth, 2015).

Ward, Catherine, 'Desperate Remedies': A Historical Overview of Women's Methods of Procuring Abortion' (unpublished MA dissertation, Wellcome Institute for the History of Medicine 1996).

Index

Page numbers in *italic* refer to figures in the text or *Gaol Files* in the bibliography

abandonment 29, 160, 173, 210
Abel, Anne, Carmarthenshire 174, 177, *231*
abortion 136, 137, 143, 171
accidents 169
Act for the Better Relief of the Poor of this Kingdom (1662) 23, 208
Act of Union (1536) 15
Act to Prevent the Destroying and Murthering of Bastard Children (1624) 14, 123, 175, 180
Adair, Richard 8, 16, 84; on identified paternity 11, 52, 75; on illegitimacy ratios 9–10, 47
adultery 52, 65, 73, 88, 136, 137–138
age: at death 110; of marriage 59, 66
Ajax, Elinor, midwife, Llantrisant 197
'alias', use of 17, 77
Allday, Elizabeth, Hawarden 77
Anglesey 55, 128, 198, *230*
Anglicanism 5
apprenticeships 95, 96, 97
Aristotle, *Masterpiece* 56, 57
Arthur, Jane, Llanrhaeadr ym Mochnant, Montgomeryshire *116*
Assize Courts 138, 225
attendants at births 211–212; 'gossips' 207, 208, 212; *see also* midwives; witnesses to childbirth
Axon, Deborah, Holt 78

Bamford, Anne, Trefeglys, Montgomeryshire 208
Bangor 194
baptism 5, 16, 19, 76, 109; timing of 37n99, 207

baptism registers 117, 203; and courtship and relationships 76–78, 85, 88, 95; and identified paternity 7–8, 11–12, 19–20, 25, 50–52
Barnes, Paul, St Asaph, Flintshire 132
Barret, Mary, Forden, Montgomeryshire 131, *232*
bastardy bonds 20–21, 165; prenatal and postnatal 76, 213–214; and relationships/irregular marriage 77, 78, 81–84, 86; and socioeconomic background of parents 93, 94
bastardy prone sub-society 10, 44, 73, 74, 78–79, 90
Baxter, Richard, surgeon, Berriew, Montgomeryshire 171
Bellis, Elizabeth, Denbighshire 160, 167, 172, 176, 178, 181, *231*
belly, swollen 171
Berriew, Montgomeryshire 93; care of children 95–96, 146; care of unmarried mothers 202–203, 211; and identified paternity 82, 83, 86
Berwick, William, Montgomeryshire 137, *232*
Bettws Cedewain, Montgomeryshire 82, 201, 202, 208, 212
biopower 106
birthing chamber 207, 208, 209
Bithell, Sarah, witness, Flintshire 172, 174, 175, 179
Black, John 11, 91, 94
bleeding 167, 175, 177, 178–179; *see also* menstruation
Blue Books (*Report of the Commission of Inquiry into the*

250 Index

State of Education in Wales, 1847) 6–7, 55
Board of Guardians, Llanfyllin 59
bodies: in infanticide cases 157, 158, 159, 161–162, 179–184, 185, 204; reproductive 155–185; *see also* reproductive knowledge
Bolanson, Francis, London 169, 188n106
bonding 108
Bowen, Anne, Wrexham, Denbighshire 77
breasts 160, 163, 175, 176–177, 178
Brecon/Breconshire: infanticide 130–131, 162, *230*; murder of pregnant women 53, 139–140, 141, 143, *230*
Brees, Ann, Berriew, Montgomeryshire 83
Brewster, Jane, Cardiganshire 172, 174
Bright, Edward, surgeon, Montgomeryshire 137
Brown, Jerimiah, Berriew, Montgomeryshire 86
Brown, Mary and Thomas 22, *231*
Brown, Richard, Llandinam, Montgomeryshire 83
Brueton, Anna 46, 80, 95, 224
Bryan, Mary, attendant, Flintshire 182
bundling 53–55, 56–57, 67, 222
burial of infants 110, 112, 113, 146
burial registers 18, 20, 107, 109–110
Burke, Peter 29
Butler, Hannah, London 172
Butler, Sara 143

Caernarfon 87, *231*
Cambridge Group for the History of Population and Social Structure 8, 109
Cardigan/Cardiganshire 87, 230–231; infanticide 160, 172, 174, 181, *230*, *231*
care of illegitimate children 95–96, 145–146
care of unmarried mothers 26, 133, 145–147, 164, 192–216, 223–224; and midwives 24, 200; Montgomeryshire 202–203, 211, 212; in poor law accounts 24, 118, 185
Carmarthen/Carmarthenshire 95; murder of pregnant women 55, *231*; and prostitution 88, *231*; *see also* infanticide, Carmarthenshire
Carno, Montgomeryshire 17, 18
Castell Caereinion, Montgomeryshire 146, 201, 203, 211, 212, 213
Ceri/Kerry, Montgomeryshire 76, 81, 208
Chandley, William 81
change, cultural and socioeconomic 43
charitable societies 29, 195
childbirth: attendants at births/witnesses to 175, 207, 208, 211–212; birthing chamber 207, 208, 209; ceremony of 193, 206–214; complications 114, 203, 205; concealed 128–129, 130–131, 133, 175–179, 180, 223; death of child in 209; death of mother in 203, 205; lying-in 195, 207, 210–211, 214–215; signs of 155–156, 160, 163–164, 167, 170–172, 173–174, 175–179; *see also* care of unmarried mothers; midwives
children, illegitimate 10, 94–97, 143; care of 95–96, 145–146; discrimination of/stigmatisation 96–97, 98, 224; mortality penalty of 118–119, 147
Chirk, Denbighshire 61, 64
church courts 28, 58; *see also* ecclesiastical regulation
churching 207, 214
churchwarden accounts 19, 23, 30–31, 77, 202
Clark family, Marchwiel, Denbighshire 108
Clyro, Radnorshire 66, 115, 209
Cody, Lisa Forman 28, 166
cohabitation 44, 73, 75–76, 77, 78, 80–84, 86
Colborne, Raleigh, medical practioner 160, 176
compassion 127–131, 134, 145, 146, 147–148, 184
concubines 78, 80–81, 108
confessions 21–22, 23, 143, 158, 165
Coram, Thomas 29
coroners 21, 126
Court of Great Sessions 21–22, 25–26, 30, 122, 144; and midwives 160, 194, 199, 204; and murder

of pregnant women 53, 117–118, 135–136, 138–139, 225; and non-consensual sex 85, 100n83; and reproductive knowledge 185, 225
Court of Great Sessions, infanticide cases 14, 123–124, 156, 160, 186n16, 194, 216n9; examination of infant bodies 180, 182, 204; *see also* infanticide
court records 21–23, 44; courtship/pre-marital sex 53, 55; Quarter Sessions 194, 209; relationships within neighbourhood 4, 209
courtship 25, 44, 52–57, 75, 97, 124; and baptism registers 76–78, 85, 88, 95; bundling 53–55, 56–57, 67, 222; and court records 53, 55; courtship-led marriage 43, 62, 67, 222, 223
'courtship intensity' hypothesis 59
Crawford, Patricia 27, 166
criminal justice systems 144
Cromwell, Thomas 15
crop failure 62
Culcheth, Lancashire 63

Dabhoiwala, Faramerz 57–58
David, Barbara, Glamorganshire 182, *232*
David, Elizabeth, Breconshire 173, 175, 177–178
David, Gwenllian, Breconshire 171, 199–200, *230*
David, Hannah, Carmarthenshire 174
David, Joan, Swansea 177
David, Oliver, Trefeglwys 78
David, Sarah, Cardiganshire 160, *231*
Davies, Anne, Llanrhaeadr ym Mochnant, Montgomeryshire 80, *116*
Davies, Edward, Llandinam, Montgomeryshire 86, 100n83
Davies, Elizabeth, Merionethshire 199, 232
Davies, Elizabeth, midwife 202
Davies, Ellen, midwife, Merionethshire 199
Davies, John, Norton, Radnorshire 79, 82
Davies, Margaret, midwife, Radnorshire 199
Davies, Margaret, Montgomeryshire 171, 174

Davies, Mary, Flintshire 160, 172, 176–177, *231*
Davies, Mary, Trefeglwys, Montgomeryshire 127–128
Davies, Rebecca, midwife, Newtown, Montgomeryshire 196, 197, 198
Davies, Thomas, Trefeglwys, Montgomeryshire 81–82, 88
Davies, William, Forden, Montgomeryshire 131
death penalty 124, 145, 184
Dell, Mary, Montgomeryshire 134, 178, 182
demographic data 26, 110
Denbighshire 5; care of unmarried mothers and illegitimate children 96, 214; and economics and industrialization 60, 61, 62–65, 67; and identified paternity *51*, 52, 64–65, 67, 78, 82, 93; illegitimacy levels 6, 48–49, 63, 64, 222; murder of pregnant women 131, 142, 143, *231*; poor law accounts 6, 64; *see also* individual places; infanticide, Denbighshire; Roberts, Catherine, Abergele, Denbighshire
deviance of unmarried mothers 2, 143–144, 145, 147–148, 179–180, 185, 223
discrimination 31, 96–97
disease 107
dissection 162, 183
divorce 88
Donnison, Jean 204
double standards 98, 144
Drew, John and David, Llandegley, Radnorshire 83

ecclesiastical regulation 28, 58, 67; and midwives 196, 198, 199
economics: economic dependence of women 60, 66, 163; economic stability 30, 59, 60, 62; and illegitimacy 29, 45, 49, 97–98, 222; and marriage 59–60, 62
Edwards, Anne, Llanrhaeadr ym Mochnant, Montgomeryshire *116*
Edwards, Anne, midwife, Breconshire 199, 200
Edwards, Dorothy ferch, midwife, Flintshire 162, 182, 199
Edwards, Edward, Wrexham, Denbighshire 78

Index

Edwards, Jane, Denbighshire 140, *231*
Edwards, Roger and Jane, Oswestry, Shropshire 85
Elis y Cowper (Ellis Roberts) 126–127
Ellis, Margaret 79
Emerson, Joseph, Halkyn, Flintshire 131, *231*
employers 131, 132–133
employment opportunities 60, 61, 63, 64, 66
Encyclopaedia Britannica 28
English illegitimacy 2, 3, 45–46; English illegitimacy ratios 9; *see also* London
espousals 75–76
Evans, David, Montgomeryshire 172
Evans, Edward, Hawarden, Flintshire 77
Evans, Eliza, Trefeglwys, Montgomeryshire 210
Evans, Elizabeth, Aberhafesp/Llanwnog, Montgomeryshire 53, 115, 117–118, 138–139, 143, *232*
Evans, Jane, Llanrhaeadr ym Mochnant, Montgomeryshire *116*
Evans, Joyce, Carno, Montgomeryshire 18
Evans, Lydia, Gladestry, Radnorshire 80
Evans, Margaret, Berriew, Montgomeryshire 171, 173, 174, *232*
Evans, Mary, Llanrhaeadr ym Mochnant, Montgomeryshire *116*
Evans, Mary and Samuel, Buttington, Montgomeryshire 77
Evans, Robert, Abergele, Denbighshire 155–156, 163, 164, 172
Evans, Tanya 12–13
Evenden, Doreen 195–196
experience, lived 12–13, 53, 108–109; and infanticide 125, 126; of unmarried mothers 4, 26, 192, 215–216

famine 45, 62
fathers: and infanticide 130–131; and murder of older children 143; and murder of pregnant women 135–145; and reproductive knowledge 159; socioeconomic background of 11–12, 50, 74, 86, 89–92, 93, 225; survival strategies 223; unidentified 87; and violence 15, 135, 136, 147; *see also* bastardy bonds; maintenance payments; paternity, identified
fees, midwives' 200–206
filiation orders 20–21, 82, 212
fines, for rape 85, 100n83
Flintshire *see* individual places; infanticide
Follyman, Elizabeth, Holt, Denbighshire 82
Foucault, Michel 27, 28, 30, 106
Foulkes, Elizabeth, midwife, Flintshire 182
Foulkes, Mary, Llanfyllin, Montgomeryshire 79
Foundling Hospital 29, 60, 62
Francis, Richard, Llandinam, Montgomeryshire 86
French Revolution 29

Gabriel, Edward, Denbighshire 64
Gabrielle, Jane, Gresford, Denbighshire 96
George, Elizabeth, Cardiganshire 87, 230, *231*
Gillis, John 75, 76, 106
Gladestry, Radnorshire 17, 80, 214
Glamorganshire 95; infanticide 167, 170–171, 173, 176, 182, 200, *232*
Glascwm, Radnorshire 108, 130; illegitimacy rates 78, 79, 81
Goodwyn, Mary, midwife, Berriew, Montgomeryshire 200, 202–203
Goose, Nigel 60
Gowing, Laura 13, 163, 181; on ceremony of childbirth 193, 207–208; on infanticide 14, 123, 129; on symptoms of pregnancy 166, 171
grain prices 60, 62
Graunt, John 28
Gresford, Denbighshire 211; care of unmarried mothers and illegitimate children 96, 214; illegitimacy levels 63, 64
Grey, Daniel 166
Griffin, Emma 44, 53, 59, 60, 63
Griffith, Elizabeth John, midwife, Anglesey 198–199
Griffith, Jane, St Asaph, Flintshire 132, 162, 168–170, 188n106, 199, *231*; examination of infant's body 180, 182

Index 253

Griffiths, John, Berriew, Montgomeryshire 86
Griffiths, Mary 77
Gwyn, John and Catherine, Glascwym, Radnorshire 108
Gwynn, Gwenith 76

Harley, David 195
Harrington, Jane, Radnorshire 199, 232
Harris, Mary, Brecon 130–131, 163, 230
Harry, Catherine, Llangadfan, Montgomeryshire 77
Harry, Wenllian, midwife, Whitchurch, Glamorgan 197, 201
Hawarden, Flintshire 7, 77
Henllan, Denbighshire 64–65, 77
Herefordshire 6
Herrup, Cynthia 144
Hertfordshire 6
highland regions 10, 47
Hill, Bridget 63
Hitchcock, Tim 56, 57
Hoare family, Colyton, Devon 10
Hoddall, Judith, New Radnor 31
Holt, Denbighshire 78, 82, 93
Hopkins, David Williams, surgeon 183
Howard, Sharon 13, 144
'How to Live in Britain: A handbook for students from overseas' 7
Hughes, Ann, Cardiganshire 172, 174, 230
Hughes, Frances, midwife, Haverfordwest 200, 218n52
Hughes, Samuel, Wrexham, Denbighshire 77
Humphrey, Catherine, Llanrhaeadr ym Mochnant, Montgomeryshire 116
Humphreys, Edward, Llangollen, Denbighshire 88
Humphreys, Judith, Berriew, Montgomeryshire 95
Humphreys, Melvin 113
Hunt, Mary, Flintshire 180, 231

illegitimacy 7–11; definition 1; and economics 29, 45, 49, 97–98, 222; English 2, 3, 9, 45–46, 63; Scottish 3, 9, 12, 109; see also children, illegitimate; infanticide; London; murder of pregnant women; paternity, identified
illegitimacy, repeated 77, 78–80, 132
Illegitimacy in Britain, 1700–1920 12
illegitimacy levels 6, 8–11, 25, 43–68; Denbighshire 6, 48–49, 63, 64, 222; illegitimacy rates 18; illegitimacy ratios 3, 18, 45–50, 62–64, 222–223; Montgomeryshire 6, 48–49, 222; Radnorshire 6, 48–49, 78, 79, 81
incest 52, 65, 72n119, 73, 85–86
industrialisation 43, 44, 60–65, 67
Industrial Revolution 29
infanticide 13, 14, 26, 122–134, 145, 168–184; and compassion 127–131, 134; convictions 188n106; infant bodies in 157, 158, 159, 161–162, 179–184, 185, 204; and law 14, 123, 133–134, 168, 175, 180; in literature 25; and lived experience 125, 126; London 169, 172, 188n106; and witnesses/attendants 126, 128, 129, 174, 175, 211–212; see also Court of Great Sessions, infanticide cases
infanticide, Breconshire 162; Elizabeth Morris 167, 172, 230; Elizabeth Williams 169, 170; Gwellian Powell 175, 230; Mary Harris 130–131, 163
infanticide, Cardiganshire: Ann Hughes 172, 174, 230; Maria Morris 181, 231; Sarah David 160, 231
infanticide, Carmarthenshire: Anne Abel 174, 177, 231; Anne John 167, 169, 188n106, 231; Hannah John 161, 169, 188n106, 199, 231; Jane Thomas 179, 180–181, 231
infanticide, Denbighshire: Ann Parry 169, 188n106, 231; Elizabeth Bellis 160, 167, 172, 176, 178, 181, 231; Jane Edwards 140, 231; Jane Williams 131, 132, 171–172, 176, 181, 231; Mary Owen 126–127, 161, 231; Mary Philips 177, 231; Sarah Owen 85, 130, 131, 132, 210, 231; see also Roberts, Catherine, Abergele, Denbighshire
infanticide, Flintshire: Eleanor Jones 161, 179, 231; Elizabeth Jones 169, 170, 171, 231; Elizabeth Williams

254 Index

170–171, 176, 177; Jane Griffith 132, 168–169, 170, 180, 182, 188n106, 199; Joseph Emerson 131, *231*; Margaret Jones 131, 160, 172; Margaret Parker 179, *231*; Mary Davies 160, 172, 176–177, *231*; Mary Hunt 180, *231*; Mary Jones 174, 175, 179, *231*; *see also* Griffith, Jane, St Asaph, Flintshire

infanticide, Glamorganshire: Barbara David 182, *232*; Jannet John 170–171, 176, *232*; Margaret Lewis 167, *232*; Mary Morgan 173, 200, *232*; Mary Richard 182, *232*

infanticide, Montgomeryshire: Ann Owen 132, 133, 176; Elinor Pugh 134, *232*; Jane Williams 162, 171–172, 173–174, 179, 183, 184, *232*; Margaret Evans 171, 173, 174, *232*; Margaret Lewis 133, 134, 176, *232*; Mary Barret 131, *232*; Mary Dell 134, 178, 182; *see also* Jenkin, Margaret, Trefeglwys, Montgomeryshire

infanticide, Radnorshire: Hannah Morris 174, 178, *232*; Jane Harrington 199, *232*; Margaret Thomas Preece 130, 133, 179; Mary Powell 115, 117–118, 209, *232*

infants, bodies of 179–184

Isle of Skye 109

Jackson, Mark 14, 123, 161, 166, 175

Jenkin, Margaret, Trefeglwys, Montgomeryshire 127–128, 180, *232*; medical examination of 163–164, 176; suspected pregnancy 171, 173, 174

Jenkins, Evan, Llanwnog, Montgomeryshire 53, 138–139, *232*

Jenkyn, Margaret, Llanwnog, Montgomeryshire 80

John, Anne, Carmarthenshire 167, 169, 188n106, *231*

John, Hannah, Carmarthenshire 161, 169, 188n106, 199, *231*

John, James, Breconshire 143, *231*

John, Jannet, Glamorgan 170–171, 176, *232*

John, Jennet, Breconshire 171

Jones, Bridget, Machynlleth, Montgomeryshire 77

Jones, Catherine, Llangyniew, Montgomeryshire 77

Jones, Catherine, Llanrhaeadr ym Mochnant, Montgomeryshire *116*

Jones, Edward, Gresford, Denbighshire 64

Jones, Eleanor, Flintshire 161, 179, *231*

Jones, Elinor, Llandrindod, Radnorshire 214

Jones, Elizabeth, Carmarthenshire 55, *231*

Jones, Elizabeth, Flintshire 169, 170, 171, *231*

Jones, Evan, Ystradfellte, Brecon 141

Jones, Griffith 29, 58

Jones, Jane, Castell Caereinion, Montgomeryshire 214

Jones, John, Llanfair Caereinion, Montgomeryshire 77

Jones, John, Llangollen, Denbighshire 88

Jones, Lucy, midwife, Breconshire 177

Jones, Margaret, Halkyn, Flintshire 131, 160

Jones, Margaret, Llanrhaeadr ym Mochnant, Montgomeryshire *116*

Jones, Mary, Erbistock, Denbighshire 131, 142, 143, *231*

Jones, Mary, Flintshire 172, 174, 175, 179, *231*

Jones, Mary, Llanraieadr ym Mochnant, Montgomeryshire 88

Jones, Richard, Llandegley, Radnorshire 82

Jones, Roger, Wrexham, Denbighshire 77

Jones, Thomas, Llangadfan, Montgomeryshire 77

Jones, Ursula, Berriew, Montgomeryshire 86

Jones, William, Manafon, Montgomeryshire 83

Jones, William, surgeon 161, 183, 199, 205

Josselin, Ralph 207

Kenyon, Lloyd and George, Flintshire 30

Kerry, Alice, Flintshire 161, 176, 177

Kerry, John, man-midwife, Flintshire 161, 204

Kilday, Anne-Marie 14, 123

Index 255

King, Gregory 28
King, Helen 204
King, Peter 144
King, Steven 78, 83
Kinsey, Elizabeth, Aberhafesp, Montgomeryshire 81
Kinsey, Elizabeth, Berriew, Montgomeryshire 95
Kitson, Peter 13–14

labour pains 170–171
lactation 176, 178
Laqueur, Thomas 129, 183–184
Laslett, Peter 26, 31, 59, 75; on bastardy prone sub-society 10, 44, 73, 78–79; on illegitimacy ratios 8, 9, 45
law: and infanticide 14, 123, 133–134, 168, 175, 180; and poor relief 23, 208
Leneman, Leah and Mitchison, Rosalind 8–9
Levene, Alysa 14
Levine, David 59
Lewis, Alice, Llandegley, Radnorshire 83, 84
Lewis, David, Meifod, Montgomeryshire 96
Lewis, Elizabeth, Carmarthen 88, 231
Lewis, Margaret, Glamorgan 167, 232
Lewis, Margaret, Montgomeryshire 133, 134, 176, 232
Lewis, Rachel, Breconshire 163
licencing of midwives 194, 195, 196–206; fees 200–206
literacy 93, 94, 198
literature, popular 24–25, 123; ballads 25, 125–126
Llanarmon Dyffrin Ceiriog, Denbighshire 214
Llanbister, Radnorshire 95
Llandaff, diocese of 194, 195
Llandegley, Radnorshire 77, 82, 83
Llandinam, Montgomeryshire 83, 86, 93, 208
Llanfair Caereinion, Montgomeryshire 77
Llanfihangel Nant Melan, Radnorshire 79, 80, 108–109
Llanfihangel-yng-Ngwynfa, Montgomeryshire 205
Llanfyllin, Denbighshire 59, 79

Llangadfan, Montgomeryshire 77
Llangollen, Denbighshire 64, 85, 86, 88, 90
Llangyniew, Montgomeryshire 77, 96
Llanrhaeadr ym Mochnant, Montgomberyshire 20, 88, 107, 115–116, 117, 118
Llansilin, Denbighshire 72n119
Llanwnog, Montgomeryshire 81, 88, 115, 138–139
Lloyd, Catherine, Llanrhaeadr ym Mochnant, Montgomeryshire 116
Lloyd, Elizabeth 78, 79
Lloyd, Harry, Llangyniew, Montgomeryshire 96
Lloyd, John, Llangyniew, Montgomeryshire 77
Lloyd, Richard, surgeon 162, 183
Lloyd, William, medical practioner 160
London 115, 144, 172, 195–196; and cultural and socioeconomic background 12–14, 43, 60, 62, 67, 91, 94; infanticide 169, 172, 188n106
Loudon, Irvine 14
Lowe, Estar, Llandinam, Montgomeryshire 208, 210
Lumley, Sarah, Berriew, Montgomeryshire 168
Luscott, Sarah, Berriew, Montgomeryshire 86
lying-in 207, 210–211, 214–215; lying-in charities 195
Lynstone, Lettice, midwife, Breconshire 199

Machynlleth, Montgomeryshire 63, 65, 72n112, 77, 128
Maddock, Watkin, Holt, Denbighshire 78
Maesmawr estate, Llandinam 86
magistrates/justices of the peace 31, 128, 214
maintenance payments 113, 145; and identified paternity 20–21, 65–66, 72n125, 81–82, 142–143, 147
male power, abuse of 21
malnutrition 14, 166
Malthus, Thomas 30
Manafon, Montgomeryshire 83, 208
Manchester 212
man-midwives 160–161, 162, 194, 198, 204–205, 206, 225

256 Index

Mantle, Elizabeth, Llandegley, Radnorshire 82
Marchwiel, Denbighshire 31, 63–64, 108
marriage 59–67; age of 59, 66; coerced 77; cost of 75; courtship-led 2, 43, 62, 67, 222, 223; informal/cohabitation 44, 73, 75–76, 77, 78, 80–84, 86; intention of 53, 139, 141; *see also* courtship
Massy, Elizabeth 77
masturbation 44, 56–57
Matthews, George, Holt, Denbighshire 82
Matthews, Margaret, New Radnor, Radnorshire 78
Matthews, Margaret, Old Radnor, Radnorshire 53, 140, 143, *232*
Matthews, Thomas and Johan, Glascwyn, Radnorshire 108
McClive, Cathy 182
medical examinations: of bodies of babies 161–162, 182–184; of women 160–161, 176–177, 184
medical practitioners, male 182–183, 194, 203–204; man-midwives 160–161, 162, 194, 198, 204–206, 225; and reproductive knowledge 159, 160–162
Meifod, Montgomeryshire 63, 65, 72n112, 96, 146, 205, 209
menstruation 164, 165, 166–167
mental health of unmarried mothers 183–184
Meredith, Elizabeth, Llandegley, Radnorshire 82
Meredith, Mary, Caernarfon 87, *231*
Methodism 58
midwives 5, 193–206; and care of unmarried mothers 24, 200; and ceremony of childbirth 207, 208; and Court of Great Sessions 160, 194, 199, 204; and ecclesiastical regulation 196, 198, 199; fees 200–206; and identified paternity 212–213; and infanticide 134, 162, 182; inferior 200; licencing of 194, 195, 196–206; in London 195–196; man-midwives 160–161, 162, 194, 198, 204–206, 225; marital status 196–197; and medical examinations 161, 162, 184; oath 134, 195, 196, 199, 200–201, 212–213; and poor relief *201*, 202–203; and reproductive knowledge 159, 160, 162, 197, 225; reputation 197–200; socioeconomic background 198–200, 218n52; widows as 196, 217n25; working relationships 205–206
migration 66–67
Miles, Ann, Llandegley, Radnorshire 77
mining 49, 61, 63, 67
miscarriage 169, 179, 180, 181
Montgomeryshire 5, 58, 194; care of children 95–96, 146; care of unmarried mothers 202–203, 211; and economics and industrialization 60, 61, 62–63; illegitimacy levels 6, 48–49, 222; and infant mortality 110–111, 112–113, 117; mortality crisis 45; murder of pregnant women 53, 115, 117–118, 137, 138–139, 143, *232*; and right of settlement 208, 210; *see also* Berriew, Montgomeryshire; individual places; infanticide; Jenkin, Margaret, Trefeglwys, Montgomeryshire; paternity, identified; Williams, Jane, Montgomeryshire
moral regulation 27, 29, 58, 67, 145, 147
Morgan, Jane, midwife, Llantrisant, Glamorgan 197, 198
Morgan, Mary, Glamorganshire 173, 200, *232*
Morgan, Reverend James 6–7
Morgan, Susan, Llandinam, Montgomeryshire 86
Morrice, Martha, Berriew, Montgomeryshire 211
Morris, Catherine, Bettws Cedewain, Montgomeryshire 212, 214
Morris, Elizabeth, Breconshire 167, 172, *230*
Morris, Hannah, Radnorshire 174, 178, *232*
Morris, Maria, Cardiganshire 181, *231*
Morris, Matthew, Llansilin, Denbighshire 72n119, 86
Morris, William, Llangadfan, Montgomeryshire 77

Index

mortality 105–119; mortality crisis 45, 62; Mortality Rates 106
mortality, infant 13–14, 20, 25, 105–114; burials/burial registers 20, 107, 109–110, 112, 113; Infant Mortality Rates 106; perinatal 17, 20; and poverty 109, 118–119
mortality, maternal 14, 20, 25, 105, 114–117; in Llanrhaeadr ym Mochnant 88, 107, 115–116, 117, 118
mortality penalty 4, 13–15, 25, 105–148; *see also* infanticide; mortality, infant; mortality, maternal; murder of pregnant women
Mortan, Edward, Llandegley, Radnorshire 82
mothers, unmarried: condemnation of 31, 97–98, 107, 125–128, 184; lived experience of 4, 26, 192, 215–216; socioeconomic background of 74, 86, 90–91, 94, 215, 224–225
Mrs, use of 79
murder 135; murder trials 22, 53, 118, 122, 144–145, 147; of older children 143, *230*; *see also* infanticide
murder of pregnant women 53, 135–145; and adultery 136, 137–138; Breconshire 53, 139–140, 141, 143, *230*; Carmarthenshire 55, *231*; and Court of Great Sessions 53, 117–118, 135–136, 138–139, 225; Denbighshire 131, 142, 143, *231*; Montgomeryshire 53, 115, 117–118, 137, 138–139, 143, *232*; and moral regulation 145, 147; Pembrokeshire 137, *232*; Radnorshire 53, 140, 143, *232*; and social control 145, 147

National Library of Wales 194, 225
Neals, Edward, surgeon, Montgomeryshire 162, 183
New Radnor, Radnorshire 31, 77, 79
Newtown, Montgomeryshire 208
Nichols, Elizabeth, Llanrhaeadr ym Mochnant, Montgomeryshire *116*
noises, loud 169
nonconformism, religious 58
Norwich 115

Nutt, Richard, Bettws Cedewain, Montgomeryshire 82
Nutt, Thomas 11

oath, midwives' 134, 195, 196, 199, 200–201, 212–213
obstetrics 24, 194, 204
occupation 11–12, 91–92
Old Bailey 135, 161, 173, 183, 184
Old Radnor, Radnorshire 66, 140
Oliver, Elizabeth, midwife, Castell Caereinion, Montgomeryshire 203
Onania, or the Henious Sin of Self-Pollution and all its Frightful Consequences in both Sexes 56
Oosterveen, Karen, Smith, Richard M and Stewart, Susan 91
Owen, Ann, Montgomeryshire 132, 133, 176, *232*
Owen, Jane, Trefeglwys, Montgomeryshire 78
Owen, John, Llandegley, Radnorshire 82
Owen, Margaret, Llanrhaeadr ym Mochnant, Montgomeryshire *116*
Owen, Mary, Llansantffried Glan, Denbyshire 126–127, 161, *231*
Owen, Sarah, Llangollen, Denbighshire 85, 130, 131, 132, 210, *231*

Paré, Ambroise 169
parish records 5, 15–19, 31, 44, 74, 88; burial registers 18, 20, 107, 109–110; churchwarden accounts 19, 23, 30–31, 77, 202; marriage registers 76; and midwives 194, 202–203; *see also* baptism registers; poor law
Parker, Margaret, Flintshire 179, *231*
Parry, Ann, Denbighshire 169, 188n106, *231*
Parry, David, surgeon 162, 183
Parry, Elizabeth, Glascwm, Radnorshire 79
Parry, John, Denbighshire 180
Parry, Mary, Llanrhaeadr ym Mochnant, Montgomeryshire *116*, 117
Parry, Thomas, Glascwym, Radnorshire 78, 79, 108
parturition *see* childbirth
paternity, biological 82–83

paternity, identified 25, 97; and baptism registers 7–8, 11–12, 19–20, 25, 50–52; and bastardy bonds 83; and Denbighshire *51, 52*, 64–65, 67, 78, 82, 93; and incest 65, 72n119; and infant mortality 105, 106–107, 112–113, 118; and maintenance and support 20–21, 65–66, 72n125, 81–82, 142–143, 147; and midwives 212–213; and Montgomeryshire *51, 52*, 65–66, 112–113; and murder of pregnant women 136–137; in parish records 4, 7–8, 11–12, 18–20, 25, 50–52, 64–65; and Radnorshire *51, 52*, 65–66, 112–114; and rape 65; and social control 113–114; survival strategies 223; *see also* Berriew, Montgomeryshire; socioeconomic background; Trefeglwys, Montgomeryshire

patriarchy 90, 142–143, 144, 163, 164

patronymics, Welsh 17, 76

Payton, Robert and Eleanor, Erbistock, Denbighshire 142

Pembrokeshire 57; murder of pregnant women 137, *232*

phallo-centrism 56, 57

Philips, Mary, Denbighshire 177, *231*

Pierce, Mary, Llanrhaeadr ym Mochnant, Montgomeryshire *116*

placentas 182, 183

poisoning 22, 137–138

Poole, Anthony, surgeon, Montgomeryshire 163, 180

poor law: poor law legislation 23, 65, 208; poor law officials 59, 64, 81–82, 208–209

poor law accounts 4, 6, 12, 23–24, 64–66, 74, 82, 146; care of unmarried mothers 24, 118, 185

poor relief 6, 29, 95, 192; and midwives 201, 202–203; and right of settlement 16, 23, 208–210

Porter, Roy 4

postpartum depression/psychosis 123

poverty 24, 25, 43–68, 73–98, 131–132; famine 45, 62; and illegitimacy ratios 45, 49; and infant mortality 109, 118–119; Radnorshire 66, 113–114; *see also* poor law; poor relief; socioeconomic background

Powell, Anne, Castell Caereinion, Montgomeryshire 211

Powell, Gwenllian, Breconshire 175, *230*

Powell, Mary, Clyro, Radnorshire 115, 117–118, 209, *232*

Powell, Sarah, Narberth, Pembrokeshire 137, *232*

Powell, William, Brecon 130–131

Preece, Margaret Thomas, Glascwym, Radnorshire 130, 133, 179

Prees, Evan, Glascwym, Radnorshire 130, 179

pregnancy 155–159; bridal 75, 76–77

pregnancy, concealed 13, 131, 165, 171–175, 185, 210, 223; Catherine Roberts 155, 163; Margaret Jenkin 171, 173, 174

pregnancy, symptoms of 156, 160, 165–174, 175; Catherine Roberts 155–156, 163–164, 167, 171, 173, 175–176; Jane Williams 171–172, 173–174, 179; menstruation 164, 165, 166–167; quickening 157, 168–170; swollen bellies 172–173, 175, 177; vomiting 166

prejudice 31, 144–145, 147

Price, James, Carmarthen 88

Price, Phoebe, Llanfihangel Nant Melon, Radnorshire 80

Price, Reverend Rees, Brecknock 7

Probert, Jane, Glascwym, Radnorshire 108

prostitution 52, 74, 87–88

Pryce, Evan 77

Pryce, Richard, Berriew, Montgomeryshire 168, *232*

Pugh, Abraham, Machynlleth, Montgomeryshire 77

Pugh, David, Garthbeibio, Montgomeryshire 77

Pugh, Edward, Old Radnor, Radnorshire 53, 140, *232*

Pugh, Elinor, Montgomeryshire 134, *232*

Pugh, Margaret, Llangadfan, Montgomeryshire 77

Pugh, Richard, Llanwnog, Montgomeryshire 80

Quarter Sessions 100n83, 194, 209

quickening 157, 168–170

Rabin, Dana 142
Radnorshire 5; and economics and industrialization 60, 61, 62–63; and identified paternity 51, 52, 65–66, 112–114; illegitimacy levels 6, 48–49, 78, 79, 81; and infant mortality 111, 112–114; murder of pregnant women 53, 140, 143, *232*; poverty 6, 66, 113–114; *see also* individual places
Ranson, Thomas 77
rape 52, 65, 73, 84–85, 87, 100n75, 177; Sarah Owen 85, 131
Read, Elizabeth, Holt, Denbighshire 94
Read, Sara 166
Reay, Barry 89
Reece, Thomas, Berriew, Montgomeryshire 82
Reekie, Gail 27
Rees, Elizabeth, Trefeglwys, Montgomeryshire 83
Rees, Mary, Garthbeibio, Montgomeryshire 80
Rees, Rees Thomas, Carmarthenshire 55, *231*
Reeves, Jane, Wrexham, Denbighshire 77
reform movements 29
relationships 25, 73–98; exploitational 21, 52, 84, 86–87; *see also* courtship
remorsefulness 127, 128
removal orders 114–115
reproductive knowledge 158–165; and fathers 159; and married women 159, 163, 165; and midwives 159, 160–162, 197, 225; and single women 159–160, 164–165, 181, 185
rheumatism 171
Rice, Evan, Llanfyllin, Denbighshire 79, 90
Richard, Adam, Manafon, Montgomeryshire 208–209
Richard, Mary, Glamorgan 182, *232*
Richard, Richard, Llandinam, Montgomeryshire 93
Richards, John 76
Robert, Jennet, midwife, Cardiff 197–198
Roberts, Catherine, Abergele, Denbighshire 161, *231*; symptoms of pregnancy and childbirth 155–156, 163–164, 167, 171, 173, 175–176
Roberts, Elizabeth, Llangollen, Denbighshire 86
Roberts, Ellis *see* Elis y Cowper (Ellis Roberts)
Roberts, Griffith, Anglesey 55, 88, *230*
Roberts, Jane, Llanrhaeadr ym Mochnant, Montgomeryshire *116*
Roberts, Jane, Oswestry, Shropshire 85
Roberts, Martha, midwife, Montgomeryshire 134, 178, 182
Roberts, Thomas, Henllan, Denbighshire 65
Roberts, Thomas, Trefeglwys, Montgomeryshire 83
Roberts, Ursula, Llanrhaeadr ym Mochnant, Montgomeryshire *116*
Rogers, Elizabeth, Llangyniew, Montgomeryshire 77
Rogers, Jane, Castell Caereinion, Montgomeryshire 203, 212, 213
Rogers, Nicholas 82, 94
Rogers, Samuel, Erbistock, Denbighshire 142, *231*
Rogers, Simon, Llangollen, Denbighshire 86
Rosser, Siwan 125
Rowlands, Mary, Berriew, Montgomeryshire 203
Rowton, Edward, Berriew, Montgomeryshire 83
Royal Proclamation (1787) 29
Ruabon, Denbighshire 64
Rural and Town Queries (1834) 55, 65–66, 113, 224
rural areas 60, 62, 195

Samuel, Sarah, Wrexham, Denbighshire 78
Saunders, Hugh, New Radnor 77
Schofield, Roger 14, 116
schools, circulating 29, 58
Scotland 3, 9, 12, 109
Second Annual Report of the Poor Law Commission (1836) 6
servants 12, 21, 59, 80, 90, 131, 137
settlement, right of 16, 23, 208–210
sex: consensual 52, 74, 89, 90, 91; extramarital 50, 58, 80, 88; non-consensual 84–89, 132; premarital penetrative 27, 52, 53, 55–58, 59, 66, 67

260 Index

sexual exploitation 21, 52, 84, 86–87
sexual morality 129–130
sexual practice/behaviour 27, 31, 44, 50, 55–59
sexual propriety 130, 160
shame 132, 137
Sharp, Jane 165, 166, 169, 181
Shepard, Alexandra 12
Shorter, Edward 60
Shrewsbury Drapers Company 61
Shropshire 6, 49
Simon, Thomas, surgeon 162, 183
Smellie, William, man-midwife 204
Smith, Mary, Swansea 177
Smyth, Margaret, Trefeglwys, Montgomeryshire 87
social control 27, 29, 43, 113–114, 123, 156; and murder of pregnant women 145, 147
social problem of illegitimacy 26–32, 106
Society for the Promotion of Christian Knowledge (SPCK) 29, 56, 57
Society for the Reformation of Manners 29
socioeconomic background 74, 89–97, 124–125; and bastardy bonds 93, 94; of fathers 11–12, 50, 74, 86, 89–92, 93, 225; and London 12–14, 43, 60, 62, 67, 91, 94; of midwives 198–200, 218n52; of mothers 74, 86, 90–91, 94, 215, 224–225; occupation 11–12, 91–92; and poor law accounts 12, 23–24, 74; and use of man-midwives 204, 205, 206
Solomon, of the Bible 127, 149n31
Sommers, Sheena 161, 183
St Asaph, Flintshire 132, 194
St Peters, Carmarthen 7
stability, economic 30, 59, 60, 62
statistics 30
stigmatisation 98, 114, 123, 132, 145, 209, 224
stillbirths 110, 115, 117, 168–169, 181, 211–212; testing for 162, 187n40
Stocks, Hannah 138
stomach upsets 170–171
straw plait trade 60
suicide 138, 142
survival strategies 13, 223
Swift, Anne, Llanfyllin, Denbighshire 79

Tattum, Mary, midwife, Flintshire 161
Taylor, William, surgeon, Flintshire 160, 177
testimonials 196, 197–198
Thomas, Anne, Trefeglwys, Montgomeryshire 127–128
Thomas, David, Meifod, Montgomeryshire 205
Thomas, Gwen, Meifod, Montgomeryshire 214
Thomas, Honoratus Leigh, medical practitioner, Hawarden, Flintshire 161, 204
Thomas, James, Talley, Carmarthenshire 146
Thomas, Jane, Cardiff 197–198
Thomas, Jane, Carmarthenshire 179, 180–181, *231*
Thomas, John, man-midwife, Cardiganshire 181
Thomas, Margaret, Ystradfellte, Brecon 53, 141, 143, *230*
Thomas, Peter and Mary, Llanfihangel Nant, Radnorshire 108
Thomas, Sophia, Radnorshire *232*
Tilley, Louise A, Scott, Joah W and Cohen, Miriam 60
Tissot, Samuel Auguste, *Onanism: or a Treatise upon the Disorders Produced by Masturbation* 56
Tomley, Elizabeth, Montgomeryshire 209, 210
Tonman, Roger and Theodosia, Llanfihangel Nant, Radnorshire 108–109
Toulalan, Sarah 57, 177
Townsend, Joseph 29
travel writing 24–25, 54
Trefeglwys, Montgomeryshire: identified paternity 78, 81–82, 83, 87, 88; and right of settlement 208, 210; *see also* Jenkin, Margaret, Trefeglwys, Montgomeryshire
Tregynon, Montgomeryshire 76
Tuders, Martha, Ceri, Montgomeryshire 76
twins 108, 204, 205

United States 135

vaginas 178, 190n190
Valentine, Martha, Glamorganshire 172
Vaughan, Elizabeth, Llanrhaeadr ym Mochnant, Montgomeryshire *116*

Vaughan, Thomas, Montgomeryshire 137, *232*
Venette, Nicholas, *Tableau de l'amour conjugal* 56
victim precipitation 144
violence 147; fatal 4, 14–15, 22, 25–26, 122–148, 225; non-fatal 136; partner 15, 135, 136; *see also* infanticide; murder of pregnant women
vomiting 166

Walker, Garthine 129
Walter, Richard, Wrexham, Denbighshire 80
Walter, William, Breconshire 139–140, *230*
Ward, Samuel, Meifod, Montgomeryshire 205
Watkin, Ann, Breconshire 139–140, 143, *230*
Welsh language 57
wet nurses 95, 107, 214
Weyman, Ellen, Flintshire 182
Whittingham, Rachel, Montgomeryshire 137
widows, as midwives 196, 217n25
Williams, Ann, Merioneth 183, *232*
Williams, Arabella, Llanbedr-Goch, Anglesey 128–129, *230*
Williams, David, Gladestry, Radnorshire 80
Williams, Elizabeth, Breconshire 169, 170, 188n106
Williams, Elizabeth, Flintshire 161, 170–171, 176, 177
Williams, George, apothecary/surgeon 162, 183
Williams, George, Narberth, Pembrokeshire 137
Williams, Jane, Denbighshire 131, 132, 171–172, 176, 181, *231*
Williams, Jane, Montgomeryshire *232*; examination of infant's body 162, 183, 184; symptoms of pregnancy and childbirth 171–172, 173–174, 179
Williams, John, medical practitioner, Cardiganshire 160
Williams, Margaret and Jane, Anglesey 128–129
Williams, Margaret, Breconshire 177
Williams, Margaret, midwife, Carmarthenshire 161, 199, 205
Williams, Margaret, midwife, Denbighshire 177, 199
Williams, Mary, Breconshire 167
Williams, Mary, midwife, Carmarthenshire 199
Williams, Mary, midwife, Denbighshire 155, 164, 167, 199
Williams, Rachel, Breconshire 140
Williams, Richard, medical practitioner 7
Williams, Samantha 13, 20, 82
Williams, Thomas, Bettws Cedewain, Montgomeryshire 210–211
Williams, William, Berriew, Montgomeryshire 93
Williams, William, medical practitioner, Cardiganshire 160
Williams, William, Ystradfellte, Brecon 53, 141, *230*
Wilson, Adrian 13, 44, 163; on ceremony of childbirth 193, 207; on economics and poverty 59–60, 62; on midwives 201, 202–203, 204
Wiltshire 6
Winn, Mary, midwife, Cardiff 197–198, 200
witnesses to childbirth 175, 211, 212
witness statements 143, 165; and infanticide 126, 128, 129, 174, 175, 211–212
Woodward, Josiah, *Rebuke of the Sin of Uncleanness* 56, 57
Woodward, Nick 14, 123
Woola, Elizabeth, Trefeglwys, Montgomeryshire 83
woollen trade 49, 61, 63
workhouse 59
World Health Organisation 135
Wrightson, Keith 14, 123

yeomen 92–93